A Guide to the

Project Management Body of Knowledge

Third Edition

(PMBOK® Guide)

an American National Standard
ANSI/PMI 99-001-2004

Library of Congress Cataloging-in-Publication Data

A guide to the project management body of knowledge: PMBOK® guide. – 3rd ed.
    p. cm
    Includes index.
    ISBN 1-930699-45-X
      1. Project management. I. Title: PMBOK guide. II. Project Management Institute.

    HD69.P75G845 2004
    658.4'04—dc22

                                                                                    2004058697

ISBN 10: 1-930699-45-X (paperback)
ISBN 13: 978-1-930699-45-8 (paperback)
ISBN 10: 1-930699-50-6 (CD-ROM)
ISBN 13: 978-1-930699-50-2 (CD-ROM)

Published by: Project Management Institute, Inc.
                                Four Campus Boulevard
                                Newtown Square, Pennsylvania 19073-3299 USA
                                Phone: +610-356-4600
                                Fax: +610-356-4647
                                E-mail customercare@pmi.org
                                Internet: www.PMI.org/Marketplace

PMI Publications welcomes corrections and comments on its books. Please feel free to send comments on typographical, formatting, or other errors. Simply make a copy of the relevant page of the book, mark the error, and send it to: Book Editor, PMI Publications, 14 Campus Boulevard, Newtown Square, PA 19073-3299 USA.

To inquire about discounts for resale or educational purposes, please contact the PMI Book Service Center.
PMI Book Service Center
P. O. Box 932683, Atlanta, GA 31193-2683 USA
Phone: 1-866-276-4764 (within the U. S. or Canada) or +1-770-280-4129 (globally)
Fax: +1-770-280-4113
E-mail: book orders@pmi.org

NOTICE

The Project Management Institute, Inc. (PMI) standards and guideline publications, of which the document contained herein is one, are developed through a voluntary consensus standards development process. This process brings together volunteers and/or seeks out the views of persons who have an interest in the topic covered by this publication. While PMI administers the process and establishes rules to promote fairness in the development of consensus, it does not write the document and it does not independently test, evaluate, or verify the accuracy or completeness of any information or the soundness of any judgments contained in its standards and guideline publications.

PMI disclaims liability for any personal injury, property or other damages of any nature whatsoever, whether special, indirect, consequential or compensatory, directly or indirectly resulting from the publication, use of application, or reliance on this document. PMI disclaims and makes no guaranty or warranty, expressed or implied, as to the accuracy or completeness of any information published herein, and disclaims and makes no warranty that the information in this document will fulfill any of your particular purposes or needs. PMI does not undertake to guarantee the performance of any individual manufacturer or seller's products or services by virtue of this standard or guide.

In publishing and making this document available, PMI is not undertaking to render professional or other services for or on behalf of any person or entity, nor is PMI undertaking to perform any duty owed by any person or entity to someone else. Anyone using this document should rely on his or her own independent judgment or, as appropriate, seek the advice of a competent professional in determining the exercise of reasonable care in any given circumstances. Information and other standards on the topic covered by this publication may be available from other sources, which the user may wish to consult for additional views or information not covered by this publication.

PMI has no power, nor does it undertake to police or enforce compliance with the contents of this document. PMI does not certify, tests, or inspect products, designs, or installations for safety or health purposes. Any certification or other statement of compliance with any health or safety-related information in this document shall not be attributable to PMI and is solely the responsibility of the certifier or maker of the statement.

CONTENTS

Preface.. vii

The Project Management Framework 1

Introduction 3
  1.1 Purpose of the *PMBOK® GUIDE* 3
  1.2 What is a Project?...5
  1.3 What is Project Management?..8
  1.4 The *PMBOK® GUIDE* Structure 9
  1.5 Areas of Expertise...12
  1.6 Project Management Context 16

Project Life Cycle and Organization 19
  2.1 The Project Life Cycle..19
  2.2 Project Stakeholders...24
  2.3 Organizational Influences 27

The Standard for Project Management of a Project 35

Project Management Processes for a Project... 37
  3.1 Project Management Processes 39
  3.2 Project management Process Groups..40
  3.3 Process Interactions..67
  3.4 Project Management Process Mapping..69

The Project Management Knowledge Areas 71

Introduction 73
  Process Flow Diagrams..73
  Major Project Documents 76

Project Integration Management 77
  4.1 Develop Project Charter...81
  4.2 Develop Preliminary Project Scope Statement...86
  4.3 Develop Project Management Plan 88
  4.4 Direct and Manage Project Execution...91
  4.5 Monitor and Control Project Work..94
  4.6 Integrated Change Control...96
  4.7 Close Project..100

Project Scope Management 103
  5.1 Scope Planning..107
  5.2 Scope Definition..109
  5.3 Create WBS..112
  5.4 Scope Verification...118
  5.5 Scope Control..119

Project Time Management.. 123
  6.1 Activity Definition...127
  6.2 Activity Sequencing..130

    6.3 Activity Resource Estimating 135
    6.4 Activity Duration Estimating 139
    6.5 Schedule Development 143
    6.6 Schedule Control...152

Project Cost Management... 157
    7.1 Cost Estimating 161
    7.2 Cost Budgeting..167
    7.3 Cost Control 171

Project Quality Management... 179
    8.1 Quality Planning 183
    8.2 Perform Quality Assurance 187
    8.3 Perform Quality Control 190

Project Human Resource Management 199
    9.1 Human Resource Planning...202
    9.2 Acquire Project Team...209
    9.3 Develop Project Team 212
    9.4 Manage Project Team..215

Project Communications Management... 221
    10.1 Communications Planning 225
    10.2 Information Distribution..228
    10.3 Performance Reporting..231
    10.4 Manage Stakeholders 235

Project Risk Management 237
    11.1 Risk Management Planning..242
    11.2 Risk Identification..246
    11.3 Qualitative Risk Analysis 249
    11.4 Quantitative Risk Analysis 254
    11.5 Risk Response Planning...260
    11.6 Risk Monitoring and Control 264

Project Procurement Management... 269
    12.1 Plan Purchases and Acquisitions 274
    12.2 Plan Contracting..281
    12.3 Request Seller Responses 284
    12.4 Select Sellers 286
    12.5 Contract Administration 290
    12.6 Contract Closure 295

Appendices 299

Third Edition Changes... 301

Evolution of PMI's *A Guide to the Project Management Body of Knowledge* 309

Contributors and Reviewers of *PMBOK*® *Guide* – Third Edition.................. 321

Application Area Extensions 329

Additional Sources of Information on Project Management 333

Summary of Project Management Knowledge Areas................................... 337

Glossary and Index 343

References 345

Glossary 347

Index 381

LIST OF TABLES AND FIGURES

Figure 1-1. Overview of Project Management Knowledge Areas
and Project Management Processes 11
Figure 1-2. Areas of Expertise Needed by the Project Management Team 13
Figure 2-1. Typical Project Cost and Staffing Level Across the
Project Life Cycle..21
Figure 2-2. Stakeholders' Influence Over Time 21
Figure 2-3. Typical Sequence of Phases in a Project Life Cycle...........................23
Figure 2-4. Relationship Between the Product and the Project Life Cycles 24
Figure 2-5. The Relationship Between Stakeholders and the Project 25
Figure 2-6. Organizational Structure Influences on Projects 28
Figure 2-7. Functional Organization..29
Figure 2-8. Projectized Organization 29
Figure 2-9. Weak Matrix Organization 30
Figure 2-10. Balanced Matrix Organization 30
Figure 2-11. Strong Matrix Organization...31
Figure 2-12. Composite Organization..31
Figure 3-1. The Plan-Do-Check-Act Cycle...39
Figure 3-2. Project Management Process Groups Mapped to the
Plan-Do-Check-Act Cycle...40
Figure 3-3. Flow Chart Legend 41
Figure 3-4. High Level Summary of Process Groups' Interactions........................42
Figure 3-5. Project Boundaries 43
Figure 3-6. Initiating Process Group 44
Table 3-1. Develop Project Charter: Inputs and Outputs....................................45
Table 3-2. Develop Preliminary Project Scope: Inputs and Outputs 45
Figure 3-7. Planning Process Group...47
Table 3-3. Develop Project Management Plan: Inputs and Outputs 48
Table 3-4. Scope Planning: Inputs and Outputs 48
Table 3-5. Scope Definition: Inputs and Outputs 49
Table 3-6. Create WBS: Inputs and Outputs 49
Table 3-7. Activity Definition: Inputs and Outputs..49
Table 3-8. Activity Sequencing: Inputs and Outputs...50
Table 3-9. Activity Resource Estimating: Inputs and Outputs..............................50
Table 3-10. Activity Duration Estimating: Inputs and Outputs 50
Table 3-11. Schedule Development: Inputs and Outputs 51
Table 3-12. Cost Estimating: Inputs and Outputs 51
Table 3-13. Cost Budgeting: Inputs and Outputs..51
Table 3-14. Quality Planning: Inputs and Outputs 52
Table 3-15. Human Resource Planning: Inputs and Outputs 52
Table 3-16. Communications Planning: Inputs and Outputs 52
Table 3-17. Risk Management Planning: Inputs and Outputs 53
Table 3-18. Risk Identification: Inputs and Outputs 53
Table 3-19. Qualitative Risk Analysis: Inputs and Outputs....................................53
Table 3-20. Quantitative Risk Analysis: Inputs and Outputs..................................54

Contents

Table 3-21. Risk Response Planning: Inputs and Outputs 54
Table 3-22. Plan Purchases and Acquisitions: Inputs and Outputs.....................54
Table 3-23. Plan Contracting: Inputs and Outputs...55
Figure 3-8. Executing Process Group..55
Table 3-24. Direct and Manage Project Execution: Inputs and Outputs...............56
Table 3-25. Perform Quality Assurance: Inputs and Outputs 56
Table 3-26. Acquire Project Team: Inputs and Outputs......................................57
Table 3-27. Develop Project Team: Inputs and Outputs.....................................57
Table 3-28. Information Distribution: Inputs and Outputs 57
Table 3-29. Request Seller Responses: Inputs and Outputs................................58
Table 3-30. Select Sellers: Inputs and Outputs 58
Figure 3-9. Monitoring and Controlling Process Group 60
Table 3-31. Monitor and Control Project Work: Inputs and Outputs.....................61
Table 3-32. Integrated Change Control: Inputs and Outputs...............................61
Table 3-33. Scope Verification: Inputs and Outputs 62
Table 3-34. Scope Control: Inputs and Outputs 62
Table 3-35. Schedule Control: Inputs and Outputs 62
Table 3-36. Cost Control: Inputs and Outputs 63
Table 3-37. Perform Quality Control: Inputs and Outputs...................................63
Table 3-38. Manage Project Team: Inputs and Outputs 63
Table 3-39. Performance Reporting: Inputs and Outputs....................................64
Table 3-40. Manage Stakeholders: Inputs and Outputs 64
Table 3-41. Risk Monitoring and Control: Inputs and Outputs.............................65
Table 3-42. Contract Administration: Inputs and Outputs...................................65
Figure 3-10. Closing Process Group...66
Table 3-43. Close Project: Inputs and Outputs 67
Table 3-44. Contract Closure: Inputs and Outputs 67
Figure 3-11. Process Groups Interact in a Project..68
Figure 3-12. Project Management Process Group Triangle 69
Table 3-45. Mapping of the Project Management Processes to the
    Project Management Process Groups and the Knowledge Areas 70
Figure III-1. Process Flow Diagram Legend 73
Figure III-2. Three Major Project Documents and their Relationship to their
    Components 75
Figure 4-1. Project Integration Management Overview 79
Figure 4-2. Project Integration Management Processes Flow Diagram 80
Figure 4-3. Develop Project Charter:
    Inputs, Tools & Techniques, and Outputs 82
Figure 4-4. Develop Preliminary Project Scope Statement:
    Inputs, Tools & Techniques, and Outputs 87
Figure 4-5. Develop Project Management Plan:
    Inputs, Tools & Techniques, and Outputs 89
Figure 4-6. Direct and Manage Project Execution:
    Inputs, Tools & Techniques, and Outputs 92
Figure 4-7. Monitor and Control Project Work:
    Inputs, Tools & Techniques, and Outputs 95
Figure 4-8. Integrated Change Control:
    Inputs, Tools & Techniques, and Outputs 98
Figure 4-9. Close Project: Inputs, Tools & Techniques, and Outputs..................100
Figure 5-1. Project Scope Management Overview 105
Figure 5-2. Project Scope Management Process Flow Diagram.........................106
Figure 5-3. Scope Planning: Inputs, Tools & Techniques, and Outputs...............107
Figure 5-4. Scope Definition: Inputs, Tools & Techniques, and Outputs.............109
Figure 5-5. Create WBS: Inputs, Tools & Techniques, and Outputs 113
Figure 5-6. Sample Work Breakdown Structure with Some Branches
    Decomposed Down Through Work Packages 114

A Guide to the Project Management Body of Knowledge (PMBOK® Guide) Third Edition
©2004 Project Management Institute, Four Campus Boulevard, Newtown Square, PA 19073-3299 USA

Figure 5-7. Sample Work Breakdown Structure Organized by Phase 116
Figure 5-8. Sample Work Breakdown for Defense Materiel Items........................116
Figure 5-9. Scope Verification: Inputs, Tools & Techniques, and Outputs 118
Figure 5-10. Scope Control: Inputs, Tools & Techniques, and Outputs 120
Figure 6-1. Project Time Management Overview 125
Figure 6-2. Project Time Management Process Flow Diagram..........................126
Figure 6-3. Activity Definition: Inputs, Tools & Techniques, and Outputs 127
Figure 6-4. Activity Sequencing: Inputs, Tools & Techniques, and Outputs 130
Figure 6-5. Precedence Diagram Method...131
Figure 6-6. Arrow Diagram Method..132
Figure 6-7. Activity Resource Estimating:
    Inputs, Tools & Techniques, and Outputs 136
Figure 6-8. Activity Duration Estimating:
    Inputs, Tools & Techniques, and Outputs 139
Figure 6-9. Schedule Development Overview:
    Inputs, Tools & Techniques, and Outputs 143
Figure 6-10. Project Schedule – Graphic Examples...150
Figure 6-11. Schedule Control Overview:
    Inputs, Tools & Techniques, and Outputs 152
Figure 7-1. Project Cost Management Overview..159
Figure 7-2. Project Cost Management Process Flow Diagram..........................160
Figure 7-3. Cost Estimating: Inputs, Tools & Techniques, and Outputs...............162
Figure 7-4. Cost Budgeting: Inputs, Tools & Techniques, and Outputs 167
Figure 7-5. Cash Flow, Cost Baseline and Funding Display 170
Figure 7-6. Cost Control: Inputs, Tools & Techniques, and Outputs 171
Figure 7-7. Illustrative Graphic Performance Report 174
Figure 8-1. Project Quality Management Overview 182
Figure 8-2. Project Quality Management Process Flow Diagram........................183
Figure 8-3. Quality Planning: Inputs, Tools & Techniques, and Outputs..............184
Figure 8-4. Perform Quality Assurance:
    Inputs, Tools & Techniques, and Outputs 188
Figure 8-5. Perform Quality Control:
    Inputs, Tools & Techniques, and Outputs 191
Figure 8-6. Cause and Effect Diagram 192
Figure 8-7. Example of a Control Chart of Project Schedule Performance..........193
Figure 8-8. Sample Process Flowchart..194
Figure 8-9. Pareto Diagram (Chart) 195
Figure 9-1. Project Human Resource Management Overview 201
Figure 9-2. Project Human Resource Management Process Flow Diagram........202
Figure 9-3. Human Resource Planning:
    Inputs, Tools & Techniques, and Outputs 203
Figure 9-4. Roles and Responsibility Definition Formats.......................................205
Figure 9-5. Responsibility Assignment Matrix (RAM) Using a RACI Format........206
Figure 9-6. Illustrative Resource Histogram 208
Figure 9-7. Acquire Project Team: Inputs, Tools & Techniques, and Outputs 209
Figure 9-8. Develop Project Team: Inputs, Tools & Techniques, and Outputs 212
Figure 9-9. Manage Project Team: Inputs, Tools & Techniques, and Outputs.....215
Figure 10-1. Project Communications Management Overview 222
Figure 10-2. Project Communications Management Process Flow Diagram 223
Figure 10-3. Communication – Basic Model...224
Figure 10-4. Communications Planning:
    Inputs, Tools & Techniques, and Outputs 225
Figure 10-5. Information Distribution: Inputs, Tools & Techniques, and Outputs ... 228
Figure 10-6. Performance Reporting: Inputs, Tools & Techniques, and Outputs ...231
Figure 10-7 Tabular Performance Report Sample...234
Figure 10-8. Manage Stakeholders: Inputs, Tools & Techniques, and Outputs ...235

Figure 11-1. Project Risk Management Overview 239
Figure 11-2. Project Risk Management Process Flow Diagram 241
Figure 11-3. Risk Management Planning:
   Inputs, Tools & Techniques, and Outputs 242
Figure 11-4. Example of a Risk Breakdown Structure (RBS) 244
Figure 11-5. Definition of Impact Scales for Four Project Objectives 245
Figure 11-6. Risk Identification: Inputs, Tools & Techniques, and Outputs 246
Figure 11-7. Qualitative Risk Analysis:
   Inputs, Tools & Techniques, and Outputs 250
Figure 11-8. Probability and Impact Matrix 252
Figure 11-9. Quantitative Risk Analysis:
   Inputs, Tools & Techniques, and Outputs 254
Figure 11-10. Range of Project Cost Estimates Collected During the
   Risk Interview 256
Figure 11-11. Examples of Commonly Used Probability Distributions 256
Figure 11-12. Decision Tree Diagram..258
Figure 11-13 Cost Risk Simulation Results 259
Figure 11-14. Risk Response Planning:
   Inputs, Tools & Techniques, and Outputs 260
Figure 11-15. Risk Monitoring and Control:
   Inputs, Tools & Techniques, and Outputs 265
Figure 12-1. Project Procurement Management Overview.................................272
Figure 12-2. Project Procurement Management Process Flow Diagram 273
Figure 12-3. Plan Purchases and Acquisitions:
   Inputs, Tools & Techniques, and Outputs 274
Figure 12-4. Plan Contracting: Inputs, Tools & Techniques, and Outputs 281
Figure 12-5. Request Seller Responses:
   Inputs, Tools & Techniques, and Outputs 284
Figure 12.6. Select Sellers: Inputs, Tools & Techniques, and Outputs 287
Figure 12-7. Contract Administration:
   Inputs, Tools & Techniques, and Outputs 291
Figure 12-8. Contract Closure: Inputs, Tools & Techniques, and Outputs..........296
Table 1 – Structural Changes 301
Table 2 – Chapter 4 Changes..304
Table 3 – Chapter 5 Changes..304
Table 4 – Chapter 6 Changes..305
Table 5 – Chapter 7 Changes..305
Table 6 – Chapter 8 Changes..306
Table 7 – Chapter 9 Changes..306
Table 8 – Chapter 10 Changes..306
Table 9 – Chapter 11 Changes 307
Table 10 – Chapter 12 Changes...307

Preface to the Third Edition

This document supersedes *A Guide to the Project Management Body of Knowledge (PMBOK® Guide)* – 2000 Edition, which was published as the second edition of the *PMBOK® Guide*. In the time since its publication, the Project Management Institute (PMI) received thousands of valuable recommendations for improvements to the *PMBOK® Guide* – 2000 Edition that have since been reviewed and, as appropriate, incorporated into the third edition.

As a result of those inputs and growth of the Project Management Body of Knowledge, PMI volunteers prepared an updated version of the *PMBOK® Guide*. The project charter to update the *PMBOK® Guide* – 2000 Edition was to:

- Change the criteria for the inclusion of material from "generally accepted on most projects most of the time" to "generally recognized as good practice on most projects most of the time." Generally recognized means that the knowledge and practices described are applicable to most projects most of the time, and that there is widespread consensus about their value and usefulness.
- Add new material reflecting the growth of the knowledge and practices in the field of project management by documenting those practices, tools, techniques, and other relevant items that are generally recognized as good practice.
- Expand the emphasis on and treatment of the Project Management Process Groups.
- Expand the treatment of integration and more appropriately convey its importance to a project.
- Expand treatment of the Initiating Process Group to more accurately describe the front-end of the project and the start of each phase.
- Expand the closing processes.
- Evaluate all processes to ensure that they are properly placed, complete, and clear.
- Review all text to make sure it is clear, complete, and relevant.
- Ensure consistent terminology and placement of project inputs, outputs, and tools and techniques. Identify the origin of all inputs and the destination of all outputs.
- Change text, where possible, to improve the translatability of the document and consider changing words and phrases with negative cultural connotations.
- Expand the index and glossary.
- Correct existing errors in the predecessor document.

The *PMBOK® Guide* 2004 Update Project Team complied with its charter as described above. To assist practitioners and other interested parties who may be familiar with the *PMBOK® Guide* – 2000 Edition, the major differences between the editions are summarized below:

1. Across the entire third edition, in most instances when a new process was introduced, and in other selected cases where existing process names were revised, such process names are in a verb-object format for clarity.
2. The writing style was generally changed to the active voice.
3. The distinction between project life cycles and product life cycles was clarified.
4. The number of processes increased from 39 to 44. Seven processes were added, two processes were deleted, and 13 processes were renamed for a net gain of five new processes.
5. All graphics were numbered and labeled as either a table or figure.
6. The distinction between Project Management Process Groups and the Knowledge Areas was clarified. A greater emphasis was placed on the importance of Process Groups.
7. Chapter 3 was renamed "Project Management Processes for a Project" and moved from Section I to a new Section II, which is now called "The Standard for Project Management of a Project." As part of this change, Chapter 3 was extensively revised to indicate that the Process Groups and inputs and outputs in the chapter are the basis of the standard for project management of a single project.
8. The project management processes were mapped to show process integration.
9. The glossary was significantly revised and augmented. Appropriate terms have been categorized to avoid confusion.
10. The following processes were added:
    *   Develop Project Charter (Section 4.1)
    *   Develop Preliminary Project Scope Statement (Section 4.2)
    *   Monitor and Control Project Work (Section 4.5)
    *   Close Project (Section 4.7)
    *   Create Work Breakdown Structure (Section 5.3)
    *   Manage Project Team (Section 9.4)
    *   Manage Stakeholders (Section 10.4)
11. All of the process inputs, tools, techniques, and outputs have been revised to support the improved integration and mapping of the processes.
12. Process flow diagrams have been added to Chapters 4 through 12 to provide added support to the integration of processes.
13. An introduction has been added to Section III to describe the process flow diagrams and provide a legend of the symbols.

Appendix A – Third Edition Changes details the changes made in the chapters.

The *PMBOK® Guide* – Third Edition was presented in an exposure draft document at the end of calendar year 2003, and a significant number of the comments sent in by reviewers were incorporated into this final release.

Dennis Bolles, PMP
Project Manager
PMBOK® Guide 2004 Update Project Team

Steve Fahrenkrog, PMP
PMI Standards Manager

Section I

The Project Management Framework

Chapter 1   Introduction

Chapter 2   Project Life Cycle and Organization

CHAPTER 1

Introduction

The Project Management Body of Knowledge is the sum of knowledge within the profession of project management. As with other professions such as law, medicine, and accounting, the body of knowledge rests with the practitioners and academics who apply and advance it. The complete Project Management Body of Knowledge includes proven traditional practices that are widely applied, as well as innovative practices that are emerging in the profession, including published and unpublished material. As a result, the Project Management Body of Knowledge is constantly evolving.

This chapter defines several key terms and provides an overview of the rest of *A Guide to the Project Management Body of Knowledge (PMBOK® Guide)* in the following major sections:

1.1   **Purpose of the *PMBOK® Guide***
1.2   **What Is a Project?**
1.3   **What Is Project Management?**
1.4   **The *PMBOK® Guide* Structure**
1.5   **Areas of Expertise**
1.6   **Project Management Context**

1.1   Purpose of the *PMBOK® GUIDE*

The primary purpose of the *PMBOK® Guide* is to identify that subset of the Project Management Body of Knowledge that is generally recognized as good practice. "Identify" means to provide a general overview as opposed to an exhaustive description. "Generally recognized" means that the knowledge and practices described are applicable to most projects most of the time, and that there is widespread consensus about their value and usefulness. "Good practice" means that there is general agreement that the correct application of these skills, tools, and techniques can enhance the chances of success over a wide range of different projects. Good practice does not mean that the knowledge described should always be applied uniformly on all projects; **the project management team is responsible for determining what is appropriate for any given project.**

The *PMBOK® Guide* also provides and promotes a common lexicon for discussing, writing, and applying project management. Such a standard lexicon is an essential element of a profession.

The Project Management Institute uses this document as a foundational, but not the sole, project management reference for its professional development programs including:

- Project Management Professional (PMP®) certification
- Project management education and training offered by PMI Registered Education Providers (R.E.P.s)
- Accreditation of educational programs in project management.

As a foundational reference, this standard is neither comprehensive nor all-inclusive. Appendix D discusses application area extensions, while Appendix E lists sources of further information on project management.

This standard addresses only single projects and the project management processes that are generally recognized as good practice. There are other standards on organizational project management maturity, project manager competency, and other topics that address what is generally recognized as good practices in those areas. Some of the material in those other standards impacts single projects. The other standards should be consulted for additional information and understanding of the broader context in which projects are accomplished.

Project management standards do not address all details of every topic. Topics that are not mentioned should not be considered unimportant. There are several reasons why a topic may not be included in a standard: it may be included within some other related standard; it may be so general that there is nothing uniquely applicable to project management; or there is insufficient consensus on a topic. The lack of consensus means there are variations in the profession regarding how, when or where within the organization, as well as who within the organization, should perform that specific project management activity. The organization or the project management team must decide how those activities are going to be addressed in the context and the circumstances of the project for which the *PMBOK® Guide* is being used.

1.1.1 Audience for the *PMBOK® Guide*

This standard provides a foundational reference for anyone interested in the profession of project management. This includes, but is not limited to:

- Senior executives
- Program managers and managers of project managers
- Project managers and other project team members
- Members of a project management office
- Customers and other stakeholders
- Functional managers with employees assigned to project teams
- Educators teaching project management and related subjects
- Consultants and other specialists in project management and related fields
- Trainers developing project management educational programs
- Researchers analyzing project management.

A Guide to the Project Management Body of Knowledge (PMBOK® Guide) Third Edition
©2004 Project Management Institute, Four Campus Boulevard, Newtown Square, PA 19073-3299 USA

1.2   What is a Project?

1.2.1   Project Characteristics

A project is a temporary endeavor undertaken to create a unique product, service, or result.

.1   Temporary

Temporary means that every project has a definite beginning and a definite end. The end is reached when the project's objectives have been achieved, or it becomes clear that the project objectives will not or cannot be met, or the need for the project no longer exists and the project is terminated. Temporary does not necessarily mean short in duration; many projects last for several years. In every case, however, the duration of a project is finite. Projects are not ongoing efforts.

In addition, temporary does not generally apply to the product, service or result created by the project. Most projects are undertaken to create a lasting outcome. For example, a project to erect a national monument will create a result expected to last centuries. Projects also may often have intended and unintended social, economic and environmental impacts that far outlast the projects themselves.

The temporary nature of projects may apply to other aspects of the endeavor as well:

- The opportunity or market window is usually temporary—some projects have a limited time frame in which to produce their product or service.

- The project team, as a working unit, seldom outlives the project—a team created for the sole purpose of performing the project will perform that project, and then the team is disbanded and the team members reassigned when the project ends.

.2   Unique Products, Services, or Results

A project creates unique deliverables, which are products, services, or results. Projects can create:

- A product or artifact that is produced, is quantifiable, and can be either an end item in itself or a component item

- A capability to perform a service, such as business functions supporting production or distribution

- A result, such as outcomes or documents. For example, a research project develops knowledge that can be used to determine whether or not a trend is present or a new process will benefit society.

Uniqueness is an important characteristic of project deliverables. For example, many thousands of office buildings have been developed, but each individual facility is unique—different owner, different design, different location, different contractors, and so on. The presence of repetitive elements does not change the fundamental uniqueness of the project work.

.3 Progressive Elaboration

Progressive elaboration is a characteristic of projects that accompanies the concepts of temporary and unique. Progressive elaboration means developing in steps, and continuing by increments[1]. For example, the project scope will be broadly described early in the project and made more explicit and detailed as the project team develops a better and more complete understanding of the objectives and deliverables. Progressive elaboration should not be confused with scope creep (Section 5.5).

Progressive elaboration of a project's specifications needs to be carefully coordinated with proper project scope definition, particularly if the project is performed under contract. When properly defined, the scope of the project—the work to be done—should be controlled as the project and product specifications are progressively elaborated. The relationship between product scope and project scope is discussed further in the Chapter 5 introductory material.

The following examples illustrate progressive elaboration in two different application areas:

- Development of a chemical processing plant begins with process engineering to define the characteristics of the process. These characteristics are used to design the major processing units. This information becomes the basis for engineering design, which defines both the detailed plant layout and the mechanical characteristics of the process units and ancillary facilities. All of this results in design drawings that are elaborated to produce fabrication and construction drawings. During construction, interpretations and adaptations are made as needed and are subject to proper approval. This further elaboration of the deliverables is captured in as-built drawings, and final operating adjustments are made during testing and turnover.

- The product of an economic development project may initially be defined as: "Improve the quality of life of the lowest income residents of community X." As the project proceeds, the products may be described more specifically as, for example: "Provide access to food and water to 500 low-income residents in community X." The next round of progressive elaboration might focus exclusively on increasing agriculture production and marketing, with provision of water deemed to be a secondary priority to be initiated once the agricultural component is well under way.

1.2.2 Projects vs. Operational Work

Organizations perform work to achieve a set of objectives. Generally, work can be categorized as either projects or operations, although the two sometimes overlap. They share many of the following characteristics:

- Performed by people
- Constrained by limited resources
- Planned, executed, and controlled.

Projects and operations differ primarily in that operations are ongoing and repetitive, while projects are temporary and unique.

A Guide to the Project Management Body of Knowledge (PMBOK® Guide) Third Edition
©2004 Project Management Institute, Four Campus Boulevard, Newtown Square, PA 19073-3299 USA

The objectives of projects and operations are fundamentally different. The purpose of a project is to attain its objective and then terminate. Conversely, the objective of an ongoing operation is to sustain the business. Projects are different because the project concludes when its specific objectives have been attained, while operations adopt a new set of objectives and the work continues.

Projects are undertaken at all levels of the organization and they can involve a single person or many thousands. Their duration ranges from a few weeks to several years. Projects can involve one or many organizational units, such as joint ventures and partnerships. Examples of projects include, but are not limited to:

- Developing a new product or service
- Effecting a change in structure, staffing, or style of an organization
- Designing a new transportation vehicle
- Developing or acquiring a new or modified information system
- Constructing a building or facility
- Building a water system for a community
- Running a campaign for political office
- Implementing a new business procedure or process
- Responding to a contract solicitation.

1.2.3 Projects and Strategic Planning

Projects are a means of organizing activities that cannot be addressed within the organization's normal operational limits. Projects are, therefore, often utilized as a means of achieving an organization's strategic plan, whether the project team is employed by the organization or is a contracted service provider.

Projects are typically authorized as a result of one or more of the following strategic considerations:

- A market demand (e.g., an oil company authorizes a project to build a new refinery in response to chronic gasoline shortages)
- An organizational need (e.g., a training company authorizes a project to create a new course in order to increase its revenues)
- A customer request (e.g., an electric utility authorizes a project to build a new substation to serve a new industrial park)
- A technological advance (e.g., a software firm authorizes a new project to develop a new generation of video games after the introduction of new game-playing equipment by electronics firms)
- A legal requirement (e.g., a paint manufacturer authorizes a project to establish guidelines for the handling of a new toxic material).

1.3 What is Project Management?

Project management is the application of knowledge, skills, tools and techniques to project activities to meet project requirements. Project management is accomplished through the application and integration of the project management processes of initiating, planning, executing, monitoring and controlling, and closing. The project manager is the person responsible for accomplishing the project objectives.

Managing a project includes:

- Identifying requirements
- Establishing clear and achievable objectives
- Balancing the competing demands for quality, scope, time and cost
- Adapting the specifications, plans, and approach to the different concerns and expectations of the various stakeholders.

Project managers often talk of a "triple constraint"—project scope, time and cost—in managing competing project requirements. Project quality is affected by balancing these three factors (Chapters 5 through 7). High quality projects deliver the required product, service or result within scope, on time, and within budget. The relationship among these factors is such that if any one of the three factors changes, at least one other factor is likely to be affected. Project managers also manage projects in response to uncertainty. Project risk is an uncertain event or condition that, if it occurs, has a positive or negative effect on at least one project objective.

The project management team has a professional responsibility to its stakeholders including customers, the performing organization, and the public. PMI members adhere to a "Code of Ethics" and those with the Project Management Professional (PMP®) certification adhere to a "Code of Professional Conduct." Project team members who are PMI members and/or PMPs are obligated to adhere to the current versions of these codes.

It is important to note that many of the processes within project management are iterative because of the existence of, and necessity for, progressive elaboration in a project throughout the project's life cycle. That is, as a project management team learns more about a project, the team can then manage to a greater level of detail.

The term "project management" is sometimes used to describe an organizational or managerial approach to the management of projects and some ongoing operations, which can be redefined as projects, that is also referred to as "management by projects." An organization that adopts this approach defines its activities as projects in a way that is consistent with the definition of a project provided in Section 1.2.2. There has been a tendency in recent years to manage more activities in more application areas using project management. More organizations are using "management by project." This is not to say that all operations can or should be organized into projects. The adoption of "management by project" is also related to the adoption of an organizational culture that is close to the project management culture described in Section 2.3. Although, an understanding of project management is critical to an organization that is using "management by projects," a detailed discussion of the approach itself is outside the scope of this standard.

1.4 The *PMBOK® Guide* Structure

The *PMBOK® Guide* is organized into three sections.

1.4.1 Section I: The Project Management Framework

Section I, The Project Management Framework, provides a basic structure for understanding project management.

Chapter 1, **Introduction**, defines key terms and provides an overview for the rest of the *PMBOK® Guide*.

Chapter 2, **Project Life Cycle and Organization,** describes the environment in which projects operate. The project management team should understand this broader context. Managing the day-to-day activities of the project is necessary, but not sufficient, to ensure success.

1.4.2 Section II: The Standard for Project Management of a Project

Section II, The Standard for Project Management of a Project, specifies all the project management processes that are used by the project team to manage a project.

Chapter 3, **Project Management Processes for a Project**, describes the five required Project Management Process Groups for any project and their constituent project management processes. This chapter describes the multi-dimensional nature of project management.

1.4.3 Section III: The Project Management Knowledge Areas

Section III, The Project Management Knowledge Areas, organizes the 44 project management processes from the Chapter 3 Project Management Process Groups into nine Knowledge Areas, as described below. An introduction to Section III describes the legend for the process flow diagrams used in each Knowledge Area chapter and introductory material applicable to all the Knowledge Areas.

Chapter 4, **Project Integration Management**, describes the processes and activities that integrate the various elements of project management, which are identified, defined, combined, unified and coordinated within the Project Management Process Groups. It consists of the Develop Project Charter, Develop Preliminary Project Scope Statement, Develop Project Management Plan, Direct and Manage Project Execution, Monitor and Control Project Work, Integrated Change Control, and Close Project project management processes.

Chapter 5, **Project Scope Management,** describes the processes involved in ascertaining that the project includes all the work required, and only the work required, to complete the project successfully. It consists of the Scope Planning, Scope Definition, Create WBS, Scope Verification, and Scope Control project management processes.

Chapter 6, **Project Time Management**, describes the processes concerning the timely completion of the project. It consists of the Activity Definition, Activity Sequencing, Activity Resource Estimating, Activity Duration Estimating, Schedule Development, and Schedule Control project management processes.

Chapter 7, **Project Cost Management**, describes the processes involved in planning, estimating, budgeting, and controlling costs so that the project is completed within the approved budget. It consists of the Cost Estimating, Cost Budgeting, and Cost Control project management processes.

Chapter 8, **Project Quality Management,** describes the processes involved in assuring that the project will satisfy the objectives for which it was undertaken. It consists of the Quality Planning, Perform Quality Assurance, and Perform Quality Control project management processes.

Chapter 9, **Project Human Resource Management,** describes the processes that organize and manage the project team. It consists of the Human Resource Planning, Acquire Project Team, Develop Project Team, and Manage Project Team project management processes.

Chapter 10, **Project Communications Management**, describes the processes concerning the timely and appropriate generation, collection, dissemination, storage and ultimate disposition of project information. It consists of the Communications Planning, Information Distribution, Performance Reporting, and Manage Stakeholders project management processes.

Chapter 11, **Project Risk Management,** describes the processes concerned with conducting risk management on a project. It consists of the Risk Management Planning, Risk Identification, Qualitative Risk Analysis, Quantitative Risk Analysis, Risk Response Planning, and Risk Monitoring and Control project management processes.

Chapter 12, **Project Procurement Management**, describes the processes that purchase or acquire products, services or results, as well as contract management processes. It consists of the Plan Purchases and Acquisitions, Plan Contracting, Request Seller Responses, Select Sellers, Contract Administration, and Contract Closure project management processes.

A Guide to the Project Management Body of Knowledge (PMBOK® Guide) Third Edition
©2004 Project Management Institute, Four Campus Boulevard, Newtown Square, PA 19073-3299 USA

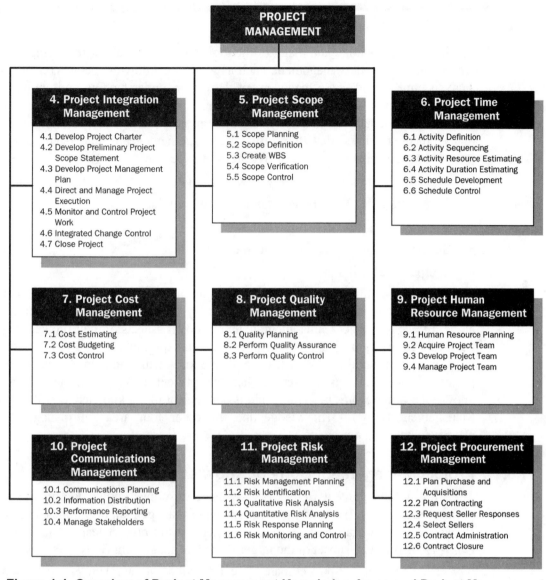

Figure 1-1. Overview of Project Management Knowledge Areas and Project Management Processes

1.5   Areas of Expertise

Much of the knowledge and many of the tools and techniques for managing projects are unique to project management, such as work breakdown structures, critical path analysis, and earned value management. However, understanding and applying the knowledge, skills, tools, and techniques, which are generally recognized as good practice, are not sufficient alone for effective project management. Effective project management requires that the project management team understand and use knowledge and skills from at least five areas of expertise:

- The Project Management Body of Knowledge
- Application area knowledge, standards, and regulations
- Understanding the project environment
- General management knowledge and skills
- Interpersonal skills.

Figure 1-2 illustrates the relationship among these five areas of expertise. Although they appear as discrete elements, they generally overlap; none can stand alone. Effective project teams integrate them into all aspects of their project. It is not necessary for every project team member to be an expert in all five areas. In fact, it is unlikely that any one person will have all the knowledge and skills needed for the project. However, it is important that the project management team has full knowledge of the *PMBOK® Guide* and is conversant in the knowledge of the Project Management Body of Knowledge and the other four areas of management to effectively manage a project.

1.5.1   Project Management Body of Knowledge

The Project Management Body of Knowledge describes knowledge unique to the project management field and that overlaps other management disciplines. Figure 1-2 shows the common areas of expertise needed by the project team. The *PMBOK® Guide* is, therefore, a subset of the larger Project Management Body of Knowledge.

The knowledge of project management described in the *PMBOK® Guide* consists of:

- Project life cycle definition (Chapter 2)
- Five Project Management Process Groups (Chapter 3)
- Nine Knowledge Areas (Chapters 4-12).

A Guide to the Project Management Body of Knowledge (PMBOK® Guide) Third Edition
©2004 Project Management Institute, Four Campus Boulevard, Newtown Square, PA 19073-3299 USA

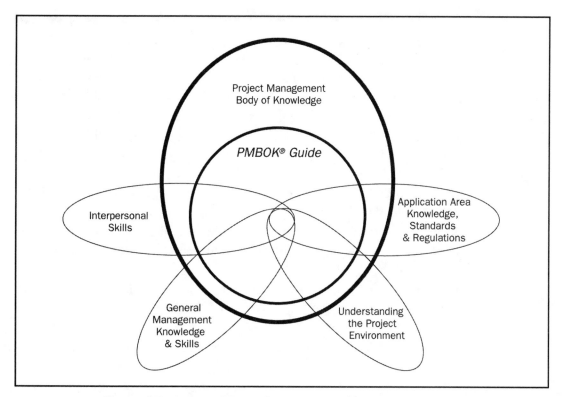

Figure 1-2. Areas of Expertise Needed by the Project Team

1.5.2 Application Area Knowledge, Standards and Regulations

Application areas are categories of projects that have common elements significant in such projects, but are not needed or present in all projects. Application areas are usually defined in terms of:

- Functional departments and supporting disciplines, such as legal, production and inventory management, marketing, logistics, and personnel

- Technical elements, such as software development or engineering, and sometimes a specific kind of engineering, such as water and sanitation engineering or construction engineering

- Management specializations, such as government contracting, community development, and new product development

- Industry groups, such as automotive, chemical, agriculture, and financial services.

Each application area generally has a set of accepted standards and practices, often codified in regulations. The International Organization for Standardization (ISO) differentiates between standards and regulations as follows[2]:

- A standard is a "document established by consensus and approved by a recognized body that provides, for common and repeated use, rules, guidelines or characteristics for activities or their results, aimed at the achievement of the optimum degree of order in a given context." Some examples of standards are computer disk sizes and the thermal stability specifications of hydraulic fluids.

- A regulation is a government-imposed requirement, which specifies product, process or service characteristics, including the applicable administrative provisions, with which compliance is mandatory. Building codes are an example of regulations.

There is an overlap in the concepts of standards and regulations that cause confusion. For example:

- Standards often begin as guidelines that describe a preferred approach and later, with widespread adoption, become generally accepted as if they were regulations

- Different organizational levels can mandate compliance, such as when a government agency, the management of the performing organization, or the project management team establishes specific policies and procedures.

A more detailed discussion of project management application areas appears in Appendix D.

1.5.3 Understanding the Project Environment

Virtually all projects are planned and implemented in a social, economic, and environmental context, and have intended and unintended positive and/or negative impacts. The project team should consider the project in its cultural, social, international, political, and physical environmental contexts.

- **Cultural and social environment.** The team needs to understand how the project affects people and how people affect the project. This may require an understanding of aspects of the economic, demographic, educational, ethical, ethnic, religious, and other characteristics of the people whom the project affects or who may have an interest in the project. The project manager should also examine the organizational culture and determine whether project management is recognized as a valid role with accountability and authority for managing the project.

- **International and political environment.** Some team members may need to be familiar with applicable international, national, regional, and local laws and customs, as well as the political climate that could affect the project. Other international factors to consider are time-zone differences, national and regional holidays, travel requirements for face-to-face meetings, and the logistics of teleconferencing.

- **Physical environment.** If the project will affect its physical surroundings, some team members should be knowledgeable about the local ecology and physical geography that could affect the project or be affected by the project.

A Guide to the Project Management Body of Knowledge (PMBOK® Guide) Third Edition
©2004 Project Management Institute, Four Campus Boulevard, Newtown Square, PA 19073-3299 USA

1.5.4 General Management Knowledge and Skills

General management encompasses planning, organizing, staffing, executing, and controlling the operations of an ongoing enterprise. It includes supporting disciplines such as:

- Financial management and accounting
- Purchasing and procurement
- Sales and marketing
- Contracts and commercial law
- Manufacturing and distribution
- Logistics and supply chain
- Strategic planning, tactical planning, and operational planning
- Organizational structures, organizational behavior, personnel administration, compensation, benefits, and career paths
- Health and safety practices
- Information technology.

General management provides the foundation for building project management skills and is often essential for the project manager. On any given project, skill in any number of general management areas may be required. General management literature documents these skills, and their application is fundamentally the same on a project.

1.5.5 Interpersonal Skills

The management of interpersonal relationships includes:

- **Effective communication.** The exchange of information
- **Influencing the organization.** The ability to "get things done"
- **Leadership.** Developing a vision and strategy, and motivating people to achieve that vision and strategy
- **Motivation.** Energizing people to achieve high levels of performance and to overcome barriers to change
- **Negotiation and conflict management.** Conferring with others to come to terms with them or to reach an agreement
- **Problem solving.** The combination of problem definition, alternatives identification and analysis, and decision-making.

1.6 Project Management Context

Project management exists in a broader context that includes program management, portfolio management and project management office. Frequently, there is a hierarchy of strategic plan, portfolio, program, project and subproject, in which a program consisting of several associated projects will contribute to the achievement of a strategic plan.

1.6.1 Programs and Program Management

A program is a group of related projects managed in a coordinated way to obtain benefits and control not available from managing them individually[3]. Programs may include elements of related work outside of the scope of the discrete projects in the program. For example:

- A new car model program can be broken up into projects for the design and upgrades of each major component (for example, transmission, engine, interior, exterior) while the ongoing manufacturing occurs on the assembly line

- Many electronics firms have program managers who are responsible for both individual product releases (projects) and the coordination of multiple releases over a period of time (an ongoing operation).

Programs also involve a series of repetitive or cyclical undertakings. For example:

- Utilities often speak of an annual "construction program," a series of projects built on previous efforts

- Many nonprofit organizations have a "fundraising program," to obtain financial support involving a series of discrete projects, such as a membership drive or an auction

- Publishing a newspaper or magazine is also a program with each individual issue managed as a project. This is an example of where general operations can become "management by projects" (Section 1.3).

In contrast with project management, program management is the centralized, coordinated management of a group of projects to achieve the program's strategic objectives and benefits.

1.6.2 Portfolios and Portfolio Management

A portfolio is a collection of projects or programs and other work that are grouped together to facilitate effective management of that work to meet strategic business objectives. The projects or programs in the portfolio may not necessarily be interdependent or directly related. Funding and support can be assigned on the basis of risk/reward categories, specific lines of business, or general types of projects, such as infrastructure and internal process improvement.

A Guide to the Project Management Body of Knowledge (PMBOK® Guide) Third Edition
©2004 Project Management Institute, Four Campus Boulevard, Newtown Square, PA 19073-3299 USA

Organizations manage their portfolios based on specific goals. One goal of portfolio management is to maximize the value of the portfolio by careful examination of candidate projects and programs for inclusion in the portfolio and the timely exclusion of projects not meeting the portfolio's strategic objectives. Other goals are to balance the portfolio among incremental and radical investments and for efficient use of resources. Senior managers or senior management teams typically take on the responsibility of portfolio management for an organization.

1.6.3 Subprojects

Projects are frequently divided into more manageable components or subprojects, although the individual subprojects can be referred to as projects and managed as such. Subprojects are often contracted to an external enterprise or to another functional unit in the performing organization. Examples include:

- Subprojects based on the project process, such as a single phase in the project life cycle

- Subprojects according to human resource skill requirements, such as plumbers or electricians needed on a construction project

- Subprojects involving specialized technology, such as the automated testing of computer programs on a software development project.

On very large projects, the subprojects can consist of a series of even smaller subprojects.

1.6.4 Project Management Office

A project management office (PMO) is an organizational unit to centralize and coordinate the management of projects under its domain. A PMO can also be referred to as a "program management office," "project office," or "program office." A PMO oversees the management of projects, programs, or a combination of both. The projects supported or administered by the PMO may not be related other than by being managed together. Some PMOs, however, do coordinate and manage related projects. In many organizations, those projects are indeed grouped or are related in some manner based on the way the PMO will coordinate and manage those projects. The PMO focuses on the coordinated planning, prioritization and execution of projects and subprojects that are tied to the parent organization's or client's overall business objectives.

PMOs can operate on a continuum, from providing project management support functions in the form of training, software, standardized policies, and procedures, to actual direct management and responsibility for achieving the project objectives. A specific PMO can receive delegated authority to act as an integral stakeholder and a key decision-maker during the initiation stage of each project, can have the authority to make recommendations, or can terminate projects to keep the business objectives consistent. In addition, the PMO can be involved in the selection, management, and redeployment, if necessary, of shared project personnel and, where possible, dedicated project personnel.

Some of the key features of a PMO include, but are not limited to:

- Shared and coordinated resources across all projects administered by the PMO
- Identification and development of project management methodology, best practices, and standards
- Clearinghouse and management for project policies, procedures, templates, and other shared documentation
- Centralized configuration management for all projects administered by the PMO
- Centralized repository and management for both shared and unique risks for all projects
- Central office for operation and management of project tools, such as enterprise-wide project management software
- Central coordination of communication management across projects
- A mentoring platform for project managers
- Central monitoring of all PMO project timelines and budgets, usually at the enterprise level
- Coordination of overall project quality standards between the project manager and any internal or external quality personnel or standards organization.

Differences between project managers and a PMO may include the following:

- Project managers and PMOs pursue different objectives and, as such, are driven by different requirements. All of these efforts, however, are aligned with the strategic needs of the organization.
- A project manager is responsible for delivering specific project objectives within the constraints of the project, while a PMO is an organizational structure with specific mandates that can include an enterprisewide perspective.
- The project manager focuses on the specified project objectives, while the PMO manages major program scope changes and can view them as potential opportunities to better achieve business objectives.
- The project manager controls the assigned project resources to best meet project objectives, while the PMO optimizes the use of shared organizational resources across all projects.
- The project manager manages the scope, schedule, cost, and quality of the products of the work packages, while the PMO manages overall risk, overall opportunity, and the interdependencies among projects.
- The project manager reports on project progress and other project specific information, while the PMO provides consolidated reporting and an enterprise view of projects under its purview.

A Guide to the Project Management Body of Knowledge (PMBOK® Guide) Third Edition
©2004 Project Management Institute, Four Campus Boulevard, Newtown Square, PA 19073-3299 USA

CHAPTER 2

Project Life Cycle and Organization

Projects and project management are carried out in an environment broader than that of the project itself. The project management team must understand this broader context so it can select the life cycle phases, processes, and tools and techniques that appropriately fit the project. This chapter describes some key aspects of the project management context. The topics included here are:

2.1 The Project Life Cycle

2.2 Project Stakeholders

2.3 Organizational Influences

2.1 The Project Life Cycle

Project managers or the organization can divide projects into phases to provide better management control with appropriate links to the ongoing operations of the performing organization. Collectively, these phases are known as the project life cycle. Many organizations identify a specific set of life cycles for use on all of their projects.

2.1.1 Characteristics of the Project Life Cycle

The project life cycle defines the phases that connect the beginning of a project to its end. For example, when an organization identifies an opportunity to which it would like to respond, it will often authorize a feasibility study to decide whether it should undertake the project. The project life cycle definition can help the project manager clarify whether to treat the feasibility study as the first project phase or as a separate, stand-alone project. Where the outcome of such a preliminary effort is not clearly identifiable, it is best to treat such efforts as a separate project. The phases of a project life cycle are not the same as the Project Management Process Groups described in detail in Chapter 3.

The transition from one phase to another within a project's life cycle generally involves, and is usually defined by, some form of technical transfer or handoff. Deliverables from one phase are usually reviewed for completeness and accuracy and approved before work starts on the next phase. However, it is not uncommon for a phase to begin prior to the approval of the previous phase's deliverables, when the risks involved are deemed acceptable. This practice of overlapping phases, normally done in sequence, is an example of the application of the schedule compression technique called fast tracking.

There is no single best way to define an ideal project life cycle. Some organizations have established policies that standardize all projects with a single life cycle, while others allow the project management team to choose the most appropriate life cycle for the team's project. Further, industry common practices will often lead to the use of a preferred life cycle within that industry.

Project life cycles generally define:

- What technical work to do in each phase (for example, in which phase should the architect's work be performed?)
- When the deliverables are to be generated in each phase and how each deliverable is reviewed, verified, and validated
- Who is involved in each phase (for example, concurrent engineering requires that the implementers be involved with requirements and design)
- How to control and approve each phase.

Project life cycle descriptions can be very general or very detailed. Highly detailed descriptions of life cycles can include forms, charts, and checklists to provide structure and control.

Most project life cycles share a number of common characteristics:

- Phases are generally sequential and are usually defined by some form of technical information transfer or technical component handoff.
- Cost and staffing levels are low at the start, peak during the intermediate phases, and drop rapidly as the project draws to a conclusion. Figure 2-1 illustrates this pattern.

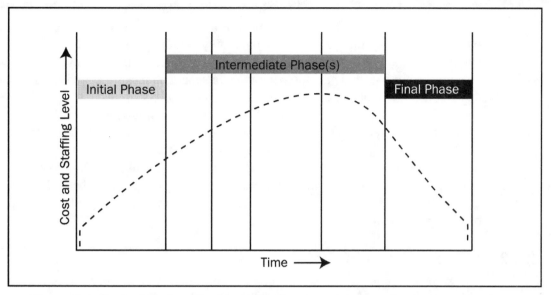

Figure 2-1. Typical Project Cost and Staffing Level Across the Project Life Cycle

- The level of uncertainty is highest and, hence, risk of failing to achieve the objectives is greatest at the start of the project. The certainty of completion generally gets progressively better as the project continues.

- The ability of the stakeholders to influence the final characteristics of the project's product and the final cost of the project is highest at the start, and gets progressively lower as the project continues. Figure 2-2 illustrates this. A major contributor to this phenomenon is that the cost of changes and correcting errors generally increases as the project continues.

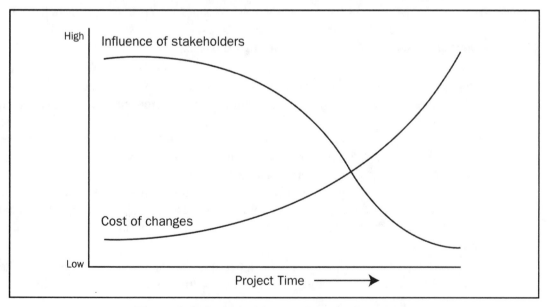

Figure 2-2. Stakeholders' Influence Over Time

Although many project life cycles have similar phase names with similar deliverables, few life cycles are identical. Some can have four or five phases, but others may have nine or more. Single application areas are known to have significant variations. One organization's software development life cycle can have a single design phase, while another can have separate phases for architectural and detailed design. Subprojects can also have distinct project life cycles. For example, an architectural firm hired to design a new office building is first involved in the owner's definition phase while doing the design, and in the owner's implementation phase while supporting the construction effort. The architect's design project, however, will have its own series of phases from conceptual development, through definition and implementation, to closure. The architect can even treat designing the facility and supporting the construction as separate projects, each with its own set of phases.

2.1.2 Characteristics of Project Phases

The completion and approval of one or more deliverables characterizes a project phase. A deliverable is a measurable, verifiable work product such as a specification, feasibility study report, detailed design document, or working prototype. Some deliverables can correspond to the project management process, whereas others are the end products or components of the end products for which the project was conceived. The deliverables, and hence the phases, are part of a generally sequential process designed to ensure proper control of the project and to attain the desired product or service, which is the objective of the project.

In any specific project, for reasons of size, complexity, level of risk, and cash flow constraints, phases can be further subdivided into subphases. Each subphase is aligned with one or more specific deliverables for monitoring and control. The majority of these subphase deliverables are related to the primary phase deliverable, and the phases typically take their names from these phase deliverables: requirements, design, build, test, startup, turnover, and others, as appropriate.

A project phase is generally concluded with a review of the work accomplished and the deliverables to determine acceptance, whether extra work is still required, or whether the phase should be considered closed. A management review is often held to reach a decision to start the activities of the next phase without closing the current phase, for example, when the project manager chooses fast tracking as the course of action. Another example is when an information technology company chooses an iterative life cycle where more than one phase of the project might progress simultaneously. Requirements for a module can be gathered and analyzed before the module is designed and constructed. While analysis of a module is being done, the requirements gathering for another module could also start in parallel.

Similarly, a phase can be closed without the decision to initiate any other phases. For example, the project is completed or the risk is deemed too great for the project to be allowed to continue.

A Guide to the Project Management Body of Knowledge (PMBOK® Guide) Third Edition
©2004 Project Management Institute, Four Campus Boulevard, Newtown Square, PA 19073-3299 USA

Formal phase completion does not include authorizing the subsequent phase. For effective control, each phase is formally initiated to produce a phase-dependent output of the Initiating Process Group, specifying what is allowed and expected for that phase, as shown in Figure 2-3. A phase-end review can be held with the explicit goals of obtaining authorization to close the current phase and to initiate the subsequent one. Sometimes both authorizations can be gained at one review. Phase-end reviews are also called phase exits, phase gates, or kill points.

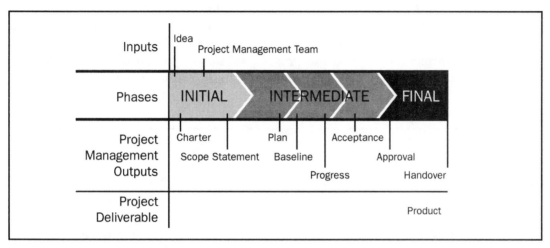

Figure 2-3. Typical Sequence of Phases in a Project Life Cycle

2.1.3 Project Life Cycle and Product Life Cycle Relationships

Many projects are linked to the ongoing work of the performing organization. Some organizations formally approve projects only after completion of a feasibility study, a preliminary plan, or some other equivalent form of analysis; in these cases, the preliminary planning or analysis takes the form of a separate project. For example, additional phases could come from developing and testing a prototype prior to initiating the project for the development of the final product. Some types of projects, especially internal service or new product development projects, can be initiated informally for a limited amount of time to secure formal approval for additional phases or activities.

The driving forces that create the stimuli for a project are typically referred to as problems, opportunities, or business requirements. The effect of these pressures is that management generally must prioritize this request with respect to the needs and resource demands of other potential projects.

The project life cycle definition will also identify which transitional actions at the end of the project are included or not included, in order to link the project to the ongoing operations of the performing organization. Examples would be when a new product is released to manufacturing, or a new software program is turned over to marketing. Care should be taken to distinguish the project life cycle from the product life cycle. For example, a project undertaken to bring a new desktop computer to market is only one aspect of the product life cycle. Figure 2-4 illustrates the product life cycle starting with the business plan, through idea, to product, ongoing operations and product divestment. The project life cycle goes through a series of phases to create the product. Additional projects can include a performance upgrade to the product. In some application areas, such as new product development or software development, organizations consider the project life cycle as part of the product life cycle.

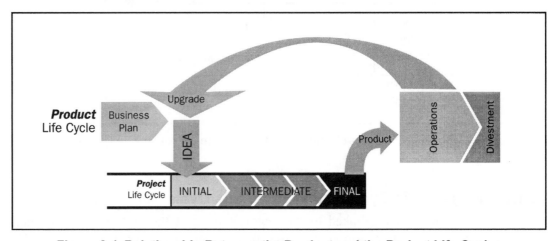

Figure 2-4. Relationship Between the Product and the Project Life Cycles

2.2 Project Stakeholders

Project stakeholders are individuals and organizations that are actively involved in the project, or whose interests may be affected as a result of project execution or project completion. They may also exert influence over the project's objectives and outcomes. The project management team must identify the stakeholders, determine their requirements and expectations, and, to the extent possible, manage their influence in relation to the requirements to ensure a successful project. Figure 2-5 illustrates the relationship between stakeholders and the project team.

A Guide to the Project Management Body of Knowledge (PMBOK® Guide) Third Edition
©2004 Project Management Institute, Four Campus Boulevard, Newtown Square, PA 19073-3299 USA

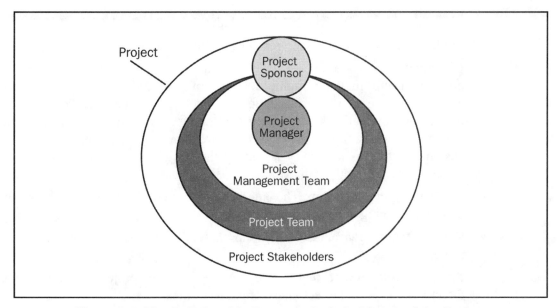

Figure 2-5. The Relationship Between Stakeholders and the Project

Stakeholders have varying levels of responsibility and authority when participating on a project and these can change over the course of the project's life cycle. Their responsibility and authority range from occasional contributions in surveys and focus groups to full project sponsorship, which includes providing financial and political support. Stakeholders who ignore this responsibility can have a damaging impact on the project objectives. Likewise, project managers who ignore stakeholders can expect a damaging impact on project outcomes.

Sometimes, stakeholder identification can be difficult. For example, some would argue that an assembly-line worker whose future employment depends on the outcome of a new product-design project is a stakeholder. Failure to identify a key stakeholder can cause major problems for a project. For example, late recognition that the legal department was a significant stakeholder in a year 2000 rollover (Y2K) software upgrade project caused many additional documentation tasks to be added to the project's requirements.

Stakeholders may have a positive or negative influence on a project. Positive stakeholders are those who would normally benefit from a successful outcome from the project, while negative stakeholders are those who see negative outcomes from the project's success. For example, business leaders from a community that will benefit from an industrial expansion project may be positive stakeholders because they see economic benefit to the community from the project's success. Conversely, environmental groups could be negative stakeholders if they view the project as doing harm to the environment. In the case of positive stakeholders, their interests are best served by helping the project succeed, for example, helping the project obtain the needed permits to proceed. The negative stakeholders' interest would be better served by impeding the project's progress by demanding more extensive environmental reviews. Negative stakeholders are often overlooked by the project team at the risk of failing to bring their projects to a successful end.

Key stakeholders on every project include:

- **Project manager.** The person responsible for managing the project.
- **Customer/user.** The person or organization that will use the project's product. There may be multiple layers of customers. For example, the customers for a new pharmaceutical product can include the doctors who prescribe it, the patients who take it and the insurers who pay for it. In some application areas, customer and user are synonymous, while in others, customer refers to the entity acquiring the project's product and users are those who will directly utilize the project's product.
- **Performing organization.** The enterprise whose employees are most directly involved in doing the work of the project.
- **Project team members.** The group that is performing the work of the project.
- **Project management team.** The members of the project team who are directly involved in project management activities.
- **Sponsor.** The person or group that provides the financial resources, in cash or in kind, for the project.
- **Influencers.** People or groups that are not directly related to the acquisition or use of the project's product, but due to an individual's position in the customer organization or performing organization, can influence, positively or negatively, the course of the project.
- **PMO.** If it exists in the performing organization, the PMO can be a stakeholder if it has direct or indirect responsibility for the outcome of the project.

In addition to these key stakeholders, there are many different names and categories of project stakeholders, including internal and external, owners and investors, sellers and contractors, team members and their families, government agencies and media outlets, individual citizens, temporary or permanent lobbying organizations, and society-at-large. The naming or grouping of stakeholders is primarily an aid to identifying which individuals and organizations view themselves as stakeholders. Stakeholder roles and responsibilities can overlap, such as when an engineering firm provides financing for a plant that it is designing.

Project managers must manage stakeholder expectations, which can be difficult because stakeholders often have very different or conflicting objectives. For example:

- The manager of a department that has requested a new management information system may desire low cost, the system architect may emphasize technical excellence, and the programming contractor may be most interested in maximizing its profit.
- The vice president of research at an electronics firm may define new product success as state-of-the-art technology, the vice president of manufacturing may define it as world-class practices, and the vice president of marketing may be primarily concerned with the number of new features.

A Guide to the Project Management Body of Knowledge (PMBOK® Guide) **Third Edition**
©2004 Project Management Institute, Four Campus Boulevard, Newtown Square, PA 19073-3299 USA

- The owner of a real estate development project may be focused on timely performance, the local governing body may desire to maximize tax revenue, an environmental group may wish to minimize adverse environmental impacts, and nearby residents may hope to relocate the project.

2.3 Organizational Influences

Projects are typically part of an organization that is larger than the project. Examples of organizations include corporations, government agencies, healthcare institutions, international bodies, professional associations, and others. Even when the project is external (joint ventures, partnering), the project will still be influenced by the organization or organizations that initiated it. The maturity of the organization with respect to its project management system, culture, style, organizational structure and project management office can also influence the project. The following sections describe key aspects of these larger organizational structures that are likely to influence the project.

2.3.1 Organizational Systems

Project-based organizations are those whose operations consist primarily of projects. These organizations fall into two categories:

- Organizations that derive their revenue primarily from performing projects for others under contract – architectural firms, engineering firms, consultants, construction contractors, and government contractors.

- Organizations that have adopted management by projects (Section 1.3). These organizations tend to have management systems in place to facilitate project management. For example, their financial systems are often specifically designed for accounting, tracking, and reporting on multiple, simultaneous projects.

   Non-project-based organizations often may lack management systems designed to support project needs efficiently and effectively. The absence of project-oriented systems usually makes project management more difficult. In some cases, non-project-based organizations will have departments or other sub-units that operate as project-based organizations with systems to support them. The project management team should be aware of how its organization's structure and systems affect the project.

2.3.2 Organizational Cultures and Styles

Most organizations have developed unique and describable cultures. These cultures are reflected in numerous factors, including, but not limited to:

- Shared values, norms, beliefs, and expectations
- Policies and procedures
- View of authority relationships
- Work ethic and work hours.

Organizational cultures often have a direct influence on the project. For example:

- A team proposing an unusual or high-risk approach is more likely to secure approval in an aggressive or entrepreneurial organization

- A project manager with a highly participative style is apt to encounter problems in a rigidly hierarchical organization, while a project manager with an authoritarian style will be equally challenged in a participative organization.

2.3.3 Organizational Structure

The structure of the performing organization often constrains the availability of resources in a spectrum from functional to projectized, with a variety of matrix structures in between. Figure 2-6 shows key project-related characteristics of the major types of organizational structures.

Organization Structure / Project Characteristics	Functional	Matrix			Projectized
		Weak Matrix	Balanced Matrix	Strong Matrix	
Project Manager's Authority	Little or None	Limited	Low to Moderate	Moderate to High	High to Almost Total
Resource Availability	Little or None	Limited	Low to Moderate	Moderate to High	High to Almost Total
Who controls the project budget	Functional Manager	Functional Manager	Mixed	Project Manager	Project Manager
Project Manager's Role	Part-time	Part-time	Full-time	Full-time	Full-time
Project Management Administrative Staff	Part-time	Part-time	Part-time	Full-time	Full-time

Figure 2-6. Organizational Structure Influences on Projects

The classic functional organization, shown in Figure 2-7, is a hierarchy where each employee has one clear superior. Staff members are grouped by specialty, such as production, marketing, engineering, and accounting at the top level. Engineering may be further subdivided into functional organizations that support the business of the larger organization, such as mechanical and electrical. Functional organizations still have projects, but the scope of the project is usually limited to the boundaries of the function. The engineering department in a functional organization will do its project work independent of the manufacturing or marketing departments. When new product development is undertaken in a purely functional organization, the design phase, often called a design project, includes only engineering department staff. Then, when questions about manufacturing arise, they are passed up the organizational hierarchy to the department head, who consults with the head of the manufacturing department. The engineering department head then passes the answer back down the hierarchy to the engineering functional manager.

A Guide to the Project Management Body of Knowledge (PMBOK® Guide) Third Edition
©2004 Project Management Institute, Four Campus Boulevard, Newtown Square, PA 19073-3299 USA

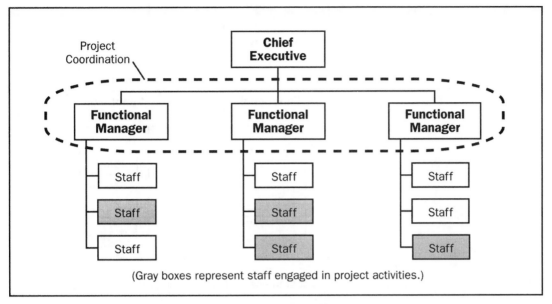

(Gray boxes represent staff engaged in project activities.)

Figure 2-7. Functional Organization

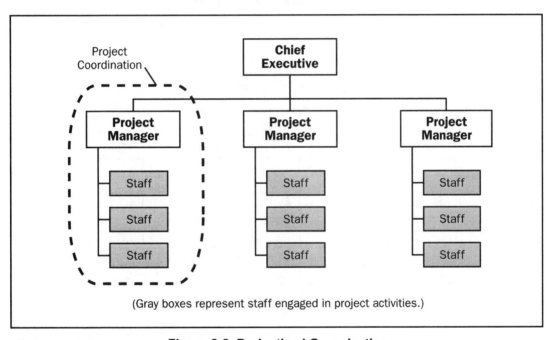

(Gray boxes represent staff engaged in project activities.)

Figure 2-8. Projectized Organization

At the opposite end of the spectrum is the projectized organization, shown in Figure 2-8. In a projectized organization, team members are often collocated. Most of the organization's resources are involved in project work, and project managers have a great deal of independence and authority. Projectized organizations often have organizational units called departments, but these groups either report directly to the project manager or provide support services to the various projects.

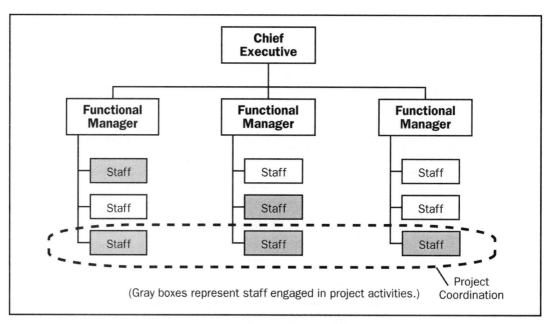

Figure 2-9. Weak Matrix Organization

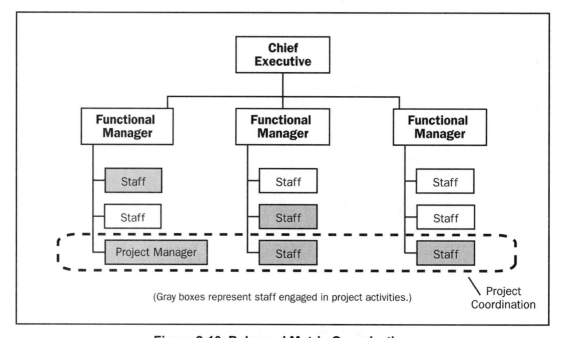

Figure 2-10. Balanced Matrix Organization

Matrix organizations, as shown in Figures 2-9 through 2-11, are a blend of functional and projectized characteristics. Weak matrices maintain many of the characteristics of a functional organization and the project manager role is more that of a coordinator or expediter than that of a manager. In similar fashion, strong matrices have many of the characteristics of the projectized organization, and can have full-time project managers with considerable authority and full-time project administrative staff. While the balanced matrix organization recognizes the need for a project manager, it does not provide the project manager with the full authority over the project and project funding (Figure 2-6).

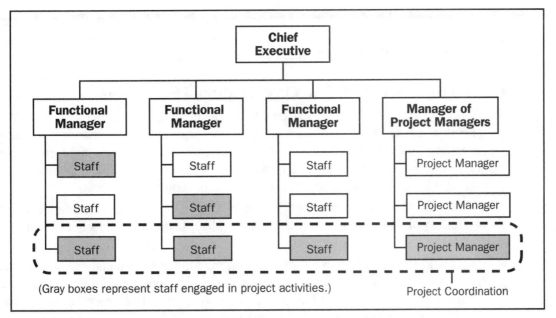

Figure 2-11. Strong Matrix Organization

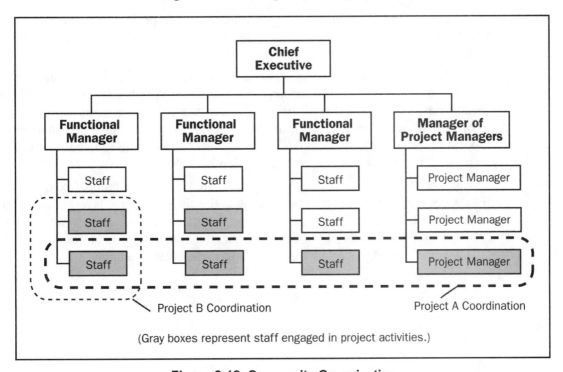

Figure 2-12. Composite Organization

Most modern organizations involve all these structures at various levels, as shown in Figure 2-12 (Composite Organization). For example, even a fundamentally functional organization may create a special project team to handle a critical project. Such a team may have many of the characteristics of a project team in a projectized organization. The team may include full-time staff from different functional departments, may develop its own set of operating procedures and may operate outside the standard, formalized reporting structure.

2.3.4 The Role of the PMO in Organizational Structures

Many organizations realize the benefit of developing and implementing a PMO (Section 1.6.4). This is often true of those organizations employing a matrix organizational structure, and almost always true of those employing a projectized organizational structure, especially when the parent organization is involved with the simultaneous management of multiple and/or sequential projects.

A PMO can exist in any of the organizational structures, including those with a functional organization, with increasing likelihood of occurrence toward the rightmost columns in Figure 2-6.

A PMO's function in an organization may range from an advisory influence, limited to the recommendation of specific policies and procedures on individual projects, to a formal grant of authority from executive management. In such cases, the PMO may, in turn, delegate its authority to the individual project manager. The project manager will have administrative support from the PMO either through dedicated staff or through a shared staff member. The project team members will either be dedicated to the project or might include staff members who are shared with other projects and, in turn, are managed by the PMO.

Project team members will report either directly to the project manager or, if shared, to the PMO. The project manager reports directly to the PMO. Additionally, the flexibility of the PMO's centralized management can offer the project manager a greater opportunity for advancement within the organization. Specialty project team members can also be exposed to alternative project management career options in organizations with PMOs.

Note that if a PMO exists, Figure 2-8 would have an additional box, labeled PMO, between the project manager layer and the chief executive layer. Similarly in Figures 2-11 and 2-12, the "manager of project managers" would normally be the PMO manager, whereas in the other organizational structures (Figures 2-9 and 2-10), the PMO usually does not directly report to the chief executive.

2.3.5 Project Management System

The project management system is the set of tools, techniques, methodologies, resources, and procedures used to manage a project. It can be formal or informal and aids a project manager in effectively guiding a project to completion. The system is a set of processes and the related control functions that are consolidated and combined into a functioning, unified whole.

The project management plan describes how the project management system will be used. The project management system content will vary depending upon the application area, organizational influence, complexity of the project, and availability of existing systems. The organizational influences shape the system for executing projects within that organization. The system will adjust or adapt to accommodate any influence imposed by the organization.

If a PMO exists in the performing organization, one of the functions of the PMO would typically be to manage the project management system, in order to ensure consistency in application and continuity on the various projects being performed.

Section II

The Standard for Project Management of a Project

Chapter 3   Project Management Processes for a Project

CHAPTER 3

Project Management Processes for a Project

Project management is the application of knowledge, skills, tools, and techniques to project activities to meet project requirements. Project management is accomplished through processes, using project management knowledge, skills, tools, and techniques that receive inputs and generate outputs.

In order for a project to be successful, the project team must:

- Select appropriate processes within the Project Management Process Groups (also known as Process Groups) that are required to meet the project objectives
- Use a defined approach to adapt the product specifications and plans to meet project and product requirements
- Comply with requirements to meet stakeholder needs, wants and expectations
- Balance the competing demands of scope, time, cost, quality, resources, and risk to produce a quality product.

This standard documents information needed to initiate, plan, execute, monitor and control, and close a single project, and identifies those project management processes that have been recognized as good practice on most projects most of the time. These processes apply globally and across industry groups. Good practice means there is general agreement that the application of those project management processes has been shown to enhance the chances of success over a wide range of projects.

This does not mean that the knowledge, skills and processes described should always be applied uniformly on all projects. The project manager, in collaboration with the project team, is always responsible for determining what processes are appropriate, and the appropriate degree of rigor for each process, for any given project.

In fact, project managers and their teams are advised to carefully consider addressing each process and its constituent inputs and outputs. Project managers and their teams should use this chapter as a high-level guide for those processes that they must consider in managing their project. This effort is known as tailoring.

A process is a set of interrelated actions and activities that are performed to achieve a pre-specified set of products, results, or services. The project processes are performed by the project team, and generally fall into one of two major categories:

- The project management processes common to most projects most of the time are associated with each other by their performance for an integrated purpose. The purpose is to initiate, plan, execute, monitor and control, and close a project. These processes interact with each other in complex ways that cannot be completely explained in a document or with graphics. However, an example of the interactions among the Process Groups is shown in Figure 3-4. The processes may also interact in relation to project scope, cost, schedule, etc., which are called Knowledge Areas, and are described in Chapters 4 through 12.

- Product-oriented processes specify and create the project's product. Product-oriented processes are typically defined by the project life cycle (discussed in Section 2.1) and vary by application area. Project management processes and product-oriented processes overlap and interact throughout the project. For example, the scope of the project cannot be defined in the absence of some basic understanding of how to create the specified product.

Project management is an integrative undertaking. Project management integration requires each project and product process to be appropriately aligned and connected with the other processes to facilitate their coordination. These process interactions often require tradeoffs among project requirements and objectives. A large and complex project may have some processes that will have to be iterated several times to define and meet stakeholder requirements and reach agreement on the processes outcome. Failure to take action during one process will usually affect that process and other related processes. For example, a scope change will almost always affect project cost, but the scope change may or may not affect team morale or product quality. The specific performance tradeoffs will vary from project to project and organization to organization. Successful project management includes actively managing these interactions to successfully meet sponsor, customer and other stakeholder requirements.

This standard describes the nature of project management processes in terms of the integration between the processes, the interactions within them, and the purposes they serve. These processes are aggregated into five groups, defined as the Project Management Process Groups:

- Initiating Process Group
- Planning Process Group
- Executing Process Group
- Monitoring and Controlling Process Group
- Closing Process Group.

This chapter provides information about project management of a single project as a number of interlinked processes, and includes the following major sections:

3.1 Project Management Processes

3.2 Project Management Process Groups

3.3 Process Interactions

3.4 Project Management Process Mapping

3.1 Project Management Processes

The project management processes are presented as discrete elements with well-defined interfaces. However, in practice they overlap and interact in ways that are not completely detailed here. Most experienced project management practitioners recognize there is more than one way to manage a project. The specifics for a project are defined as objectives that must be accomplished based on complexity, risk, size, time frame, project team's experience, access to resources, amount of historical information, the organization's project management maturity, and industry and application area. The required Process Groups and their constituent processes are guides to apply appropriate project management knowledge and skills during the project. In addition, the application of the project management processes to a project is iterative and many processes are repeated and revised during the project. The project manager and the project team are responsible for determining what processes from the Process Groups will be employed, by whom, and the degree of rigor that will be applied to the execution of those processes to achieve the desired project objective.

An underlying concept for the interaction among the project management processes is the plan-do-check-act cycle (as defined by Shewhart and modified by Deming, in the ASQ Handbook, pages 13–14, American Society for Quality, 1999). This cycle is linked by results – the result from one part of the cycle becomes the input to another. See Figure 3-1.

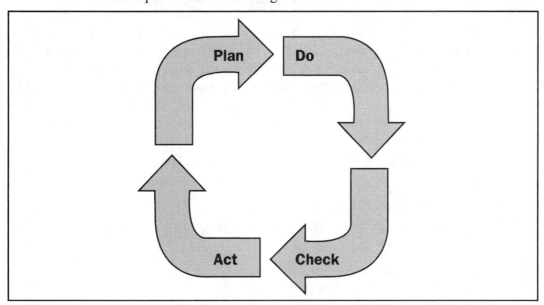

Figure 3-1. The Plan-Do-Check-Act Cycle

The integrative nature of the Process Groups is more complex than the basic plan-do-check-act cycle (see Figure 3-2). However, the enhanced cycle can be applied to the interrelationships within and among the Process Groups. The Planning Process Group corresponds to the "plan" component of the plan-do-check-act cycle. The Executing Process Group corresponds to the "do" component and the Monitoring and Controlling Process Group corresponds to the "check and act" components. In addition, since management of a project is a finite effort, the Initiating Process Group starts these cycles and the Closing Process Group ends them. The integrative nature of project management requires the Monitoring and Controlling Process Group interaction with every aspect of the other Process Groups.

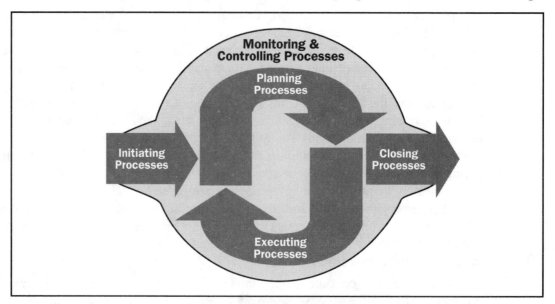

Figure 3-2. Project Management Process Groups Mapped to the Plan-Do-Check-Act Cycle

3.2 Project Management Process Groups

This section identifies and describes the five Project Management Process Groups required for any project. These five Process Groups have clear dependencies and are performed in the same sequence on each project. They are independent of application areas or industry focus. Individual Process Groups and individual constituent processes are often iterated prior to completing the project. Constituent processes also can have interactions both within a Process Group and among Process Groups.

The symbols for the process flow diagrams are shown in Figure 3-3:

• Process Groups

• Processes within the Process Groups

• Organizational Process Assets and Enterprise Environmental Factors, shown as inputs to and outputs from the Process Groups, but external to the processes

• Arrows or line arrows indicate process or data flow among or within the Process Groups.

Note: Not all process interactions and data flow among the processes are shown in an effort to make the diagrams more readable.

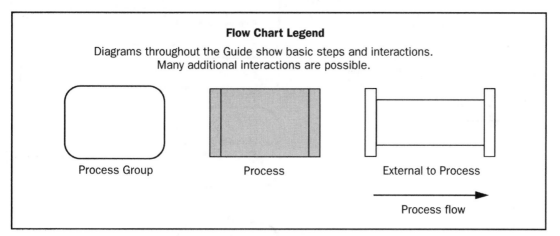

Flow Chart Legend

Diagrams throughout the Guide show basic steps and interactions.
Many additional interactions are possible.

Process Group

Process

External to Process

Process flow

Figure 3-3. Flow Chart Legend

The process flow diagram, Figure 3-4, provides an overall summary of the basic flow and interactions among the Process Groups. An individual process may define and constrain how inputs are used to produce outputs for that Process Group. A Process Group includes the constituent project management processes that are linked by the respective inputs and outputs, that is, the result or outcome of one process becomes the input to another. The Monitoring and Controlling Process Group, for example, not only monitors and controls the work being done during a Process Group, but also monitors and controls the entire project effort. The Monitoring and Controlling Process Group must also provide feedback to implement corrective or preventive actions to bring the project into compliance with the project management plan or to appropriately modify the project management plan. Many additional interactions among the Process Groups are likely. **The Process Groups are not project phases.** Where large or complex projects may be separated into distinct phases or sub-projects such as feasibility study, concept development, design, prototype, build, test, etc. all of the Process Group processes would normally be repeated for each phase or subproject.

The five Process Groups are:

- **Initiating Process Group.** Defines and authorizes the project or a project phase.

- **Planning Process Group.** Defines and refines objectives, and plans the course of action required to attain the objectives and scope that the project was undertaken to address.

- **Executing Process Group.** Integrates people and other resources to carry out the project management plan for the project.

- **Monitoring and Controlling Process Group.** Regularly measures and monitors progress to identify variances from the project management plan so that corrective action can be taken when necessary to meet project objectives.

- **Closing Process Group.** Formalizes acceptance of the product, service or result and brings the project or a project phase to an orderly end.

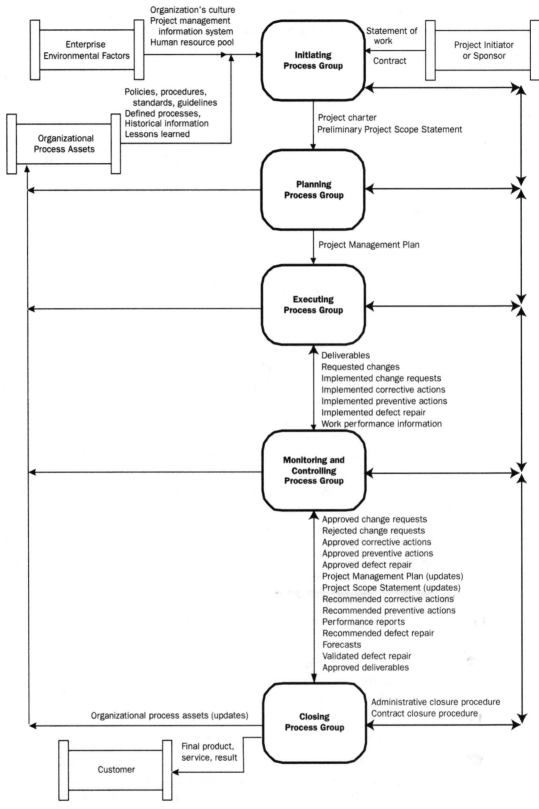

Note: Not all process interactions and data flow among the Process Groups are shown.

Figure 3-4. High Level Summary of Process Groups' Interactions

3.2.1 Initiating Process Group

The Initiating Process Group consists of the processes that facilitate the formal authorization to start a new project or a project phase. Initiating processes are often done external to the project's scope of control by the organization or by program or portfolio processes (Figure 3-5), which may blur the project boundaries for the initial project inputs. For example, before beginning the Initiation Process Group activities, the organization's business needs or requirements are documented. The feasibility of the new undertaking may be established through a process of evaluating alternatives to pick the best one. Clear descriptions of the project objectives are developed, including the reasons why a specific project is the best alternative solution to satisfy the requirements. The documentation for this decision also contains a basic description of the project scope, the deliverables, project duration, and a forecast of the resources for the organization's investment analysis. The framework of the project can be clarified by documenting the project selection processes. The relationship of the project to the organization's strategic plan identifies the management responsibilities within the organization. In multi-phase projects, initiating processes are carried out during subsequent phases to validate the assumptions and decisions made during the original Develop Project Charter and Develop Preliminary Project Scope Statement processes.

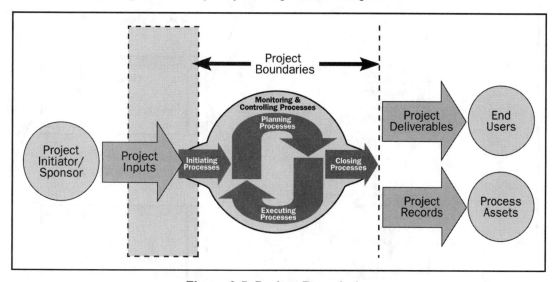

Figure 3-5. Project Boundaries

The initial scope description and the resources that the organization is willing to invest are further refined during the initiation process. If not already assigned, the project manager will be selected. Initial assumptions and constraints will also be documented. This information is captured in the Project Charter and, when it is approved, the project becomes officially authorized. Although the project management team may help write the Project Charter, approval and funding are handled external to the project boundaries.

As part of the Initiating Process Group, many large or complex projects may be divided into phases. Reviewing the initiating processes at the start of each phase helps to keep project focused on the business need that the project was undertaken to address. The entry criteria are verified, including the availability of required resources. A decision is then made whether or not the project is ready to continue or whether the project should be delayed or discontinued. During subsequent project phases, further validation and development of the project scope for that phase is performed. Repeating the initiating processes at each subsequent phase also enables the project to be halted if the business need no longer exists or if the project is deemed unable to satisfy that business need.

Involving the customers and other stakeholders during initiation generally improves the probability of shared ownership, deliverable acceptance, and customer and other stakeholder satisfaction. Such acceptance is critical to project success. The Initiating Process Group (Figure 3-6) starts a project or project phase, and the output defines the project's purpose, identifies objectives, and authorizes the project manager to start the project.

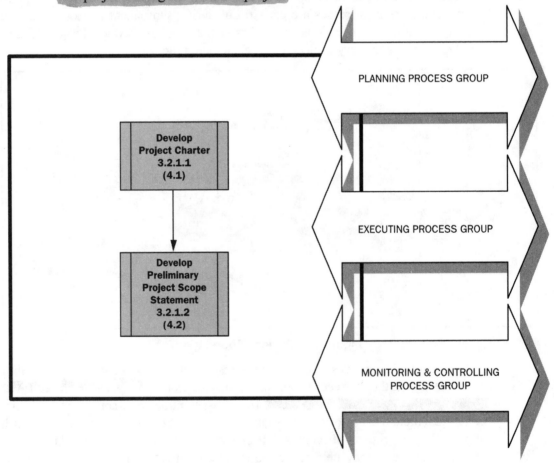

Figure 3-6. Initiating Process Group

The Initiating Process Group includes the following project management processes:

.1 Develop Project Charter

This process is primarily concerned with authorizing the project or, in a multi-phase project, a project phase. It is the process necessary for documenting the business needs and the new product, service, or other result that is intended to satisfy those requirements. This chartering links the project to the ongoing work of the organization and authorizes the project. Projects are chartered and authorized external to the project by the organization, a program or portfolio management body. In multi-phase projects, this process is used to validate or refine the decisions made during the previous Develop Project Charter process.

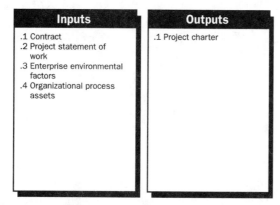

Table 3-1. Develop Project Charter: Inputs and Outputs

.2 Develop Preliminary Project Scope Statement

This is the process necessary for producing a preliminary high-level definition of the project using the Project Charter with other inputs to the initiating processes. This process addresses and documents the project and deliverable requirements, product requirements, boundaries of the project, methods of acceptance, and high-level scope control. In multi-phase projects, this process validates or refines the project scope for each phase.

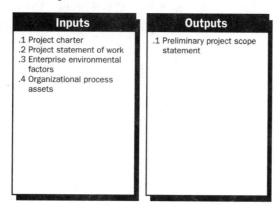

Table 3-2. Develop Preliminary Project Scope: Inputs and Outputs

3.2.2 Planning Process Group

The project management team uses the Planning Process Group and its constituent processes and interactions to plan and manage a successful project for the organization. The Planning Process Group helps gather information from many sources with each having varying levels of completeness and confidence. The planning processes develop the project management plan. These processes also identify, define, and mature the project scope, project cost, and schedule the project activities that occur within the project. As new project information is discovered, additional dependencies, requirements, risks, opportunities, assumptions, and constraints will be identified or resolved. The multi-dimensional nature of project management causes repeated feedback loops for additional analysis. As more project information or characteristics are gathered and understood, follow-on actions may be required. Significant changes occurring throughout the project life cycle trigger a need to revisit one or more of the planning processes and, possibly, some of the initiating processes.

The frequency of iterating the planning processes is also affected. For example, the project management plan, developed as an output of the Planning Process Group, will have an emphasis on exploring all aspects of the scope, technology, risks, and costs. Updates arising from approved changes during project execution may significantly impact parts of the project management plan. Project management plan updates provide greater precision with respect to schedule, costs, and resource requirements to meet the defined project scope as a whole. Updates can be limited to the activities and issues associated with the execution of a specific phase. This progressive detailing of the project management plan is often called "rolling wave planning," indicating that planning is an iterative and ongoing process (see Figure 3-7).

While planning the project, the project team should involve all appropriate stakeholders, depending upon their influence on the project and its outcomes. The project team should use stakeholders in project planning since the stakeholders have skills and knowledge that can be leveraged in developing the project management plan and any subsidiary plans. The project team must create an environment in which stakeholders can contribute appropriately.

Since the feedback and refinement process cannot continue indefinitely, procedures set by the organization identify when the planning effort ends. These procedures will be affected by the nature of the project, the established project boundaries, appropriate monitoring and controlling activities, as well as the environment in which the project will be performed.

Other interactions among the processes within the Planning Process Group are dependent on the nature of the project. For example, on some projects there will be little or no identifiable risk until after most of the planning has been done. At that time, the team might recognize that the cost and schedule targets are overly aggressive, thus involving considerably more risk than previously understood. The results of the iterations are documented as updates to the project management plan.

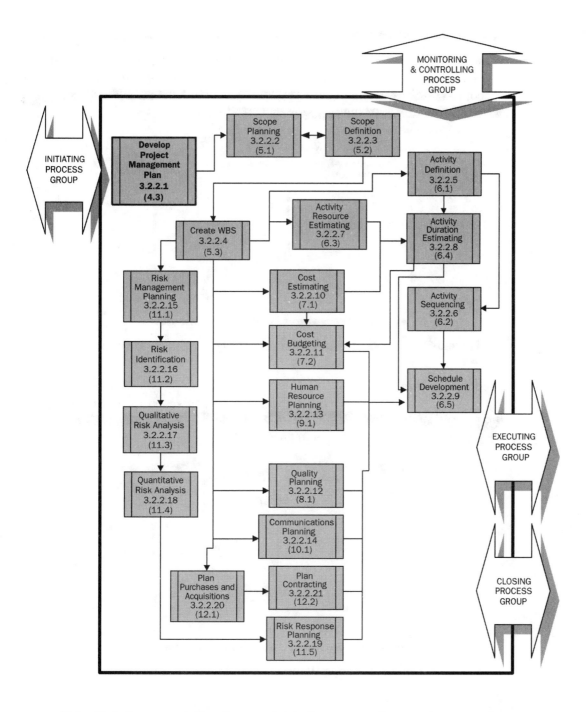

Note: Not all process interactions and data flow among the processes are shown.

Figure 3-7. Planning Process Group

The Planning Process Group facilitates project planning across multiple processes. The following list identifies the processes the project team should address during the planning process to decide if they need to be done, and if so, by whom. The Planning Process Group includes the following project management processes:

.1 Develop Project Management Plan

This is the process necessary for defining, preparing, integrating and coordinating all subsidiary plans into a project management plan. The project management plan becomes the primary source of information for how the project will be planned, executed, monitored and controlled, and closed.

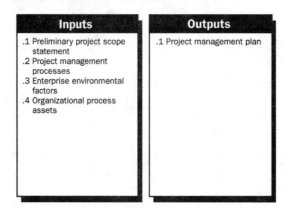

Inputs	Outputs
.1 Preliminary project scope statement .2 Project management processes .3 Enterprise environmental factors .4 Organizational process assets	.1 Project management plan

Table 3-3. Develop Project Management Plan: Inputs and Outputs

.2 Scope Planning

This is the process necessary for creating a project scope management plan that documents how the project scope will be defined, verified and controlled, and how the work breakdown structure will be created and defined.

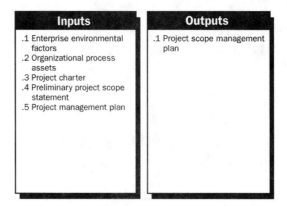

Inputs	Outputs
.1 Enterprise environmental factors .2 Organizational process assets .3 Project charter .4 Preliminary project scope statement .5 Project management plan	.1 Project scope management plan

Table 3-4. Scope Planning: Inputs and Outputs

.3   Scope Definition

This is the process necessary for developing a detailed project scope statement as the basis for future project decisions.

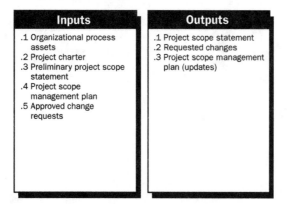

Inputs	Outputs
.1 Organizational process assets .2 Project charter .3 Preliminary project scope statement .4 Project scope management plan .5 Approved change requests	.1 Project scope statement .2 Requested changes .3 Project scope management plan (updates)

Table 3-5. Scope Definition: Inputs and Outputs

.4   Create WBS

This is the process necessary for subdividing the major project deliverables and project work into smaller, more manageable components.

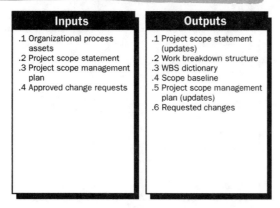

Inputs	Outputs
.1 Organizational process assets .2 Project scope statement .3 Project scope management plan .4 Approved change requests	.1 Project scope statement (updates) .2 Work breakdown structure .3 WBS dictionary .4 Scope baseline .5 Project scope management plan (updates) .6 Requested changes

Table 3-6. Create WBS: Inputs and Outputs

.5   Activity Definition

This is the process necessary for identifying the specific activities that need to be performed to produce the various project deliverables.

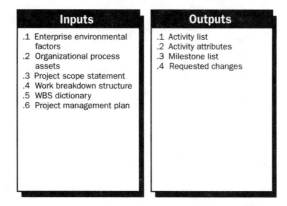

Inputs	Outputs
.1 Enterprise environmental factors .2 Organizational process assets .3 Project scope statement .4 Work breakdown structure .5 WBS dictionary .6 Project management plan	.1 Activity list .2 Activity attributes .3 Milestone list .4 Requested changes

Table 3-7. Activity Definition: Inputs and Outputs

.6   Activity Sequencing

This is the process necessary for identifying and documenting dependencies among schedule activities.

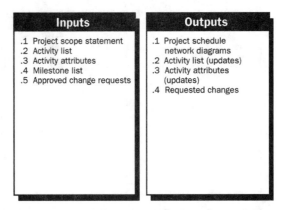

Table 3-8. Activity Sequencing: Inputs and Outputs

.7   Activity Resource Estimating

This is the process necessary for estimating the type and quantities of resources required to perform each schedule activity.

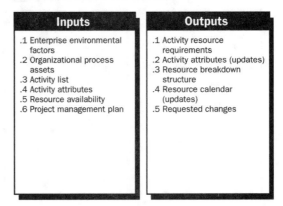

Table 3-9. Activity Resource Estimating: Inputs and Outputs

.8   Activity Duration Estimating

This is the process necessary for estimating the number of work periods that will be needed to complete individual schedule activities.

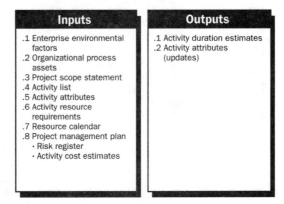

Table 3-10. Activity Duration Estimating: Inputs and Outputs

.9 Schedule Development

This is the process necessary for analyzing activity sequences, durations, resource requirements, and schedule constraints to create the project schedule.

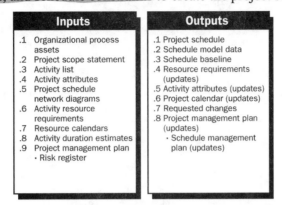

Inputs	Outputs
.1 Organizational process assets .2 Project scope statement .3 Activity list .4 Activity attributes .5 Project schedule network diagrams .6 Activity resource requirements .7 Resource calendars .8 Activity duration estimates .9 Project management plan · Risk register	.1 Project schedule .2 Schedule model data .3 Schedule baseline .4 Resource requirements (updates) .5 Activity attributes (updates) .6 Project calendar (updates) .7 Requested changes .8 Project management plan (updates) · Schedule management plan (updates)

Table 3-11. Schedule Development: Inputs and Outputs

.10 Cost Estimating

This is the process necessary for developing an approximation of the costs of the resources needed to complete project activities.

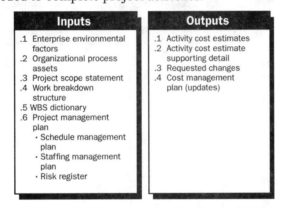

Inputs	Outputs
.1 Enterprise environmental factors .2 Organizational process assets .3 Project scope statement .4 Work breakdown structure .5 WBS dictionary .6 Project management plan · Schedule management plan · Staffing management plan · Risk register	.1 Activity cost estimates .2 Activity cost estimate supporting detail .3 Requested changes .4 Cost management plan (updates)

Table 3-12. Cost Estimating: Inputs and Outputs

.11 Cost Budgeting

This is the process necessary for aggregating the estimated costs of individual activities or work packages to establish a cost baseline.

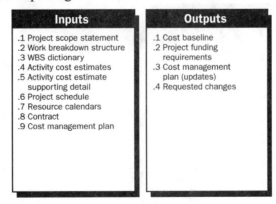

Inputs	Outputs
.1 Project scope statement .2 Work breakdown structure .3 WBS dictionary .4 Activity cost estimates .5 Activity cost estimate supporting detail .6 Project schedule .7 Resource calendars .8 Contract .9 Cost management plan	.1 Cost baseline .2 Project funding requirements .3 Cost management plan (updates) .4 Requested changes

Table 3-13. Cost Budgeting: Inputs and Outputs

.12 Quality Planning

This is the process necessary for identifying which quality standards are relevant to the project and determining how to satisfy them.

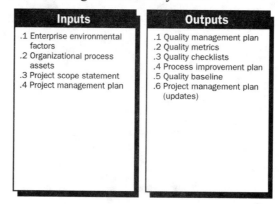

Inputs	Outputs
.1 Enterprise environmental factors .2 Organizational process assets .3 Project scope statement .4 Project management plan	.1 Quality management plan .2 Quality metrics .3 Quality checklists .4 Process improvement plan .5 Quality baseline .6 Project management plan (updates)

Table 3-14. Quality Planning: Inputs and Outputs

.13 Human Resource Planning

This is the process necessary for identifying and documenting project roles, responsibilities and reporting relationships, as well as creating the staffing management plan.

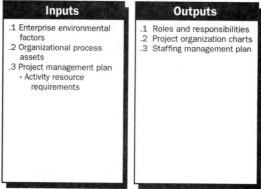

Inputs	Outputs
.1 Enterprise environmental factors .2 Organizational process assets .3 Project management plan • Activity resource requirements	.1 Roles and responsibilities .2 Project organization charts .3 Staffing management plan

Table 3-15. Human Resource Planning: Inputs and Outputs

.14 Communications Planning

This is the process necessary for determining the information and communication needs of the project stakeholders.

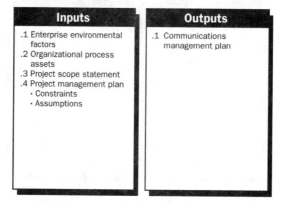

Inputs	Outputs

.1 Enterprise environmental factors
.2 Organizational process assets
.3 Project scope statement
.4 Project management plan
  • Constraints
  • Assumptions
	.1 Communications management plan

Table 3-16. Communications Planning: Inputs and Outputs

A Guide to the Project Management Body of Knowledge (PMBOK® Guide) Third Edition
©2004 Project Management Institute, Four Campus Boulevard, Newtown Square, PA 19073-3299 USA

.15   Risk Management Planning
This is the process necessary for deciding how to approach, plan and execute the risk management activities for a project.

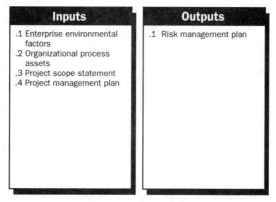

Inputs	Outputs
.1 Enterprise environmental factors .2 Organizational process assets .3 Project scope statement .4 Project management plan	.1 Risk management plan

Table 3-17. Risk Management Planning: Inputs and Outputs

.16   Risk Identification
This is the process necessary for determining which risks might affect the project and documenting their characteristics.

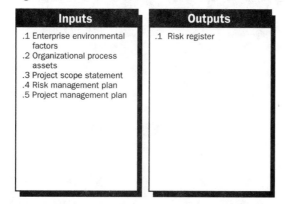

Inputs	Outputs
.1 Enterprise environmental factors .2 Organizational process assets .3 Project scope statement .4 Risk management plan .5 Project management plan	.1 Risk register

Table 3-18. Risk Identification: Inputs and Outputs

.17   Qualitative Risk Analysis
This is the process necessary for prioritizing risks for subsequent further analysis or action by assessing and combining their probability of occurrence and impact.

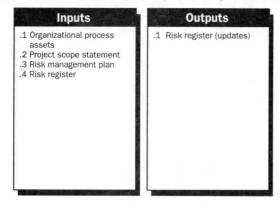

Inputs	Outputs
.1 Organizational process assets .2 Project scope statement .3 Risk management plan .4 Risk register	.1 Risk register (updates)

Table 3-19. Qualitative Risk Analysis: Inputs and Outputs

.18 Quantitative Risk Analysis

This is the process necessary for numerically analyzing the effect on overall project objectives of identified risks.

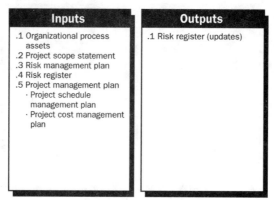

Table 3-20. Quantitative Risk Analysis: Inputs and Outputs

.19 Risk Response Planning

This is the process necessary for developing options and actions to enhance opportunities and to reduce threats to project objectives.

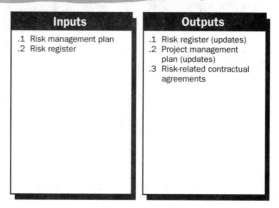

Table 3-21. Risk Response Planning: Inputs and Outputs

.20 Plan Purchases and Acquisitions

This is the process necessary for determining what to purchase or acquire, and determining when and how.

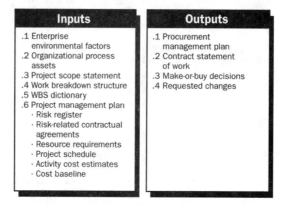

Table 3-22. Plan Purchases and Acquisitions: Inputs and Outputs

.21 Plan Contracting

This is the process necessary for documenting products, services, and results requirements and identifying potential sellers.

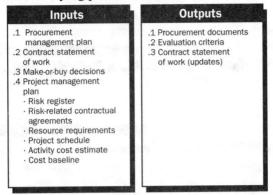

Inputs	Outputs
.1 Procurement management plan	.1 Procurement documents
.2 Contract statement of work	.2 Evaluation criteria
.3 Make-or-buy decisions	.3 Contract statement of work (updates)
.4 Project management plan	
· Risk register	
· Risk-related contractual agreements	
· Resource requirements	
· Project schedule	
· Activity cost estimate	
· Cost baseline	

Table 3-23. Plan Contracting: Inputs and Outputs

3.2.3 Executing Process Group

The Executing Process Group consists of the processes used to complete the work defined in the project management plan to accomplish the project's requirements. The project team should determine which of the processes are required for the team's specific project. This Process Group involves coordinating people and resources, as well as integrating and performing the activities of the project in accordance with the project management plan. This Process Group also addresses the scope defined in the project scope statement and implements approved changes (see Figure 3-8).

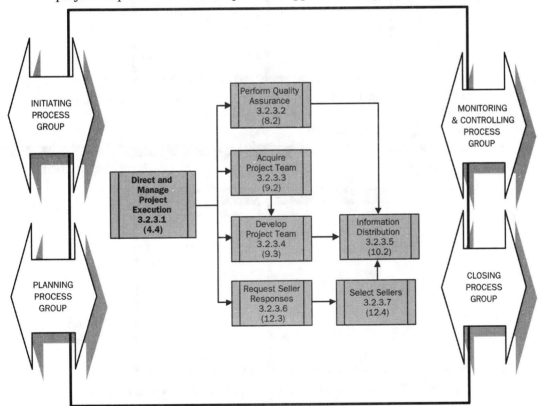

Note: Not all process interactions and data flow among the processes are shown.

Figure 3-8. Executing Process Group

Normal execution variances will cause some replanning. These variances can include activity durations, resource productivity and availability and unanticipated risks. Such variances may or may not affect the project management plan, but can require an analysis. The results of the analysis can trigger a change request that, if approved, would modify the project management plan and possibly require establishing a new baseline. The vast majority of the project's budget will be expended in performing the Executing Process Group processes. The Executing Process Group includes the following project management processes:

.1 Direct and Manage Project Execution

This is the process necessary for directing the various technical and organizational interfaces that exist in the project to execute the work defined in the project management plan. The deliverables are produced as outputs from the processes performed as defined in the project management plan. Information on the completion status of the deliverables and what work has been accomplished are collected as part of project execution and input to the performance reporting process.

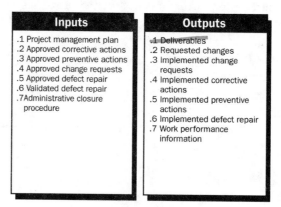

Inputs	Outputs
.1 Project management plan	.1 Deliverables
.2 Approved corrective actions	.2 Requested changes
.3 Approved preventive actions	.3 Implemented change requests
.4 Approved change requests	.4 Implemented corrective actions
.5 Approved defect repair	.5 Implemented preventive actions
.6 Validated defect repair	.6 Implemented defect repair
.7 Administrative closure procedure	.7 Work performance information

Table 3-24. Direct and Manage Project Execution: Inputs and Outputs

.2 Perform Quality Assurance

This is the process necessary for applying the planned, systematic quality activities to ensure that the project employs all processes needed to meet requirements.

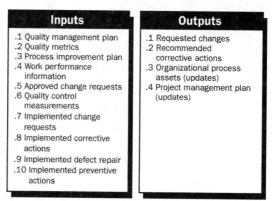

Inputs	Outputs
.1 Quality management plan	.1 Requested changes
.2 Quality metrics	.2 Recommended corrective actions
.3 Process improvement plan	.3 Organizational process assets (updates)
.4 Work performance information	.4 Project management plan (updates)
.5 Approved change requests	
.6 Quality control measurements	
.7 Implemented change requests	
.8 Implemented corrective actions	
.9 Implemented defect repair	
.10 Implemented preventive actions	

Table 3-25. Perform Quality Assurance: Inputs and Outputs

A Guide to the Project Management Body of Knowledge (PMBOK® Guide) Third Edition
©2004 Project Management Institute, Four Campus Boulevard, Newtown Square, PA 19073-3299 USA

.3 Acquire Project Team

This is the process necessary for obtaining the human resources needed to complete the project.

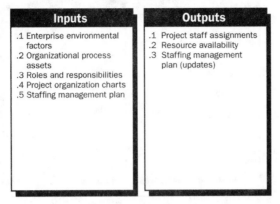

Table 3-26. Acquire Project Team: Inputs and Outputs

Inputs	Outputs
.1 Enterprise environmental factors	.1 Project staff assignments
.2 Organizational process assets	.2 Resource availability
.3 Roles and responsibilities	.3 Staffing management plan (updates)
.4 Project organization charts	
.5 Staffing management plan	

.4 Develop Project Team

This is the process necessary for improving the competencies and interaction of team members to enhance project performance.

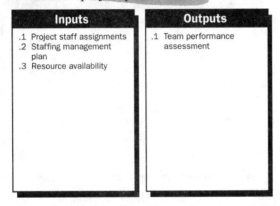

Table 3-27. Develop Project Team: Inputs and Outputs

Inputs	Outputs
.1 Project staff assignments	.1 Team performance assessment
.2 Staffing management plan	
.3 Resource availability	

.5 Information Distribution

This is the process necessary for making information available to project stakeholders in a timely manner.

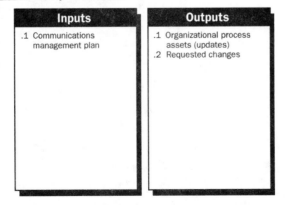

Table 3-28. Information Distribution: Inputs and Outputs

Inputs	Outputs
.1 Communications management plan	.1 Organizational process assets (updates)
	.2 Requested changes

.6 Request Seller Responses

This is the process necessary for obtaining information, quotations, bids, offers or proposals.

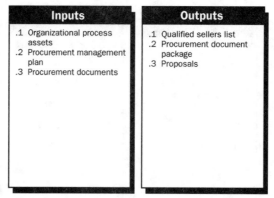

Inputs	Outputs
.1 Organizational process assets	.1 Qualified sellers list
.2 Procurement management plan	.2 Procurement document package
.3 Procurement documents	.3 Proposals

Table 3-29. Request Seller Responses: Inputs and Outputs

.7 Select Sellers

This is the process necessary for reviewing offers, choosing from among potential sellers, and negotiating a written contract with the seller.

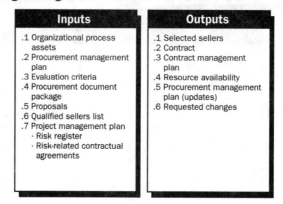

Inputs	Outputs
.1 Organizational process assets	.1 Selected sellers
.2 Procurement management plan	.2 Contract
.3 Evaluation criteria	.3 Contract management plan
.4 Procurement document package	.4 Resource availability
.5 Proposals	.5 Procurement management plan (updates)
.6 Qualified sellers list	.6 Requested changes
.7 Project management plan · Risk register · Risk-related contractual agreements	

Table 3-30. Select Sellers: Inputs and Outputs

A Guide to the Project Management Body of Knowledge (PMBOK® Guide) Third Edition
©2004 Project Management Institute, Four Campus Boulevard, Newtown Square, PA 19073-3299 USA

3.2.4 Monitoring and Controlling Process Group

The Monitoring and Controlling Process Group consists of those processes performed to observe project execution so that potential problems can be identified in a timely manner and corrective action can be taken, when necessary, to control the execution of the project. The project team should determine which of the processes are required for the team's specific project. The key benefit of this Process Group is that project performance is observed and measured regularly to identify variances from the project management plan. The Monitoring and Controlling Process Group also includes controlling changes and recommending preventive action in anticipation of possible problems. The Monitoring and Controlling Processes Group includes, for example:

- Monitoring the ongoing project activities against the project management plan and the project performance baseline

- Influencing the factors that could circumvent integrated change control so only approved changes are implemented.

This continuous monitoring provides the project team insight into the health of the project and highlights any areas that require additional attention. The Monitoring and Controlling Process Group not only monitors and controls the work being done within a Process Group, but also monitors and controls the entire project effort. In multi-phase projects, the Monitoring and Controlling Process Group also provides feedback between project phases, in order to implement corrective or preventive actions to bring the project into compliance with the project management plan. When variances jeopardize the project objectives, appropriate project management processes within the Planning Process Group are revisited as part of the modified plan-do-check-act cycle. This review can result in recommended updates to the project management plan. For example, a missed activity finish date can require adjustments to the current staffing plan, reliance on overtime, or tradeoffs between budget and schedule objectives. Figure 3-9 indicates some of the process interactions that are essential to this Process Group.

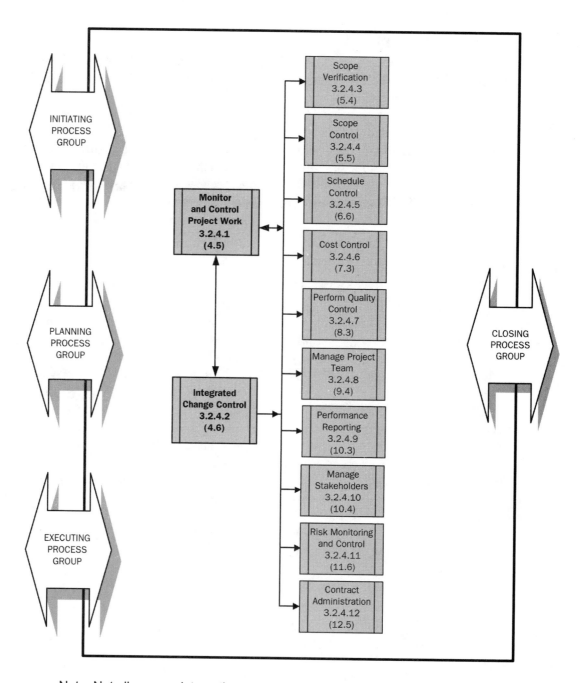

Note: Not all process interactions and data flow among the processes are shown.

Figure 3-9. Monitoring and Controlling Process Group

The Monitoring and Controlling Process Group includes the following project management processes:

A Guide to the Project Management Body of Knowledge (PMBOK® Guide) Third Edition
©2004 Project Management Institute, Four Campus Boulevard, Newtown Square, PA 19073-3299 USA

.1 Monitor and Control Project Work

This is the process necessary for collecting, measuring, and disseminating performance information, and assessing measurements and trends to effect process improvements. This process includes risk monitoring to ensure that risks are identified early, their status is reported, and appropriate risk plans are being executed. Monitoring includes status reporting, progress measurement, and forecasting. Performance reports provide information on the project's performance with regard to scope, schedule, cost, resources, quality, and risk.

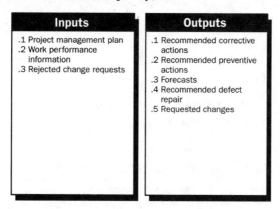

Inputs	Outputs
.1 Project management plan .2 Work performance information .3 Rejected change requests	.1 Recommended corrective actions .2 Recommended preventive actions .3 Forecasts .4 Recommended defect repair .5 Requested changes

Table 3-31. Monitor and Control Project Work: Inputs and Outputs

.2 Integrated Change Control

This is the process necessary for controlling factors that create changes to make sure those changes are beneficial, determining whether a change has occurred, and managing the approved changes, including when they occur. This process is performed throughout the project, from project initiation through project closure.

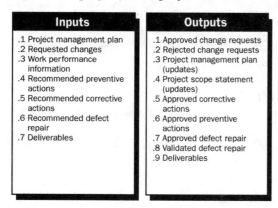

Inputs	Outputs
.1 Project management plan .2 Requested changes .3 Work performance information .4 Recommended preventive actions .5 Recommended corrective actions .6 Recommended defect repair .7 Deliverables	.1 Approved change requests .2 Rejected change requests .3 Project management plan (updates) .4 Project scope statement (updates) .5 Approved corrective actions .6 Approved preventive actions .7 Approved defect repair .8 Validated defect repair .9 Deliverables

Table 3-32. Integrated Change Control: Inputs and Outputs

.3 Scope Verification

This is the process necessary for formalizing acceptance of the completed project deliverables.

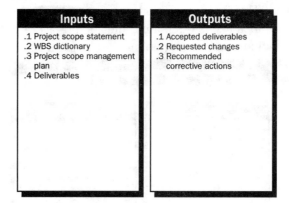

Inputs	Outputs
.1 Project scope statement	.1 Accepted deliverables
.2 WBS dictionary	.2 Requested changes
.3 Project scope management plan	.3 Recommended corrective actions
.4 Deliverables	

Table 3-33. Scope Verification: Inputs and Outputs

.4 Scope Control

This is the process necessary for controlling changes to the project scope.

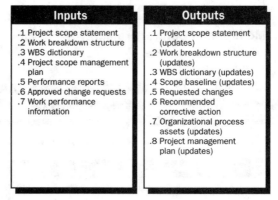

Inputs	Outputs
.1 Project scope statement	.1 Project scope statement (updates)
.2 Work breakdown structure	.2 Work breakdown structure (updates)
.3 WBS dictionary	.3 WBS dictionary (updates)
.4 Project scope management plan	.4 Scope baseline (updates)
.5 Performance reports	.5 Requested changes
.6 Approved change requests	.6 Recommended corrective action
.7 Work performance information	.7 Organizational process assets (updates)
	.8 Project management plan (updates)

Table 3-34. Scope Control: Inputs and Outputs

.5 Schedule Control

This is the process necessary for controlling changes to the project schedule.

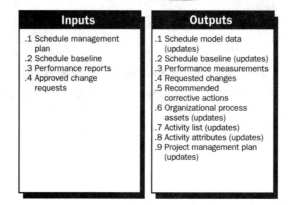

Inputs	Outputs
.1 Schedule management plan	.1 Schedule model data (updates)
.2 Schedule baseline	.2 Schedule baseline (updates)
.3 Performance reports	.3 Performance measurements
.4 Approved change requests	.4 Requested changes
	.5 Recommended corrective actions
	.6 Organizational process assets (updates)
	.7 Activity list (updates)
	.8 Activity attributes (updates)
	.9 Project management plan (updates)

Table 3-35. Schedule Control: Inputs and Outputs

.6 Cost Control

The process of influencing the factors that create variances, and controlling changes to the project budget.

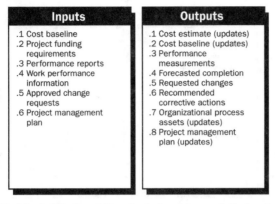

Table 3-36. Cost Control: Inputs and Outputs

.7 Perform Quality Control

This is the process necessary for monitoring specific project results to determine whether they comply with relevant quality standards and identifying ways to eliminate causes of unsatisfactory performance.

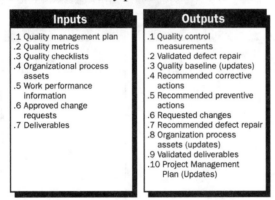

Table 3-37. Perform Quality Control: Inputs and Outputs

.8 Manage Project Team

This is the process necessary for tracking team member performance, providing feedback, resolving issues, and coordinating changes to enhance project performance.

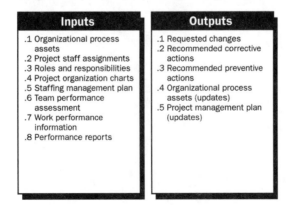

Table 3-38. Manage Project Team: Inputs and Outputs

.9 Performance Reporting

This is the process necessary for collecting and distributing performance information. This includes status reporting, progress measurement, and forecasting.

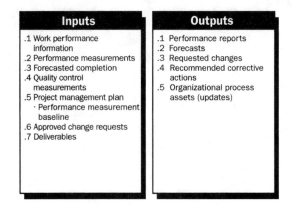

Inputs	Outputs
.1 Work performance information .2 Performance measurements .3 Forecasted completion .4 Quality control measurements .5 Project management plan · Performance measurement baseline .6 Approved change requests .7 Deliverables	.1 Performance reports .2 Forecasts .3 Requested changes .4 Recommended corrective actions .5 Organizational process assets (updates)

Table 3-39. Performance Reporting: Inputs and Outputs

.10 Manage Stakeholders

This is the process necessary for managing communications to satisfy the requirements of, and resolve issues with, project stakeholders.

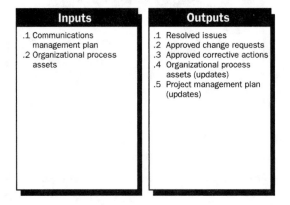

Inputs	Outputs
.1 Communications management plan .2 Organizational process assets	.1 Resolved issues .2 Approved change requests .3 Approved corrective actions .4 Organizational process assets (updates) .5 Project management plan (updates)

Table 3-40. Manage Stakeholders: Inputs and Outputs

.11 Risk Monitoring and Control

This is the process necessary for tracking identified risks, monitoring residual risks, identifying new risks, executing risk response plans, and evaluating their effectiveness throughout the project life cycle.

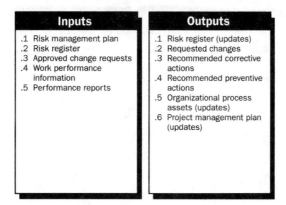

Inputs	Outputs
.1 Risk management plan	.1 Risk register (updates)
.2 Risk register	.2 Requested changes
.3 Approved change requests	.3 Recommended corrective actions
.4 Work performance information	.4 Recommended preventive actions
.5 Performance reports	.5 Organizational process assets (updates)
	.6 Project management plan (updates)

Table 3-41. Risk Monitoring and Control: Inputs and Outputs

.12 Contract Administration

This is the process necessary for managing the contract and relationship between the buyer and seller, reviewing and documenting how a seller is performing or has performed and, when appropriate, managing the contractual relationship with the outside buyer of the project.

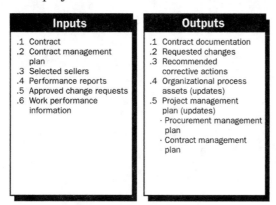

Inputs	Outputs
.1 Contract	.1 Contract documentation
.2 Contract management plan	.2 Requested changes
.3 Selected sellers	.3 Recommended corrective actions
.4 Performance reports	.4 Organizational process assets (updates)
.5 Approved change requests	.5 Project management plan (updates)
.6 Work performance information	· Procurement management plan
	· Contract management plan

Table 3-42. Contract Administration: Inputs and Outputs

3.2.5   Closing Process Group

The Closing Process Group includes the processes used to formally terminate all activities of a project or a project phase, hand off the completed product to others or close a cancelled project. This Process Group, when completed, verifies that the defined processes are completed within all the Process Groups to close the project or a project phase, as appropriate, and formally establishes that the project or project phase is finished. See Figure 3-10.

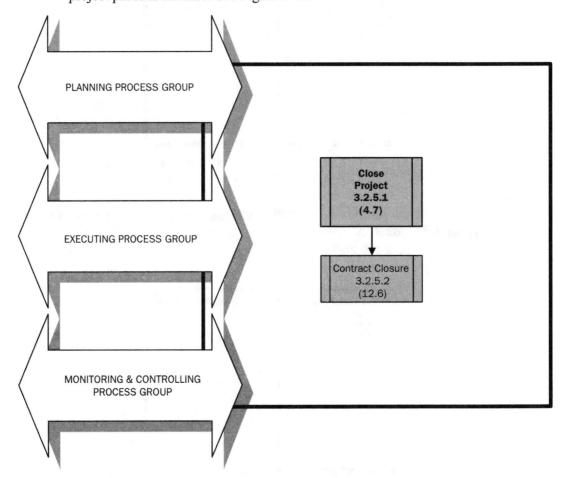

Figure 3-10. Closing Process Group

A Guide to the Project Management Body of Knowledge (PMBOK® Guide) Third Edition
©2004 Project Management Institute, Four Campus Boulevard, Newtown Square, PA 19073-3299 USA

The Closing Process Group includes the following project management processes:

.1 Close Project

This is the process necessary to finalize all activities across all of the Process Groups to formally close the project or a project phase.

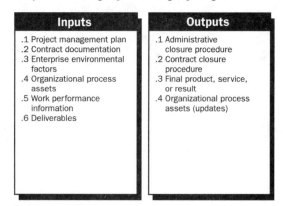

Table 3-43. Close Project: Inputs and Outputs

.2 Contract Closure

This is the process necessary for completing and settling each contract, including the resolution of any open items, and closing each contract applicable to the project or a project phase.

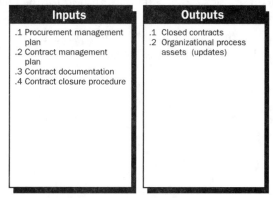

Table 3-44. Contract Closure: Inputs and Outputs

3.3 Process Interactions

Project Management Process Groups are linked by the objectives they produce. The output of one process generally becomes an input to another process or is a deliverable of the project. The Planning Process Group provides the Executing Process Group a documented project management plan and project scope statement, and often updates the project management plan as the project progresses. In addition, the Process Groups are seldom either discrete or one-time events; they are overlapping activities that occur at varying levels of intensity throughout the project. Figure 3-11 illustrates how the Process Groups interact and the level of overlap at varying times within a project. If the project is divided into phases, the Process Groups interact within a project phase and also may cross the project phases.

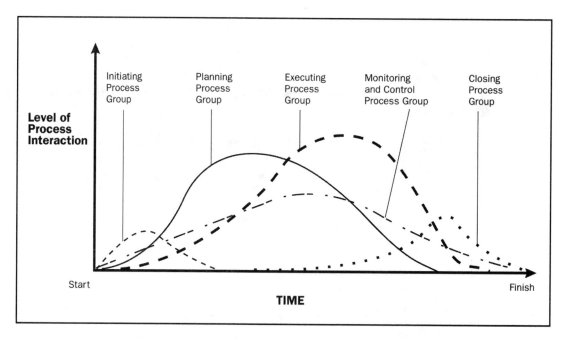

Figure 3-11. Process Groups Interact in a Project

Among the Process Groups and their processes, the process outputs are related and have an impact on the other Process Groups. For example, closing a design phase requires customer acceptance of the design document. Then, the design document defines the product description for the ensuing Executing Process Group. When a project is divided into phases, the Process Groups are normally repeated within each phase throughout the project's life to effectively drive the project to completion. The Process Groups and their relationships are illustrated in Figure 3-12.

A Guide to the Project Management Body of Knowledge (PMBOK® Guide) Third Edition
©2004 Project Management Institute, Four Campus Boulevard, Newtown Square, PA 19073-3299 USA

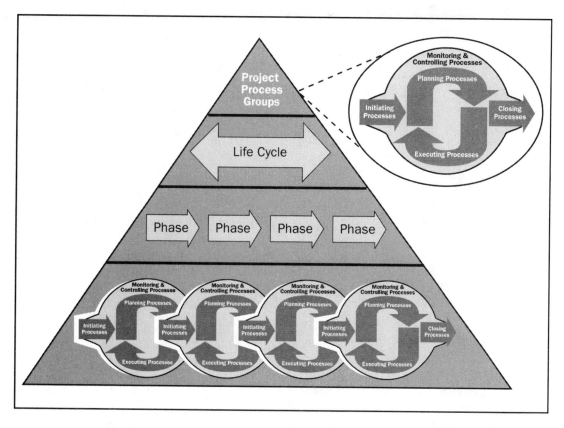

Figure 3-12. Project Management Process Group Triangle

However, just as not all of the processes will be needed on all projects, not all of the interactions will apply to all projects or project phases. For example:

- Projects that are dependent upon unique resources (e.g., commercial software development and biopharmaceuticals) can define roles and responsibilities prior to scope definition, since what can be done is dependent on who is available to do it.

- Some process inputs are predefined as constraints. For example, management can specify a target completion date rather than allowing that date to be determined by the planning process. An imposed completion date will often require scheduling backward from that date and can increase project risk, add cost, and compromise quality, or, in extreme cases, require a significant change in scope.

3.4 Project Management Process Mapping

Table 3-45 reflects the mapping of the 44 project management processes into the five Project Management Process Groups and the nine Project Management Knowledge Areas. Each of the required project management processes is shown in the Process Group in which **most** of the activity takes place. For instance, when a process that normally takes place during planning is revisited or updated during execution, it is still the same process that was performed in the planning process, not an additional, new process.

Knowledge Area Processes	Project Management Process Groups				
	Initiating Process Group	Planning Process Group	Executing Process Group	Monitoring & Controlling Process Group	Closing Process Group
4. Project Integration Management	Develop Project Charter 3.2.1.1 (4.1) Develop Preliminary Project Scope Statement 3.2.1.2 (4.2)	Develop Project Management Plan 3.2.2.1 (4.3)	Direct and Manage Project Execution 3.2.3.1 (4.4)	Monitor and Control Project Work 3.2.4.1 (4.5) Integrated Change Control 3.2.4.2 (4.6)	Close Project 3.2.5.1 (4.7)
5. Project Scope Management		Scope Planning 3.2.2.2 (5.1) Scope Definition 3.2.2.3 (5.2) Create WBS 3.2.2.4 (5.3)		Scope Verification 3.2.4.3 (5.4) Scope Control 3.2.4.4 (5.5)	
6. Project Time Management		Activity Definition 3.2.2.5 (6.1) Activity Sequencing 3.2.2.6 (6.2) Activity Resource Estimating 3.2.2.7 (6.3) Activity Duration Estimating 3.2.2.8 (6.4) Schedule Development 3.2.2.9 (6.5)		Schedule Control 3.2.4.5 (6.6)	
7. Project Cost Management		Cost Estimating 3.2.2.10 (7.1) Cost Budgeting 3.2.2.11 (7.2)		Cost Control 3.2.4.6 (7.3)	
8. Project Quality Management		Quality Planning 3.2.2.12 (8.1)	Perform Quality Assurance 3.2.3.2 (8.2)	Perform Quality Control 3.2.4.7 (8.3)	
9. Project Human Resource Management		Human Resource Planning 3.2.2.13 (9.1)	Acquire Project Team 3.2.3.3 (9.2) Develop Project Team 3.2.3.4 (9.3)	Manage Project Team 3.2.4.8 (9.4)	
10. Project Communications Management		Communications Planning 3.2.2.14 (10.1)	Information Distribution 3.2.3.5 (10.2)	Performance Reporting 3.2.4.9 (10.3) Manage Stakeholders 3.2.4.10 (10.4)	
11. Project Risk Management		Risk Management Planning 3.2.2.15 (11.1) Risk Identification 3.2.2.16 (11.2) Qualitative Risk Analysis 3.2.2.17 (11.3) Quantative Risk Analysis 3.2.2.18 (11.4) Risk Response Planning 3.2.2.19 (11.5)		Risk Monitoring and Control 3.2.4.11 (11.6)	
12. Project Procurement Management		Plan Purchases and Acquisitions 3.2.2.20 (12.1) Plan Contracting 3.2.2.21 (12.2)	Request Seller Responses 3.2.3.6 (12.3) Select Sellers 3.2.3.7 (12.4)	Contract Administration 3.2.4.12 (12.5)	Contract Closure 3.2.5.2 (12.6)

Table 3-45. Mapping of the Project Management Processes to the Project Management Process Groups and the Knowledge Areas

A Guide to the Project Management Body of Knowledge (PMBOK® Guide) Third Edition
©2004 Project Management Institute, Four Campus Boulevard, Newtown Square, PA 19073-3299 USA

Section III

The Project Management Knowledge Areas

Section III   Introduction

Chapter 4   Project Integration Management

Chapter 5   Project Scope Management

Chapter 6   Project Time Management

Chapter 7   Project Cost Management

Chapter 8   Project Quality Management

Chapter 9   Project Human Resource Management

Chapter 10   Project Communications Management

Chapter 11   Project Risk Management

Chapter 12   Project Procurement Management

SECTION III

Introduction

Process Flow Diagrams

A process flow diagram is provided in each Knowledge Area chapter (Chapters 4 through 12). The process flow diagram is a summary level depiction of the process inputs and process outputs that flow down through all the processes within a specific Knowledge Area. Although the processes are presented here as discrete elements with well-defined interfaces, in practice they are iterative and can overlap and interact in ways not detailed here.

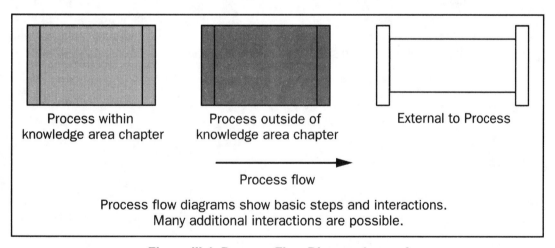

Figure III-1. Process Flow Diagram Legend

The symbols for the process flow diagrams are explained in Figure III-1 and depict three types of information:

1.   Knowledge Area processes, their interaction with other processes within the Knowledge Area, and their outputs to Chapter 4 integration processes.

2.   Processes external to the Knowledge Area, whose outputs are used as inputs to the Knowledge Area processes under discussion.

3.   Organizational process assets and enterprise environmental factors are shown as inputs to the first process.

The project management plan, and its subsidiary plans and components that are external to the Knowledge Area, **are provided as input into the first process of the diagram, and are considered to be available in each subsequent process in their latest updated form**.

The organizational process assets and enterprise environmental factors are shown as inputs to the first process to provide those items of information, policy, and procedure that are external to the project, but can impact the project planning and execution. These assets and factors, plus **the external process outputs used as an input to a Knowledge Area process, are also considered to be available in each subsequent process in their latest updated form**.

The process flow diagram is not detailed and does not show all the possible interfaces with all external processes. It also does not show possible alternate process flow paths or feedback loops among the specific Knowledge Area processes or with processes external to the Knowledge Area. The iterative nature of most projects makes the permutations of the process flows and feedback loops very complex. Therefore, in the interest of keeping the flow diagrams easier to follow, alternate or iterative paths were not included with the diagrams.

A Guide to the Project Management Body of Knowledge (PMBOK® Guide) Third Edition
©2004 Project Management Institute, Four Campus Boulevard, Newtown Square, PA 19073-3299 USA

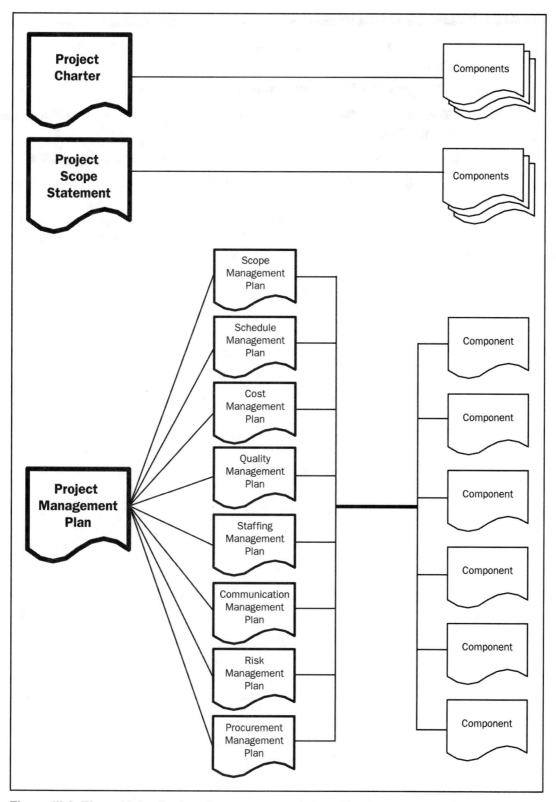

Figure III-2. Three Major Project Documents and their Relationship to their Components

Major Project Documents

There are three major documents described within the *PMBOK® Guide* and each has a specific purpose:

- **Project Charter. Formally authorizes the project.**

- **Project Scope Statement. States what work is** to be accomplished and what **deliverables** need to be produced.

- **Project Management Plan. States how the work will be performed.**

Figure III-2 depicts these three documents and their relationship to their components.

The project management plan is composed of the plans and documents generated by the various processes. Those items are the subsidiary plans and components of the project management plan.

A Guide to the Project Management Body of Knowledge (PMBOK® Guide) Third Edition
©2004 Project Management Institute, Four Campus Boulevard, Newtown Square, PA 19073-3299 USA

CHAPTER 4

Project Integration Management

The Project Integration Management Knowledge Area includes the processes and activities needed to identify, define, combine, unify, and coordinate the various processes and project management activities within the Project Management Process Groups. In the project management context, integration includes characteristics of unification, consolidation, articulation, and integrative actions that are crucial to project completion, successfully meeting customer and other stakeholder requirements, and managing expectations. Integration, in the context of managing a project, is making choices about where to concentrate resources and effort on any given day, anticipating potential issues, dealing with these issues before they become critical, and coordinating work for the overall project good. The integration effort also involves making trade-offs among competing objectives and alternatives. The project management processes are usually presented as discrete components with well-defined interfaces while, in practice, they overlap and interact in ways that cannot be completely detailed in the *PMBOK® Guide*.

The need for integration in project management becomes evident in situations where individual processes interact. For example, a cost estimate needed for a contingency plan involves integration of the planning processes described in greater detail in the Project Cost Management processes, Project Time Management processes, and Project Risk Management processes. When additional risks associated with various staffing alternatives are identified, then one or more of those processes must be revisited. The project deliverables also need to be integrated with ongoing operations of either the performing organization or the customer's organization, or with the long-term strategic planning that takes future problems and opportunities into consideration.

Most experienced project management practitioners know there is no single way to manage a project. They apply project management knowledge, skills, and processes in different orders and degrees of rigor to achieve the desired project performance. However, the perception that a particular process is not required does not mean that it should not be addressed. The project manager and project team must address every process, and the level of implementation for each process must be determined for each specific project.

The integrative nature of projects and project management can be better understood if we think of the other activities performed while completing a project. For example, some activities performed by the project management team could be to:

- Analyze and understand the scope. This includes the project and product requirements, criteria, assumptions, constraints, and other influences related to a project, and how each will be managed or addressed within the project.

- Document specific criteria of the product requirements.

- Understand how to take the identified information and transform it into a project management plan using the Planning Process Group described in the *PMBOK® Guide*.

- Prepare the work breakdown structure.

- Take appropriate action to have the project performed in accordance with the project management plan, the planned set of integrated processes, and the planned scope.

- Measure and monitor project status, processes and products.

- Analyze project risks.

Among the processes in the Project Management Process Groups, the links are often iterated. The Planning Process Group provides the Executing Process Group with a documented project management plan early in the project and then facilitates updates to the project management plan if changes occur as the project progresses.

Integration is primarily concerned with effectively integrating the processes among the Project Management Process Groups that are required to accomplish project objectives within an organization's defined procedures. Figure 4-1 provides an overview of the major project management integrative processes. Figure 4-2 provides a process flow diagram of those processes and their inputs, outputs and other related Knowledge Area processes. The integrative project management processes include:

4.1 Develop Project Charter – developing the project charter that formally authorizes a project or a project phase.

4.2 Develop Preliminary Project Scope Statement – developing the preliminary project scope statement that provides a high-level scope narrative.

4.3 Develop Project Management Plan – documenting the actions necessary to define, prepare, integrate, and coordinate all subsidiary plans into a project management plan.

4.4 Direct and Manage Project Execution – executing the work defined in the project management plan to achieve the project's requirements defined in the project scope statement.

4.5 Monitor and Control Project Work – monitoring and controlling the processes used to initiate, plan, execute, and close a project to meet the performance objectives defined in the project management plan.

4.6 Integrated Change Control – reviewing all change requests, approving changes, and controlling changes to the deliverables and organizational process assets.

4.7 Close Project – finalizing all activities across all of the Project Management Process Groups to formally close the project or a project phase.

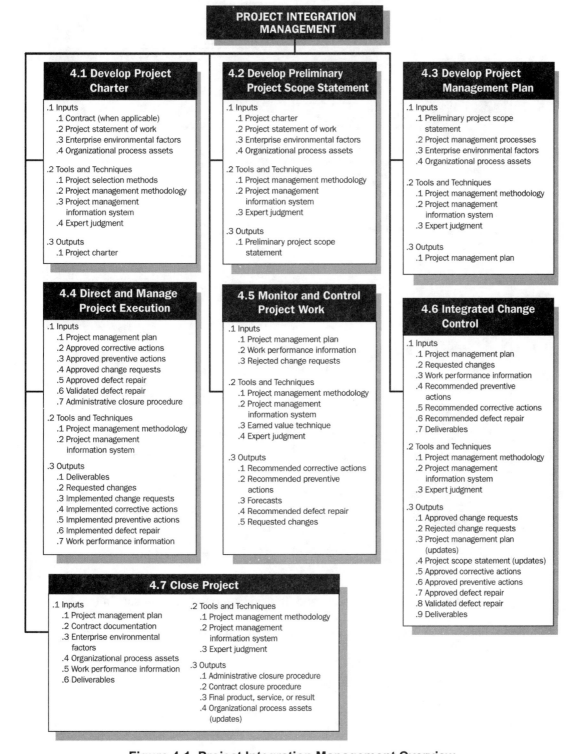

Figure 4-1. Project Integration Management Overview

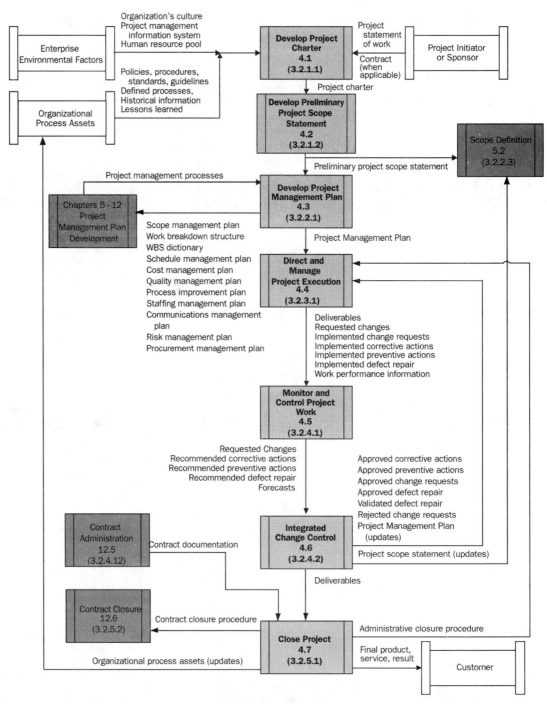

Note: Not all process interactions and data flow among the processes are shown.

Figure 4-2. Project Integration Management Processes Flow Diagram

A Guide to the Project Management Body of Knowledge (PMBOK® Guide) Third Edition
©2004 Project Management Institute, Four Campus Boulevard, Newtown Square, PA 19073-3299 USA

4.1 Develop Project Charter

The project charter is the document that formally authorizes a project. The project charter provides the project manager with the authority to apply organizational resources to project activities. A project manager is identified and assigned as early in the project as is feasible. The project manager should always be assigned prior to the start of planning, and preferably while the project charter is being developed.

A project initiator or sponsor external to the project organization, at a level that is appropriate to funding the project, issues the project charter. Projects are usually chartered and authorized external to the project organization by an enterprise, a government agency, a company, a program organization, or a portfolio organization, as a result of one or more of the following:

- A market demand (e.g., a car company authorizing a project to build more fuel-efficient cars in response to gasoline shortages)

- A business need (e.g., a training company authorizing a project to create a new course to increase its revenues)

- A customer request (e.g., an electric utility authorizing a project to build a new substation to serve a new industrial park)

- A technological advance (e.g., an electronics firm authorizing a new project to develop a faster, cheaper, and smaller laptop after advances in computer memory and electronics technology)

- A legal requirement (e.g., a paint manufacturer authorizing a project to establish guidelines for handling toxic materials)

- A social need (e.g., a nongovernmental organization in a developing country authorizing a project to provide potable water systems, latrines, and sanitation education to communities suffering from high rates of cholera).

These stimuli can also be called problems, opportunities, or business requirements. The central theme of all these stimuli is that management must make a decision about how to respond and what projects to authorize and charter. Project selection methods involve measuring value or attractiveness to the project owner or sponsor and may include other organizational decision criteria. Project selection also applies to choosing alternative ways of executing the project.

Chartering a project links the project to the ongoing work of the organization. In some organizations, a project is not formally chartered and initiated until completion of a needs assessment, feasibility study, preliminary plan, or some other equivalent form of analysis that was separately initiated. Developing the project charter is primarily concerned with documenting the business needs, project justification, current understanding of the customer's requirements, and the new product, service, or result that is intended to satisfy those requirements. The project charter, either directly, or by reference to other documents, should address the following information:

- Requirements that satisfy customer, sponsor, and other stakeholder needs, wants and expectations
- Business needs, high-level project description, or product requirements that the project is undertaken to address
- Project purpose or justification
- Assigned Project Manager and authority level
- Summary milestone schedule
- Stakeholder influences
- Functional organizations and their participation
- Organizational, environmental and external assumptions
- Organizational, environmental and external constraints
- Business case justifying the project, including return on investment
- Summary budget.

During subsequent phases of multi-phase projects, the Develop Project Charter process validates the decisions made during the original chartering of the project. If required, it also authorizes the next project phase, and updates the charter.

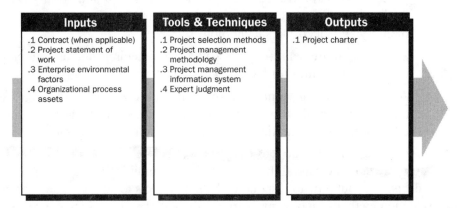

Inputs	Tools & Techniques	Outputs
.1 Contract (when applicable) .2 Project statement of work .3 Enterprise environmental factors .4 Organizational process assets	.1 Project selection methods .2 Project management methodology .3 Project management information system .4 Expert judgment	.1 Project charter

Figure 4-3. Develop Project Charter: Inputs, Tools & Techniques, and Outputs

4.1.1 Develop Project Charter: Inputs

.1 Contract (When Applicable)
A contract from the customer's acquiring organization is an input if the project is being done for an external customer.

.2 Project Statement of Work
The statement of work (SOW) is a narrative description of products or services to be supplied by the project. For internal projects, the project initiator or sponsor provides the statement of work based on business needs, product, or service requirements. For external projects, the statement of work can be received from the customer as part of a bid document, for example, request for proposal, request for information, request for bid, or as part of a contract. The SOW indicates a:

A Guide to the Project Management Body of Knowledge (PMBOK® Guide) Third Edition
 ©2004 Project Management Institute, Four Campus Boulevard, Newtown Square, PA 19073-3299 USA

- Business need – an organization's business need can be based on needed training, market demand, technological advance, legal requirement, or governmental standard.

- Product scope description – documents the product requirements and characteristics of the product or service that the project will be undertaken to create. The product requirements will generally have less detail during the initiation process and more detail during later processes, as the product characteristics are progressively elaborated. These requirements should also document the relationship among the products or services being created and the business need or other stimulus that causes the need. While the form and substance of the product requirements document will vary, it should always be detailed enough to support later project planning.

- Strategic plan – all projects should support the organization's strategic goals. The strategic plan of the performing organization should be considered as a factor when making project selection decisions.

.3 Enterprise Environmental Factors

When developing the project charter, any and all of the organization's enterprise environmental factors and systems that surround and influence the project's success must be considered. This includes items such as, but not limited to:

- Organizational or company culture and structure

- Governmental or industry standards (e.g., regulatory agency regulations, product standards, quality standards, and workmanship standards)

- Infrastructure (e.g., existing facilities and capital equipment)

- Existing human resources (e.g., skills, disciplines, and knowledge, such as design, development, legal, contracting, and purchasing)

- Personnel administration (e.g., hiring and firing guidelines, employee performance reviews, and training records)

- Company work authorization system

- Marketplace conditions

- Stakeholder risk tolerances

- Commercial databases (e.g., standardized cost estimating data, industry risk study information, and risk databases)

- Project management information systems (e.g., an automated tool suite, such as a scheduling software tool, a configuration management system, an information collection and distribution system, or web interfaces to other online automated systems).

.4 Organizational Process Assets

When developing the project charter and subsequent project documentation, any and all of the assets that are used to influence the project's success can be drawn from organizational process assets. Any and all of the organizations involved in the project can have formal and informal policies, procedures, plans, and guidelines whose effects must be considered. Organizational process assets also represent the organizations' learning and knowledge from previous projects; for example, completed schedules, risk data, and earned value data. Organizational process assets can be organized differently, depending on the type of industry, organization, and application area. For example, the organizational process assets could be grouped into two categories:

- Organization's processes and procedures for conducting work:
    - Organizational standard processes, such as standards, policies (e.g., safety and health policy, and project management policy), standard product and project life cycles, and quality policies and procedures (e.g., process audits, improvement targets, checklists, and standardized process definitions for use in the organization)
    - Standardized guidelines, work instructions, proposal evaluation criteria, and performance measurement criteria
    - Templates (e.g., risk templates, work breakdown structure templates, and project schedule network diagram templates)
    - Guidelines and criteria for tailoring the organization's set of standard processes to satisfy the specific needs of the project
    - Organization communication requirements (e.g., specific communication technology available, allowed communication media, record retention, and security requirements)
    - Project closure guidelines or requirements (e.g., final project audits, project evaluations, product validations, and acceptance criteria)
    - Financial controls procedures (e.g., time reporting, required expenditure and disbursement reviews, accounting codes, and standard contract provisions)
    - Issue and defect management procedures defining issue and defect controls, issue and defect identification and resolution, and action item tracking
    - Change control procedures, including the steps by which official company standards, policies, plans, and procedures—or any project documents—will be modified, and how any changes will be approved and validated
    - Risk control procedures, including risk categories, probability definition and impact, and probability and impact matrix
    - Procedures for approving and issuing work authorizations.

A Guide to the Project Management Body of Knowledge (PMBOK® Guide) Third Edition
©2004 Project Management Institute, Four Campus Boulevard, Newtown Square, PA 19073-3299 USA

- Organizational corporate knowledge base for storing and retrieving information:
    - Process measurement database used to collect and make available measurement data on processes and products
    - Project files (e.g., scope, cost, schedule, and quality baselines, performance measurement baselines, project calendars, project schedule network diagrams, risk registers, planned response actions, and defined risk impact)
    - Historical information and lessons learned knowledge base (e.g., project records and documents, all project closure information and documentation, information about both the results of previous project selection decisions and previous project performance information, and information from the risk management effort)
    - Issue and defect management database containing issue and defect status, control information, issue and defect resolution, and action item results
    - Configuration management knowledge base containing the versions and baselines of all official company standards, policies, procedures, and any project documents
    - Financial database containing information such as labor hours, incurred costs, budgets, and any project cost overruns.

4.1.2 Develop Project Charter: Tools and Techniques

.1 Project Selection Methods

Project selection methods are used to determine which project the organization will select. These methods generally fall into one of two broad categories[4]:

- Benefit measurement methods that are comparative approaches, scoring models, benefit contribution, or economic models.
- Mathematical models that use linear, nonlinear, dynamic, integer, or multi-objective programming algorithms.

.2 Project Management Methodology

A project management methodology defines a set of Project Management Process Groups, their related processes and the related control functions that are consolidated and combined into a functioning unified whole. A project management methodology may or may not be an elaboration of a project management standard. A project management methodology can be either a formal mature process or an informal technique that aids a project management team in effectively developing a project charter.

.3 Project Management Information System

The Project Management Information System (PMIS) is a standardized set of automated tools available within the organization and integrated into a system. The PMIS is used by the project management team to support generation of a project charter, facilitate feedback as the document is refined, control changes to the project charter, and release the approved document.

.4 Expert Judgment

Expert judgment is often used to assess the inputs needed to develop the project charter. Such judgment and expertise is applied to any technical and management details during this process. Such expertise is provided by any group or individual with specialized knowledge or training, and is available from many sources, including:

- Other units within the organization
- Consultants
- Stakeholders, including customers or sponsors
- Professional and technical associations
- Industry groups.

4.1.3 Develop Project Charter: Outputs

.1 Project Charter

Described in the introduction to Section 4.1.

4.2 Develop Preliminary Project Scope Statement

The project scope statement is the definition of the project—what needs to be accomplished. The Develop Preliminary Project Scope Statement process addresses and documents the characteristics and boundaries of the project and its associated products and services, as well as the methods of acceptance and scope control. A project scope statement includes:

- Project and product objectives
- Product or service requirements and characteristics
- Product acceptance criteria
- Project boundaries
- Project requirements and deliverables
- Project constraints
- Project assumptions
- Initial project organization
- Initial defined risks
- Schedule milestones
- Initial WBS
- Order of magnitude cost estimate
- Project configuration management requirements

● Approval requirements.

The preliminary project scope statement is developed from information provided by the initiator or sponsor. The project management team in the Scope Definition process further refines the preliminary project scope statement into the project scope statement. The project scope statement content will vary depending upon the application area and complexity of the project and can include some or all of the components identified above. During subsequent phases of multi-phase projects, the Develop Preliminary Project Scope Statement process validates and refines, if required, the project scope defined for that phase.

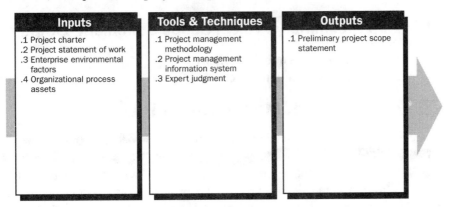

Figure 4-4. Develop Preliminary Project Scope Statement: Inputs, Tools & Techniques, and Outputs

4.2.1 Develop Preliminary Project Scope Statement: Inputs

.1 Project Charter
Described in Section 4.1.

.2 Project Statement of Work
Described in Section 4.1.1.2.

.3 Enterprise Environmental Factors
Described in Section 4.1.1.3.

.4 Organizational Process Assets
Described in Section 4.1.1.4.

4.2.2 Develop Preliminary Project Scope Statement: Tools and Techniques

.1 Project Management Methodology
The project management methodology defines a process that aids a project management team in developing and controlling changes to the preliminary project scope statement.

.2 Project Management Information System

The project management information system, an automated system, is used by the project management team to support generation of a preliminary project scope statement, facilitate feedback as the document is refined, control changes to the project scope statement, and release the approved document.

.3 Expert Judgment

Expert judgment is applied to any technical and management details to be included in the preliminary project scope statement.

4.2.3 Develop Preliminary Project Scope Statement: Outputs

.1 Preliminary Project Scope Statement

Described in the introduction to Section 4.2.

4.3 Develop Project Management Plan

The Develop Project Management Plan process includes the actions necessary to define, integrate, and coordinate all subsidiary plans into a project management plan. The project management plan content will vary depending upon the application area and complexity of the project. This process results in a project management plan that is updated and revised through the Integrated Change Control process. The project management plan defines how the project is executed, monitored and controlled, and closed. The project management plan documents the collection of outputs of the planning processes of the Planning Process Group and includes:

- The project management processes selected by the project management team
- The level of implementation of each selected process
- The descriptions of the tools and techniques to be used for accomplishing those processes
- How the selected processes will be used to manage the specific project, including the dependencies and interactions among those processes, and the essential inputs and outputs
- How work will be executed to accomplish the project objectives
- How changes will be monitored and controlled
- How configuration management will be performed
- How integrity of the performance measurement baselines will be maintained and used
- The need and techniques for communication among stakeholders
- The selected project life cycle and, for multi-phase projects, the associated project phases
- Key management reviews for content, extent, and timing to facilitate addressing open issues and pending decisions.

A Guide to the Project Management Body of Knowledge (PMBOK® Guide) Third Edition
©2004 Project Management Institute, Four Campus Boulevard, Newtown Square, PA 19073-3299 USA

The project management plan can be either summary level or detailed, and can be composed of one or more subsidiary plans and other components. Each of the subsidiary plans and components is detailed to the extent required by the specific project. These subsidiary plans include, but are not limited to:

- Project scope management plan (Section 5.1.3.1)
- Schedule management plan (Chapter 6 introductory material)
- Cost management plan (Chapter 7 introductory material)
- Quality management plan (Section 8.1.3.1)
- Process improvement plan (Section 8.1.3.4)
- Staffing management plan (Section 9.1.3.3)
- Communication management plan (Section 10.1.3.1)
- Risk management plan (Section 11.1.3.1)
- Procurement management plan (Section 12.1.3.1).

  These other components include, but are not limited to:

- Milestone list (Section 6.1.3.3)
- Resource calendar (Section 6.3.3.4)
- Schedule baseline (Section 6.5.3.3)
- Cost baseline (Section 7.2.3.1)
- Quality baseline (Section 8.1.3.5)
- Risk register (Section 11.2.3.1)

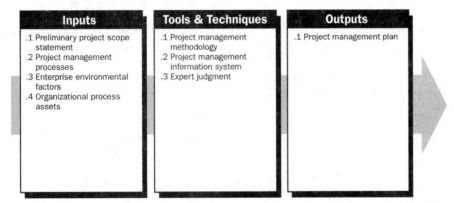

Figure 4-5. Develop Project Management Plan: Inputs, Tools & Techniques, and Outputs

4.3.1 Develop Project Management Plan: Inputs

.1 Preliminary Project Scope Statement
Described in Section 4.2.

.2 Project Management Processes
Described in Chapters 5 through 12.

.3 **Enterprise Environmental Factors**
Described in Section 4.1.1.3.

.4 **Organizational Process Assets**
Described in Section 4.1.1.4.

4.3.2 Develop Project Management Plan: Tools and Techniques

.1 **Project Management Methodology**
The project management methodology defines a process, which aids a project management team in developing and controlling changes to the project management plan.

.2 **Project Management Information System**
The project management information system, an automated system, is used by the project management team to support generation of the project management plan, facilitate feedback as the document is developed, control changes to the project management plan, and release the approved document.

• **Configuration Management System**
The configuration management system is a subsystem of the overall project management information system. The system includes the process for submitting proposed changes, tracking systems for reviewing and approving proposed changes, defining approval levels for authorizing changes, and providing a method to validate approved changes. In most application areas, the configuration management system includes the change control system. The configuration management system is also a collection of formal documented procedures used to apply technical and administrative direction and surveillance to:

♦ Identify and document the functional and physical characteristics of a product or component

♦ Control any changes to such characteristics

♦ Record and report each change and its implementation status

♦ Support the audit of the products or components to verify conformance to requirements.

• **Change Control System**
The change control system is a collection of formal documented procedures that define how project deliverables and documentation are controlled, changed, and approved. The change control system is a subsystem of the configuration management system. For example, for information technology systems, a change control system can include the specifications (scripts, source code, data definition language, etc.) for each software component.

.3 **Expert Judgment**
Expert judgment is applied to develop technical and management details to be included in the project management plan.

A Guide to the Project Management Body of Knowledge (PMBOK® Guide) Third Edition
©2004 Project Management Institute, Four Campus Boulevard, Newtown Square, PA 19073-3299 USA

4.3.3 Develop Project Management Plan: Outputs

.1 Project Management Plan

Described in the introduction to Section 4.3.

4.4 Direct and Manage Project Execution

The Direct and Manage Project Execution process requires the project manager and the project team to perform multiple actions to execute the project management plan to accomplish the work defined in the project scope statement. Some of those actions are:

- Perform activities to accomplish project objectives
- Expend effort and spend funds to accomplish the project objectives
- Staff, train, and manage the project team members assigned to the project
- Obtain quotations, bids, offers, or proposals as appropriate
- Select sellers by choosing from among potential sellers
- Obtain, manage, and use resources including materials, tools, equipment, and facilities
- Implement the planned methods and standards
- Create, control, verify, and validate project deliverables
- Manage risks and implement risk response activities
- Manage sellers
- Adapt approved changes into the project's scope, plans, and environment
- Establish and manage project communication channels, both external and internal to the project team
- Collect project data and report cost, schedule, technical and quality progress, and status information to facilitate forecasting
- Collect and document lessons learned, and implement approved process improvement activities.

The project manager, along with the project management team, directs the performance of the planned project activities, and manages the various technical and organizational interfaces that exist within the project. The Direct and Manage Project Execution process is most directly affected by the project application area. Deliverables are produced as outputs from the processes performed to accomplish the project work planned and scheduled in the project management plan. Work performance information about the completion status of the deliverables, and what has been accomplished, is collected as part of project execution and is fed into the performance reporting process. Although the products, services, or results of the project are frequently in the form of tangible deliverables such as buildings, roads, etc., intangible deliverables, such as training, can also be provided.

Direct and Manage Project Execution also requires implementation of:

- Approved corrective actions that will bring anticipated project performance into compliance with the project management plan
- Approved preventive actions to reduce the probability of potential negative consequences
- Approved defect repair requests to correct product defects found by the quality process.

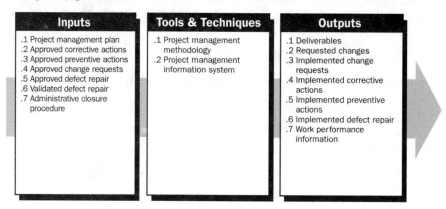

Inputs	Tools & Techniques	Outputs
.1 Project management plan .2 Approved corrective actions .3 Approved preventive actions .4 Approved change requests .5 Approved defect repair .6 Validated defect repair .7 Administrative closure procedure	.1 Project management methodology .2 Project management information system	.1 Deliverables .2 Requested changes .3 Implemented change requests .4 Implemented corrective actions .5 Implemented preventive actions .6 Implemented defect repair .7 Work performance information

Figure 4-6. Direct and Manage Project Execution: Inputs, Tools & Techniques, and Outputs

4.4.1   Direct and Manage Project Execution: Inputs

.1   Project Management Plan
Described in the introduction to Section 4.3.

.2   Approved Corrective Actions
Approved corrective actions are documented, authorized directions required to bring expected future project performance into conformance with the project management plan.

.3   Approved Preventive Actions
Approved preventive actions are documented, authorized directions that reduce the probability of negative consequences associated with project risks.

.4   Approved Change Requests
Approved change requests are the documented, authorized changes to expand or contract project scope. The approved change requests can also modify policies, project management plans, procedures, costs or budgets, or revise schedules. Approved change requests are scheduled for implementation by the project team.

.5   Approved Defect Repair
The approved defect repair is the documented, authorized request for product correction of a defect found during the quality inspection or the audit process.

A Guide to the Project Management Body of Knowledge (PMBOK® Guide) Third Edition
©2004 Project Management Institute, Four Campus Boulevard, Newtown Square, PA 19073-3299 USA

.6 Validated Defect Repair

Notification that reinspected repaired items have either been accepted or rejected.

.7 Administrative Closure Procedure

The administrative closure procedure documents all the activities, interactions, and related roles and responsibilities needed in executing the administrative closure procedure for the project.

4.4.2 Direct and Manage Project Execution: Tools and Techniques

.1 Project Management Methodology

The project management methodology defines a process that aids a project team in executing the project management plan.

.2 Project Management Information System

The project management information system is an automated system used by the project management team to aid execution of the activities planned in the project management plan.

4.4.3 Direct and Manage Project Execution: Outputs

.1 Deliverables

A deliverable is any unique and verifiable product, result or capability to perform a service that is identified in the project management planning documentation, and must be produced and provided to complete the project.

.2 Requested Changes

Changes requested to expand or reduce project scope, to modify policies or procedures, to modify project cost or budget, or to revise the project schedule are often identified while project work is being performed. Requests for a change can be direct or indirect, externally or internally initiated, and can be optional or legally/contractually mandated.

.3 Implemented Change Requests

Approved change requests that have been implemented by the project management team during project execution.

.4 Implemented Corrective Actions

The approved corrective actions that have been implemented by the project management team to bring expected future project performance into conformance with the project management plan.

.5 Implemented Preventive Actions

The approved preventive actions that have been implemented by the project management team to reduce the consequences of project risks.

.6 Implemented Defect Repair

During project execution, the project management team has implemented approved product defect corrections.

.7 Work Performance Information

Information on the status of the project activities being performed to accomplish the project work is routinely collected as part of the project management plan execution. This information includes, but is not limited to:

- Schedule progress showing status information
- Deliverables that have been completed and those not completed
- Schedule activities that have started and those that have been finished
- Extent to which quality standards are being met
- Costs authorized and incurred
- Estimates to complete the schedule activities that have started
- Percent physically complete of the in-progress schedule activities
- Documented lessons learned posted to the lessons learned knowledge base
- Resource utilization detail.

4.5 Monitor and Control Project Work

The Monitor and Control Project Work process is performed to monitor project processes associated with initiating, planning, executing, and closing. Corrective or preventive actions are taken to control the project performance. Monitoring is an aspect of project management performed throughout the project. Monitoring includes collecting, measuring, and disseminating performance information, and assessing measurements and trends to effect process improvements. Continuous monitoring gives the project management team insight into the health of the project, and identifies any areas that can require special attention. The Monitor and Control Project Work process is concerned with:

- Comparing actual project performance against the project management plan
- Assessing performance to determine whether any corrective or preventive actions are indicated, and then recommending those actions as necessary
- Analyzing, tracking, and monitoring project risks to make sure the risks are identified, their status is reported, and that appropriate risk response plans are being executed
- Maintaining an accurate, timely information base concerning the project's product(s) and their associated documentation through project completion
- Providing information to support status reporting, progress measurement, and forecasting
- Providing forecasts to update current cost and current schedule information
- Monitoring implementation of approved changes when and as they occur.

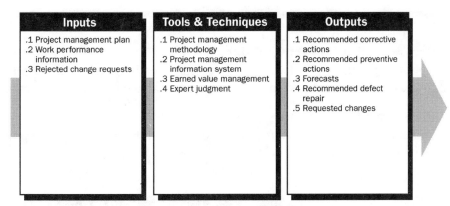

Figure 4-7. Monitor and Control Project Work: Inputs, Tools & Techniques, and Outputs

4.5.1 Monitor and Control Project Work: Inputs

.1 Project Management Plan
Described in the introduction to Section 4.3.

.2 Work Performance Information
Described in Section 4.4.3.7.

.3 Rejected Change Requests
Rejected change requests include the change requests, their supporting documentation, and their change review status showing a disposition of rejected change requests.

4.5.2 Monitor and Control Project Work: Tools and Techniques

.1 Project Management Methodology
The project management methodology defines a process that aids a project management team in monitoring and controlling the project work being performed in accordance with the project management plan.

.2 Project Management Information System
The project management information system (PMIS), an automated system, is used by the project management team to monitor and control the execution of activities that are planned and scheduled in the project management plan. The PMIS is also used to create new forecasts as needed.

.3 Earned Value Technique
The earned value technique measures performance of the project as it moves from project initiation through project closure. The earned value management methodology also provides a means to forecast future performance based upon past performance.

4 Expert Judgment
Expert judgment is used by the project management team to monitor and control project work.

4.5.3 Monitor and Control Project Work: Outputs

.1 Recommended Corrective Actions

Corrective actions are documented recommendations required to bring expected future project performance into conformance with the project management plan.

.2 Recommended Preventive Actions

Preventive actions are documented recommendations that reduce the probability of negative consequences associated with project risks.

.3 Forecasts

Forecasts include estimates or predictions of conditions and events in the project's future, based on information and knowledge available at the time of the forecast. Forecasts are updated and reissued based on work performance information provided as the project is executed. This information is about the project's past performance that could impact the project in the future; for example, estimate at completion and estimate to complete.

.4 Recommended Defect Repair

Some defects, which are found during the quality inspection and audit process, are recommended for correction.

.5 Requested Changes

Described in Section 4.4.3.2.

4.6 Integrated Change Control

The Integrated Change Control process is performed from project inception through completion. Change control is necessary because projects seldom run exactly according to the project management plan. The project management plan, the project scope statement, and other deliverables must be maintained by carefully and continuously managing changes, either by rejecting changes or by approving changes so those approved changes are incorporated into a revised baseline. The Integrated Change Control process includes the following change management activities in differing levels of detail, based upon the completion of project execution:

- Identifying that a change needs to occur or has occurred.

- Influencing the factors that circumvent integrated change control so that only approved changes are implemented.

- Reviewing and approving requested changes.

- Managing the approved changes when and as they occur, by regulating the flow of requested changes.

- Maintaining the integrity of baselines by releasing only approved changes for incorporation into project products or services, and maintaining their related configuration and planning documentation.

- Reviewing and approving all recommended corrective and preventive actions.

- Controlling and updating the scope, cost, budget, schedule and quality requirements based upon approved changes, by coordinating changes across the entire project. For example, a proposed schedule change will often affect cost, risk, quality, and staffing.

- Documenting the complete impact of requested changes.

- Validating defect repair.

- Controlling project quality to standards based on quality reports.

Proposed changes can require new or revised cost estimates, schedule activity sequences, schedule dates, resource requirements, and analysis of risk response alternatives. These changes can require adjustments to the project management plan, project scope statement, or other project deliverables. The configuration management system with change control provides a standardized, effective, and efficient process to centrally manage changes within a project. Configuration management with change control includes identifying, documenting, and controlling changes to the baseline. The applied level of change control is dependent upon the application area, complexity of the specific project, contract requirements, and the context and environment in which the project is performed.

Project-wide application of the configuration management system, including change control processes, accomplishes three main objectives:

- Establishes an evolutionary method to consistently identify and request changes to established baselines, and to assess the value and effectiveness of those changes

- Provides opportunities to continuously validate and improve the project by considering the impact of each change

- Provides the mechanism for the project management team to consistently communicate all changes to the stakeholders.

Some of the configuration management activities included in the integrated change control process are:

- **Configuration Identification.** Providing the basis from which the configuration of products is defined and verified, products and documents are labeled, changes are managed, and accountability is maintained.

- **Configuration Status Accounting.** Capturing, storing, and accessing configuration information needed to manage products and product information effectively.

- **Configuration Verification and Auditing.** Establishing that the performance and functional requirements defined in the configuration documentation have been met.

Every documented requested change must be either accepted or rejected by some authority within the project management team or an external organization representing the initiator, sponsor, or customer. Many times, the Integrated Change Control process includes a change control board responsible for approving and rejecting the requested changes. The roles and responsibilities of these boards are clearly defined within the configuration control and change control procedures, and are agreed to by the sponsor, customer, and other stakeholders. Many large organizations provide for a multi-tiered board structure, separating responsibilities among the boards. If the project is being provided under a contract, then some proposed changes would need to be approved by the customer.

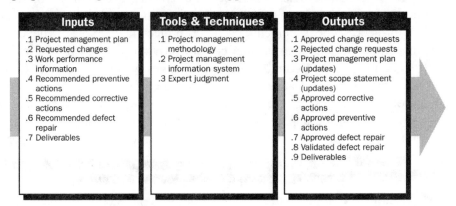

Figure 4-8. Integrated Change Control: Inputs, Tools & Techniques, and Outputs

4.6.1 Integrated Change Control: Inputs

.1 Project Management Plan
Described in the introduction to Section 4.3.

.2 Requested Changes
Described in Section 4.4.3.2.

.3 Work Performance Information
Described in Section 4.4.3.7.

.4 Recommended Preventive Actions
Described in Section 4.5.3.2.

.5 Recommended Corrective Actions
Described in Section 4.5.3.1.

.6 Recommended Defect Repair
Described in Section 4.5.3.4.

.7 Deliverables
Described in Section 4.4.3.1.

4.6.2 Integrated Change Control: Tools and Techniques

.1 Project Management Methodology
The project management methodology defines a process that aids a project management team in implementing Integrated Change Control for the project.

.2 Project Management Information System
The project management information system, an automated system, is used by the project management team as an aid for implementing an Integrated Change Control process for the project, facilitating feedback for the project and controlling changes across the project.

.3 Expert Judgment
The project management team uses stakeholders with expert judgment on the change control board to control and approve all requested changes to any aspect of the project.

4.6.3 Integrated Change Control: Outputs

.1 Approved Change Requests
Described in Section 4.4.1.4.

.2 Rejected Change Requests
Described in Section 4.5.1.3.

.3 Project Management Plan (Updates)
Described in the introduction to Section 4.3.

.4 Project Scope Statement (Updates)
Described in Section 5.3.3.1.

.5 Approved Corrective Actions
Described in Section 4.4.1.2.

.6 Approved Preventive Actions
Described in Section 4.4.1.3.

.7 Approved Defect Repair
Described in Section 4.4.1.5.

.8 Validated Defect Repair
Described in Section 4.4.1.6.

.9 Deliverables
Described in Section 4.4.3.1 and approved by the Integrated Change Control process (Section 4.6).

4.7 Close Project

The Close Project process involves performing the project closure portion of the project management plan. In multi-phase projects, the Close Project process closes out the portion of the project scope and associated activities applicable to a given phase. This process includes finalizing all activities completed across all Project Management Process Groups to formally close the project or a project phase, and transfer the completed or cancelled project as appropriate. The Close Project process also establishes the procedures to coordinate activities needed to verify and document the project deliverables, to coordinate and interact to formalize acceptance of those deliverables by the customer or sponsor, and to investigate and document the reasons for actions taken if a project is terminated before completion.

Two procedures are developed to establish the interactions necessary to perform the closure activities across the entire project or for a project phase:

- **Administrative closure procedure.** This procedure details all the activities, interactions, and related roles and responsibilities of the project team members and other stakeholders involved in executing the administrative closure procedure for the project. Performing the administrative closure process also includes integrated activities needed to collect project records, analyze project success or failure, gather lessons learned, and archive project information for future use by the organization.

- **Contract closure procedure.** Includes all activities and interactions needed to settle and close any contract agreement established for the project, as well as define those related activities supporting the formal administrative closure of the project. This procedure involves both product verification (all work completed correctly and satisfactorily) and administrative closure (updating of contract records to reflect final results and archiving that information for future use). The contract terms and conditions can also prescribe specifications for contract closure that must be part of this procedure. Early termination of a contract is a special case of contract closure that could involve, for example, the inability to deliver the product, a budget overrun, or lack of required resources. This procedure is an input to the Close Contract process.

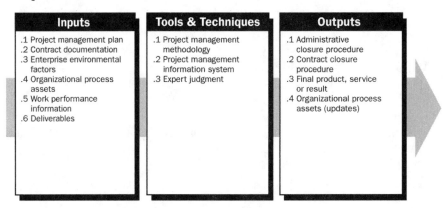

Inputs	Tools & Techniques	Outputs
.1 Project management plan .2 Contract documentation .3 Enterprise environmental factors .4 Organizational process assets .5 Work performance information .6 Deliverables	.1 Project management methodology .2 Project management information system .3 Expert judgment	.1 Administrative closure procedure .2 Contract closure procedure .3 Final product, service or result .4 Organizational process assets (updates)

Figure 4-9. Close Project: Inputs, Tools & Techniques, and Outputs

A Guide to the Project Management Body of Knowledge (PMBOK® Guide) Third Edition
©2004 Project Management Institute, Four Campus Boulevard, Newtown Square, PA 19073-3299 USA

4.7.1 Close Project: Inputs

.1 Project Management Plan
Described in the introduction to Section 4.3.

.2 Contract Documentation
Contract documentation is an input used to perform the contract closure process, and includes the contract itself, as well as changes to the contract and other documentation (such as the technical approach, product description, or deliverable acceptance criteria and procedures).

.3 Enterprise Environmental Factors
Described in Section 4.1.1.3.

.4 Organizational Process Assets
Described in Section 4.1.1.4.

.5 Work Performance Information
Described in Section 4.4.3.7.

.6 Deliverables
Described in Section 4.4.3.1 and approved by the Integrated Change Control process (Section 4.6).

4.7.2 Close Project: Tools and Techniques

.1 Project Management Methodology
The project management methodology defines a process that aids a project management team in performing both administrative and contract closure procedures for the project.

.2 Project Management Information System
The project management team uses the project management information system to perform both administrative and contract closure procedures across the project.

.3 Expert Judgment
Expert judgment is applied in developing and performing both the administrative and contract closure procedures.

4.7.3 Close Project: Outputs

.1 Administrative Closure Procedure
This procedure contains all the activities and the related roles and responsibilities of the project team members involved in executing the administrative closure procedure. The procedures to transfer the project products or services to production and/or operations are developed and established. This procedure provides a step-by-step methodology for administrative closure that addresses:

- Actions and activities to define the stakeholder approval requirements for changes and all levels of deliverables
- Actions and activities that are necessary to confirm that the project has met all sponsor, customer, and other stakeholders' requirements, verify that all deliverables have been provided and accepted, and validate that completion and exit criteria have been met
- Actions and activities necessary to satisfy completion or exit criteria for the project.

.2 Contract Closure Procedure

This procedure is developed to provide a step-by-step methodology that addresses the terms and conditions of the contracts and any required completion or exit criteria for contract closure. It contains all activities and related responsibilities of the project team members, customers, and other stakeholders involved in the contract closure process. The actions performed formally close all contracts associated with the completed project.

.3 Final Product, Service, or Result

Formal acceptance and handover of the final product, service, or result that the project was authorized to produce. The acceptance includes receipt of a formal statement that the terms of the contract have been met.

.4 Organizational Process Assets (Updates)

Closure will include the development of the index and location of project documentation using the configuration management system (Section 4.3).

- **Formal Acceptance Documentation.** Formal confirmation has been received from the customer or sponsor that customer requirements and specifications for the project's product, service, or result have been met. This document formally indicates that the customer or sponsor has officially accepted the deliverables.
- **Project Files.** Documentation resulting from the project's activities; for example, project management plan, scope, cost, schedule and quality baselines, project calendars, risk registers, planned risk response actions, and risk impact.
- **Project Closure Documents.** Project closure documents consist of formal documentation indicating completion of the project and the transfer of the completed project deliverables to others, such as an operations group. If the project was terminated prior to completion, the formal documentation indicates why the project was terminated, and formalizes the procedures for the transfer of the finished and unfinished deliverables of the cancelled project to others.
- **Historical Information.** Historical information and lessons learned information are transferred to the lessons learned knowledge base for use by future projects.

CHAPTER 5

Project Scope Management

Project Scope Management includes the processes required to ensure that the project includes all the work required, and only the work required, to complete the project successfully[5]. Project scope management is primarily concerned with defining and controlling what is and is not included in the project. Figure 5-1 provides an overview of the Project Scope Management processes, and Figure 5-2 provides a process flow diagram of those processes and their inputs, outputs, and other related Knowledge Area processes.

5.1 Scope Planning – creating a project scope management plan that documents how the project scope will be defined, verified, controlled, and how the work breakdown structure (WBS) will be created and defined.

5.2 Scope Definition – developing a detailed project scope statement as the basis for future project decisions.

5.3 Create WBS – subdividing the major project deliverables and project work into smaller, more manageable components.

5.4 Scope Verification – formalizing acceptance of the completed project deliverables.

5.5 Scope Control – controlling changes to the project scope.

These processes interact with each other and with processes in the other Knowledge Areas as well. Each process can involve effort from one or more persons or groups of persons, based on the needs of the project. Each process occurs at least once in every project and occurs in one or more project phases, if the project is divided into phases. Although the processes are presented here as discrete components with well-defined interfaces, in practice they can overlap and interact in ways not detailed here. Process interactions are discussed in detail in Chapter 3.

In the project context, the term scope can refer to:

- **Product scope.** The features and functions that characterize a product, service, or result

- **Project scope.** The work that needs to be accomplished to deliver a product, service, or result with the specified features and functions.

This chapter focuses on the processes used to manage the project scope. These project scope management processes, and their associated tools and techniques, vary by application area, are usually defined as part of the project life cycle (Section 2.1), and are documented in the project scope management plan. The approved detailed project scope statement and its associated WBS and WBS dictionary are the scope baseline for the project.

A project generally results in a single product, but that product can include subsidiary components, each with its own separate, but interdependent, product scope. For example, a new telephone system would generally include four subsidiary components—hardware, software, training, and implementation.

Completion of the project scope is measured against the project management plan (Section 4.3), the project scope statement, and its associated WBS and WBS dictionary, but completion of the product scope is measured against the product requirements. Project scope management needs to be well integrated with the other Knowledge Area processes, so that the work of the project will result in delivery of the specified product scope.

A Guide to the Project Management Body of Knowledge (PMBOK® Guide) Third Edition
©2004 Project Management Institute, Four Campus Boulevard, Newtown Square, PA 19073-3299 USA

PROJECT SCOPE MANAGEMENT

5.1 Scope Planning

.1 Inputs
  .1 Enterprise environmental factors
  .2 Organizational process assets
  .3 Project charter
  .4 Preliminary project scope statement
  .5 Project management plan

.2 Tools and Techniques
  .1 Expert judgment
  .2 Templates, forms, standards

.3 Outputs
  .1 Project scope management plan

5.2 Scope Definition

.1 Inputs
  .1 Organizational process assets
  .2 Project charter
  .3 Preliminary project scope statement
  .4 Project scope management plan
  .5 Approved change requests

.2 Tools and Techniques
  .1 Product analysis
  .2 Alternatives identification
  .3 Expert judgment
  .4 Stakeholder analysis

.3 Outputs
  .1 Project scope statement
  .2 Requested changes
  .3 Project scope management plan (updates)

5.3 Create WBS

.1 Inputs
  .1 Organizational process assets
  .2 Project scope statement
  .3 Project scope management plan
  .4 Approved change requests

.2 Tools and Techniques
  .1 Work breakdown structure templates
  .2 Decomposition

.3 Outputs
  .1 Project scope statement (updates)
  .2 Work breakdown structure
  .3 WBS dictionary
  .4 Scope baseline
  .5 Project scope management plan (updates)
  .6 Requested changes

5.4 Scope Verification

.1 Inputs
  .1 Project scope statement
  .2 WBS dictionary
  .3 Project scope management plan
  .4 Deliverables

.2 Tools and Techniques
  .1 Inspection

.3 Outputs
  .1 Accepted deliverables
  .2 Requested changes
  .3 Recommended corrective actions

5.5 Scope Control

.1 Inputs
  .1 Project scope statement
  .2 Work breakdown structure
  .3 WBS dictionary
  .4 Project scope management plan
  .5 Performance reports
  .6 Approved change requests
  .7 Work performance information

.2 Tools and Techniques
  .1 Change control system
  .2 Variance analysis
  .3 Replanning
  .4 Configuration management system

.3 Outputs
  .1 Project scope statement (updates)
  .2 Work breakdown structure (updates)
  .3 WBS dictionary (updates)
  .4 Scope baseline (updates)
  .5 Requested changes
  .6 Recommended corrective action
  .7 Organizational process assets (updates)
  .8 Project management plan (updates)

Figure 5-1. Project Scope Management Overview

5

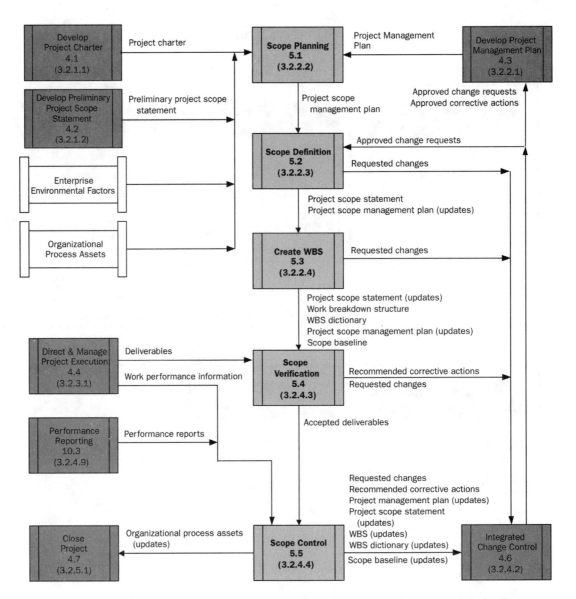

Note: Not all process interactions and data flow among the processes are shown.

Figure 5-2. Project Scope Management Process Flow Diagram

5.1 Scope Planning

Defining and managing the project scope influences the project's overall success. Each project requires a careful balance of tools, data sources, methodologies, processes and procedures, and other factors to ensure that the effort expended on scoping activities is commensurate with the project's size, complexity, and importance. For example, a critical project could merit formal, thorough, and time-intensive scoping activities, while a routine project could require substantially less documentation and scrutiny. The project management team documents these scope management decisions in the project scope management plan. The project scope management plan is a planning tool describing how the team will define the project scope, develop the detailed project scope statement, define and develop the work breakdown structure, verify the project scope, and control the project scope. The development of the project scope management plan and the detailing of the project scope begin with the analysis of information contained in the project charter (Section 4.1), the preliminary project scope statement (Section 4.2), the latest approved version of the project management plan (Section 4.3), historical information contained in the organizational process assets (Section 4.1.1.4), and any relevant enterprise environmental factors (Section 4.1.1.3).

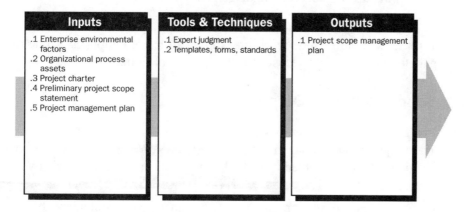

Inputs	Tools & Techniques	Outputs
.1 Enterprise environmental factors .2 Organizational process assets .3 Project charter .4 Preliminary project scope statement .5 Project management plan	.1 Expert judgment .2 Templates, forms, standards	.1 Project scope management plan

Figure 5-3. Scope Planning: Inputs, Tools & Techniques, and Outputs

5.1.1 Scope Planning: Inputs

.1 Enterprise Environmental Factors

Enterprise environmental factors include items such as the organization's culture, infrastructure, tools, human resources, personnel policies, and marketplace conditions that could affect how project scope is managed.

.2 Organizational Process Assets

Organizational process assets are the formal and informal policies, procedures, and guidelines that could impact how the project's scope is managed. Those of particular interest to project scope planning include:

- Organizational policies as they pertain to project scope planning and management
- Organizational procedures related to project scope planning and management
- Historical information about previous projects that may be located in the lessons learned knowledge base.

.3 Project Charter
Described in Section 4.1.

.4 Preliminary Project Scope Statement
Described in Section 4.2.

.5 Project Management Plan
Described in the introduction to Section 4.3.

5.1.2 Scope Planning: Tools and Techniques

.1 Expert Judgment
Expert judgment related to how equivalent projects have managed scope is used in developing the project scope management plan.

.2 Templates, Forms, Standards
Templates could include work breakdown structure templates, scope management plan templates, and project scope change control forms.

5.1.3 Scope Planning: Outputs

.1 Project Scope Management Plan
The project scope management plan provides guidance on how project scope will be defined, documented, verified, managed, and controlled by the project management team. The components of a project scope management plan include:

- A process to prepare a detailed project scope statement based upon the preliminary project scope statement
- A process that enables the creation of the WBS from the detailed project scope statement, and establishes how the WBS will be maintained and approved
- A process that specifies how formal verification and acceptance of the completed project deliverables will be obtained
- A process to control how requests for changes to the detailed project scope statement will be processed. This process is directly linked to the integrated change control process (Section 4.6).

A project scope management plan is contained in, or is a subsidiary of, the project management plan. The project scope management plan can be informal and broadly framed, or formal and highly detailed, based on the needs of the project.

5.2 Scope Definition

The preparation of a detailed project scope statement is critical to project success and builds upon the major deliverables, assumptions, and constraints that are documented during project initiation in the preliminary project scope statement. During planning, the project scope is defined and described with greater specificity because more information about the project is known. Stakeholder needs, wants, and expectations are analyzed and converted into requirements. The assumptions and constraints are analyzed for completeness, with additional assumptions and constraints added as necessary. The project team and other stakeholders, who have additional insight into the preliminary project scope statement, can perform and prepare the analyses.

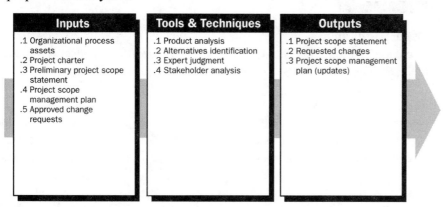

Figure 5-4. Scope Definition: Inputs, Tools & Techniques, and Outputs

5.2.1 Scope Definition: Inputs

.1 Organizational Process Assets
Described in Section 4.1.1.4.

.2 Project Charter
If a project charter is not used in a performing organization, then comparable information needs to be acquired or developed, and used to develop the detailed project scope statement.

.3 Preliminary Project Scope Statement
If a preliminary project scope statement is not used in a performing organization, then comparable information, including the product scope description, needs to be acquired or developed and used to develop the detailed project scope statement.

.4 Project Scope Management Plan
Described in Section 5.1.3.1.

.5 Approved Change Requests
Approved change requests (Section 4.4) can cause a change to project scope, project quality, estimated costs, or project schedule. Changes are often identified and approved while the work of the project is ongoing.

5.2.2 Scope Definition: Tools and Techniques

.1 Product Analysis

Each application area has one or more generally accepted methods for translating project objectives into tangible deliverables and requirements. Product analysis includes techniques such as product breakdown, systems analysis, systems engineering, value engineering, value analysis, and functional analysis.

.2 Alternatives Identification

Identifying alternatives is a technique used to generate different approaches to execute and perform the work of the project. A variety of general management techniques is often used here, the most common of which are brainstorming and lateral thinking.

.3 Expert Judgment

Each application area has experts who can be used to develop portions of the detailed project scope statement.

.4 Stakeholder Analysis

Stakeholder analysis identifies the influence and interests of the various stakeholders and documents their needs, wants, and expectations. The analysis then selects, prioritizes, and quantifies the needs, wants, and expectations to create requirements. Unquantifiable expectations, such as customer satisfaction, are subjective and entail a high risk of being successfully accomplished. Stakeholders' interests may be positively or negatively affected by execution or completion of the project and they may also exert influence over the project and its deliverables.

5.2.3 Scope Definition: Outputs

.1 Project Scope Statement

The project scope statement describes, in detail, the project's deliverables and the work required to create those deliverables. The project scope statement also provides a common understanding of the project scope among all project stakeholders and describes the project's major objectives. It also enables the project team to perform more detailed planning, guides the project team's work during execution, and provides the baseline for evaluating whether requests for changes or additional work are contained within or outside the project's boundaries.

The degree and level of detail to which the project scope statement defines what work will be performed and what work is excluded can determine how well the project management team can control the overall project scope. Managing the project scope, in turn, can determine how well the project management team can plan, manage, and control the execution of the project. The detailed project scope statement includes, either directly or by reference to other documents:

- **Project objectives.** Project objectives include the measurable success criteria of the project. Projects may have a wide variety of business, cost, schedule, technical, and quality objectives. Project objectives can also include cost, schedule, and quality targets. Each project objective has attributes such as cost, a metric such as United States dollars, and an absolute or relative value such as less than 1.5 million dollars.

- **Product scope description.** Describes the characteristics of the product, service, or result that the project was undertaken to create. These characteristics will generally have less detail in early phases and more detail in later phases as the product characteristics are progressively elaborated. While the form and substance of the characteristics will vary, the scope description should always provide sufficient detail to support later project scope planning.

- **Project requirements.** Describes the conditions or capabilities that must be met or possessed by the deliverables of the project to satisfy a contract, standard, specification, or other formally imposed documents. Stakeholder analyses of all stakeholder needs, wants, and expectations are translated into prioritized requirements.

- **Project boundaries.** Identifies generally what is included within the project. It states explicitly what is excluded from the project, if a stakeholder might assume that a particular product, service, or result could be a component of the project.

- **Project deliverables.** Deliverables (Section 4.4.3.1) include both the outputs that comprise the product or service of the project, as well as ancillary results, such as project management reports and documentation. Depending on the project scope statement, the deliverables may be described at a summary level or in great detail.

- **Product acceptance criteria.** Defines the process and criteria for accepting completed products.

- **Project constraints.** Lists and describes the specific project constraints associated with the project scope that limit the team's options. For example, a predefined budget or any imposed dates (schedule milestones) that are issued by the customer or performing organization are included. When a project is performed under contract, contractual provisions will generally be constraints. The constraints listed in the detailed project scope statement are typically more numerous and more detailed than the constraints listed in the project charter.

- **Project assumptions.** Lists and describes the specific project assumptions associated with the project scope and the potential impact of those assumptions if they prove to be false. Project teams frequently identify, document, and validate assumptions as part of their planning process. The assumptions listed in the detailed project scope statement are typically more numerous and more detailed than the assumptions listed in the project charter.

- **Initial project organization.** The members of the project team, as well as stakeholders, are identified. The organization of the project is also documented.

- **Initial defined risks.** Identifies the known risks.

- **Schedule milestones.** The customer or performing organization can identify milestones and can place imposed dates on those schedule milestones. These dates can be addressed as schedule constraints.

- **Fund limitation.** Describes any limitation placed upon funding for the project, whether in total value or over specified time frames.

- **Cost estimate.** The project's cost estimate factors into the project's expected overall cost, and is usually preceded by a modifier that provides some indication of accuracy, such as conceptual or definitive.

- **Project configuration management requirements.** Describes the level of configuration management and change control to be implemented on the project.

- **Project specifications.** Identifies those specification documents with which the project should comply.

- **Approval requirements.** Identifies approval requirements that can be applied to items such as project objectives, deliverables, documents, and work.

.2 Requested Changes

Requested changes to the project management plan and its subsidiary plans may be developed during the Scope Definition process. Requested changes are processed for review and disposition through the Integrated Change Control process.

.3 Project Scope Management Plan (Updates)

The project scope management plan component of the project management plan may need to be updated to include approved change requests resulting from the project's Scope Definition process.

5.3 Create WBS

The WBS is a deliverable-oriented hierarchical decomposition of the work to be executed by the project team, to accomplish the project objectives and create the required deliverables. The WBS organizes and defines the total scope of the project. The WBS subdivides the project work into smaller, more manageable pieces of work, with each descending level of the WBS representing an increasingly detailed definition of the project work. The planned work contained within the lowest-level WBS components, which are called work packages, can be scheduled, cost estimated, monitored, and controlled.

The WBS represents the work specified in the current approved project scope statement. Components comprising the WBS assist the stakeholders in viewing the deliverables (Section 4.4.3.1) of the project.

A Guide to the Project Management Body of Knowledge (PMBOK® Guide) Third Edition
©2004 Project Management Institute, Four Campus Boulevard, Newtown Square, PA 19073-3299 USA

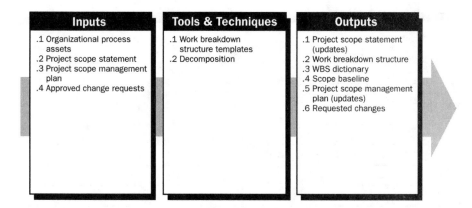

Inputs	Tools & Techniques	Outputs
.1 Organizational process assets .2 Project scope statement .3 Project scope management plan .4 Approved change requests	.1 Work breakdown structure templates .2 Decomposition	.1 Project scope statement (updates) .2 Work breakdown structure .3 WBS dictionary .4 Scope baseline .5 Project scope management plan (updates) .6 Requested changes

Figure 5-5. Create WBS: Inputs, Tools & Techniques, and Outputs

5.3.1 Create WBS: Inputs

.1 Organizational Process Assets
Described in Section 4.1.1.4.

.2 Project Scope Statement
Described in Section 5.2.3.1.

.3 Project Scope Management Plan
Described in Section 5.2.1.4.

.4 Approved Change Requests
Described in Section 4.4.1.4.

5.3.2 Create WBS: Tools and Techniques

.1 Work Breakdown Structure Templates
Although each project is unique, a WBS from a previous project can often be used as a template for a new project, since some projects will resemble another prior project to some extent. For example, most projects within a given organization will have the same or similar project life cycles and, therefore, have the same or similar deliverables required from each phase. Many application areas or performing organizations have standard WBS templates.

The Project Management Institute Practice Standard for Work Breakdown Structures provides guidance for the generation, development, and application of work breakdown structures. This publication contains industry-specific examples of WBS templates that can be tailored to specific projects in a particular application area. A portion of a WBS example, with some branches of the WBS decomposed down through the work package level, is shown in Figure 5-6.

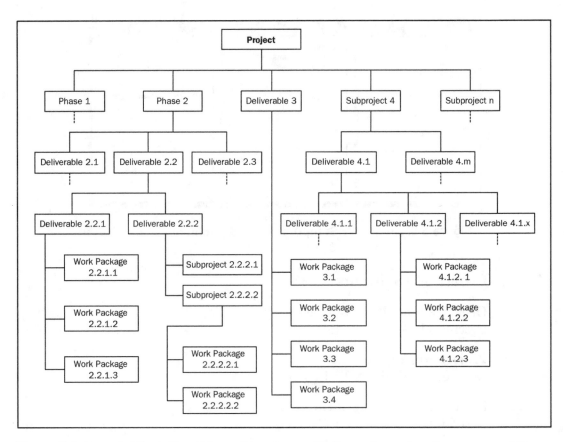

Figure 5-6. Sample Work Breakdown Structure with Some Branches Decomposed Down Through Work Packages

.2   Decomposition

Decomposition is the subdivision of project deliverables into smaller, more manageable components until the work and deliverables are defined to the work package level. The work package level is the lowest level in the WBS, and is the point at which the cost and schedule for the work can be reliably estimated. The level of detail for work packages will vary with the size and complexity of the project.

Decomposition may not be possible for a deliverable or subproject that will be accomplished far into the future. The project management team usually waits until the deliverable or subproject is clarified so the details of the WBS can be developed. This technique is sometimes referred to as rolling wave planning.

Different deliverables can have different levels of decomposition. To arrive at a manageable work effort (i.e., a work package), the work for some deliverables needs to be decomposed only to the next level, while others need more levels of decomposition. As the work is decomposed to lower levels of detail, the ability to plan, manage, and control the work is enhanced. However, excessive decomposition can lead to non-productive management effort, inefficient use of resources, and decreased efficiency in performing the work. The project team needs to seek a balance between too little and too much in the level of WBS planning detail.

A Guide to the Project Management Body of Knowledge (PMBOK® Guide) Third Edition
©2004 Project Management Institute, Four Campus Boulevard, Newtown Square, PA 19073-3299 USA

Decomposition of the total project work generally involves the following activities:

- Identifying the deliverables and related work
- Structuring and organizing the WBS
- Decomposing the upper WBS levels into lower level detailed components
- Developing and assigning identification codes to the WBS components
- Verifying that the degree of decomposition of the work is necessary and sufficient.

Identifying the major deliverables of the project and the work needed to produce those deliverables requires analyzing the detailed project scope statement. This analysis requires a degree of expert judgment to identify all the work including project management deliverables and those deliverables required by contract.

Structuring and organizing the deliverables and associated project work into a WBS that can meet the control and management requirements of the project management team is an analytical technique that may be done with the use of a WBS template. The resulting structure can take a number of forms, such as:

- Using the major deliverables and subprojects as the first level of decomposition, as shown in Figure 5-6.

- Using subprojects as illustrated in Figure 5-6, where the subprojects may be developed by organizations outside the project team. For example, in some application areas, the project WBS can be defined and developed in multiple parts, such as a project summary WBS with multiple subprojects within the WBS that can be contracted out. The seller then develops the supporting contract work breakdown structure as part of the contracted work.

- Using the phases of the project life cycle as the first level of decomposition, with the project deliverables inserted at the second level, as shown in Figure 5-7.

- Using different approaches within each branch of the WBS, as illustrated in Figure 5-8, where test and evaluation is a phase, the air vehicle is a product, and training is a supporting service.

Decomposition of the upper level WBS components requires subdividing the work for each of the deliverables or subprojects into its fundamental components, where the WBS components represent verifiable products, services, or results. Each component should be clearly and completely defined and assigned to a specific performing organizational unit that accepts responsibility for the WBS component's completion. The components are defined in terms of how the work of the project will actually be executed and controlled. For example, the status-reporting component of project management could include weekly status reports, while a product to be manufactured might include several individual physical components plus the final assembly.

Verifying the correctness of the decomposition requires determining that the lower-level WBS components are those that are necessary and sufficient for completion of the corresponding higher-level deliverables.

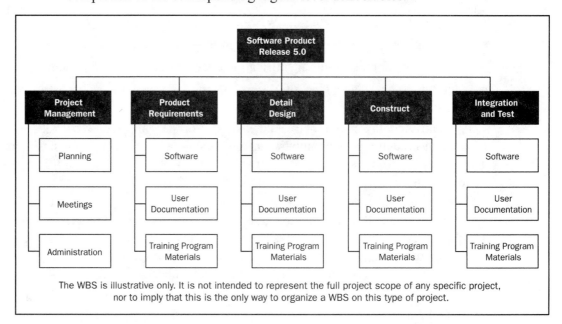

Figure 5-7. Sample Work Breakdown Structure Organized by Phase

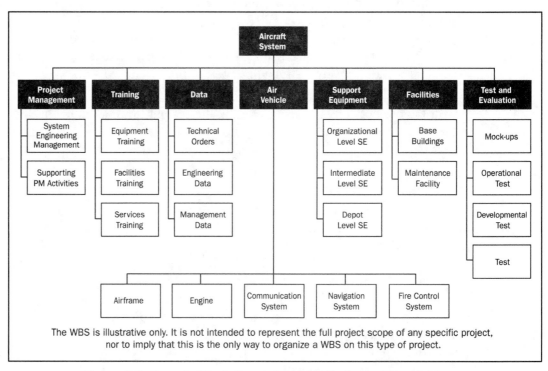

Figure 5-8. Sample Work Breakdown for Defense Materiel Items

5.3.3 Create WBS: Outputs

.1 Project Scope Statement (Updates)

If approved change requests result from the Create WBS process, then the project scope statement is updated to include those approved changes.

.2 Work Breakdown Structure

The key document generated by the Create WBS process is the actual WBS. Each WBS component, including work package and control accounts within a WBS, is generally assigned a unique identifier from a code of accounts. These identifiers provide a structure for hierarchical summation of costs, schedule, and resource information.

The WBS should not be confused with other kinds of breakdown structures used to present project information. Other structures used in some application areas or other Knowledge Areas include:

- **Organizational Breakdown Structure (OBS).** Provides a hierarchically organized depiction of the project organization arranged so that the work packages can be related to the performing organizational units.

- **Bill of Materials (BOM).** Presents a hierarchical tabulation of the physical assemblies, subassemblies, and components needed to fabricate a manufactured product.

- **Risk Breakdown Structure (RBS).** A hierarchically organized depiction of the identified project risks arranged by risk category.

- **Resource Breakdown Structure (RBS).** A hierarchically organized depiction of the resources by type to be used on the project.

.3 WBS Dictionary

The document generated by the Create WBS process that supports the WBS is called the WBS dictionary and is a companion document to the WBS. The detailed content of the components contained in a WBS, including work packages and control accounts, can be described in the WBS dictionary. For each WBS component, the WBS dictionary includes a code of account identifier, a statement of work, responsible organization, and a list of schedule milestones. Other information for a WBS component can include contract information, quality requirements, and technical references to facilitate performance of the work. Other information for a control account would be a charge number. Other information for a work package can include a list of associated schedule activities, resources required, and an estimate of cost. Each WBS component is cross-referenced, as appropriate, to other WBS components in the WBS dictionary.

.4 Scope Baseline

The approved detailed project scope statement (Section 5.2.3.1) and its associated WBS and WBS dictionary are the scope baseline for the project.

.5 Project Scope Management Plan (Updates)

If approved change requests result from the Create WBS process, then the project scope management plan may need to be updated to include approved changes.

.6 Requested Changes

Requested changes to the project scope statement and its components may be generated from the Create WBS process, and are processed for review and approval through the integrated change control process.

5.4 Scope Verification

Scope verification is the process of obtaining the stakeholders' formal acceptance of the completed project scope and associated deliverables. Verifying the project scope includes reviewing deliverables to ensure that each is completed satisfactorily. If the project is terminated early, the project scope verification process should establish and document the level and extent of completion. Scope verification differs from quality control in that scope verification is primarily concerned with acceptance of the deliverables, while quality control is primarily concerned with meeting the quality requirements specified for the deliverables. Quality control is generally performed before scope verification, but these two processes can be performed in parallel.

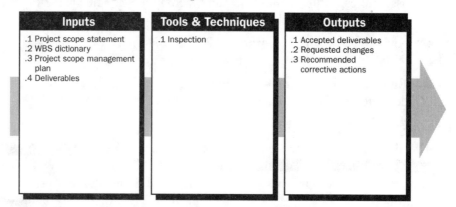

Figure 5-9. Scope Verification: Inputs, Tools & Techniques, and Outputs

5.4.1 Scope Verification: Inputs

.1 Project Scope Statement

The project scope statement includes the product scope description that describes the project's product to be reviewed and the product acceptance criteria.

.2 WBS Dictionary

The WBS dictionary is a component of the detailed project scope definition, and is used to verify that the deliverables being produced and accepted are included in the approved project scope.

A Guide to the Project Management Body of Knowledge (PMBOK® Guide) Third Edition
©2004 Project Management Institute, Four Campus Boulevard, Newtown Square, PA 19073-3299 USA

.3   Project Scope Management Plan
Described in Section 5.1.3.1.

.4   Deliverables
The deliverables are those that have been fully or partially completed, and are an output of the Direct and Manage Project Execution process (Section 4.4).

5.4.2   Scope Verification: Tools and Techniques

.1   Inspection
Inspection includes activities such as measuring, examining, and verifying to determine whether work and deliverables meet requirements and product acceptance criteria. Inspections are variously called reviews, product reviews, audits, and walkthroughs. In some application areas, these different terms have narrow and specific meanings.

5.4.3   Scope Verification: Outputs

.1   Accepted Deliverables
The Scope Verification process documents those completed deliverables that have been accepted. Those completed deliverables that have not been accepted are documented, along with the reasons for non-acceptance. Scope verification includes supporting documentation received from the customer or sponsor and acknowledging stakeholder acceptance of the project's deliverables.

.2   Requested Changes
Requested changes may be generated from the Scope Verification process, and are processed for review and disposition through the Integrated Change Control process.

.3   Recommended Corrective Actions
Described in Section 4.5.3.1.

5.5   Scope Control

Project scope control is concerned with influencing the factors that create project scope changes and controlling the impact of those changes. Scope control assures all requested changes and recommended corrective actions are processed through the project Integrated Change Control process. Project scope control is also used to manage the actual changes when they occur and is integrated with the other control processes. Uncontrolled changes are often referred to as project scope creep. Change is inevitable, thereby mandating some type of change control process.

Inputs	Tools & Techniques	Outputs
.1 Project scope statement .2 Work breakdown structure .3 WBS dictionary .4 Project scope management plan .5 Performance reports .6 Approved change requests .7 Work performance information	.1 Change control system .2 Variance analysis .3 Replanning .4 Configuration management system	.1 Project scope statement (updates) .2 Work breakdown structure (updates) .3 WBS dictionary (updates) .4 Scope baseline (updates) .5 Requested changes .6 Recommended corrective action .7 Organizational process assets (updates) .8 Project management plan (updates)

Figure 5-10. Scope Control: Inputs, Tools & Techniques, and Outputs

5.5.1 Scope Control: Inputs

.1 Project Scope Statement
The project scope statement, along with its associated WBS and WBS dictionary (Section 5.3), defines the project's scope baseline and product scope.

.2 Work Breakdown Structure
Described in Section 5.3.3.2.

.3 WBS Dictionary
Described in Section 5.3.3.3.

.4 Project Scope Management Plan
Described in Section 5.1.3.1.

.5 Performance Reports
Performance reports provide information on project work performance, such as interim deliverables that have been completed.

.6 Approved Change Requests
An approved change request (Section 4.4.1.4) impacting project scope is any modification to the agreed-upon project scope baseline, as defined by the approved project scope statement, WBS, and WBS dictionary.

.7 Work Performance Information
Described in Section 4.4.3.7.

A Guide to the Project Management Body of Knowledge (PMBOK® Guide) Third Edition
©2004 Project Management Institute, Four Campus Boulevard, Newtown Square, PA 19073-3299 USA

5.5.2 Scope Control: Tools and Techniques

.1 Change Control System

A project scope change control system, documented in the project scope management plan, defines the procedures by which the project scope and product scope can be changed. The system includes the documentation, tracking systems, and approval levels necessary for authorizing changes. The scope change control system is integrated with any overall project management information system (Section 4.6.2.2) to control project scope. When the project is managed under a contract, the change control system also complies with all relevant contractual provisions.

.2 Variance Analysis

Project performance measurements are used to assess the magnitude of variation. Important aspects of project scope control include determining the cause of variance relative to the scope baseline (Section 5.3.3.4) and deciding whether corrective action is required.

.3 Replanning

Approved change requests affecting the project scope can require modifications to the WBS and WBS dictionary, the project scope statement, and the project scope management plan. These approved change requests can cause updates to components of the project management plan.

.4 Configuration Management System

A formal configuration management system (Section 4.3.2.2) provides procedures for the status of the deliverables, and assures that requested changes to the project scope and product scope are thoroughly considered and documented before being processed through the Integrated Change Control process.

5.5.3 Scope Control: Outputs

.1 Project Scope Statement (Updates)

If the approved change requests have an effect upon the project scope, then the project scope statement is revised and reissued to reflect the approved changes. The updated project scope statement becomes the new project scope baseline for future changes.

.2 Work Breakdown Structure (Updates)

If the approved change requests have an effect upon the project scope, then the WBS is revised and reissued to reflect the approved changes.

.3 WBS Dictionary (Updates)

If the approved change requests have an effect upon the project scope, then the WBS dictionary is revised and reissued to reflect the approved changes.

.4   Scope Baseline (Updates)

Described in Section 5.3.3.4.

.5   Requested Changes

The results of project scope control can generate requested changes, which are processed for review and disposition according to the project Integrated Change Control process.

.6   Recommended Corrective Action

A recommended corrective action is any step recommended to bring expected future project performance in line with the project management plan and project scope statement.

.7   Organizational Process Assets (Updates)

The causes of variances, the reasoning behind the corrective action chosen, and other types of lessons learned from project scope change control are documented and updated in the historical database of the organizational process assets.

.8   Project Management Plan (Updates)

If the approved change requests have an effect on the project scope, then the corresponding component documents and cost baseline, and schedule baselines of the project management plan, are revised and reissued to reflect the approved changes.

A Guide to the Project Management Body of Knowledge (PMBOK® Guide) Third Edition
©2004 Project Management Institute, Four Campus Boulevard, Newtown Square, PA 19073-3299 USA

CHAPTER 6

Project Time Management

Project Time Management includes the processes required to accomplish timely completion of the project. Figure 6-1 provides an overview of the Project Time Management processes and Figure 6-2 provides a process flow diagram of those processes and their inputs, outputs, and other related Knowledge Area processes. The Project Time Management processes include the following:

6.1 Activity Definition – identifying the specific schedule activities that need to be performed to produce the various project deliverables.

6.2 Activity Sequencing – identifying and documenting dependencies among schedule activities.

6.3 Activity Resource Estimating – estimating the type and quantities of resources required to perform each schedule activity.

6.4 Activity Duration Estimating – estimating the number of work periods that will be needed to complete individual schedule activities.

6.5 Schedule Development – analyzing activity sequences, durations, resource requirements, and schedule constraints to create the project schedule.

6.6 Schedule Control – controlling changes to the project schedule.

These processes interact with each other and with processes in the other Knowledge Areas as well. Each process can involve effort from one or more persons or groups of persons, based on the needs of the project. Each process occurs at least once in every project and occurs in one or more project phases, if the project is divided into phases. Although the processes are presented here as discrete components with well-defined interfaces, in practice they can overlap and interact in ways not detailed here. Process interactions are discussed in detail in Chapter 3.

On some projects, especially ones of smaller scope, activity sequencing, activity resource estimating, activity duration estimating, and schedule development are so tightly linked that they are viewed as a single process that can be performed by a person over a relatively short period of time. These processes are presented here as distinct processes because the tools and techniques for each are different.

Although not shown here as a discrete process, the work involved in performing the six processes of Project Time Management is preceded by a planning effort by the project management team. This planning effort is part of the Develop Project Management Plan process (Section 4.3), which produces a schedule management plan that sets the format and establishes criteria for developing and controlling the project schedule. The project time management processes, and their associated tools and techniques, vary by application area, are usually defined as part of the project life cycle (Section 2.1), and are documented in the schedule management plan. The schedule management plan is contained in, or is a subsidiary plan of, the project management plan (introduction to Section 4.3), and may be formal or informal, highly detailed or broadly framed, based upon the needs of the project.

A Guide to the Project Management Body of Knowledge (PMBOK® Guide) Third Edition
©2004 Project Management Institute, Four Campus Boulevard, Newtown Square, PA 19073-3299 USA

PROJECT TIME MANAGEMENT

6.1 Activity Definition

.1 Inputs
   .1 Enterprise environmental factors
   .2 Organizational process assets
   .3 Project scope statement
   .4 Work breakdown structure
   .5 WBS dictionary
   .6 Project management plan

.2 Tools and Techniques
   .1 Decomposition
   .2 Templates
   .3 Rolling wave planning
   .4 Expert judgment
   .5 Planning component

.3 Outputs
   .1 Activity list
   .2 Activity attributes
   .3 Milestone list
   .4 Requested changes

6.2 Activity Sequencing

.1 Inputs
   .1 Project scope statement
   .2 Activity list
   .3 Activity attributes
   .4 Milestone list
   .5 Approved change requests

.2 Tools and Techniques
   .1 Precedence Diagramming Method (PDM)
   .2 Arrow Diagramming Method (ADM)
   .3 Schedule network templates
   .4 Dependency determination
   .5 Applying leads and lags

.3 Outputs
   .1 Project schedule network diagrams
   .2 Activity list (updates)
   .3 Activity attributes (updates)
   .4 Requested changes

6.3 Activity Resource Estimating

.1 Inputs
   .1 Enterprise environmental factors
   .2 Organizational process assets
   .3 Activity list
   .4 Activity attributes
   .5 Resouce availability
   .6 Project management plan

.2 Tools and Techniques
   .1 Expert judgment
   .2 Alternatives analysis
   .3 Published estimating data
   .4 Project management software
   .5 Bottom-up estimating

.3 Outputs
   .1 Activity resource requirements
   .2 Activity attributes (updates)
   .3 Resource breakdown structure
   .4 Resource calendars (updates)
   .5 Requested changes

6.4 Activity Duration Estimating

.1 Inputs
   .1 Enterprise environmental factors
   .2 Organizational process assets
   .3 Project scope statement
   .4 Activity list
   .5 Activity attributes
   .6 Activity resource requirements
   .7 Resource calendars
   .8 Project management plan
      · Risk register
      · Activity cost estimates

.2 Tools and Techniques
   .1 Expert judgment
   .2 Analogous estimating
   .3 Parametric estimating
   .4 Three-point estimates
   .5 Reserve analysis

.3 Outputs
   .1 Activity duration estimates
   .2 Activity attributes (updates)

6.5 Schedule Development

.1 Inputs
   .1 Organizational process assets
   .2 Project scope statement
   .3 Activity list
   .4 Activity attributes
   .5 Project schedule network diagrams
   .6 Activity resource requirements
   .7 Resource calendars
   .8 Activity duration estimates
   .9 Project management plan
      · Risk register

.2 Tools and Techniques
   .1 Schedule network analysis
   .2 Critical path method
   .3 Schedule compression
   .4 What-if scenario analysis
   .5 Resource leveling
   .6 Critical chain method
   .7 Project management software
   .8 Applying calendars
   .9 Adjusting leads and lags
   .10 Schedule model

.3 Outputs
   .1 Project schedule
   .2 Schedule model data
   .3 Schedule baseline
   .4 Resource requirements (updates)
   .5 Activity attributes (updates)
   .6 Project calendar (updates)
   .7 Requested changes
   .8 Project management plan (updates)
      · Schedule management plan (updates)

6.6 Schedule Control

.1 Inputs
   .1 Schedule management plan
   .2 Schedule baseline
   .3 Performance reports
   .4 Approved change requests

.2 Tools and Techniques
   .1 Progress reporting
   .2 Schedule change control system
   .3 Performance measurement
   .4 Project management software
   .5 Variance analysis
   .6 Schedule comparison bar charts

.3 Outputs
   .1 Schedule model data (updates)
   .2 Schedule baseline (updates)
   .3 Performance measurements
   .4 Requested changes
   .5 Recommended corrective actions
   .6 Organizational process assets (updates)
   .7 Activity list (updates)
   .8 Activity attributes (updates)
   .9 Project management plan (updates)

6

Figure 6-1. Project Time Management Overview

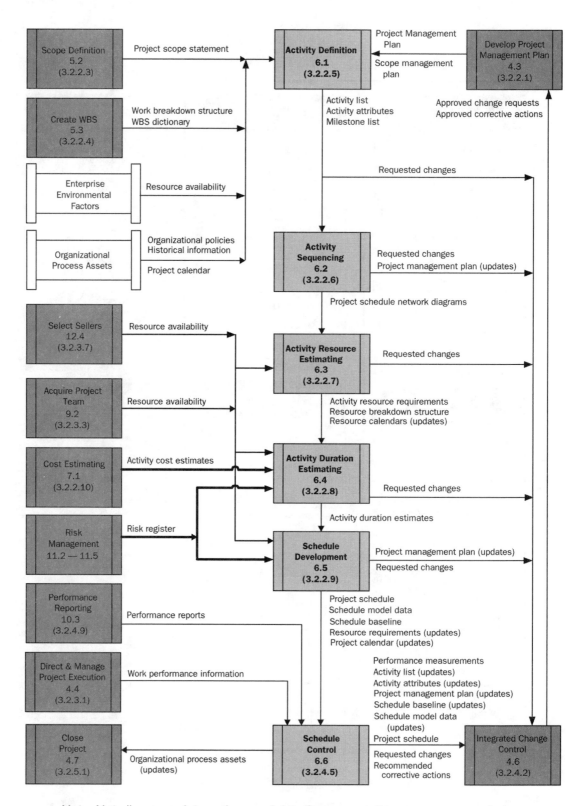

Note: Not all process interactions and data flow among the processes are shown.

Figure 6-2. Project Time Management Process Flow Diagram

A Guide to the Project Management Body of Knowledge (PMBOK® Guide) Third Edition
©2004 Project Management Institute, Four Campus Boulevard, Newtown Square, PA 19073-3299 USA

6.1 Activity Definition

Defining the schedule activities involves identifying and documenting the work that is planned to be performed. The Activity Definition process will identify the deliverables at the lowest level in the work breakdown structure (WBS), which is called the work package. Project work packages are planned (decomposed) into smaller components called schedule activities to provide a basis for estimating, scheduling, executing, and monitoring and controlling the project work. Implicit in this process is defining and planning the schedule activities such that the project objectives will be met.

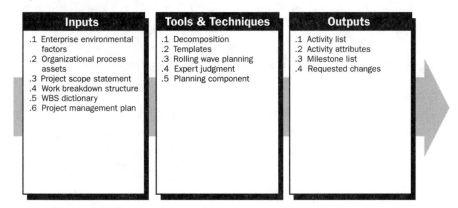

Figure 6-3. Activity Definition: Inputs, Tools & Techniques, and Outputs

6.1.1 Activity Definition: Inputs

.1 Enterprise Environmental Factors
Enterprise environmental factors (Section 4.1.1.3) that can be considered include availability of project management information systems and scheduling software tools.

.2 Organizational Process Assets
Organizational process assets (Section 4.1.1.4) contain the existing formal and informal activity planning-related policies, procedures, and guidelines that are considered in developing the activity definitions. The lessons-learned knowledge base contains historical information regarding activities lists used by previous similar projects that can be considered when defining project schedule activities.

.3 Project Scope Statement
The project deliverables, constraints, and assumptions documented in the project scope statement (Section 5.2.3.1) are considered explicitly during activity definition. Constraints are factors that will limit the project management team's options, such as schedule milestones with imposed completion dates that are required either by management or contract. Assumptions are factors that are considered to be true for project schedule planning, such as work hours per week or the time of the year that construction work will be performed.

.4   Work Breakdown Structure

The work breakdown structure (Section 5.3.3.2) is a primary input to schedule activity definition.

.5   WBS Dictionary

The WBS dictionary (Section 5.3.3.3) is a primary input to schedule activity definition.

.6   Project Management Plan

The project management plan contains the schedule management plan (Chapter 6 introductory material), which provides guidance on the development and planning of schedule activities and the project scope management plan.

6.1.2   Activity Definition: Tools and Techniques

.1   Decomposition

The technique of decomposition, as it is applied to activity definition, involves subdividing the project work packages into smaller, more manageable components called schedule activities. The Activity Definition process defines the final outputs as schedule activities rather than as deliverables, as is done in the Create WBS process (Section 5.3).

The activity list, WBS, and WBS dictionary can be developed either sequentially or concurrently, with the WBS and WBS dictionary being the basis for development of the final activity list. Each work package within the WBS is decomposed into the schedule activities required to produce the work package deliverables. This activity definition is often performed by the project team members responsible for the work package.

.2   Templates

A standard activity list or a portion of an activity list from a previous project is often usable as a template (Section 4.1.1.4) for a new project. The related activity attributes information in the templates can also contain a list of resource skills and their required hours of effort, identification of risks, expected deliverables, and other descriptive information. Templates can also be used to identify typical schedule milestones.

.3   Rolling Wave Planning

The WBS and WBS dictionary reflect the project scope evolution as it becomes more detailed until the work package level is reached. Rolling wave planning is a form of progressive elaboration (Section 1.2.1.3) planning where the work to be accomplished in the near term is planned in detail at a low level of the WBS, while work far in the future is planned for WBS components that are at a relatively high level of the WBS. The work to be performed within another one or two reporting periods in the near future is planned in detail as work is being completed during the current period. Therefore, schedule activities can exist at various levels of detail in the project's life cycle. During early strategic planning, when information is less defined, activities might be kept at the milestone level.

.4 Expert Judgment

Project team members or other experts who are experienced and skilled in developing detailed project scope statements, WBSs, and project schedules can provide expertise in defining activities.

.5 Planning Component

When insufficient definition of the project scope is available to decompose a branch of the WBS down to the work package level, the last component in that branch of the WBS can be used to develop a high-level project schedule for that component. These planning components are selected and used by the project team to plan and schedule future work at various higher levels within the WBS. The schedule activities used for these planning components may be summary activities that are not enough to support detailed estimating, scheduling, executing, monitoring, or controlling of the project work. Two planning components are:

- **Control Account.** A management control point can be placed at selected management points (specific components at selected levels) of the work breakdown structure above the work package level. These control points are used as a basis for planning when associated work packages have not yet been planned. All work and effort performed within a control account is documented in a control account plan.
- **Planning Package.** A planning package is a WBS component below the control account, but above the work package. This component is used for planning known work content that does not have detailed schedule activities.

6.1.3 Activity Definition: Outputs

.1 Activity List

The activity list is a comprehensive list including all schedule activities that are planned to be performed on the project. The activity list does not include any schedule activities that are not required as part of the project scope. The activity list includes the activity identifier and a scope of work description for each schedule activity in sufficient detail to ensure that project team members understand what work is required to be completed. The schedule activity's scope of work can be in physical terms, such as linear feet of pipe to be installed, designated placement of concrete, number of drawings, lines of computer program code, or chapters in a book. The activity list is used in the schedule model and is a component of the project management plan (Section 4.3). The schedule activities are discrete components of the project schedule, but are not components of the WBS.

.2 Activity Attributes

These activity attributes are an extension of the activity attributes in the activity list and identify the multiple attributes associated with each schedule activity. Activity attributes for each schedule activity include the activity identifier, activity codes, activity description, predecessor activities, successor activities, logical relationships, leads and lags, resource requirements, imposed dates, constraints, and assumptions. Activity attributes can also include the person responsible for executing the work, geographic area or place where the work has to be performed, and schedule activity type such as level of effort, discrete effort, and apportioned effort. These attributes are used for project schedule development and for selecting, ordering, and sorting the planned schedule activities in various ways within reports. The number of attributes varies by application area. The activity attributes are used in the schedule model.

.3 Milestone List

The list of schedule milestones identifies all milestones and indicates whether the milestone is mandatory (required by the contract) or optional (based upon project requirements or historical information). The milestone list is a component of the project management plan (Section 4.3) and the milestones are used in the schedule model.

.4 Requested Changes

The Activity Definition process can generate requested changes (Section 4.4.3.2) that can affect the project scope statement and WBS. Requested changes are processed for review and disposition through the Integrated Change Control process (Section 4.6).

6.2 Activity Sequencing

Activity sequencing involves identifying and documenting the logical relationships among schedule activities. Schedule activities can be logically sequenced with proper precedence relationships, as well as leads and lags to support later development of a realistic and achievable project schedule. Sequencing can be performed by using project management software or by using manual techniques. Manual and automated techniques can also be used in combination.

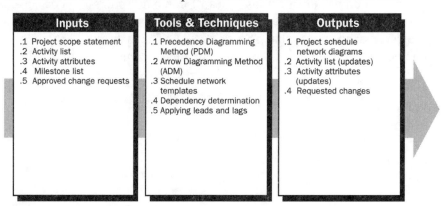

Inputs	Tools & Techniques	Outputs
.1 Project scope statement .2 Activity list .3 Activity attributes .4 Milestone list .5 Approved change requests	.1 Precedence Diagramming Method (PDM) .2 Arrow Diagramming Method (ADM) .3 Schedule network templates .4 Dependency determination .5 Applying leads and lags	.1 Project schedule network diagrams .2 Activity list (updates) .3 Activity attributes (updates) .4 Requested changes

Figure 6-4. Activity Sequencing: Inputs, Tools & Techniques, and Outputs

A Guide to the Project Management Body of Knowledge (PMBOK® Guide) Third Edition
©2004 Project Management Institute, Four Campus Boulevard, Newtown Square, PA 19073-3299 USA

6.2.1 Activity Sequencing: Inputs

.1 Project Scope Statement

The project scope statement (Section 5.2.3.1) contains the product scope description, which includes product characteristics that often can affect activity sequencing, such as the physical layout of a plant to be constructed or subsystem interfaces on a software project. While these effects are often apparent in the activity list, the product scope description is generally reviewed to ensure accuracy.

.2 Activity List

Described in Section 6.1.3.1.

.3 Activity Attributes

Described in Section 6.1.3.2.

.4 Milestone List

Described in Section 6.1.3.3.

.5 Approved Change Requests

Described in Section 4.4.1.4.

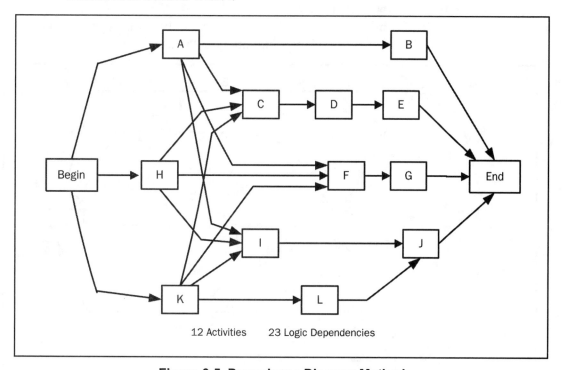

Figure 6-5. Precedence Diagram Method

6.2.2 Activity Sequencing: Tools and Techniques

.1 Precedence Diagramming Method (PDM)

PDM is a method of constructing a project schedule network diagram that uses boxes or rectangles, referred to as nodes, to represent activities and connects them with arrows that show the dependencies. Figure 6-5 shows a simple project schedule network diagram drawn using PDM. This technique is also called activity-on-node (AON), and is the method used by most project management software packages.

PDM includes four types of dependencies or precedence relationships:

- **Finish-to-Start.** The initiation of the successor activity depends upon the completion of the predecessor activity.
- **Finish-to-Finish.** The completion of the successor activity depends upon the completion of the predecessor activity.
- **Start-to-Start.** The initiation of the successor activity depends upon the initiation of the predecessor activity.
- **Start-to-Finish.** The completion of the successor activity depends upon the initiation of the predecessor activity.

In PDM, finish-to-start is the most commonly used type of precedence relationship. Start-to-finish relationships are rarely used.

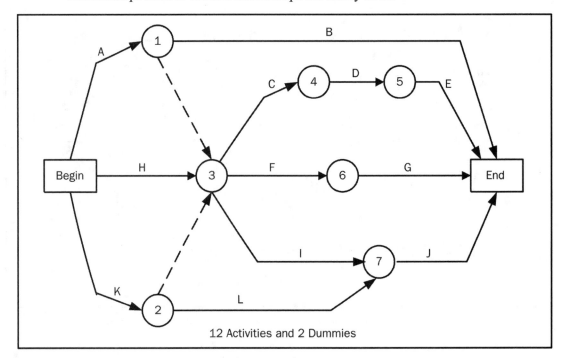

Figure 6-6. Arrow Diagram Method

A Guide to the Project Management Body of Knowledge (PMBOK® Guide) Third Edition
©2004 Project Management Institute, Four Campus Boulevard, Newtown Square, PA 19073-3299 USA

.2 Arrow Diagramming Method (ADM)

ADM is a method of constructing a project schedule network diagram that uses arrows to represent activities and connects them at nodes to show their dependencies. Figure 6-6 shows a simple network logic diagram drawn using ADM. This technique is also called activity-on-arrow (AOA) and, although less prevalent than PDM, it is still used in teaching schedule network theory and in some application areas.

ADM uses only finish-to-start dependencies and can require the use of "dummy" relationships called dummy activities, which are shown as dashed lines, to define all logical relationships correctly. Since dummy activities are not actual schedule activities (they have no work content), they are given a zero value duration for schedule network analysis purposes. For example, in Figure 6-6 schedule activity "F" is dependent upon the completion of schedule activities "A" and "K," in addition to the completion of schedule activity "H."

.3 Schedule Network Templates

Standardized project schedule network diagram templates can be used to expedite the preparation of networks of project schedule activities. They can include an entire project or only a portion of it. Portions of a project schedule network diagram are often referred to as a subnetwork or a fragment network. Subnetwork templates are especially useful when a project includes several identical or nearly identical deliverables, such as floors on a high-rise office building, clinical trials on a pharmaceutical research project, coding program modules on a software project, or the start-up phase of a development project.

.4 Dependency Determination

Three types of dependencies are used to define the sequence among the activities.

- **Mandatory dependencies.** The project management team determines which dependencies are mandatory during the process of establishing the sequence of activities. Mandatory dependencies are those that are inherent in the nature of the work being done. Mandatory dependencies often involve physical limitations, such as on a construction project, where it is impossible to erect the superstructure until after the foundation has been built, or on an electronics project, where a prototype must be built before it can be tested. Mandatory dependencies are also sometimes referred to as hard logic.

- **Discretionary dependencies.** The project management team determines which dependencies are discretionary during the process of establishing the sequence of activities. Discretionary dependencies are fully documented since they can create arbitrary total float values and can limit later scheduling options. Discretionary dependencies are sometimes referred to as preferred logic, preferential logic or soft logic. Discretionary dependencies are usually established based on knowledge of best practices within a particular application area or some unusual aspect of the project where a specific sequence is desired, even though there are other acceptable sequences. Some discretionary dependencies include preferred schedule activity sequences based upon previous experience on a successful project performing the same type of work.

- **External dependencies.** The project management team identifies external dependencies during the process of establishing the sequence of activities. External dependencies are those that involve a relationship between project activities and non-project activities. For example, the testing schedule activity in a software project can be dependent on delivery of hardware from an external source, or governmental environmental hearings may need to be held before site preparation can begin on a construction project. This input can be based on historical information (Section 4.1.1.4) from previous projects of a similar nature or from seller contracts or proposals (Section 12.4.3.2).

.5 Applying Leads and Lags

The project management team determines the dependencies (Section 6.2.2.4) that may require a lead or a lag to accurately define the logical relationship. The use of leads and lags and their related assumptions are documented.

A lead allows an acceleration of the successor activity. For example, a technical writing team can begin writing the second draft of a large document (the successor activity) fifteen days before they finish writing the entire first draft (the predecessor activity). This could be accomplished by a finish-to-start relationship with a fifteen-day lead time.

A lag directs a delay in the successor activity. For example, to account for a ten-day curing period for concrete, a ten-day lag on a finish-to-start relationship could be used, which means the successor activity cannot start until ten days after the predecessor is completed.

A Guide to the Project Management Body of Knowledge (PMBOK® Guide) Third Edition
©2004 Project Management Institute, Four Campus Boulevard, Newtown Square, PA 19073-3299 USA

6.2.3 Activity Sequencing: Outputs

.1 Project Schedule Network Diagrams

Project schedule network diagrams are schematic displays of the project's schedule activities and the logical relationships among them, also referred to as dependencies. Figures 6-5 and 6-6 illustrate two different approaches to drawing a project schedule network diagram. A project schedule network diagram can be produced manually or by using project management software. The project schedule network diagram can include full project details, or have one or more summary activities. A summary narrative accompanies the diagram and describes the basic approach used to sequence the activities. Any unusual activity sequences within the network are fully described within the narrative.

.2 Activity List (Updates)

If approved change requests (Section 4.4.1.4) result from the Activity Sequencing process, then the activity list (Section 6.1.3.1) is updated to include those approved changes.

.3 Activity Attributes (Updates)

The activity attributes (Section 6.1.3.2) are updated to include the defined logical relationships and any associated leads and lags. If approved change requests (Section 4.4.1.4) resulting from the Activity Sequencing process affect the activity list, then the related items in the activity attributes are updated to include those approved changes.

.4 Requested Changes

Preparation of project logical relationships, leads, and lags might reveal instances that can generate a requested change (Section 4.4.3.2) to the activity list or the activity attributes. Examples include where a schedule activity can be divided or otherwise redefined, where dependencies can be refined, or where a lead or lag is adjusted to adequately diagram the correct logical relationships. Requested changes are processed for review and disposition through the Integrated Change Control process (Section 4.6).

6.3 Activity Resource Estimating

Estimating schedule activity resources involves determining what resources (persons, equipment, or materiel) and what quantities of each resource will be used, and when each resource will be available to perform project activities. The Activity Resource Estimating process is closely coordinated with the Cost Estimating process (Section 7.1). For example:

- A construction project team will need to be familiar with local building codes. Such knowledge is often readily available from local sellers. However, if the local labor pool lacks experience with unusual or specialized construction techniques, the additional cost for a consultant might be the most effective way to secure knowledge of the local building codes.

- An automotive design team will need to be familiar with the latest in automated assembly techniques. The requisite knowledge might be obtained by hiring a consultant, by sending a designer to a seminar on robotics, or by including someone from manufacturing as a member of the project team.

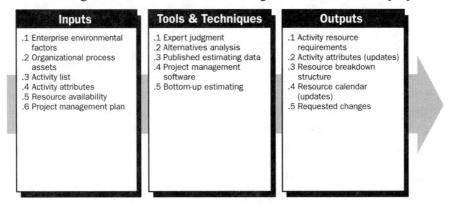

Inputs	Tools & Techniques	Outputs
.1 Enterprise environmental factors .2 Organizational process assets .3 Activity list .4 Activity attributes .5 Resource availability .6 Project management plan	.1 Expert judgment .2 Alternatives analysis .3 Published estimating data .4 Project management software .5 Bottom-up estimating	.1 Activity resource requirements .2 Activity attributes (updates) .3 Resource breakdown structure .4 Resource calendar (updates) .5 Requested changes

Figure 6-7. Activity Resource Estimating: Inputs, Tools & Techniques, and Outputs

6.3.1 Activity Resource Estimating: Inputs

.1 Enterprise Environmental Factors

The Activity Resource Estimating process uses the infrastructure resource availability information included in enterprise environmental factors (Section 4.1.1.3).

.2 Organizational Process Assets

Organizational process assets (Section 4.1.1.4) provide the policies of the performing organization regarding staffing and the rental or purchase of supplies and equipment that are considered during activity resource estimating. If available, historical information regarding what types of resources were required for similar work on previous projects are reviewed.

.3 Activity List

The activity list (Section 6.1.3.1) identifies the schedule activities for resources that are estimated.

.4 Activity Attributes

The activity attributes (Section 6.1.3.2) developed during the activity definition process provide the primary data input for use in estimating those resources required for each schedule activity in the activity list.

A Guide to the Project Management Body of Knowledge (PMBOK® Guide) Third Edition
©2004 Project Management Institute, Four Campus Boulevard, Newtown Square, PA 19073-3299 USA

.5 Resource Availability

Information on which resources (such as people, equipment, and materiel) are potentially available (Sections 9.2.3.2 and 12.4.3.4) is used for estimating the resource types. This knowledge includes consideration of various geographical locations from which the resources originate and when they may be available. For example, during the early phases of an engineering design project, the pool of resources might include junior and senior engineers in large numbers. During later phases of the same project, however, the pool can be limited to those individuals who are knowledgeable about the project as a result of having worked on the earlier phases of the project.

.6 Project Management Plan

The schedule management plan is a component part of the project management plan (Section 4.3) that is used in Activity Resource Estimating.

6.3.2 Activity Resource Estimating: Tools and Techniques

.1 Expert Judgment

Expert judgment is often required to assess the resource-related inputs to this process. Any group or person with specialized knowledge in resource planning and estimating can provide such expertise.

.2 Alternatives Analysis

Many schedule activities have alternative methods of accomplishment. They include using various levels of resource capability or skills, different size or type of machines, different tools (hand versus automated), and make-or-buy decisions regarding the resource (Section 12.1.3.3).

.3 Published Estimating Data

Several companies routinely publish updated production rates and unit costs of resources for an extensive array of labor trades, materiel, and equipment for different countries and geographical locations within countries.

.4 Project Management Software

Project management software has the capability to help plan, organize, and manage resource pools and develop resource estimates. Depending upon the sophistication of the software, resource breakdown structures, resource availabilities, and resource rates can be defined, as well as various resource calendars.

.5 Bottom-up Estimating

When a schedule activity cannot be estimated with a reasonable degree of confidence, the work within the schedule activity is decomposed into more detail. The resource needs of each lower, more detailed piece of work are estimated, and these estimates are then aggregated into a total quantity for each of the schedule activity's resources. Schedule activities may or may not have dependencies between them that can affect the application and use of resources. If there are dependencies, this pattern of resource usage is reflected in the estimated requirements of the schedule activity and is documented.

6.3.3 Activity Resource Estimating: Outputs

.1 Activity Resource Requirements

The output of the Activity Resource Estimating process is an identification and description of the types and quantities of resources required for each schedule activity in a work package. These requirements can then be aggregated to determine the estimated resources for each work package. The amount of detail and the level of specificity of the resource requirement descriptions can vary by application area. The resource requirements documentation for each schedule activity can include the basis of estimate for each resource, as well as the assumptions that were made in determining which types of resources are applied, their availability, and what quantity are used. The Schedule Development process (Section 6.5) determines when the resources are needed.

.2 Activity Attributes (Updates)

The types and quantities of resources required for each schedule activity are incorporated into the activity attributes. If approved change requests (Section 4.6.3.1) result from the Activity Resource Estimating process, then the activity list (Section 6.2.3.2) and activity attributes (Section 6.2.3.3) are updated to include those approved changes.

.3 Resource Breakdown Structure

The resource breakdown structure (RBS) is a hierarchical structure of the identified resources by resource category and resource type.

.4 Resource Calendar (Updates)

A composite resource calendar for the project documents working days and nonworking days that determine those dates on which a specific resource, whether a person or materiel, can be active or is idle. The project resource calendar typically identifies resource-specific holidays and resource availability periods. The project resource calendar identifies the quantity of each resource available during each availability period.

.5 Requested Changes

The Activity Resource Estimating process can result in requested changes (Section 4.4.3.2) to add or delete planned schedule activities within the activity list. Requested changes are processed for review and disposition through the Integrated Change Control process (Section 4.6).

A Guide to the Project Management Body of Knowledge (PMBOK® Guide) Third Edition
©2004 Project Management Institute, Four Campus Boulevard, Newtown Square, PA 19073-3299 USA

6.4 Activity Duration Estimating

The process of estimating schedule activity durations uses information on schedule activity scope of work, required resource types, estimated resource quantities, and resource calendars with resource availabilities. The inputs for the estimates of schedule activity duration originate from the person or group on the project team who is most familiar with the nature of the work content in the specific schedule activity. The duration estimate is progressively elaborated, and the process considers the quality and availability of the input data. For example, as the project engineering and design work evolves, more detailed and precise data is available, and the accuracy of the duration estimates improves. Thus, the duration estimate can be assumed to be progressively more accurate and of better quality.

The Activity Duration Estimating process requires that the amount of work effort required to complete the schedule activity is estimated, the assumed amount of resources to be applied to complete the schedule activity is estimated, and the number of work periods needed to complete the schedule activity is determined. All data and assumptions that support duration estimating are documented for each activity duration estimate.

Estimating the number of work periods required to complete a schedule activity can require consideration of elapsed time as a requirement related to a specific type of work. Most project management software for scheduling will handle this situation by using a project calendar and alternative work-period resource calendars that are usually identified by the resources that require specific work periods. The schedule activities will be worked according to the project calendar, and the schedule activities to which the resources are assigned will also be worked according to the appropriate resource calendars.

Overall project duration is calculated as an output of the Schedule Development process (Section 6.5).

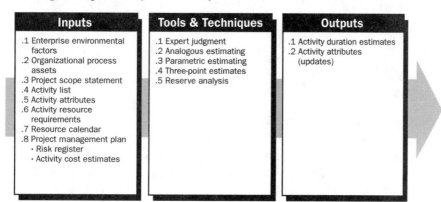

Inputs	Tools & Techniques	Outputs
.1 Enterprise environmental factors .2 Organizational process assets .3 Project scope statement .4 Activity list .5 Activity attributes .6 Activity resource requirements .7 Resource calendar .8 Project management plan • Risk register • Activity cost estimates	.1 Expert judgment .2 Analogous estimating .3 Parametric estimating .4 Three-point estimates .5 Reserve analysis	.1 Activity duration estimates .2 Activity attributes (updates)

Figure 6-8. Activity Duration Estimating: Inputs, Tools & Techniques, and Outputs

6.4.1 Activity Duration Estimating: Inputs

.1 Enterprise Environmental Factors

One or more of the organizations involved in the project may maintain duration estimating databases and other historical reference data. This type of reference information is also available commercially. These databases tend to be especially useful when activity durations are not driven by the actual work content (e.g., how long it takes concrete to cure or how long a government agency usually takes to respond to certain types of requests).

.2 Organizational Process Assets

Historical information (Section 4.1.1.4) on the likely durations of many categories of activities is often available. One or more of the organizations involved in the project may maintain records of previous project results that are detailed enough to aid in developing duration estimates. In some application areas, individual team members may maintain such records. The organizational process assets (Section 4.1.1.4) of the performing organization may have some asset items that can be used in Activity Duration Estimating, such as the project calendar (a calendar of working days or shifts on which schedule activities are worked, and nonworking days on which schedule activities are idle).

.3 Project Scope Statement

The constraints and assumptions from the project scope statement (Section 5.2.3.1) are considered when estimating the schedule activity durations. An example of an assumption would be the length of the reporting periods for the project that could dictate maximum schedule activity durations. An example of a constraint would be document submittals, reviews, and similar non-deliverable schedule activities that often have frequency and durations specified by contract or within the performing organization's policies.

.4 Activity List

Described in Section 6.1.3.1.

.5 Activity Attributes

Described in Section 6.1.3.2.

.6 Activity Resource Requirements

The estimated activity resource requirements (Section 6.3.3.1) will have an effect on the duration of the schedule activity, since the resources assigned to the schedule activity, and the availability of those resources, will significantly influence the duration of most activities. For example, if a schedule activity requires two engineers working together to efficiently complete a design activity, but only one person is applied to the work, the schedule activity will generally take at least twice as much time to complete. However, as additional resources are added or lower skilled resources are applied to some schedule activities, projects can experience a reduction in efficiency. This inefficiency, in turn, could result in a work production increase of less than the equivalent percentage increase in resources applied.

.7 Resource Calendar

The composite resource calendar (Section 6.3), developed as part of the Activity Resource Estimating process, includes the availability, capabilities, and skills of human resources (Section 9.2). The type, quantity, availability, and capability, when applicable, of both equipment and materiel resources (Section 12.4) that could significantly influence the duration of schedule activities are also considered. For example, if a senior and junior staff member are assigned full time, a senior staff member can generally be expected to complete a given schedule activity in less time than a junior staff member.

.8 Project Management Plan

The project management plan contains the risk register (Sections 11.2 through 11.6) and project cost estimates (Section 7.1).

- **Risk Register.** The risk register has information on identified project risks that the project team considers when producing estimates of activity durations and adjusting those durations for risks. The project team considers the extent to which the effects of risks are included in the baseline duration estimate for each schedule activity, in particular those risks with ratings of high probability or high impact.

- **Activity Cost Estimates.** The project activity cost estimates, if already completed, can be developed in sufficient detail to provide estimated resource quantities for each schedule activity in the project activity list.

6.4.2 Activity Duration Estimating: Tools and Techniques

.1 Expert Judgment

Activity durations are often difficult to estimate because of the number of factors that can influence them, such as resource levels or resource productivity. Expert judgment, guided by historical information, can be used whenever possible. The individual project team members may also provide duration estimate information or recommended maximum activity durations from prior similar projects. If such expertise is not available, the duration estimates are more uncertain and risky.

.2 Analogous Estimating

Analogous duration estimating means using the actual duration of a previous, similar schedule activity as the basis for estimating the duration of a future schedule activity. It is frequently used to estimate project duration when there is a limited amount of detailed information about the project for example, in the early phases of a project. Analogous estimating uses historical information (Section 4.1.1.4) and expert judgment.

Analogous duration estimating is most reliable when the previous activities are similar in fact and not just in appearance, and the project team members preparing the estimates have the needed expertise.

.3   Parametric Estimating

Estimating the basis for activity durations can be quantitatively determined by multiplying the quantity of work to be performed by the productivity rate. For example, productivity rates can be estimated on a design project by the number of drawings times labor hours per drawing, or a cable installation in meters of cable times labor hours per meter. The total resource quantities are multiplied by the labor hours per work period or the production capability per work period, and divided by the number of those resources being applied to determine activity duration in work periods.

.4   Three-Point Estimates

The accuracy of the activity duration estimate can be improved by considering the amount of risk in the original estimate. Three-point estimates are based on determining three types of estimates:

- **Most likely.** The duration of the schedule activity, given the resources likely to be assigned, their productivity, realistic expectations of availability for the schedule activity, dependencies on other participants, and interruptions.
- **Optimistic.** The activity duration is based on a best-case scenario of what is described in the most likely estimate.
- **Pessimistic.** The activity duration is based on a worst-case scenario of what is described in the most likely estimate.

An activity duration estimate can be constructed by using an average of the three estimated durations. That average will often provide a more accurate activity duration estimate than the single point, most-likely estimate.

.5   Reserve Analysis

Project teams can choose to incorporate additional time referred to as contingency reserves, time reserves or buffers, into the overall project schedule as recognition of schedule risk. The contingency reserve can be a percentage of the estimated activity duration, a fixed number of work periods, or developed by quantitative schedule risk analysis (Section 11.4.2.2.). The contingency reserve can be used completely or partially, or can later be reduced or eliminated, as more precise information about the project becomes available. Such contingency reserve is documented along with other related data and assumptions.

6.4.3   Activity Duration Estimating: Outputs

.1   Activity Duration Estimates

Activity duration estimates are quantitative assessments of the likely number of work periods that will be required to complete a schedule activity. Activity duration estimates include some indication of the range of possible results. For example:

- 2 weeks ± 2 days to indicate that the schedule activity will take at least eight days and no more than twelve (assuming a five-day workweek).
- 15 percent probability of exceeding three weeks to indicate a high probability—85 percent—that the schedule activity will take three weeks or less.

A Guide to the Project Management Body of Knowledge (PMBOK® Guide) Third Edition
©2004 Project Management Institute, Four Campus Boulevard, Newtown Square, PA 19073-3299 USA

.2   Activity Attributes (Updates)

The activity attributes (Section 6.1.3.2) are updated to include the durations for each schedule activity, the assumptions made in developing the activity duration estimates, and any contingency reserves.

6.5   Schedule Development

Project schedule development, an iterative process, determines planned start and finish dates for project activities. Schedule development can require that duration estimates and resource estimates are reviewed and revised to create an approved project schedule that can serve as a baseline against which progress can be tracked. Schedule development continues throughout the project as work progresses, the project management plan changes, and anticipated risk events occur or disappear as new risks are identified.

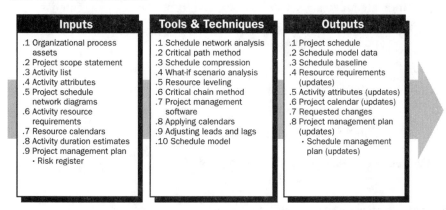

Figure 6-9. Schedule Development Overview: Inputs, Tools & Techniques, and Outputs

6.5.1   Schedule Development: Inputs

.1   Organizational Process Assets

The organizational process assets (Section 4.1.1.4) of the performing organization may have some asset items that can be used in Schedule Development, such as a project calendar (a calendar of working days or shifts that establishes dates on which schedule activities are worked, and nonworking days on which schedule activities are idle).

.2   Project Scope Statement

The project scope statement (Section 5.2.3.1) contains assumptions and constraints that can impact the development of the project schedule. Assumptions are those documented schedule-related factors that, for schedule development purposes, are considered to be true, real, or certain. Constraints are factors that will limit the project management team's options when performing schedule network analysis.

There are two major categories of time constraints considered during schedule development:

- Imposed dates on activity starts or finishes can be used to restrict the start or finish to occur either no earlier than a specified date or no later than a specified date. While several constraints are typically available in project management software, the "Start No Earlier Than" and the "Finish No Later Than" constraints are the most commonly used. Date constraints include such situations as agreed-upon contract dates, a market window on a technology project, weather restrictions on outdoor activities, government-mandated compliance with environmental remediation, and delivery of materiel from parties not represented in the project schedule.

- The project sponsor, project customer, or other stakeholders often dictate key events or major milestones affecting the completion of certain deliverables by a specified date. Once scheduled, these dates become expected and can be moved only through approved changes. Milestones can also be used to indicate interfaces with work outside of the project. Such work is typically not in the project database and milestones with constraint dates can provide the appropriate schedule interface.

.3 Activity List

Described in Section 6.1.3.1.

.4 Activity Attributes

Described in Section 6.1.3.2.

.5 Project Schedule Network Diagrams

Described in Section 6.2.3.1.

.6 Activity Resource Requirements

Described in Section 6.3.3.1.

.7 Resource Calendars

Described in Sections 6.3.3.4.

.8 Activity Duration Estimates

Described in Section 6.4.3.1.

.9 Project Management Plan

The project management plan contains the schedule management plan, cost management plan, project scope management plan, and risk management plan. These plans guide the schedule development, as well as components that directly support the Schedule Development process. One such component is the risk register.

- **Risk Register.** The risk register (Sections 11.1 through 11.5) identifies the project risks and associated risk response plans that are needed to support the Schedule Development process.

A Guide to the Project Management Body of Knowledge (PMBOK® Guide) Third Edition
©2004 Project Management Institute, Four Campus Boulevard, Newtown Square, PA 19073-3299 USA

6.5.2 Schedule Development: Tools and Techniques

.1 Schedule Network Analysis

Schedule network analysis is a technique that generates the project schedule. It employs a schedule model and various analytical techniques, such as critical path method, critical chain method, what-if analysis, and resource leveling to calculate the early and late start and finish dates, and scheduled start and finish dates for the uncompleted portions of project schedule activities. If the schedule network diagram used in the model has any network loops or network open ends, then those loops and open ends are adjusted before one of the analytical techniques is applied. Some network paths may have points of path convergence or path divergence that can be identified and used in schedule compression analysis or other analyses.

.2 Critical Path Method

The critical path method is a schedule network analysis technique that is performed using the schedule model. The critical path method calculates the theoretical early start and finish dates, and late start and finish dates, for all schedule activities without regard for any resource limitations, by performing a forward pass analysis and a backward pass analysis through the project schedule network paths. The resulting early and late start and finish dates are not necessarily the project schedule; rather, they indicate the time periods within which the schedule activity should be scheduled, given activity durations, logical relationships, leads, lags, and other known constraints.

Calculated early start and finish dates, and late start and finish dates, may or may not be the same on any network path since total float, which provides schedule flexibility, may be positive, negative, or zero. On any network path, the schedule flexibility is measured by the positive difference between early and late dates, and is termed "total float." Critical paths have either a zero or negative total float, and schedule activities on a critical path are called "critical activities." Adjustments to activity durations, logical relationships, leads and lags, or other schedule constraints may be necessary to produce network paths with a zero or positive total float. Once the total float for a network path is zero or positive, then the free float — the amount of time that a schedule activity can be delayed without delaying the early start date of any immediate successor activity within the network path — can also be determined.

.3 Schedule Compression

Schedule compression shortens the project schedule *without* changing the project scope, to meet schedule constraints, imposed dates, or other schedule objectives. Schedule compression techniques include:

- **Crashing.** Schedule compression technique in which cost and schedule tradeoffs are analyzed to determine how to obtain the greatest amount of compression for the least incremental cost. Crashing does not always produce a viable alternative and can result in increased cost.

- **Fast tracking.** A schedule compression technique in which phases or activities that normally would be done in sequence are performed in parallel. An example would be to construct the foundation for a building before all the architectural drawings are complete. Fast tracking can result in rework and increased risk. This approach can require work to be performed without completed detailed information, such as engineering drawings. It results in trading cost for time, and increases the risk of achieving the shortened project schedule.

.4 What-If Scenario Analysis

This is an analysis of the question "What if the situation represented by scenario 'X' happens?" A schedule network analysis is performed using the schedule model to compute the different scenarios, such as delaying a major component delivery, extending specific engineering durations, or introducing external factors, such as a strike or a change in the permitting process. The outcome of the what-if scenario analysis can be used to assess the feasibility of the project schedule under adverse conditions, and in preparing contingency and response plans to overcome or mitigate the impact of unexpected situations. Simulation involves calculating multiple project durations with different sets of activity assumptions. The most common technique is Monte Carlo Analysis (Section 11.4.2.2), in which a distribution of possible activity durations is defined for each schedule activity and used to calculate a distribution of possible outcomes for the total project.

.5 Resource Leveling

Resource leveling is a schedule network analysis technique applied to a schedule model that has already been analyzed by the critical path method. Resource leveling is used to address schedule activities that need to be performed to meet specified delivery dates, to address the situation where shared or critical required resources are only available at certain times or are only available in limited quantities, or to keep selected resource usage at a constant level during specific time periods of the project work. This resource usage leveling approach can cause the original critical path to change.

A Guide to the Project Management Body of Knowledge (PMBOK® Guide) Third Edition
©2004 Project Management Institute, Four Campus Boulevard, Newtown Square, PA 19073-3299 USA

The critical path method calculation (Section 6.5.2.2) produces a preliminary early start schedule and late start schedule that can require more resources during certain time periods than are available, or can require changes in resource levels that are not manageable. Allocating scarce resources to critical path activities first can be used to develop a project schedule that reflects such constraints. Resource leveling often results in a projected duration for the project that is longer than the preliminary project schedule. This technique is sometimes called the resource-based method, especially when implemented using schedule optimization project management software. Resource reallocation from non-critical to critical activities is a common way to bring the project back on track, or as close as possible, to its originally intended overall duration. Utilization of extended hours, weekends, or multiple shifts for selected resources can also be considered using different resource calendars to reduce the durations of critical activities. Resource productivity increases are another way to shorten durations that have extended the preliminary project schedule. Different technologies or machinery, such as reuse of computer code, automatic welding, electric pipe cutters, and automated processes, can all have an impact on resource productivity. Some projects can have a finite and critical project resource. In this case, the resource is scheduled in reverse from the project ending date, which is known as reverse resource allocation scheduling, and may not result in an optimal project schedule. The resource leveling technique produces a resource-limited schedule, sometimes called a resource-constrained schedule, with scheduled start dates and scheduled finish dates.

.6 Critical Chain Method

Critical chain is another schedule network analysis technique that modifies the project schedule to account for limited resources. Critical chain combines deterministic and probabilistic approaches. Initially, the project schedule network diagram is built using non-conservative estimates for activity durations within the schedule model, with required dependencies and defined constraints as inputs. The critical path is then calculated. After the critical path is identified, resource availability is entered and the resource-limited schedule result is determined. The resulting schedule often has an altered critical path.

The critical chain method adds duration buffers that are non-work schedule activities to maintain focus on the planned activity durations. Once the buffer schedule activities are determined, the planned activities are scheduled to their latest possible planned start and finish dates. Consequently, in lieu of managing the total float of network paths, the critical chain method focuses on managing the buffer activity durations and the resources applied to planned schedule activities.

.7 Project Management Software

Project management scheduling software is widely used to assist with schedule development. Other software might be capable of interacting directly or indirectly with project management software to carry out the requirements of other Knowledge Areas, such as cost estimating by time period (Section 7.1.2.5) and schedule simulation in quantitative risk analysis (Section 11.4.2.2). These products automate the calculation of the mathematical forward pass and backward pass critical path analysis and resource leveling, and, thus, allow for rapid consideration of many schedule alternatives. They are also widely used to print or display the outputs of developed schedules.

.8 Applying Calendars

Project calendars (Section 4.1.1.4) and resource calendars (Section 6.3.3.4) identify periods when work is allowed. Project calendars affect all activities. For example, it may not be possible to work on the site during certain periods of the year because of weather. Resource calendars affect a specific resource or category of resources. Resource calendars reflect how some resources work only during normal business hours, while others work three full shifts, or a project team member might be unavailable, such as on vacation or in a training program, or a labor contract can limit certain workers to certain days of the week.

.9 Adjusting Leads and Lags

Since the improper use of leads or lags can distort the project schedule, the leads or lags are adjusted during schedule network analysis to develop a viable project schedule.

.10 Schedule Model

Schedule data and information are compiled into the schedule model for the project. The schedule model tool and the supporting schedule model data are used in conjunction with manual methods or project management software to perform schedule network analysis to generate the project schedule.

6.5.3 Schedule Development: Outputs

.1 Project Schedule

The project schedule includes at least a planned start date and planned finish date for each schedule activity. If resource planning is done at an early stage, then the project schedule would remain preliminary until resource assignments have been confirmed, and scheduled start dates and finish dates are established. This process usually happens no later than completion of the project management plan (Section 4.3). A project target schedule may also be developed with defined target start dates and target finish dates for each schedule activity. The project schedule can be presented in summary form, sometimes referred to as the master schedule or milestone schedule, or presented in detail. Although a project schedule can be presented in tabular form, it is more often presented graphically, using one or more of the following formats:

- **Project schedule network diagrams.** These diagrams, with activity date information, usually show both the project network logic and the project's critical path schedule activities. These diagrams can be presented in the activity-on-node diagram format, as shown in Figure 6-5, or presented in a time-scaled schedule network diagram format that is sometimes called a logic bar chart, as shown for the detailed schedule in Figure 6-10. This example also shows how each work package is planned as a series of related schedule activities.

- **Bar charts.** These charts, with bars representing activities, show activity start and end dates, as well as expected durations. Bar charts are relatively easy to read, and are frequently used in management presentations. For control and management communication, the broader, more comprehensive summary activity, sometimes referred to as a hammock activity, is used between milestones or across multiple interdependent work packages, and is displayed in bar chart reports. An example is the summary schedule portion of Figure 6-10 that is presented in a WBS structured format.

- **Milestone charts.** These charts are similar to bar charts, but only identify the scheduled start or completion of major deliverables and key external interfaces. An example is the milestone schedule portion of Figure 6-10.

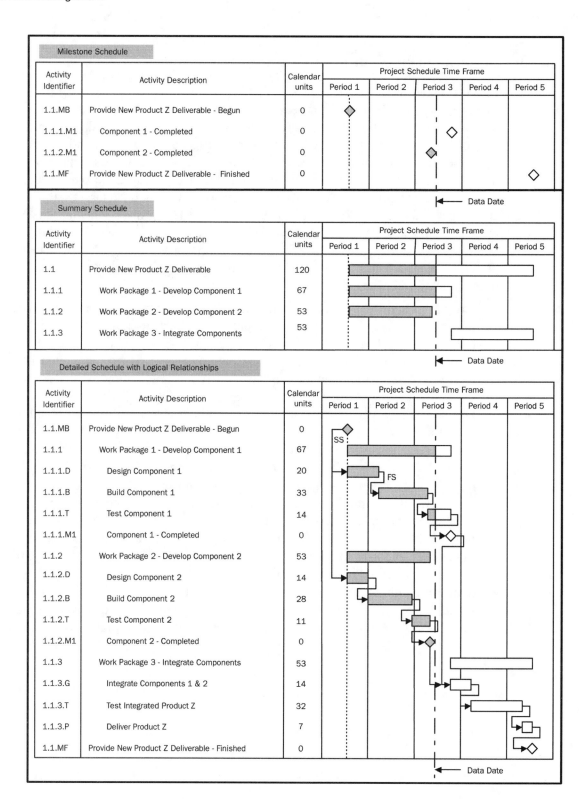

Figure 6-10. Project Schedule – Graphic Examples

Figure 6-10 shows the schedule for a sample project being executed, with the work in progress reported through the data date, which is sometimes also called the as-of date or time now date. The figure shows the actual start date, actual duration, and actual finish date for completed schedule activities, the actual start date, remaining duration, and current finish date for schedule activities with work in progress, and the current start date, original duration, and current finish date for schedule activities where work has not yet started. For a simple project schedule, Figure 6-10 gives a graphic display of a Milestone Schedule, a Summary Schedule, and a Detailed Schedule. Figure 6-10 also visually shows the relationships among the three different levels of schedule presentation.

.2 Schedule Model Data

Supporting data for the project schedule includes at least the schedule milestones, schedule activities, activity attributes and documentation of all identified assumptions and constraints. The amount of additional data varies by application area. Information frequently supplied as supporting detail includes, but is not limited to:

- Resource requirements by time period, often in the form of a resource histogram
- Alternative schedules, such as best-case or worst-case, not resource leveled, resource leveled, with or without imposed dates
- Schedule contingency reserves.

   For example, on an electronics design project, the schedule model data might include such items as human resource histograms, cash-flow projections, and order and delivery schedules.

.3 Schedule Baseline

A schedule baseline is a specific version of the project schedule developed from the schedule network analysis of the schedule model. It is accepted and approved by the project management team as the schedule baseline with baseline start dates and baseline finish dates.

.4 Resource Requirements (Updates)

Resource leveling can have a significant effect on preliminary estimates of the types and quantities of resources required. If the resource-leveling analysis changes the project resource requirements, then the resource requirements are updated.

.5 Activity Attributes (Updates)

The activity attributes (Section 6.2.3.3) are updated to include any revised resource requirements and any other related approved changes (Section 4.4.1.4) generated by the Schedule Development process.

.6 Project Calendar (Updates)

A project calendar is a calendar of working days or shifts that establishes those dates on which schedule activities are worked. It also establishes nonworking days that determine dates on which schedule activities are idle, such as holidays, weekends, and non-shift hours. The calendar for each project may use different calendar units as the basis for scheduling the project.

.7 Requested Changes

The Schedule Development process can create requested changes (Section 4.4.3.2) that are processed for review and disposition through the Integrated Change Control process (Section 4.6).

.8 Project Management Plan (Updates)

The project management plan (Section 4.3) is updated to reflect any approved changes in how the project schedule will be managed.

- **Schedule Management Plan (Updates).** If approved change requests (Section 4.4.1.4) result from the Project Time Management processes, then the schedule management plan (Chapter 6 introductory material) component of the project management plan (Section 4.3) may need to be updated to include those approved changes.

6.6 Schedule Control

Schedule control is concerned with:

- Determining the current status of the project schedule
- Influencing the factors that create schedule changes
- Determining that the project schedule has changed
- Managing the actual changes as they occur.

Schedule control is a portion of the Integrated Change Control process (Section 4.6).

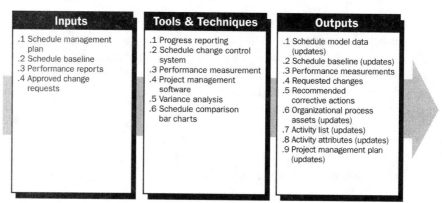

Figure 6-11. Schedule Control Overview: Inputs, Tools & Techniques, and Outputs

A Guide to the Project Management Body of Knowledge (PMBOK® Guide) Third Edition
©2004 Project Management Institute, Four Campus Boulevard, Newtown Square, PA 19073-3299 USA

6.6.1 Schedule Control: Inputs

.1 Schedule Management Plan
The project management plan (Section 4.3) contains the schedule management plan (Chapter 6 introductory material) that establishes how the project schedule will be managed and controlled.

.2 Schedule Baseline
The project schedule (Section 6.5.3.1) used for control is the approved project schedule, which is referred to as the schedule baseline (Section 6.5.3.3). The schedule baseline is a component of the project management plan (Section 4.3). It provides the basis for measuring and reporting schedule performance as part of the performance measurement baseline.

.3 Performance Reports
Performance reports (Section 10.3.3.1) provide information on schedule performance, such as which planned dates have been met and which have not. Performance reports may also alert the project team to issues that may cause schedule performance problems in the future.

.4 Approved Change Requests
Only approved change requests (Section 4.4.1.4) that have been previously processed through the Integrated Change Control process (Section 4.6) are used to update the project schedule baseline or other components of the project management plan (Section 4.3).

6.6.2 Schedule Control: Tools and Techniques

.1 Progress Reporting
The progress reporting and current schedule status includes information such as actual start and finish dates, and the remaining durations for unfinished schedule activities. If progress measurement such as earned value is also used, then the percent complete of in-progress schedule activities can also be included. To facilitate the periodic reporting of project progress, a template created for consistent use across various project organizational components can be used throughout the project life cycle. The template can be paper-based or electronic.

.2 Schedule Change Control System
The schedule change control system defines the procedures by which the project schedule can be changed. It includes the paperwork, tracking systems, and approval levels necessary for authorizing changes. The schedule change control system is operated as part of the Integrated Change Control process (Section 4.6).

.3 Performance Measurement

Performance measurement techniques produce the Schedule Variance (SV) (Section 7.3.2.2) and Schedule Performance Index (SPI) (Section 7.3.2.2), which are used to assess the magnitude of any project schedule variations that do occur. An important part of schedule control is to decide if the schedule variation requires corrective action. For example, a major delay on any schedule activity not on the critical path may have little effect on the overall project schedule, while a much shorter delay on a critical or near-critical activity may require immediate action.

.4 Project Management Software

Project management software for scheduling provides the ability to track planned dates versus actual dates, and to forecast the effects of project schedule changes, real or potential, which makes it a useful tool for schedule control.

.5 Variance Analysis

Performing the schedule variance analysis during the schedule monitoring process is a key function of schedule control. Comparing target schedule dates with the actual/forecast start and finish dates provides useful information for the detection of deviations, and for the implementation of corrective actions in case of delays. The total float variance is also an essential planning component to evaluate project time performance.

.6 Schedule Comparison Bar Charts

To facilitate analysis of schedule progress, it is convenient to use a comparison bar chart, which displays two bars for each schedule activity. One bar shows the current actual status and the other shows the status of the approved project schedule baseline. This shows graphically where the schedule has progressed as planned or where slippage has occurred.

6.6.3 Schedule Control: Outputs

.1 Schedule Model Data (Updates)

A project schedule update is any modification to the project schedule model information that is used to manage the project. Appropriate stakeholders are notified of significant modifications as they occur.

New project schedule network diagrams are developed to display approved remaining durations and modifications to the work plan. In some cases, project schedule delays can be so severe that development of a new target schedule with revised target start and finish dates is needed to provide realistic data for directing the work, and for measuring performance and progress.

.2 Schedule Baseline (Updates)

Schedule revisions are a special category of project schedule updates. Revisions are changes to the schedule's start and finish dates in the approved schedule baseline. These changes are generally incorporated in response to approved change requests (Section 4.4.1.4) related to project scope changes or changes to estimates. Development of a revised schedule baseline can only occur as a result of approved changes. The original schedule baseline and schedule model are saved before creating the new schedule baseline to prevent loss of historical data for the project schedule.

.3 Performance Measurements

The calculated schedule variance (SV) and schedule performance index (SPI) values for WBS components, in particular the work packages and control accounts, are documented and communicated (Section 10.3.3.1) to stakeholders.

.4 Requested Changes

Schedule variance analysis, along with review of progress reports, results of performance measures, and modifications to the project schedule model can result in requested changes (Section 4.4.3.2) to the project schedule baseline. Project schedule changes might or might not require adjustments to other components of the project management plan. Requested changes are processed for review and disposition through the Integrated Change Control process (Section 4.6).

.5 Recommended Corrective Actions

A corrective action is anything done to bring expected future project schedule performance in line with the approved project schedule baseline. Corrective action in the area of time management often involves expediting, which includes special actions taken to ensure completion of a schedule activity on time or with the least possible delay. Corrective action frequently requires root cause analysis to identify the cause of the variation. The analysis may address schedule activities other than the schedule activity actually causing the deviation; therefore, schedule recovery from the variance can be planned and executed using schedule activities delineated later in the project schedule.

.6 Organizational Process Assets (Updates)

Lessons learned documentation of the causes of variance, the reasoning behind the corrective actions chosen, and other types of lessons learned from schedule control are documented in the organizational process assets (Section 4.1.1.4), so that they become part of the historical database for both the project and other projects of the performing organization.

6

.7 Activity List (Updates)
Described in Section 6.1.3.1.

.8 Activity Attributes (Updates)
Described in Section 6.1.3.2.

.9 Project Management Plan (Updates)
The schedule management plan (Chapter 6 introductory material) component of the project management plan (Section 4.3) is updated to reflect any approved changes resulting from the Schedule Control process, and how the project schedule will be managed.

CHAPTER 7

Project Cost Management

Project Cost Management includes the processes involved in planning, estimating, budgeting, and controlling costs so that the project can be completed within the approved budget. Figure 7-1 provides an overview of the following three processes, while Figure 7-2 provides a process flow view of these processes and their inputs, outputs, and other related Knowledge Area processes:

7.1 Cost Estimating – developing an approximation of the costs of the resources needed to complete project activities.

7.2 Cost Budgeting – aggregating the estimated costs of individual activities or work packages to establish a cost baseline.

7.3 Cost Control – influencing the factors that create cost variances and controlling changes to the project budget.

These processes interact with each other and with processes in the other Knowledge Areas as well. Each process can involve effort from one or more persons or groups of persons based upon the needs of the project. Each process occurs at least once in every project and occurs in one or more project phases, if the project is divided into phases. Although the processes are presented here as discrete elements with well-defined interfaces, in practice they may overlap and interact in ways not detailed here. Process interactions are discussed in detail in Chapter 3.

Project Cost Management is primarily concerned with the cost of the resources needed to complete schedule activities. However, Project Cost Management should also consider the effect of project decisions on the cost of using, maintaining, and supporting the product, service, or result of the project. For example, limiting the number of design reviews can reduce the cost of the project at the expense of an increase in the customer's operating costs. This broader view of Project Cost Management is often called life-cycle costing. Life-cycle costing, together with value engineering techniques, can improve decision-making and is used to reduce cost and execution time and to improve the quality and performance of the project deliverable.

In many application areas, predicting and analyzing the prospective financial performance of the project's product is done outside the project. In others, such as a capital facilities project, Project Cost Management can include this work. When such predictions and analyses are included, Project Cost Management will address additional processes and numerous general management techniques such as return on investment, discounted cash flow, and investment payback analysis.

Project Cost Management considers the information requirements of the project stakeholders. Different stakeholders will measure project costs in different ways and at different times. For example, the cost of an acquired item can be measured when the acquisition decision is made or committed, the order is placed, the item is delivered, and the actual cost is incurred or recorded for project accounting purposes.

On some projects, especially ones of smaller scope, cost estimating and cost budgeting are so tightly linked that they are viewed as a single process that can be performed by a single person over a relatively short period of time. These processes are presented here as distinct processes because the tools and techniques for each are different. The ability to influence cost is greatest at the early stages of the project, and this is why early scope definition is critical (Section 5.2).

Although not shown here as a discrete process, the work involved in performing the three processes of Project Cost Management is preceded by a planning effort by the project management team. This planning effort is part of the Develop Project Management Plan process (Section 4.3), which produces a cost management plan that sets out the format and establishes the criteria for planning, structuring, estimating, budgeting, and controlling project costs. The cost management processes and their associated tools and techniques vary by application area, are usually selected during the project life cycle (Section 2.1) definition, and are documented in the cost management plan.

For example, the cost management plan can establish:

- **Precision level.** Schedule activity cost estimates will adhere to a rounding of the data to a prescribed precision (e.g., $100, $1,000), based on the scope of the activities and magnitude of the project, and may include an amount for contingencies.
- **Units of measure.** Each unit used in measurements is defined, such as staff hours, staff days, week, lump sum, etc., for each of the resources.
- **Organizational procedures links.** The WBS component used for the project cost accounting is called a control account (CA). Each control account is assigned a code or account number that is linked directly to the performing organization's accounting system. If cost estimates for planning packages are included in the control account, then the method for budgeting planning packages is included.
- **Control thresholds.** Variance thresholds for costs or other indicators (e.g., person-days, volume of product) at designated time points over the duration of the project can be defined to indicate the agreed amount of variation allowed.

A Guide to the Project Management Body of Knowledge (PMBOK® Guide) Third Edition
©2004 Project Management Institute, Four Campus Boulevard, Newtown Square, PA 19073-3299 USA

- **Earned value rules.** Three examples are: 1) Earned value management computation formulas for determining the estimate to complete are defined, 2) Earned value credit criteria (e.g., 0-100, 0-50-100, etc.) are established, and 3) Define the WBS level at which earned value technique analysis will be performed.
- **Reporting formats.** The formats for the various cost reports are defined.
- **Process descriptions.** Descriptions of each of the three cost management processes are documented.

All of the above, as well as other information, are included in the cost management plan, either as text within the body of the plan or as appendices. The cost management plan is contained in, or is a subsidiary plan of, the project management plan (Section 4.3) and may be formal or informal, highly detailed or broadly framed, based upon the needs of the project.

The cost management planning effort occurs early in project planning and sets the framework for each of the cost management processes, so that performance of the processes will be efficient and coordinated.

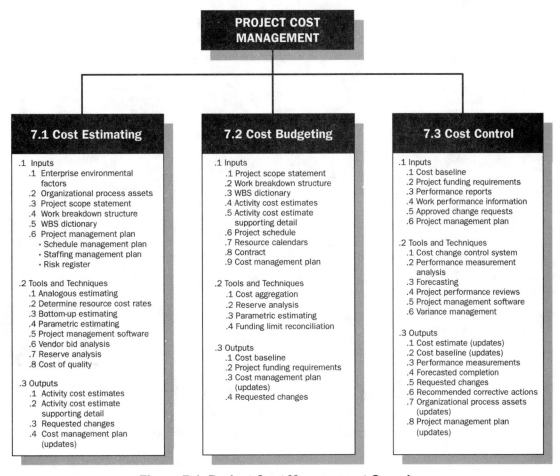

Figure 7-1. Project Cost Management Overview

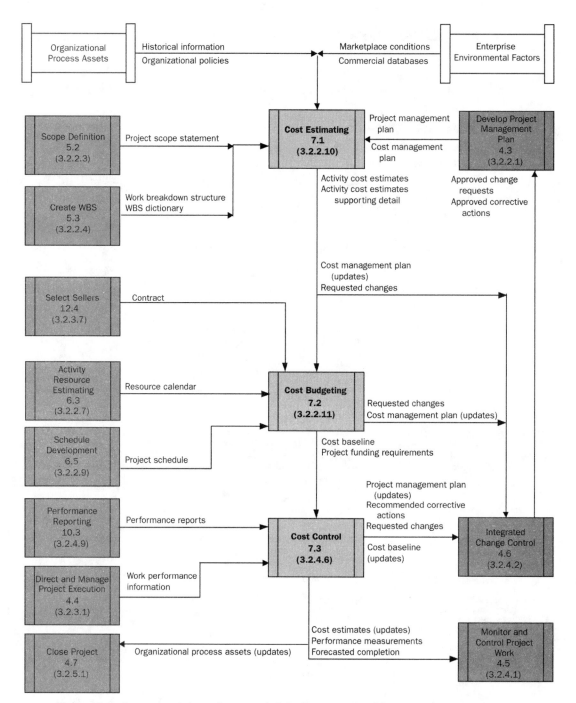

Note: Not all process interactions and data flow among the processes are shown.

Figure 7-2. Project Cost Management Process Flow Diagram

A Guide to the Project Management Body of Knowledge (PMBOK® Guide) Third Edition
©2004 Project Management Institute, Four Campus Boulevard, Newtown Square, PA 19073-3299 USA

7.1 Cost Estimating

Estimating schedule activity costs involves developing an approximation of the costs of the resources needed to complete each schedule activity. In approximating costs, the estimator considers the possible causes of variation of the cost estimates, including risks.

Cost estimating includes identifying and considering various costing alternatives. For example, in most application areas, additional work during a design phase is widely held to have the potential for reducing the cost of the execution phase and product operations. The cost estimating process considers whether the expected savings can offset the cost of the additional design work.

Cost estimates are generally expressed in units of currency (dollars, euro, yen, etc.) to facilitate comparisons both within and across projects. In some cases, the estimator can use units of measure to estimate cost, such as staff hours or staff days, along with their cost estimates, to facilitate appropriate management control.

Cost estimates can benefit from refinement during the course of the project to reflect the additional detail available. The accuracy of a project estimate will increase as the project progresses through the project life cycle. For example, a project in the initiation phase could have a rough order of magnitude (ROM) estimate in the range of -50 to +100%. Later in the project, as more information is known, estimates could narrow to a range of -10 to +15%. In some application areas, there are guidelines for when such refinements are made and for what degree of accuracy is expected.

Sources of input information come in the form of outputs from the project processes in Chapters 4 through 6 and 9 through 12. Once received, all of this information will remain available as inputs to all three of the cost management processes.

The costs for schedule activities are estimated for all resources that will be charged to the project. This includes, but is not limited to, labor, materials, equipment, services, and facilities, as well as special categories such as an inflation allowance or a contingency cost. A schedule activity cost estimate is a quantitative assessment of the likely costs of the resources required to complete the schedule activity.

If the performing organization does not have formally trained project cost estimators, then the project team will need to supply both the resources and the expertise to perform project cost estimating activities.

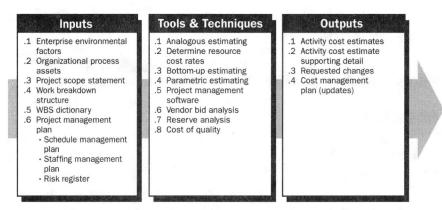

Figure 7-3. Cost Estimating: Inputs, Tools & Techniques, and Outputs

7.1.1 Cost Estimating: Inputs

.1 Enterprise Environmental Factors
The Cost Estimating process considers:

- **Marketplace conditions.** What products, services, and results are available in the marketplace, from whom, and under what terms and conditions (Section 4.1.1.3).
- **Commercial databases.** Resource cost rate information is often available from commercial databases that track skills and human resource costs, and provide standard costs for material and equipment. Published seller price lists are another source.

.2 Organizational Process Assets
Existing formal and informal cost estimating-related policies, procedures, and guidelines (Section 4.1.1) are considered in developing the cost management plan, selecting the cost estimating tools, and monitoring and reporting methods to be used.

- **Cost estimating policies.** Some organizations have predefined approaches to cost estimating. Where these exist, the project operates within the boundaries defined by these policies.
- **Cost estimating templates.** Some organizations have developed templates (or a pro forma standard) for use by the project team. The organization can continuously improve the template based on its application and usefulness in prior projects.
- **Historical information.** Information that pertains to the project's product or service, and is obtained from various sources within the organization, can influence the cost of the project.
- **Project files.** One or more of the organizations involved in the project will maintain records of previous project performance that are detailed enough to aid in developing cost estimates. In some application areas, individual team members may maintain such records.

A Guide to the Project Management Body of Knowledge (PMBOK® Guide) Third Edition
©2004 Project Management Institute, Four Campus Boulevard, Newtown Square, PA 19073-3299 USA

- **Project team knowledge.** Members of the project team may recall previous actual costs or cost estimates. While such recollections can be useful, they are generally far less reliable than documented performance.
- **Lessons learned.** Lessons learned could include cost estimates obtained from previous projects that are similar in scope and size.

.3 Project Scope Statement

The project scope statement (Section 5.2.3.1) describes the business need, justification, requirements, and current boundaries for the project. It provides important information about project requirements that is considered during cost estimating. The project scope statement includes constraints, assumptions, and requirements. Constraints are specific factors that can limit cost estimating options. One of the most common constraints for many projects is a limited project budget. Other constraints can involve required delivery dates, available skilled resources, and organizational policies. Assumptions are factors that will be considered to be true, real, or certain. Requirements with contractual and legal implications can include health, safety, security, performance, environmental, insurance, intellectual property rights, equal employment opportunity, licenses, and permits – all of which are considered when developing the cost estimates.

The project scope statement also provides the list of deliverables, and acceptance criteria for the project and its products, services, and results. All factors are considered when developing the project cost estimate. The product scope description, within the project scope statement, provides product and service descriptions, and important information about any technical issues or concerns that are considered during cost estimating.

.4 Work Breakdown Structure

The project's work breakdown structure (WBS) (Section 5.3.3.2) provides the relationship among all the components of the project and the project deliverables (Section 4.4.3.1).

.5 WBS Dictionary

The WBS dictionary (Section 5.3.3.3) and related detailed statements of work provide an identification of the deliverables and a description of the work in each WBS component required to produce each deliverable.

.6 Project Management Plan

The project management plan (Section 4.3) provides the overall plan for executing, monitoring, and controlling the project, and includes subsidiary plans that provide guidance and direction for cost management planning and control. To the extent that other planning outputs are available, they are considered during cost estimating.

- **Schedule management plan.** The type and quantity of resources and the amount of time those resources are applied to complete the work of the project is a major part of determining the project cost. Schedule activity resources and their respective durations are used as key inputs to this process. Activity Resource Estimating (Section 6.3) involves determining the availability and quantities required of staff, equipment, and materiel needed to perform schedule activities. It is closely coordinated with cost estimating. Activity Duration Estimating (Section 6.4) will affect cost estimates on any project where the project budget includes an allowance for the cost of financing, including interest charges, and where resources are applied per unit of time for the duration of the schedule activity. Schedule activity duration estimates can also affect cost estimates that have time-sensitive costs included in them, such as union labor with regularly expiring collective bargaining agreements, materials with seasonal cost variations, or cost estimates with time-related costs, such as time-related field overhead costs during construction of a project.

- **Staffing management plan.** Project staffing attributes and personnel rates (Section 9.1.3.3) are necessary components for developing the schedule cost estimates.

- **Risk register.** The cost estimator considers information on risk responses (Section 11.2.3.1) when producing cost estimates. Risks, which can be either threats or opportunities, typically have an impact on both schedule activity and project costs. As a general rule, when the project experiences a negative risk event, the cost of the project will nearly always increase, and there will be a delay in the project schedule.

7.1.2 Cost Estimating: Tools and Techniques

.1 Analogous Estimating

Analogous cost estimating means using the actual cost of previous, similar projects as the basis for estimating the cost of the current project. Analogous cost estimating is frequently used to estimate costs when there is a limited amount of detailed information about the project (e.g., in the early phases). Analogous cost estimating uses expert judgment.

Analogous cost estimating is generally less costly than other techniques, but it is also generally less accurate. It is most reliable when previous projects are similar in fact, and not just in appearance, and the persons or groups preparing the estimates have the needed expertise.

A Guide to the Project Management Body of Knowledge (PMBOK® Guide) Third Edition
©2004 Project Management Institute, Four Campus Boulevard, Newtown Square, PA 19073-3299 USA

.2 Determine Resource Cost Rates

The person determining the rates or the group preparing the estimates must know the unit cost rates, such as staff cost per hour and bulk material cost per cubic yard, for each resource to estimate schedule activity costs. Gathering quotes (Section 12.3) is one method of obtaining rates. For products, services, or results to be obtained under contract, standard rates with escalation factors can be included in the contract. Obtaining data from commercial databases and seller published price lists is another source of cost rates. If the actual rates are not known, then the rates themselves will have to be estimated.

.3 Bottom-up Estimating

This technique involves estimating the cost of individual work packages or individual schedule activities with the lowest level of detail. This detailed cost is then summarized or "rolled up" to higher levels for reporting and tracking purposes. The cost and accuracy of bottom-up cost estimating is typically motivated by the size and complexity of the individual schedule activity or work package. Generally, activities with smaller associated effort increase the accuracy of the schedule activity cost estimates.

.4 Parametric Estimating

Parametric estimating is a technique that uses a statistical relationship between historical data and other variables (e.g., square footage in construction, lines of code in software development, required labor hours) to calculate a cost estimate for a schedule activity resource. This technique can produce higher levels of accuracy depending upon the sophistication, as well as the underlying resource quantity and cost data built into the model. A cost-related example involves multiplying the planned quantity of work to be performed by the historical cost per unit to obtain the estimated cost.

.5 Project Management Software

Project management software, such as cost estimating software applications, computerized spreadsheets, and simulation and statistical tools, are widely used to assist with cost estimating. Such tools can simplify the use of some cost estimating techniques and thereby facilitate rapid consideration of various cost estimate alternatives.

.6 Vendor Bid Analysis

Other cost estimating methods include vendor bid analysis and an analysis of what the project should cost. In cases where projects are won under competitive processes, additional cost estimating work can be required of the project team to examine the price of individual deliverables, and derive a cost that supports the final total project cost.

.7 Reserve Analysis

Many cost estimators include reserves, also called contingency allowances, as costs in many schedule activity cost estimates. This has the inherent problem of potentially overstating the cost estimate for the schedule activity. Contingency reserves are estimated costs to be used at the discretion of the project manager to deal with anticipated, but not certain, events. These events are "known unknowns" and are part of the project scope and cost baselines.

One option to manage cost contingency reserves is to aggregate each schedule activity's cost contingency reserve for a group of related activities into a single contingency reserve that is assigned to a schedule activity. This schedule activity may be a zero duration activity that is placed across the network path for that group of schedule activities, and is used to hold the cost contingency reserve. An example of this solution to managing cost contingency reserves is to assign them at the work package level to a zero duration activity, which spans from the start to the end of the work package subnetwork. As the schedule activities progress, the contingency reserve, as measured by resource consumption of the non-zero duration schedule activities, can be adjusted. As a result, the activity cost variances for the related group of schedule activities are more accurate because they are based on cost estimates that are not pessimistic.

Alternatively, the schedule activity may be a buffer activity in the critical chain method, and is intentionally placed directly at the end of the network path for that group of schedule activities. As the schedule activities progress, the contingency reserve, as measured by resource consumption of the non-buffer schedule activities, can be adjusted. As a result, the activity cost variances for the related group of schedule activities are more accurate because they are based on cost estimates that are not pessimistic.

.8 Cost of Quality

Cost of quality (Section 8.1.2.4) can also be used to prepare the schedule activity cost estimate.

7.1.3 Cost Estimating: Outputs

.1 Activity Cost Estimates

An activity cost estimate is a quantitative assessment of the likely costs of the resources required to complete schedule activities. This type of estimate can be presented in summary form or in detail. Costs are estimated for all resources that are applied to the activity cost estimate. This includes, but is not limited to, labor, materials, equipment, services, facilities, information technology, and special categories such as an inflation allowance or cost contingency reserve.

A Guide to the Project Management Body of Knowledge (PMBOK® Guide) Third Edition
©2004 Project Management Institute, Four Campus Boulevard, Newtown Square, PA 19073-3299 USA

.2 Activity Cost Estimate Supporting Detail

The amount and type of additional details supporting the schedule activity cost estimate vary by application area. Regardless of the level of detail, the supporting documentation should provide a clear, professional, and complete picture by which the cost estimate was derived.

Supporting detail for the activity cost estimates should include:

- Description of the schedule activity's project scope of work
- Documentation of the basis for the estimate (i.e., how it was developed)
- Documentation of any assumptions made
- Documentation of any constraints
- Indication of the range of possible estimates (e.g., $10,000 (-10% / +15%) to indicate that the item is expected to cost between $9,000 and $11,500).

.3 Requested Changes

The Cost Estimating process may generate requested changes (Section 4.4.3.2) that may affect the cost management plan (Chapter 7 introductory material), activity resource requirements (Section 6.3.3.1), and other components of the project management plan. Requested changes are processed for review and disposition through the Integrated Change Control process (Section 4.6).

.4 Cost Management Plan (Updates)

If approved change requests (Section 4.4.1.4) result from the Cost Estimating process, then the cost management plan component of the project management plan (Chapter 7 introductory material) is updated if those approved changes impact the management of costs.

7.2 Cost Budgeting

Cost budgeting involves aggregating the estimated costs of individual schedule activities or work packages to establish a total cost baseline for measuring project performance. The project scope statement provides the summary budget. However, schedule activity or work package cost estimates are prepared prior to the detailed budget requests and work authorization.

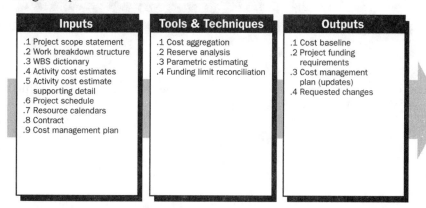

Inputs	Tools & Techniques	Outputs
.1 Project scope statement .2 Work breakdown structure .3 WBS dictionary .4 Activity cost estimates .5 Activity cost estimate supporting detail .6 Project schedule .7 Resource calendars .8 Contract .9 Cost management plan	.1 Cost aggregation .2 Reserve analysis .3 Parametric estimating .4 Funding limit reconciliation	.1 Cost baseline .2 Project funding requirements .3 Cost management plan (updates) .4 Requested changes

Figure 7-4. Cost Budgeting: Inputs, Tools & Techniques, and Outputs

7.2.1 Cost Budgeting: Inputs

.1 Project Scope Statement

Formal periodic limitations of the expenditure of project funds can be given in the project charter (Section 4.1.3.1) or contract. These funding constraints are reflected in the project scope statement, and can be due to annual funding authorizations by the buyer's organization or other entities like government agencies.

.2 Work Breakdown Structure

The project work breakdown structure (WBS) (Section 5.3.3.2) provides the relationship among all the components of the project and the project deliverables (Section 4.4.3.1).

.3 WBS Dictionary

The WBS dictionary (Section 5.3.3.3) and related detailed statements of work provide an identification of the deliverables and a description of the work in each WBS component required to produce each deliverable.

.4 Activity Cost Estimates

The cost estimates (Section 7.1.3.1) for each schedule activity within a work package are aggregated to obtain a cost estimate for each work package.

.5 Activity Cost Estimate Supporting Detail

Described in Section 7.1.3.2.

.6 Project Schedule

The project schedule (Section 6.5.3.1) includes planned start and finish dates for the project's schedule activities, schedule milestones, work packages, planning packages, and control accounts. This information is used to aggregate costs to the calendar periods when the costs are planned to be incurred.

.7 Resource Calendars

Described in Section 6.3.3.4.

.8 Contract

Contract (Section 12.4.3.2) information related to what products, services, or results have been purchased — and their costs — are used in developing the budget.

.9 Cost Management Plan

The cost management plan component of the project management plan and other subsidiary plans are considered during cost budgeting.

A Guide to the Project Management Body of Knowledge (PMBOK® Guide) Third Edition
©2004 Project Management Institute, Four Campus Boulevard, Newtown Square, PA 19073-3299 USA

7.2.2 Cost Budgeting: Tools and Techniques

.1 Cost Aggregation
Schedule activity cost estimates are aggregated by work packages in accordance with the WBS. The work package cost estimates are then aggregated for the higher component levels of the WBS, such as control accounts, and ultimately for the entire project.

.2 Reserve Analysis
Reserve analysis (Section 11.6.2.5) establishes contingency reserves, such as the management contingency reserve, that are allowances for unplanned, but potentially required, changes. Such changes may result from risks identified in the risk register

Management contingency reserves are budgets reserved for unplanned, but potentially required, changes to project scope and cost. These are "unknown unknowns," and the project manager must obtain approval before obligating or spending this reserve. Management contingency reserves are not a part of the project cost baseline, but are included in the budget for the project. They are not distributed as budget and, therefore, are not a part of the earned value calculations.

.3 Parametric Estimating
The parametric estimating technique involves using project characteristics (parameters) in a mathematical model to predict total project costs. Models can be simple (e.g., residential home construction will cost a certain amount per square foot of living space) or complex (e.g., one model of software development costs uses thirteen separate adjustment factors, each of which has five to seven points within it).

Both the cost and accuracy of parametric models vary widely. They are most likely to be reliable when:

- The historical information used to develop the model is accurate
- The parameters used in the model are readily quantifiable
- The model is scalable, such that it works for a large project as well as a small one.

.4 Funding Limit Reconciliation
Large variations in the periodic expenditure of funds are usually undesirable for organizational operations. Therefore, the expenditure of funds is reconciled with the funding limits set by the customer or performing organization on the disbursement of funds for the project. Reconciliation will necessitate the scheduling of work to be adjusted to smooth or regulate those expenditures, which is accomplished by placing imposed date constraints for some work packages, schedule milestones, or WBS components into the project schedule. Rescheduling can impact the allocation of resources. If funds were used as a limiting resource in the Schedule Development process, then the process is repeated using the new imposed date constraints. The final product of these planning iterations is a cost baseline.

7.2.3 Cost Budgeting: Outputs

.1 Cost Baseline

The cost baseline is a time-phased budget that is used as a basis against which to measure, monitor, and control overall cost performance on the project. It is developed by summing estimated costs by period and is usually displayed in the form of an S-curve, as illustrated in Figure 7-5. The cost baseline is a component of the project management plan.

Many projects, especially large ones, have multiple cost or resource baselines, and consumables production baselines (e.g., cubic yards of concrete per day) to measure different aspects of project performance. For example, management may require that the project manager track internal costs (labor) separately from external costs (contractors and construction materials) or total labor hours.

.2 Project Funding Requirements

Funding requirements, total and periodic (e.g., annual or quarterly), are derived from the cost baseline and can be established to exceed, usually by a margin, to allow for either early progress or cost overruns. Funding usually occurs in incremental amounts that are not continuous, and, therefore, appears as a step function in Figure 7-5. The total funds required are those included in the cost baseline plus the management contingency reserve amount. Some portion of the management contingency reserve can be included incrementally in each funding step or funded when needed, depending on organizational policies.

Although Figure 7-5 shows the management reserve amount at the end of the project, in reality, the cost baseline and cash flow lines would increase when a portion of the management reserve is authorized and when it is spent. Any gap at the end of a project between the funds allocated and the cost baseline and cash flow amounts shows the amount of the management reserve that was not used.

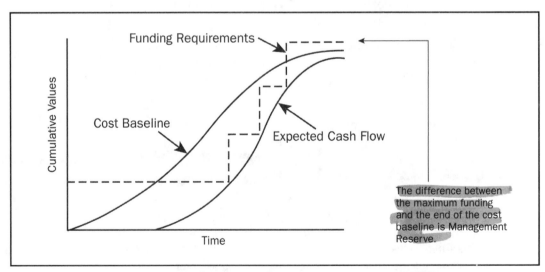

Figure 7-5. Cash Flow, Cost Baseline and Funding Display

.3 Cost Management Plan (Updates)

If approved change requests (Section 4.4.1.4) result from the Cost Budgeting process, then the cost management plan component of the project management plan is updated if those approved changes impact the management of costs.

.4 Requested Changes

The Cost Budgeting process can generate requested changes (Section 4.4.3.2) that affect the cost management plan or other components of the project management plan. Requested changes are processed for review and disposition through the Integrated Change Control process (Section 4.6).

7.3 Cost Control

Project cost control includes:

- Influencing the factors that create changes to the cost baseline
- Ensuring requested changes are agreed upon
- Managing the actual changes when and as they occur
- Assuring that potential cost overruns do not exceed the authorized funding periodically and in total for the project
- Monitoring cost performance to detect and understand variances from the cost baseline
- Recording all appropriate changes accurately against the cost baseline
- Preventing incorrect, inappropriate, or unapproved changes from being included in the reported cost or resource usage
- Informing appropriate stakeholders of approved changes
- Acting to bring expected cost overruns within acceptable limits.

Project cost control searches out the causes of positive and negative variances and is part of Integrated Change Control (Section 4.6). For example, inappropriate responses to cost variances can cause quality or schedule problems or produce an unacceptable level of risk later in the project.

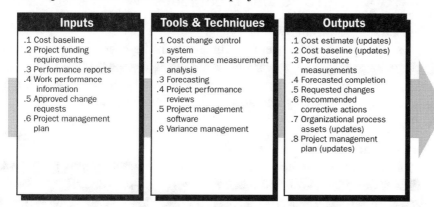

Inputs	Tools & Techniques	Outputs
.1 Cost baseline	.1 Cost change control system	.1 Cost estimate (updates)
.2 Project funding requirements	.2 Performance measurement analysis	.2 Cost baseline (updates)
.3 Performance reports	.3 Forecasting	.3 Performance measurements
.4 Work performance information	.4 Project performance reviews	.4 Forecasted completion
.5 Approved change requests	.5 Project management software	.5 Requested changes
.6 Project management plan	.6 Variance management	.6 Recommended corrective actions
		.7 Organizational process assets (updates)
		.8 Project management plan (updates)

Figure 7-6. Cost Control: Inputs, Tools & Techniques, and Outputs

7.3.1   Cost Control: Inputs

.1   Cost Baseline
Described in Section 7.2.3.1.

.2   Project Funding Requirements
Described in Section 7.2.3.2.

.3   Performance Reports
Performance reports (Section 10.3.3.1) provide information on cost and resource performance as a result of actual work progress.

.4   Work Performance Information
Work performance information (Section 4.4.3.7) pertaining to the status and cost of project activities being performed is collected. This information includes, but is not limited to:

- Deliverables that have been completed and those not yet completed
- Costs authorized and incurred
- Estimates to complete the schedule activities
- Percent physically complete of the schedule activities.

.5   Approved Change Requests
Approved change requests (Section 4.4.1.4) from the Integrated Change Control process (Section 4.6) can include modifications to the cost terms of the contract, project scope, cost baseline, or cost management plan.

.6   Project Management Plan
The project management plan and its cost management plan component and other subsidiary plans are considered when performing the Cost Control process.

7.3.2   Cost Control: Tools and Techniques

.1   Cost Change Control System
A cost change control system, documented in the cost management plan, defines the procedures by which the cost baseline can be changed. It includes the forms, documentation, tracking systems, and approval levels necessary for authorizing changes. The cost change control system is integrated with the integrated change control process (Section 4.6).

.2   Performance Measurement Analysis
Performance measurement techniques help to assess the magnitude of any variances that will invariably occur. The earned value technique (EVT) compares the value of the budgeted cost of work performed (earned) at the original allocated budget amount to both the budgeted cost of work scheduled (planned) and to the actual cost of work performed (actual). This technique is especially useful for cost control, resource management, and production.

An important part of cost control is to determine the cause of a variance, the magnitude of the variance, and to decide if the variance requires corrective action. The earned value technique uses the cost baseline (Section 7.2.3.1) contained in the project management plan (Section 4.3) to assess project progress and the magnitude of any variations that occur.

The earned value technique involves developing these key values for each schedule activity, work package, or control account:

- **Planned value (PV).** PV is the budgeted cost for the work scheduled to be completed on an activity or WBS component.
- **Earned value (EV).** EV is the budgeted amount for the work actually completed on the schedule activity or WBS component.
- **Actual cost (AC).** AC is the total cost incurred in accomplishing work on the schedule activity or WBS component. This AC must correspond in definition and coverage to whatever was budgeted for the PV and the EV (e.g., direct hours only, direct costs only, or all costs including indirect costs).
- **Estimate to complete (ETC) and estimate at completion (EAC).** See ETC and EAC development, described in the following technique on forecasting.

The PV, EV, and AC values are used in combination to provide performance measures of whether or not work is being accomplished as planned at any given point in time. The most commonly used measures are cost variance (CV) and schedule variance (SV). The amount of variance of the CV and SV values tend to decrease as the project reaches completion due to the compensating effect of more work being accomplished. Predetermined acceptable variance values that will decrease over time as the project progresses towards completion can be established in the cost management plan.

- **Cost variance (CV).** CV equals earned value (EV) minus actual cost (AC). The cost variance at the end of the project will be the difference between the budget at completion (BAC) and the actual amount spent. Formula: $CV = EV - AC$
- **Schedule variance (SV).** SV equals earned value (EV) minus planned value (PV). Schedule variance will ultimately equal zero when the project is completed because all of the planned values will have been earned. Formula: $SV = EV - PV$

These two values, the CV and SV, can be converted to efficiency indicators to reflect the cost and schedule performance of any project.

- **Cost performance index (CPI).** A CPI value less than 1.0 indicates a cost overrun of the estimates. A CPI value greater than 1.0 indicates a cost underrun of the estimates. CPI equals the ratio of the EV to the AC. The CPI is the most commonly used cost-efficiency indicator. Formula: $CPI = EV/AC$

- **Schedule performance index (SPI).** The SPI is used, in addition to the schedule status (Section 6.6.2.1), to predict the completion date and is sometimes used in conjunction with the CPI to forecast the project completion estimates. SPI equals the ratio of the EV to the PV. Formula: SPI = EV/PV

The parameters of Planed Value (PV), Earned Value (EV), and Actual Cost (AC) may be reported and used on both a period by period basis and on a cumulative basis. This allows measures such as the Cost Variance (CV), Cost Performance Index (CPI), Schedule Variance (SV), and Schedule Performance Index (SPI) to also be developed and used on both a period by period basis and on a cumulative basis.

Figure 7-7 uses S-curves to display EV data for a project that is over budget and behind the work plan.

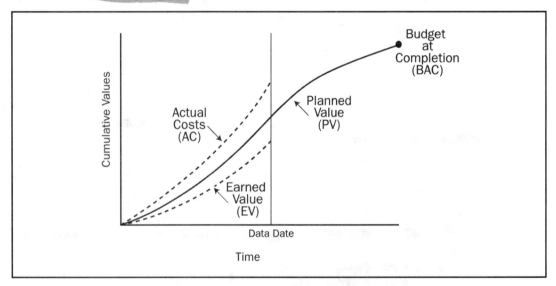

Figure 7-7. Illustrative Graphic Performance Report

The earned value technique in its various forms is a commonly used method of performance measurement. It integrates project scope, cost (or resource) and schedule measures to help the project management team assess project performance.

.3 Forecasting

Forecasting includes making estimates or predictions of conditions in the project's future based on information and knowledge available at the time of the forecast. Forecasts are generated, updated, and reissued based on work performance information (Section 4.4.3.7) provided as the project is executed and progressed. The work performance information is about the project's past performance and any information that could impact the project in the future, for example, estimate at completion and estimate to complete.

The earned value technique parameters of BAC, actual cost (AC) to date, and the CPI efficiency indicator are used to calculate ETC and EAC, where the BAC is equal to the total PV at completion for a schedule activity, work package, control account, or other WBS component. Formula: BAC = total PV at completion

Forecasting techniques help to assess the cost or the amount of work to complete schedule activities, which is called the EAC. Forecasting techniques also help to determine the ETC, which is the estimate for completing the remaining work for a schedule activity, work package, or control account. While the earned value technique of determining EAC and ETC is quick and automatic, it is not as valuable or accurate as a manual forecasting of the remaining work to be done by the project team. The ETC forecasting technique based upon the performing organization providing the estimate to complete is:

- **ETC based on new estimate.** ETC equals the revised estimate for the work remaining, as determined by the performing organization. This more accurate and comprehensive completion estimate is an independent, non-calculated estimate to complete for all the work remaining, and considers the performance or production of the resource(s) to date.

Alternatively, to calculate ETC using earned value data, one of two formulas is typically used:

- **ETC based on atypical variances.** This approach is most often used when current variances are seen as atypical and the project management team expectations are that similar variances will not occur in the future. ETC equals the BAC minus the earned value to date (EV). Formula: ETC = (BAC - EV)
- **ETC based on typical variances.** This approach is most often used when current variances are seen as typical of future variances. ETC equals the BAC minus the EV (the remaining PV) divided by the cost performance index (CPI). Formula: ETC = (BAC - EV) / CPI

An EAC is a forecast of the most likely total value based on project performance (Section 4.4) and risk quantification (Section 11.4). EAC is the projected or anticipated total final value for a schedule activity, WBS component, or project when the defined work of the project is completed. One EAC forecasting technique is based upon the performing organization providing an estimate at completion:

- **EAC using a new estimate.** EAC equals the actual costs to date (AC) plus a new ETC that is provided by the performing organization. This approach is most often used when past performance shows that the original estimating assumptions were fundamentally flawed or that they are no longer relevant due to a change in conditions. Formula: EAC = AC + ETC

7

The two most common forecasting techniques for calculating EAC using earned value data are some variation of:

- **EAC using remaining budget.** EAC equals AC plus the budget required to complete the remaining work, which is the budget at completion (BAC) minus the earned value (EV). This approach is most often used when current variances are seen as atypical and the project management team expectations are that similar variances will not occur in the future. Formula: EAC = AC + BAC – EV

- **EAC using CPI.** EAC equals actual costs to date (AC) plus the budget required to complete the remaining project work, which is the BAC minus the EV, modified by a performance factor (often the CPI). This approach is most often used when current variances are seen as typical of future variances. Formula: EAC = AC + ((BAC – EV) / CPI)

Each of these approaches can be the correct approach for any given project and will provide the project management team with a signal if the EAC forecasts are not within acceptable tolerances.

.4 Project Performance Reviews

Performance reviews compare cost performance over time, schedule activities or work packages overrunning and underrunning budget (planned value), milestones due, and milestones met.

Performance reviews are meetings held to assess schedule activity, work package, or cost account status and progress, and are typically used in conjunction with one or more of the following performance-reporting techniques:

- **Variance analysis.** Variance analysis involves comparing actual project performance to planned or expected performance. Cost and schedule variances are the most frequently analyzed, but variances from plan in the areas of project scope, resource, quality, and risk are often of equal or greater importance.

- **Trend analysis.** Trend analysis involves examining project performance over time to determine if performance is improving or deteriorating.

- **Earned value technique.** The earned value technique compares planned performance to actual performance.

.5 Project Management Software

Project management software, such as computerized spreadsheets, is often used to monitor PV versus AC, and to forecast the effects of changes or variances.

.6 Variance Management

The cost management plan (Section 7.1.3.4) describes how cost variances will be managed, for example, having different responses to major or minor problems. The amount of variance tends to decrease as more work is accomplished. The larger variances allowed at the start of the project can be decreased as the project nears completion.

7.3.3 Cost Control: Outputs

.1 Cost Estimates (Updates)
Revised schedule activity cost estimates are modifications to the cost information used to manage the project. Appropriate stakeholders are notified as needed. Revised cost estimates may require adjustments to other aspects of the project management plan.

.2 Cost Baseline (Updates)
Budget updates are changes to an approved cost baseline. These values are generally revised only in response to approved changes in project scope. However, in some cases, cost variances can be so severe that a revised cost baseline is needed to provide a realistic basis for performance measurement.

.3 Performance Measurements
The calculated CV, SV, CPI, and SPI values for WBS components, in particular the work packages and control accounts, are documented and communicated (Section 10.3.3.1) to stakeholders.

.4 Forecasted Completion
Either a calculated EAC value or a performing organization-reported EAC value is documented and the value communicated (Section 10.3.3.1) to stakeholders. Either a calculated ETC value or a reported ETC value provided by the performing organization is documented and the value communicated to stakeholders.

.5 Requested Changes
Analysis of project performance can generate a request for a change to some aspect of the project. Identified changes can require increasing or decreasing the budget. Requested changes (Section 4.4.3.2) are processed for review and disposition through the Integrated Change Control process (Section 4.6).

.6 Recommended Corrective Actions
A corrective action is anything done to bring expected future performance of the project in line with the project management plan. Corrective action in the area of cost management often involves adjusting schedule activity budgets, such as special actions taken to balance cost variances.

.7 Organizational Process Assets (Updates)
Lessons learned are documented so they can become part of the historical databases for both the project and the performing organization. Lessons learned documentation includes the root causes of variances, the reasoning behind the corrective action chosen, and other types of lessons learned from cost, resource, or resource production control.

7

.8 Project Management Plan (Updates)

Schedule activity, work package, or planning package cost estimates (Chapter 7 introductory material), as well as the cost baseline (Section 7.2.3.1), cost management plan, and project budget documents are components of the project management plan. All approved change requests (Section 4.4.1.4) affecting those documents are incorporated as updates to those documents.

CHAPTER 8

Project Quality Management

Project Quality Management processes include all the activities of the performing organization that determine quality policies, objectives, and responsibilities so that the project will satisfy the needs for which it was undertaken. It implements the quality management system through the policy, procedures, and processes of quality planning, quality assurance, and quality control, with continuous process improvement activities conducted throughout, as appropriate. Figure 8-1 provides an overview of the Project Quality Management processes, and Figure 8-2 provides a process flow diagram of those processes and their inputs, outputs, and other related Knowledge Area processes. The Project Quality Management processes include the following:

8.1 **Quality Planning** – identifying which quality standards are relevant to the project and determining how to satisfy them.

8.2 **Perform Quality Assurance** – applying the planned, systematic quality activities to ensure that the project employs all processes needed to meet requirements.

8.3 **Perform Quality Control** – monitoring specific project results to determine whether they comply with relevant quality standards and identifying ways to eliminate causes of unsatisfactory performance.

These processes interact with each other and with the processes in the other Knowledge Areas as well. Each process can involve effort from one or more persons or groups of persons based on the needs of the project. Each process occurs at least once in every project and occurs in one or more project phases, if the project is divided into phases. Although the processes are presented here as discrete elements with well-defined interfaces, in practice they may overlap and interact in ways not detailed here. Process interactions are discussed in detail in Chapter 3.

The basic approach to quality management described in this section is intended to be compatible with that of the International Organization for Standardization (ISO). This generalized approach should also be compatible with proprietary approaches to quality management such as those recommended by Deming, Juran, Crosby and others, and non-proprietary approaches such as Total Quality Management (TQM), Six Sigma, Failure Mode and Effect Analysis, Design Reviews, Voice of the Customer, Cost of Quality (COQ), and Continuous Improvement.

Project Quality Management must address the management of the project and the product of the project. While Project Quality Management applies to all projects, regardless of the nature of their product, product quality measures and techniques are specific to the particular type of product produced by the project. For example, quality management of software products entails different approaches and measures than nuclear power plants, while Project Quality Management approaches apply to both. In either case, failure to meet quality requirements in either dimension can have serious negative consequences for any or all of the project stakeholders. For example:

- Meeting customer requirements by overworking the project team may produce negative consequences in the form of increased employee attrition, unfounded errors, or rework
- Meeting project schedule objectives by rushing planned quality inspections may produce negative consequences when errors go undetected.

Quality is "the degree to which a set of inherent characteristics fulfill requirements"[6]. Stated and implied needs are the inputs to developing project requirements. A critical element of quality management in the project context is to turn stakeholder needs, wants, and expectations into requirements through Stakeholder Analysis (Section 5.2.2.4), performed during Project Scope Management.

Quality and grade are not the same. Grade is a category assigned to products or services having the same functional use but different technical characteristics[7]. Low quality is always a problem; low grade may not be. For example, a software product can be of high quality (no obvious defects, readable manual) and low grade (a limited number of features), or of low quality (many defects, poorly organized user documentation) and high grade (numerous features). The project manager and the project management team are responsible for determining and delivering the required levels of both quality and grade.

Precision and accuracy are not equivalent. Precision is consistency that the value of repeated measurements are clustered and have little scatter. Accuracy is correctness that the measured value is very close to the true value. Precise measurements are not necessarily accurate. A very accurate measurement is not necessarily precise. The project management team must determine how much accuracy or precision or both are required.

A Guide to the Project Management Body of Knowledge (PMBOK® Guide) Third Edition
©2004 Project Management Institute, Four Campus Boulevard, Newtown Square, PA 19073-3299 USA

Modern quality management complements project management. For example, both disciplines recognize the importance of:

- **Customer satisfaction.** Understanding, evaluating, defining,and managing expectations so that customer requirements are met. This requires a combination of conformance to requirements (the project must produce what it said it would produce) and fitness for use (the product or service must satisfy real needs).

- **Prevention over inspection.** The cost of preventing mistakes is generally much less than the cost of correcting them, as revealed by inspection.

- **Management responsibility.** Success requires the participation of all members of the team, but it remains the responsibility of management to provide the resources needed to succeed.

- **Continuous improvement.** The plan-do-check-act cycle is the basis for quality improvement (as defined by Shewhart and modified by Deming, in the ASQ Handbook, pages 13–14, American Society for Quality, 1999). In addition, quality improvement initiatives undertaken by the performing organization, such as TQM and Six Sigma, can improve the quality of the project's management as well as the quality of the project's product. Process improvement models include Malcolm Baldrige, CMM®, and CMMI^{SM}.

The cost of quality refers to the total cost of all efforts related to quality. Project decisions can impact operational costs of quality as a result of product returns, warranty claims, and recall campaigns. However, the temporary nature of the project means that investments in product quality improvement, especially defect prevention and appraisal, can often be borne by the acquiring organization, rather than the project, since the project may not last long enough to reap the rewards.

Figure 8-1. Project Quality Management Overview

A Guide to the Project Management Body of Knowledge (PMBOK® Guide) Third Edition
©2004 Project Management Institute, Four Campus Boulevard, Newtown Square, PA 19073-3299 USA

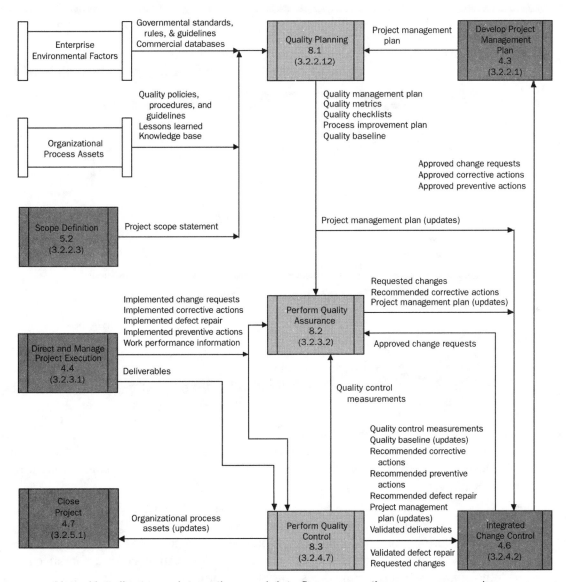

Note: Not all process interactions and data flow among the processes are shown.

Figure 8-2. Project Quality Management Process Flow Diagram

8.1   Quality Planning

Quality planning involves identifying which quality standards are relevant to the project and determining how to satisfy them. It is one of the key processes when doing the Planning Process Group (Section 3.3) and during development of the project management plan (Sections 4.3), and should be performed in parallel with the other project planning processes. For example, the required changes in the product to meet identified quality standards may require cost or schedule adjustments, or the desired product quality may require a detailed risk analysis of an identified problem.

The quality planning techniques discussed here are those techniques most frequently used on projects. There are many others that may be useful on certain projects or in some application areas. One of the fundamental tenets of modern quality management is: quality is planned, designed, and built in—not inspected in.

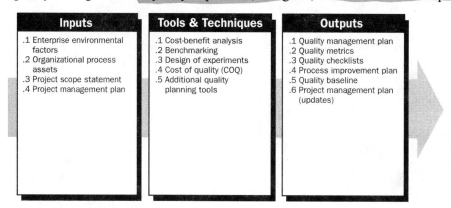

Inputs	Tools & Techniques	Outputs
.1 Enterprise environmental factors .2 Organizational process assets .3 Project scope statement .4 Project management plan	.1 Cost-benefit analysis .2 Benchmarking .3 Design of experiments .4 Cost of quality (COQ) .5 Additional quality planning tools	.1 Quality management plan .2 Quality metrics .3 Quality checklists .4 Process improvement plan .5 Quality baseline .6 Project management plan (updates)

Figure 8-3. Quality Planning: Inputs, Tools & Techniques, and Outputs

8.1.1 Quality Planning: Inputs

.1 Enterprise Environmental Factors

Governmental agency regulations, rules, standards, and guidelines specific to the application area may affect the project (Section 4.1.1.3).

.2 Organizational Process Assets

Organizational quality policies, procedures and guidelines, historical databases and lessons learned from previous projects specific to the application area may affect the project (Section 4.1.1.4).

The quality policy, as endorsed by senior management, is the intended direction of a performing organization with regard to quality. The quality policy of the performing organization for their products often can be adopted "as is" for use by the project. However, if the performing organization lacks a formal quality policy, or if the project involves multiple performing organizations (as with a joint venture), then the project management team will need to develop a quality policy for the project.

Regardless of the origin of the quality policy, the project management team is responsible for ensuring that the project stakeholders are fully aware of the policy through the appropriate distribution of information (Section 10.2.3.1).

.3 Project Scope Statement

The project scope statement (Section 5.2.3.1) is a key input to quality planning since it documents major project deliverables, the project objectives that serve to define requirements (which were derived from stakeholder needs, wants, and expectations), thresholds, and acceptance criteria.

A Guide to the Project Management Body of Knowledge (PMBOK® Guide) Third Edition
©2004 Project Management Institute, Four Campus Boulevard, Newtown Square, PA 19073-3299 USA

Thresholds, which are defined as cost, time, or resource values used as parameters, can be part of the project scope statement. If these threshold values are exceeded, it will require action from the project management team.

Acceptance criteria include performance requirements and essential conditions that must be achieved before project deliverables are accepted. The definition of acceptance criteria can significantly increase or decrease project quality costs. The result of the deliverables satisfying all acceptance criteria implies that the needs of the customer have been met. Formal acceptance (Section 5.4.3.1) validates that the acceptance criteria have been satisfied. The product scope description, embodied in the project scope statement (Section 5.2.3.1), will often contain details of technical issues and other concerns that can affect quality planning.

.4 Project Management Plan
Described in Section 4.3.

8.1.2 Quality Planning: Tools and Techniques

.1 Cost-Benefit Analysis
Quality planning must consider cost-benefits tradeoffs. The primary benefit of meeting quality requirements is less rework, which means higher productivity, lower costs, and increased stakeholder satisfaction. The primary cost of meeting quality requirements is the expense associated with Project Quality Management activities.

.2 Benchmarking
Benchmarking involves comparing actual or planned project practices to those of other projects to generate ideas for improvement and to provide a basis by which to measure performance. These other projects can be within the performing organization or outside of it, and can be within the same or in another application area.

.3 Design of Experiments
Design of experiments (DOE) is a statistical method that helps identify which factors may influence specific variables of a product or process under development or in production. It also plays a role in the optimization of products or processes. An example is where an organization can use DOE to reduce the sensitivity of product performance to sources of variations caused by environmental or manufacturing differences. The most important aspect of this technique is that it provides a statistical framework for systematically changing all of the important factors, instead of changing the factors one at a time. The analysis of the experimental data should provide the optimal conditions for the product or process, highlighting the factors that influence the results, and revealing the presence of interactions and synergisms among the factors. For example, automotive designers use this technique to determine which combination of suspension and tires will produce the most desirable ride characteristics at a reasonable cost.

.4 Cost of Quality (COQ)

Quality costs are the total costs incurred by investment in preventing nonconformance to requirements, appraising the product or service for conformance to requirements, and failing to meet requirements (rework). Failure costs are often categorized into internal and external. Failure costs are also called cost of poor quality.

.5 Additional Quality Planning Tools

Other quality planning tools are also often used to help better define the situation and help plan effective quality management activities. These include brainstorming, affinity diagrams, force field analysis, nominal group techniques, matrix diagrams, flowcharts, and prioritization matrices.

8.1.3 Quality Planning: Outputs

.1 Quality Management Plan

The quality management plan describes how the project management team will implement the performing organization's quality policy. The quality management plan is a component or a subsidiary plan of the project management plan (Section 4.3).

The quality management plan provides input to the overall project management plan and must address quality control (QC), quality assurance (QA), and continuous process improvement for the project.

The quality management plan may be formal or informal, highly detailed or broadly framed, based on the requirements of the project. The quality management plan should include efforts at the front end of a project to ensure that the earlier decisions, for example on concepts, designs and tests, are correct. These efforts should be performed through an independent peer review and not include individuals that worked on the material being reviewed. The benefits of this review can include reduction of cost and schedule overruns caused by rework.

.2 Quality Metrics

A metric is an operational definition that describes, in very specific terms, what something is and how the quality control process measures it. A measurement is an actual value. For example, it is not enough to say that meeting the planned schedule dates is a measure of management quality. The project management team must also indicate whether every activity must start on time or only finish on time and whether individual activities will be measured, or only certain deliverables and if so, which ones. Quality metrics are used in the QA and QC processes. Some examples of quality metrics include defect density, failure rate, availability, reliability, and test coverage.

A Guide to the Project Management Body of Knowledge (PMBOK® Guide) Third Edition
©2004 Project Management Institute, Four Campus Boulevard, Newtown Square, PA 19073-3299 USA

.3 Quality Checklists

A checklist is a structured tool, usually component-specific, used to verify that a set of required steps has been performed. Checklists may be simple or complex. They are usually phrased as imperatives ("Do this!") or interrogatories ("Have you done this?"). Many organizations have standardized checklists available to ensure consistency in frequently performed tasks. In some application areas, checklists are also available from professional associations or commercial service providers. Quality checklists are used in the quality control process.

.4 Process Improvement Plan

The process improvement plan is a subsidiary of the project management plan (Section 4.3). The process improvement plan details the steps for analyzing processes that will facilitate the identification of waste and non-value added activity, thus increasing customer value, such as:

- **Process boundaries.** Describes the purpose, start, and end of processes, their inputs and outputs, data required, if any, and the owner and stakeholders of processes.
- **Process configuration.** A flowchart of processes to facilitate analysis with interfaces identified.
- **Process metrics.** Maintain control over status of processes.
- **Targets for improved performance.** Guides the process improvement activities.

.5 Quality Baseline

The quality baseline records the quality objectives of the project. The quality baseline is the basis for measuring and reporting quality performance as part of the performance measurement baseline.

.6 Project Management Plan (Updates)

The project management plan will be updated through the inclusion of a subsidiary quality management plan and process improvement plan (Section 4.3). Requested changes (additions, modifications, deletions) to the project management plan and its subsidiary plans are processed by review and disposition through the Integrated Change Control process (Section 4.6).

8.2 Perform Quality Assurance

Quality assurance (QA) is the application of planned, systematic quality activities to ensure that the project will employ all processes needed to meet requirements.

A quality assurance department, or similar organization, often oversees quality assurance activities. QA support, regardless of the unit's title, may be provided to the project team, the management of the performing organization, the customer or sponsor, as well as other stakeholders not actively involved in the work of the project. QA also provides an umbrella for another important quality activity, continuous process improvement. Continuous process improvement provides an iterative means for improving the quality of all processes.

Continuous process improvement reduces waste and non-value-added activities, which allows processes to operate at increased levels of efficiency and effectiveness. Process improvement is distinguished by its identification and review of organizational business processes. It may be applied to other processes within an organization as well, from micro processes, such as the coding of modules within a software program, to macro processes, such as the opening of new markets.

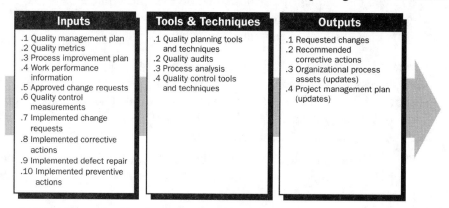

Figure 8-4. Perform Quality Assurance: Inputs, Tools & Techniques, and Outputs

8.2.1 Perform Quality Assurance: Inputs

.1 Quality Management Plan
The quality management plan describes how QA will be performed within the project (Section 8.1.3.1).

.2 Quality Metrics
Described in Section 8.1.3.2.

.3 Process Improvement Plan
Described in Section 8.1.3.4.

.4 Work Performance Information
Work performance information (Section 4.4.3.7), including technical performance measures, project deliverables status, required corrective actions, and performance reports (Section 10.3.3.1) are important inputs to QA and can be used in areas such as audits, quality reviews, and process analyses.

.5 Approved Change Requests
Approved change requests (Section 4.4.1.4) can include modifications to work methods, product requirements, quality requirements, scope, and schedule. Approved changes need to be analyzed for any effects upon the quality management plan, quality metrics, or quality checklists. Approved changes are important inputs to QA and can be used in areas such as audits, quality reviews, and process analyses. All changes should be formally documented in writing and any verbally discussed, but undocumented, changes should not be processed or implemented.

A Guide to the Project Management Body of Knowledge (PMBOK® Guide) Third Edition
©2004 Project Management Institute, Four Campus Boulevard, Newtown Square, PA 19073-3299 USA

.6 Quality Control Measurements

Quality control measurements (Section 8.3.3.1) are the results of quality control activities that are fed back to the QA process for use in re-evaluating and analyzing the quality standards and processes of the performing organization.

.7 Implemented Change Requests

Described in Section 4.4.3.3.

.8 Implemented Corrective Actions

Described in Section 4.4.3.4.

.9 Implemented Defect Repair

Described in Section 4.4.3.6.

.10 Implemented Preventive Actions

Described in Section 4.4.3.5.

8.2.2 Perform Quality Assurance: Tools and Techniques

.1 Quality Planning Tools and Techniques

The quality planning tools and techniques (Section 8.1.2) also can be used for QA activities.

.2 Quality Audits

A quality audit is a structured, independent review to determine whether project activities comply with organizational and project policies, processes, and procedures. The objective of a quality audit is to identify inefficient and ineffective policies, processes, and procedures in use on the project. The subsequent effort to correct these deficiencies should result in a reduced cost of quality and an increase in the percentage of acceptance of the product or service by the customer or sponsor within the performing organization. Quality audits may be scheduled or at random, and may be carried out by properly trained in-house auditors or by third parties, external to the performing organization.

Quality audits confirm the implementation of approved change requests, corrective actions, defect repairs, and preventive actions.

.3 Process Analysis

Process analysis follows the steps outlined in the process improvement plan to identify needed improvements from an organizational and technical standpoint. This analysis also examines problems experienced, constraints experienced, and non-value-added activities identified during process operation. Process analysis includes root cause analysis, a specific technique to analyze a problem/situation, determine the underlying causes that lead to it, and create preventive actions for similar problems.

.4 Quality Control Tools and Techniques

Described in Section 8.3.2.

8.2.3 Perform Quality Assurance: Outputs

.1 Requested Changes

Quality improvement includes taking action to increase the effectiveness and efficiency of the policies, processes, and procedures of the performing organization, which should provide added benefits to the stakeholders of all projects (Section 4.4.3.2).

.2 Recommended Corrective Actions

Quality improvement includes recommending actions to increase the effectiveness and efficiency of the performing organization. Corrective action is an action that is recommended immediately as a result of quality assurance activities, such as audits and process analyses.

.3 Organizational Process Assets (Updates)

Updated quality standards provide validation of the effectiveness and efficiency of the performing organization's quality standards and processes to meet requirements. These quality standards are used during the Perform Quality Control process (Section 8.3).

.4 Project Management Plan (Updates)

The project management plan (Section 4.3) will be updated from changes to the quality management plan that result from changes to the Perform Quality Assurance process. These updates can include incorporation of processes that have been through continuous process improvement and are ready to repeat the cycle, and improvements to processes that have been identified and measured, and are ready to be implemented. Requested changes (additions, modifications, deletions) to the project management plan and its subsidiary plans are processed by review and disposition through the Integrated Change Control process (Section 4.6).

8.3 Perform Quality Control

Performing quality control (QC) involves monitoring specific project results to determine whether they comply with relevant quality standards and identifying ways to eliminate causes of unsatisfactory results. It should be performed throughout the project. Quality standards include project processes and product goals. Project results include deliverables and project management results, such as cost and schedule performance. QC is often performed by a quality control department or similarly titled organizational unit. QC can include taking action to eliminate causes of unsatisfactory project performance.

The project management team should have a working knowledge of statistical quality control, especially sampling and probability, to help evaluate QC outputs. Among other subjects, the team may find it useful to know the differences between the following pairs of terms:

A Guide to the Project Management Body of Knowledge (PMBOK® Guide) Third Edition
©2004 Project Management Institute, Four Campus Boulevard, Newtown Square, PA 19073-3299 USA

- Prevention (keeping errors out of the process) and inspection (keeping errors out of the hands of the customer).
- Attribute sampling (the result conforms, or it does not) and variables sampling (the result is rated on a continuous scale that measures the degree of conformity).
- Special causes (unusual events) and common causes (normal process variation). Common causes are also called random causes.
- Tolerances (the result is acceptable if it falls within the range specified by the tolerance) and control limits (the process is in control if the result falls within the control limits).

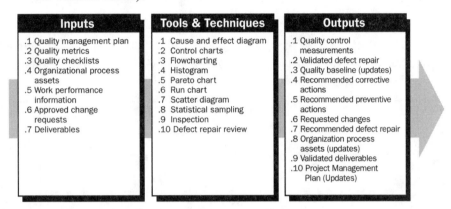

Inputs	Tools & Techniques	Outputs
.1 Quality management plan .2 Quality metrics .3 Quality checklists .4 Organizational process assets .5 Work performance information .6 Approved change requests .7 Deliverables	.1 Cause and effect diagram .2 Control charts .3 Flowcharting .4 Histogram .5 Pareto chart .6 Run chart .7 Scatter diagram .8 Statistical sampling .9 Inspection .10 Defect repair review	.1 Quality control measurements .2 Validated defect repair .3 Quality baseline (updates) .4 Recommended corrective actions .5 Recommended preventive actions .6 Requested changes .7 Recommended defect repair .8 Organization process assets (updates) .9 Validated deliverables .10 Project Management Plan (Updates)

Figure 8-5. Perform Quality Control: Inputs, Tools & Techniques, and Outputs

8.3.1 Perform Quality Control: Inputs

.1 Quality Management Plan
Described in Section 8.1.3.1.

.2 Quality Metrics
Described in Section 8.1.3.2.

.3 Quality Checklists
Described in Section 8.1.3.3.

.4 Organizational Process Assets
Described in Section 4.1.1.4.

.5 Work Performance Information
Work performance information (Section 4.4.3.7), including technical performance measures, project deliverables completion status, and the implementation of required corrective actions, are important inputs to QC. Information from the project management plan about the planned or expected results should be available along with information about the actual results and implemented change requests.

.6 Approved Change Requests

Approved change requests (Section 4.4.1.4) can include modifications such as revised work methods and revised schedule. The timely correct implementation of approved changes needs to be verified.

.7 Deliverables

Described in Section 4.4.3.1.

8.3.2 Perform Quality Control: Tools and Techniques

The first seven of these are known as the Seven Basic Tools of Quality.

.1 Cause and Effect Diagram

Cause and effect diagrams, also called Ishikawa diagrams or fishbone diagrams, illustrate how various factors might be linked to potential problems or effects. Figure 8-6 is an example of a cause and effect diagram.

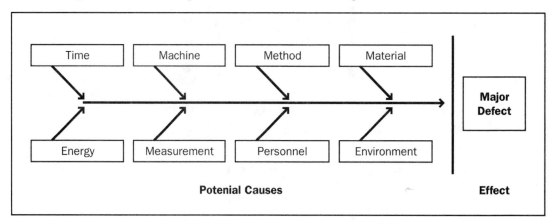

Figure 8-6. Cause and Effect Diagram

.2 Control Charts

A control chart's purpose is to determine whether or not a process is stable or has predictable performance. Control charts may serve as a data gathering tool to show when a process is subject to special cause variation, which creates an out-of-control condition. Control charts also illustrate how a process behaves over time. They are a graphic display of the interaction of process variables on a process to answer the question: Are the process variables within acceptable limits? Examination of the non-random pattern of data points on a control chart may reveal wildly fluctuating values, sudden process jumps or shifts, or a gradual trend in increased variation. By monitoring the output of a process over time, a control chart can be employed to assess whether the application of process changes resulted in the desired improvements. When a process is within acceptable limits, the process need not be adjusted. When a process is outside acceptable limits, the process should be adjusted. The upper control limit and lower control limit are usually set at +/- 3 sigma (i.e., standard deviation).

A Guide to the Project Management Body of Knowledge (PMBOK® Guide) Third Edition
©2004 Project Management Institute, Four Campus Boulevard, Newtown Square, PA 19073-3299 USA

Control charts can be used for both project and product life cycle processes. An example of project use of control charts is determining whether cost variances or schedule variances are outside of acceptable limits (for example, +/- 10 percent). An example of product use of control charts is evaluating whether the number of defects found during testing are acceptable or unacceptable in relation to the organization's standards for quality.

Control charts can be used to monitor any type of output variable. Although used most frequently to track repetitive activities, such as manufactured lots, control charts also can be used to monitor cost and schedule variances, volume and frequency of scope changes, errors in project documents, or other management results to help determine if the project management process is in control. Figure 8-7 is an example of a control chart of project schedule performance.

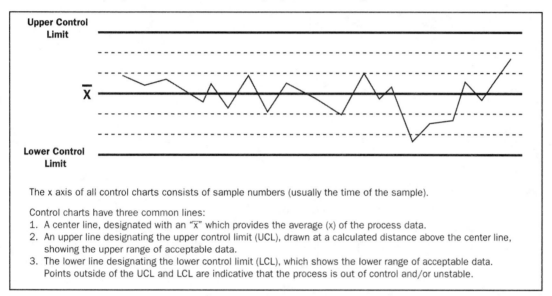

The x axis of all control charts consists of sample numbers (usually the time of the sample).

Control charts have three common lines:
1. A center line, designated with an "x̄" which provides the average (x) of the process data.
2. An upper line designating the upper control limit (UCL), drawn at a calculated distance above the center line, showing the upper range of acceptable data.
3. The lower line designating the lower control limit (LCL), which shows the lower range of acceptable data. Points outside of the UCL and LCL are indicative that the process is out of control and/or unstable.

Figure 8-7. Example of a Control Chart of Project Schedule Performance

.3 Flowcharting

Flowcharting helps to analyze how problems occur. A flowchart is a graphical representation of a process. There are many styles, but all process flowcharts show activities, decision points, and the order of processing. Flowcharts show how various elements of a system interrelate. Figure 8-8 is an example of a process flowchart for design reviews. Flowcharting can help the project team anticipate what and where quality problems might occur and, thus, can help develop approaches for dealing with them.

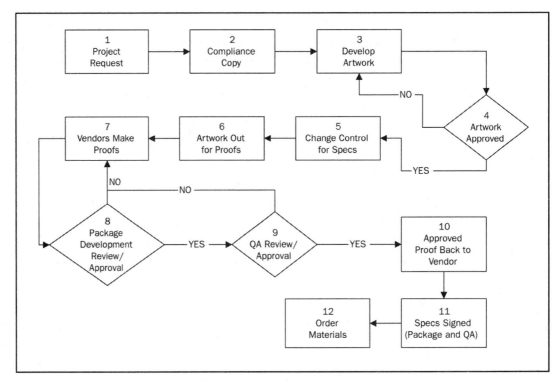

Figure 8-8. Sample Process Flowchart

.4   Histogram

A histogram is a bar chart showing a distribution of variables. Each column represents an attribute or characteristic of a problem/situation. The height of each column represents the relative frequency of the characteristic. This tool helps identify the cause of problems in a process by the shape and width of the distribution.

A Guide to the Project Management Body of Knowledge (PMBOK® Guide) Third Edition
©2004 Project Management Institute, Four Campus Boulevard, Newtown Square, PA 19073-3299 USA

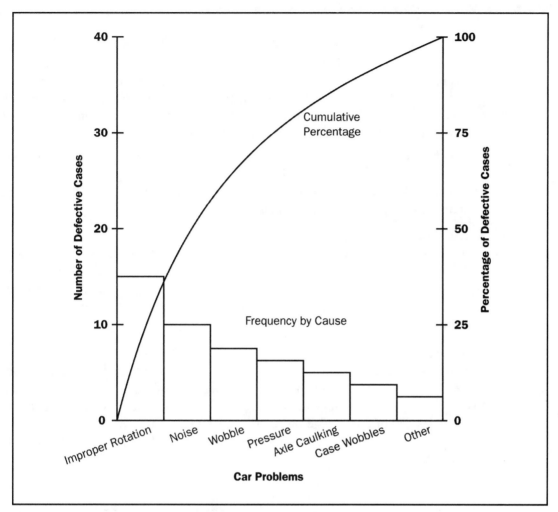

Figure 8-9. Pareto Diagram (Chart)

.5 Pareto Chart

A Pareto chart is a specific type of histogram, ordered by frequency of occurrence, which shows how many defects were generated by type or category of identified cause (Figure 8-9). The Pareto technique is used primarily to identify and evaluate nonconformities.

In Pareto diagrams, rank ordering is used to guide corrective action. The project team should take action to fix the problems that are causing the greatest number of defects first. Pareto diagrams are conceptually related to Pareto's Law, which holds that a relatively small number of causes will typically produce a large majority of the problems or defects. This is commonly referred to as the 80/20 principle, where 80 percent of the problems are due to 20 percent of the causes. Pareto diagrams also can be used to summarize all types of data for 80/20 analyses.

.6 Run Chart

A run chart shows the history and pattern of variation. A run chart is a line graph that shows data points plotted in the order in which they occur. Run charts show trends in a process over time, variation over time, or declines or improvements in a process over time. Trend analysis is performed using run charts. Trend analysis involves using mathematical techniques to forecast future outcomes based on historical results. Trend analysis is often used to monitor:

- **Technical performance.** How many errors or defects have been identified, how many remain uncorrected?
- **Cost and schedule performance.** How many activities per period were completed with significant variances?

.7 Scatter Diagram

A scatter diagram shows the pattern of relationship between two variables. This tool allows the quality team to study and identify the possible relationship between changes observed in two variables. Dependent variables versus independent variables are plotted. The closer the points are to a diagonal line, the more closely they are related.

.8 Statistical Sampling

Statistical sampling involves choosing part of a population of interest for inspection (for example, selecting ten engineering drawings at random from a list of seventy-five). Appropriate sampling can often reduce the cost of quality control. There is a substantial body of knowledge on statistical sampling; in some application areas, it may be necessary for the project management team to be familiar with a variety of sampling techniques.

.9 Inspection

An inspection is the examination of a work product to determine whether it conforms to standards. Generally, the results of an inspection include measurements. Inspections can be conducted at any level. For example, the results of a single activity can be inspected, or the final product of the project can be inspected. Inspections are also called reviews, peer reviews, audits, and walkthroughs. In some application areas, these terms have narrow and specific meanings. Inspections are also used to validate defect repairs.

.10 Defect Repair Review

Defect repair review is an action taken by the quality control department or similarly titled organization to ensure that product defects are repaired and brought into compliance with requirements or specifications.

A Guide to the Project Management Body of Knowledge (PMBOK® Guide) Third Edition
©2004 Project Management Institute, Four Campus Boulevard, Newtown Square, PA 19073-3299 USA

8.3.3 Perform Quality Control: Outputs

.1 Quality Control Measurements

Quality control measurements represent the results of QC activities that are fed back to QA (Section 8.2) to reevaluate and analyze the quality standards and processes of the performing organization.

.2 Validated Defect Repair

The repaired items are reinspected and will be either accepted or rejected before notification of the decision is provided (Section 4.4). Rejected items may require further defect repair.

.3 Quality Baseline (Updates)

Described in Section 8.1.3.5.

.4 Recommended Corrective Actions

Corrective action (Section 4.5.3.1) involves actions taken as a result of a QC measurement that indicates that the manufacturing or development process exceeds established parameters.

.5 Recommended Preventive Actions

Preventive action (Section 4.5.3.2) involves action taken to forestall a condition that may exceed established parameters in a manufacturing or development process, which may have been indicated through a QC measurement.

.6 Requested Changes

If the recommended corrective or preventive actions require a change to the project, a change request (Section 4.4.3.2) should be initiated in accordance with the defined Integrated Change Control process.

.7 Recommended Defect Repair

A defect is where a component does not meet its requirements or specifications, and needs to be repaired or replaced. Defects are identified and recommended for repair by the QC department or similarly titled organization. The project team should make every reasonable effort to minimize the errors that cause the need for defect repair. A defect log can be used to collect the set of recommended repairs. This is often implemented in an automated problem-tracking system.

.8 Organization Process Assets (Updates)

- **Completed checklists.** When checklists are used, the completed checklists should become part of the project's records (Section 4.1.1.4).
- **Lessons learned documentation.** The causes of variances, the reasoning behind the corrective action chosen, and other types of lessons learned from quality control should be documented so that they become part of the historical database for both this project and the performing organization. Lessons learned are documented throughout the project life cycle, but, at a minimum, during project closure (Section 4.1.1.4).

.9 Validated Deliverables

A goal of quality control is to determine the correctness of deliverables. The results of the execution quality control processes are validated deliverables.

.10 Project Management Plan (Updates)

The project management plan is updated to reflect changes to the quality management plan that result from changes in performing the QC process. Requested changes (additions, modifications, or deletions) to the project management plan and its subsidiary plans are processed by review and disposition through the Integrated Change Control process (Section 4.6).

CHAPTER 9

Project Human Resource Management

Project Human Resource Management includes the processes that organize and manage the project team. The project team is comprised of the people who have assigned roles and responsibilities for completing the project. While it is common to speak of roles and responsibilities being assigned, team members should be involved in much of the project's planning and decision-making. Early involvement of team members adds expertise during the planning process and strengthens commitment to the project. The type and number of project team members can often change as the project progresses. Project team members can be referred to as the project's staff.

The project management team is a subset of the project team and is responsible for project management activities such as planning, controlling, and closing. This group can be called the core, executive, or leadership team. For smaller projects, the project management responsibilities can be shared by the entire team or administered solely by the project manager. The project sponsor works with the project management team, typically assisting with matters such as project funding, clarifying scope questions, and influencing others in order to benefit the project.

Figure 9-1 provides an overview of the Project Human Resource Management processes, and Figure 9-2 provides a process flow diagram of those processes and their inputs, outputs, and other related Knowledge Area processes. The Project Human Resource Management processes include the following:

9.1 **Human Resource Planning** – Identifying and documenting project roles, responsibilities, and reporting relationships, as well as creating the staffing management plan.

9.2 **Acquire Project Team** – Obtaining the human resources needed to complete the project.

9.3 **Develop Project Team** – Improving the competencies and interaction of team members to enhance project performance.

9.4 **Manage Project Team** – Tracking team member performance, providing feedback, resolving issues, and coordinating changes to enhance project performance.

These processes interact with each other and with processes in the other Knowledge Areas as well. Each process can involve effort from one or more persons or groups of persons based on the needs of the project. Each process occurs at least once in every project, and occurs in one or more project phases, if the project is divided into phases. Although the processes are presented here as discrete elements with well-defined interfaces, in practice they may overlap and interact in ways not detailed here. Process interactions are discussed in detail in Chapter 3.

Figure 9-2 illustrates the primary ways that Project Human Resource Management interacts with other project processes. Examples of interactions that require additional planning include the following situations:

- After initial team members create a work breakdown structure, additional team members may need to be acquired
- As additional project team members are acquired, their experience level could increase or decrease project risk, creating the need for additional risk planning
- When activity durations are estimated before all project team members are known, actual competency levels of the acquired team members can cause the activity durations and schedule to change.

A Guide to the Project Management Body of Knowledge (PMBOK® Guide) Third Edition
©2004 Project Management Institute, Four Campus Boulevard, Newtown Square, PA 19073-3299 USA

PROJECT HUMAN RESOURCE MANAGEMENT

9.1 Human Resource Planning

.1 Inputs
  .1 Enterprise environmental factors
  .2 Organizational process assets
  .3 Project management plan
    · Activity resource requirements

.2 Tools and Techniques
  .1 Organization charts and position descriptions
  .2 Networking
  .3 Organizational theory

.3 Outputs
  .1 Roles and responsibilities
  .2 Project organization charts
  .3 Staffing management plan

9.2 Acquire Project Team

.1 Inputs
  .1 Enterprise environmental factors
  .2 Organizational process assets
  .3 Roles and responsibilities
  .4 Project organization charts
  .5 Staffing management plan

.2 Tools and Techniques
  .1 Pre-assignment
  .2 Negotiation
  .3 Acquisition
  .4 Virtual teams

.3 Outputs
  .1 Project staff assignments
  .2 Resource availability
  .3 Staffing management plan (updates)

9.3 Develop Project Team

.1 Inputs
  .1 Project staff assignments
  .2 Staffing management plan
  .3 Resource availability

.2 Tools and Techniques
  .1 General management skills
  .2 Training
  .3 Team-building activities
  .4 Ground rules
  .5 Co-location
  .6 Recognition and rewards

.3 Outputs
  .1 Team performance assessment

9.4 Manage Project Team

.1 Inputs
  .1 Organizational process assets
  .2 Project staff assignments
  .3 Roles and responsibilities
  .4 Project organization charts
  .5 Staffing management plan
  .6 Team performance assessment
  .7 Work performance information
  .8 Performance reports

.2 Tools and Techniques
  .1 Observation and conversation
  .2 Project performance appraisals
  .3 Conflict management
  .4 Issue log

.3 Outputs
  .1 Requested changes
  .2 Recommended corrective actions
  .3 Recommended preventive actions
  .4 Organizational process assets (updates)
  .5 Project management plan (updates)

9

Figure 9-1. Project Human Resource Management Overview

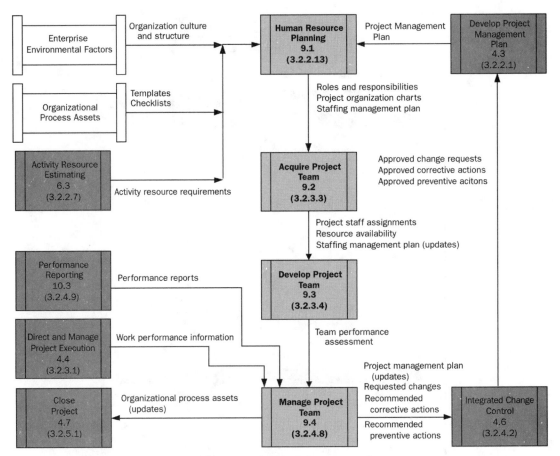

Note: Not all process interactions and data flow among the processes are shown.

Figure 9-2. Project Human Resource Management Process Flow Diagram

9.1 Human Resource Planning

Human Resource Planning determines project roles, responsibilities, and reporting relationships, and creates the staffing management plan. Project roles can be designated for persons or groups. Those persons or groups can be from inside or outside the organization performing the project. The staffing management plan can include how and when project team members will be acquired, the criteria for releasing them from the project, identification of training needs, plans for recognition and rewards, compliance considerations, safety issues, and the impact of the staffing management plan on the organization.

A Guide to the Project Management Body of Knowledge (PMBOK® Guide) Third Edition
©2004 Project Management Institute, Four Campus Boulevard, Newtown Square, PA 19073-3299 USA

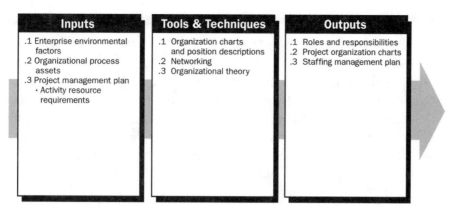

Inputs	Tools & Techniques	Outputs
.1 Enterprise environmental factors .2 Organizational process assets .3 Project management plan • Activity resource requirements	.1 Organization charts and position descriptions .2 Networking .3 Organizational theory	.1 Roles and responsibilities .2 Project organization charts .3 Staffing management plan

Figure 9-3. Human Resource Planning: Inputs, Tools & Techniques, and Outputs

9.1.1 Human Resource Planning: Inputs

.1 Enterprise Environmental Factors

The definition of project roles and responsibilities is developed with an understanding of the ways that existing organizations will be involved and how the technical disciplines and people currently interact with one another. Some of the relevant enterprise environmental factors (Section 4.1.1.3) involving organizational culture and structure are:

- **Organizational.** Which organizations or departments will be involved in the project? What are the current working arrangements among them? What formal and informal relationships exist among them?

- **Technical.** What are the different disciplines and specialties that will be needed to complete this project? Are there different types of software languages, engineering approaches, or kinds of equipment that will need to be coordinated? Do the transitions from one life cycle phase to the next present any unique challenges?

- **Interpersonal.** What types of formal and informal reporting relationships exist among people who are candidates for the project team? What are the candidates' job descriptions? What are their supervisor-subordinate relationships? What are their supplier-customer relationships? What cultural or language differences will affect working relationships among team members? What levels of trust and respect currently exist?

- **Logistical.** How much distance separates the people and units that will be part of the project? Are people in different buildings, time zones, or countries?

- **Political.** What are the individual goals and agendas of the potential project stakeholders? Which groups and people have informal power in areas important to the project? What informal alliances exist?

In addition to the factors listed above, constraints limit the project team's options. Examples of constraints that can limit flexibility in the Human Resource Planning process are:

- **Organizational structure.** An organization whose basic structure is a weak matrix means a relatively weaker role for the project manager (Section 2.3.3).
- **Collective bargaining agreements.** Contractual agreements with unions or other employee groups can require certain roles or reporting relationships.
- **Economic conditions.** Hiring freezes, reduced training funds, or a lack of travel budget are examples of economic conditions that can restrict staffing options.

.2 Organizational Process Assets

As project management methodology matures within an organization, lessons learned from past Human Resource Planning experiences are available as organizational process assets (Section 4.1.1.4) to help plan the current project. Templates and checklists reduce the amount of planning time needed at the beginning of a project and reduce the likelihood of missing important responsibilities.

- **Templates.** Templates that can be helpful in Human Resource Planning include project organization charts, position descriptions, project performance appraisals, and a standard conflict management approach.
- **Checklists.** Checklists that can be helpful in Human Resource Planning include common project roles and responsibilities, typical competencies, training programs to consider, team ground rules, safety considerations, compliance issues, and reward ideas.

.3 Project Management Plan

The project management plan (Section 4.3) includes the activity resource requirements, plus descriptions of project management activities, such as quality assurance, risk management, and procurement, that will help the project management team identify all of the required roles and responsibilities.

- **Activity Resource Requirements.** Human Resource Planning uses activity resource requirements (Section 6.3.3.1) to determine the human resource needs for the project. The preliminary requirements regarding the required people and competencies for the project team members are refined as part of the Human Resource Planning process.

9.1.2 Human Resource Planning: Tools and Techniques

.1 Organization Charts and Position Descriptions

Various formats exist to document team member roles and responsibilities. Most of the formats fall into one of three types (Figure 9-4): hierarchical, matrix, and text-oriented. Additionally, some project assignments are listed in subsidiary project plans, such as the risk, quality, or communication plans. Whichever combination of methods is used, the objective is to ensure that each work package has an unambiguous owner and that all team members have a clear understanding of their roles and responsibilities.

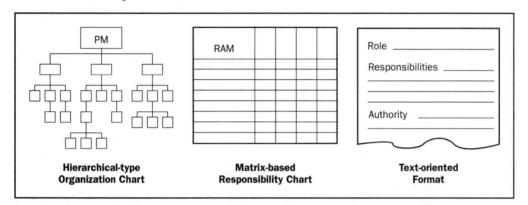

Figure 9-4. Roles and Responsibility Definition Formats

- **Hierarchical-type charts.** The traditional organization chart structure can be used to show positions and relationships in a graphic, top-down format. Work breakdown structures (WBS) that are primarily designed to show how project deliverables are broken down into work packages become one way to show high-level areas of responsibility. The organizational breakdown structure (OBS) looks similar to the WBS, but instead of being arranged according to a breakdown of project deliverables, it is arranged according to an organization's existing departments, units, or teams. The project activities or work packages are listed under each existing department. This way, an operational department such as information technology or purchasing can see all of its project responsibilities by looking at its portion of the OBS. The resource breakdown structure (RBS) is another hierarchical chart. It is used to break down the project by types of resources. For example, an RBS can depict all of the welders and welding equipment being used in different areas of a ship even though they can be scattered among different branches of the OBS and WBS. The RBS is helpful in tracking project costs, and can be aligned with the organization's accounting system. The RBS can contain resource categories other than human resources.

- **Matrix-based charts.** A responsibility assignment matrix (RAM) is used to illustrate the connections between work that needs to be done and project team members. On larger projects, RAMs can be developed at various levels. For example, a high-level RAM can define what project team group or unit is responsible for each component of the WBS, while lower-level RAMs are used within the group to designate roles, responsibilities, and levels of authority for specific activities. The matrix format, sometimes called a table, allows a person to see all activities associated with one person or to see all people associated with one activity. The matrix shown in Figure 9-5 is a type of RAM called a RACI chart because the names of roles being documented are Responsible, Accountable, Consult, and Inform. The sample chart shows the work to be done in the left column as activities, but RAMs can show responsibilities at various levels of detail. The people can be shown as persons or groups.

RACI Chart	Person				
Activity	Ann	Ben	Carlos	Dina	Ed
Define	A	R	I	I	I
Design	I	A	R	C	C
Develop	I	A	R	C	C
Test	A	I	I	R	I

R = Responsible A = Accountable C = Consult I = Inform

Figure 9-5. Responsibility Assignment Matrix (RAM) Using a RACI Format

- **Text-oriented formats.** Team member responsibilities that require detailed descriptions can be specified in text-oriented formats. Usually in outline form, the documents provide information such as responsibilities, authority, competencies, and qualifications. The documents are known by various names, including position descriptions and role-responsibility-authority forms. These descriptions and forms make excellent templates for future projects, especially when the information is updated throughout the current project by applying lessons learned.

- **Other sections of the project management plan.** Some responsibilities related to managing the project are listed and explained in other sections of the project management plan. For example, the risk register lists risk owners, the communication plan lists team members responsible for communication activities, and the quality plan designates people responsible for carrying out quality assurance and quality control activities.

.2 Networking

Informal interaction with others in an organization or industry is a constructive way to understand political and interpersonal factors that will impact the effectiveness of various staffing management options. Human resources networking activities include proactive correspondence, luncheon meetings, informal conversations, and trade conferences. While concentrated networking can be a useful technique at the beginning of a project, carrying out networking activities on a regular basis before a project begins is also effective.

.3 Organizational Theory

Organizational theory provides information regarding the ways that people, teams, and organizational units behave. Applying proven principles shortens the amount of time needed to create the Human Resource Planning outputs and improves the likelihood that the planning will be effective.

9.1.3 Human Resource Planning: Outputs

.1 Roles and Responsibilities

The following items should be addressed when listing the roles and responsibilities needed to complete the project:

- **Role.** The label describing the portion of a project for which a person is accountable. Examples of project roles are civil engineer, court liaison, business analyst, and testing coordinator. Role clarity concerning authority, responsibilities, and boundaries is essential for project success.
- **Authority.** The right to apply project resources, make decisions, and sign approvals. Examples of decisions that need clear authority include the selection of a method for completing an activity, quality acceptance, and how to respond to project variances. Team members operate best when their individual levels of authority matches their individual responsibilities.
- **Responsibility.** The work that a project team member is expected to perform in order to complete the project's activities.
- **Competency.** The skill and capacity required to complete project activities. If project team members do not possess required competencies, performance can be jeopardized. When such mismatches are identified, proactive responses such as training, hiring, schedule changes, or scope changes are initiated.

.2 Project Organization Charts

A project organization chart is a graphic display of project team members and their reporting relationships. It can be formal or informal, highly detailed or broadly framed, based on the needs of the project. For example, the project organization chart for a 3,000-person disaster response team will have greater detail than a project organization chart for an internal, twenty-person project.

.3 Staffing Management Plan

The staffing management plan, a subset of the project management plan (Section 4.3), describes when and how human resource requirements will be met. The staffing management plan can be formal or informal, highly detailed or broadly framed, based on the needs of the project. The plan is updated continually during the project to direct ongoing team member acquisition and development actions. Information in the staffing management plan varies by application area and project size, but items to consider include:

- **Staff acquisition.** A number of questions arise when planning the acquisition of project team members. For example, will the human resources come from within the organization or from external, contracted sources? Will team members need to work in a central location or can they work from distant locations? What are the costs associated with each level of expertise needed for the project? How much assistance can the organization's human resource department provide to the project management team?

- **Timetable.** The staffing management plan describes necessary time frames for project team members, either individually or collectively, as well as when acquisition activities such as recruiting should start. One tool for charting human resources is a resource histogram (Section 6.5.3.2). This bar chart illustrates the number of hours that a person, department, or entire project team will be needed each week or month over the course of the project. The chart can include a horizontal line that represents the maximum number of hours available from a particular resource. Bars that extend beyond the maximum available hours identify the need for a resource leveling strategy, such as adding more resources or extending the length of the schedule. A sample resource histogram is illustrated in Figure 9-6.

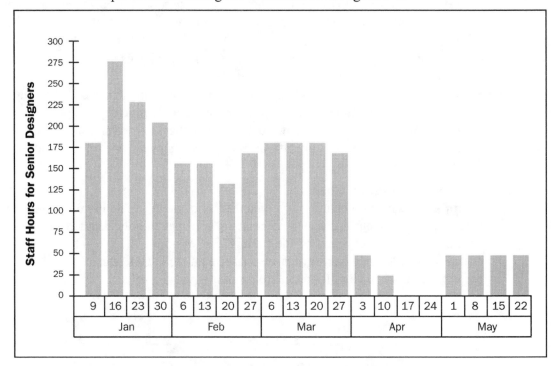

Figure 9-6. Illustrative Resource Histogram

A Guide to the Project Management Body of Knowledge (PMBOK® Guide) Third Edition
©2004 Project Management Institute, Four Campus Boulevard, Newtown Square, PA 19073-3299 USA

- **Release criteria.** Determining the method and timing of releasing team members benefits both the project and team members. When team members are released from a project at the optimum time, payments made for people who are finished with their responsibilities can be eliminated and the costs reduced. Morale is improved when smooth transitions to upcoming projects are already planned.
- **Training needs.** If the team members to be assigned are not expected to have the required competencies, a training plan can be developed as part of the project. The plan can also include ways to help team members obtain certifications that would benefit the project.
- **Recognition and rewards.** Clear criteria for rewards and a planned system for their use will promote and reinforce desired behaviors. To be effective, recognition and rewards should be based on activities and performance under a person's control. For example, a team member who is to be rewarded for meeting cost objectives should have an appropriate level of control over decisions that affect expenses. Creating a plan with established times for rewards ensures that recognition takes place and is not forgotten. Recognition and rewards are awarded as part of the Develop Project Team process (Section 9.3).
- **Compliance.** The staffing management plan can include strategies for complying with applicable government regulations, union contracts, and other established human resource policies.
- **Safety.** Policies and procedures that protect team members from safety hazards can be included in the staffing management plan as well as the risk register.

9.2 Acquire Project Team

Acquire Project Team is the process of obtaining the human resources needed to complete the project. The project management team may or may not have control over team members selected for the project.

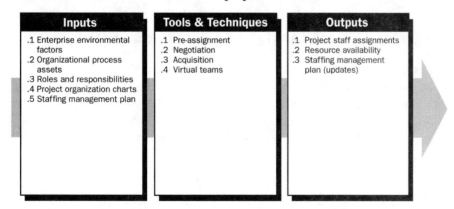

Inputs	Tools & Techniques	Outputs
.1 Enterprise environmental factors	.1 Pre-assignment	.1 Project staff assignments
.2 Organizational process assets	.2 Negotiation	.2 Resource availability
.3 Roles and responsibilities	.3 Acquisition	.3 Staffing management plan (updates)
.4 Project organization charts	.4 Virtual teams	
.5 Staffing management plan		

Figure 9-7. Acquire Project Team: Inputs, Tools & Techniques, and Outputs

9.2.1 Acquire Project Team: Inputs

.1 Enterprise Environmental Factors

Project team members are drawn from all available sources, both internal and external. When the project management team is able to influence or direct staff assignments, characteristics to consider include:

- **Availability.** Who is available and when are they available?
- **Ability.** What competencies do people possess?
- **Experience.** Have the people done similar or related work? Have they done it well?
- **Interests.** Are the people interested in working on this project?
- **Cost.** How much will each team member be paid, particularly if they are contracted from outside the organization?

.2 Organizational Process Assets

One or more of the organizations involved in the project may have policies, guidelines, or procedures governing staff assignments (Section 4.1.1.4). The human resource departments also can assist with recruitment, hiring and orientation of project team members.

.3 Roles and Responsibilities

Roles and responsibilities define the positions, skills, and competencies that the project demands (Section 9.1.3.1).

.4 Project Organization Charts

Project organization charts provide an overview regarding the number of people needed for the project (Section 9.1.3.2).

.5 Staffing Management Plan

The staffing management plan, along with the project schedule, identifies the time periods each project team member will be needed and other information important to acquiring the project team (Section 9.1.3.3).

9.2.2 Acquire Project Team: Tools and Techniques

.1 Pre-Assignment

In some cases, project team members are known in advance; that is, they are pre-assigned. This situation can occur if the project is the result of specific people being promised as part of a competitive proposal, if the project is dependent on the expertise of particular persons, or if some staff assignments are defined within the project charter.

A Guide to the Project Management Body of Knowledge (PMBOK® Guide) Third Edition
©2004 Project Management Institute, Four Campus Boulevard, Newtown Square, PA 19073-3299 USA

.2 Negotiation

Staff assignments are negotiated on many projects. For example, the project management team may need to negotiate with:

- Functional managers to ensure that the project receives appropriately competent staff in the required time frame, and that project team members will be able to work on the project until their responsibilities are completed
- Other project management teams within the performing organization to appropriately assign scarce or specialized resources.

The project management team's ability to influence others plays an important role in negotiating staff assignments, as do the politics of the organizations involved (Section 2.3.3). For example, a functional manager will weigh the benefits and visibility of competing projects when determining where to assign exceptional performers that all project teams desire.

.3 Acquisition

When the performing organization lacks the in-house staff needed to complete the project, the required services can be acquired from outside sources (Section 12.4.3.1). This can involve hiring individual consultants or subcontracting work to another organization.

.4 Virtual Teams

The use of virtual teams creates new possibilities when acquiring project team members. Virtual teams can be defined as groups of people with a shared goal, who fulfill their roles with little or no time spent meeting face to face. The availability of electronic communication, such as e-mail and video conferencing, has made such teams feasible. The virtual team format makes it possible to:

- Form teams of people from the same company who live in widespread geographic areas
- Add special expertise to a project team, even though the expert is not in the same geographic area
- Incorporate employees who work from home offices
- Form teams of people who work different shifts or hours
- Include people with mobility handicaps
- Move forward with projects that would have been ignored due to travel expenses.

Communications Planning (Section 10.1) becomes increasingly important in a virtual team environment. Additional time may be needed to set clear expectations, develop protocols for confronting conflict, include people in decision-making, and share credit in successes.

9.2.3 Acquire Project Team: Outputs

.1 Project Staff Assignments

The project is staffed when appropriate people have been assigned to work on it. Documentation can include a project team directory, memos to team members, and names inserted into other parts of the project management plan, such as project organization charts and schedules.

.2 Resource Availability

Resource availability documents the time periods each project team member can work on the project. Creating a reliable final schedule (Section 6.5.3.1) depends on having a good understanding of each person's schedule conflicts, including vacation time and commitments to other projects.

.3 Staffing Management Plan (Updates)

As specific people fill the project roles and responsibilities, changes in the staffing management plan (Section 9.1.3.3) may be needed because people seldom fit the exact staffing requirements that are planned. Other reasons for changing the staffing management plan include promotions, retirements, illnesses, performance issues, and changing workloads.

9.3 Develop Project Team

Develop Project Team improves the competencies and interaction of team members to enhance project performance. Objectives include:

- Improve skills of team members in order to increase their ability to complete project activities
- Improve feelings of trust and cohesiveness among team members in order to raise productivity through greater teamwork.

Examples of effective teamwork include assisting one another when workloads are unbalanced, communicating in ways that fit individual preferences, and sharing information and resources. Team development efforts have greater benefit when conducted early, but should take place throughout the project life cycle.

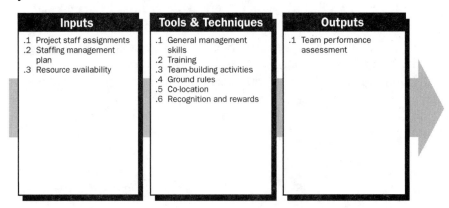

Inputs	Tools & Techniques	Outputs
.1 Project staff assignments .2 Staffing management plan .3 Resource availability	.1 General management skills .2 Training .3 Team-building activities .4 Ground rules .5 Co-location .6 Recognition and rewards	.1 Team performance assessment

Figure 9-8. Develop Project Team: Inputs, Tools & Techniques, and Outputs

9.3.1 Develop Project Team: Inputs

.1 Project Staff Assignments
Team development starts with a list of the project team members. Project staff assignment documents (Section 9.2.3.1) identify the people who are on the team.

.2 Staffing Management Plan
The staffing management plan (Section 9.1.3.3) identifies training strategies and plans for developing the project team. As the project progresses, items such as rewards, feedback, additional training, and disciplinary actions are added to the plan as a result of ongoing team performance assessments (Section 9.3.3.1) and other forms of project team management (Section 9.4.2).

.3 Resource Availability
Resource availability information (Section 9.2.3.2) identifies times that project team members can participate in team development activities.

9.3.2 Develop Project Team: Tools and Techniques

.1 General Management Skills
Interpersonal skills (Section 1.5.5), sometimes known as "soft skills," are particularly important to team development. By understanding the sentiments of project team members, anticipating their actions, acknowledging their concerns, and following up on their issues, the project management team can greatly reduce problems and increase cooperation. Skills such as empathy, influence, creativity, and group facilitation are valuable assets when managing the project team.

.2 Training
Training includes all activities designed to enhance the competencies of the project team members. Training can be formal or informal. Examples of training methods include classroom, online, computer-based, on-the-job training from another project team member, mentoring, and coaching.

If project team members lack necessary management or technical skills, such skills can be developed as part of the project work. Scheduled training takes place as stated in the staffing management plan. Unplanned training takes place as a result of observation, conversation, and project performance appraisals conducted during the controlling process of managing the project team.

.3 Team-Building Activities

Team-building activities can vary from a five-minute agenda item in a status review meeting to an off-site, professionally facilitated experience designed to improve interpersonal relationships. Some group activities, such as developing the WBS, may not be explicitly designed as team-building activities, but can increase team cohesiveness when that planning activity is structured and facilitated well. It also is important to encourage informal communication and activities because of their role in building trust and establishing good working relationships. Team-building strategies are particularly valuable when team members operate virtually from remote locations, without the benefit of face-to-face contact.

.4 Ground Rules

Ground rules establish clear expectations regarding acceptable behavior by project team members. Early commitment to clear guidelines decreases misunderstandings and increases productivity. The process of discussing ground rules allows team members to discover values that are important to one another. All project team members share responsibility for enforcing the rules once they are established.

.5 Co-Location

Co-location involves placing many or all of the most active project team members in the same physical location to enhance their ability to perform as a team. Co-location can be temporary, such as at strategically important times during the project, or for the entire project. Co-location strategy can include a meeting room, sometimes called a war room, with electronic communication devices, places to post schedules, and other conveniences that enhance communication and a sense of community. While co-location is considered good strategy, the use of virtual teams will reduce the frequency that team members are located together.

.6 Recognition and Rewards

Part of the team development process involves recognizing and rewarding desirable behavior. The original plans concerning ways to reward people are developed during Human Resource Planning (Section 9.1). Award decisions are made, formally or informally, during the process of managing the project team through performance appraisals (Section 9.4.2.2).

Only desirable behavior should be rewarded. For example, the willingness to work overtime to meet an aggressive schedule objective should be rewarded or recognized; needing to work overtime as the result of poor planning should not be rewarded. Win-lose (zero sum) rewards that only a limited number of project team members can achieve, such as team member of the month, can hurt team cohesiveness. Rewarding win-win behavior that everyone can achieve, such as turning in progress reports on time, tends to increase support among team members.

Recognition and rewards should consider cultural differences. For example, developing appropriate team rewards in a culture that encourages individualism can be difficult.

A Guide to the Project Management Body of Knowledge (PMBOK® Guide) Third Edition
©2004 Project Management Institute, Four Campus Boulevard, Newtown Square, PA 19073-3299 USA

9.3.3 Develop Project Team: Outputs

.1 Team Performance Assessment

As development efforts such as training, team building, and co-location are implemented, the project management team makes informal or formal assessments of the project team's effectiveness. Effective team development strategies and activities are expected to increase the team's performance, which increases the likelihood of meeting project objectives. The evaluation of a team's effectiveness can include indicators such as:

- Improvements in skills that allow a person to perform assigned activities more effectively
- Improvements in competencies and sentiments that help the team perform better as a group
- Reduced staff turnover rate.

9.4 Manage Project Team

Manage Project Team involves tracking team member performance, providing feedback, resolving issues, and coordinating changes to enhance project performance. The project management team observes team behavior, manages conflict, resolves issues, and appraises team member performance. As a result of managing the project team, the staffing management plan is updated, change requests are submitted, issues are resolved, input is given to organizational performance appraisals, and lessons learned are added to the organization's database.

Management of the project team is complicated when team members are accountable to both a functional manager and the project manager within a matrix organization (Section 2.3.3). Effective management of this dual reporting relationship is often a critical success factor for the project, and is generally the responsibility of the project manager.

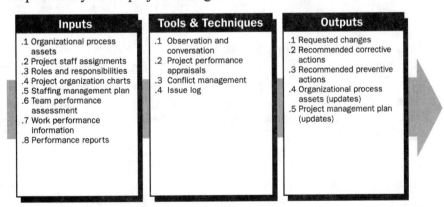

Inputs	Tools & Techniques	Outputs
.1 Organizational process assets .2 Project staff assignments .3 Roles and responsibilities .4 Project organization charts .5 Staffing management plan .6 Team performance assessment .7 Work performance information .8 Performance reports	.1 Observation and conversation .2 Project performance appraisals .3 Conflict management .4 Issue log	.1 Requested changes .2 Recommended corrective actions .3 Recommended preventive actions .4 Organizational process assets (updates) .5 Project management plan (updates)

Figure 9-9. Manage Project Team: Inputs, Tools & Techniques, and Outputs

9.4.1 Manage Project Team: Inputs

.1 Organizational Process Assets

The project management team should utilize an organization's policies, procedures, and systems for rewarding employees during the course of a project (Section 4.1.1.4). Organizational recognition dinners, certificates of appreciation, newsletters, bulletin boards, Web sites, bonus structures, corporate apparel, and other organizational perquisites should be available to the project management team as part of the project management process.

.2 Project Staff Assignments

Project staff assignments (Section 9.2.3.1) provide a list of the project team members to be evaluated during this monitoring and controlling process.

.3 Roles and Responsibilities

A list of the staff's roles and responsibilities is used to monitor and evaluate performance (Section 9.1.3.1).

.4 Project Organization Charts

Project organization charts provide a picture of the reporting relationships among project team members (Section 9.1.3.2).

.5 Staffing Management Plan

The staffing management plan lists the time periods that team members are expected to work on the project, along with information such as training plans, certification requirements, and compliance issues (Section 9.1.3.3).

.6 Team Performance Assessment

The project management team makes ongoing formal or informal assessments of the project team's performance (Section 9.3.3.1). By continually assessing the project team's performance, actions can be taken to resolve issues, modify communication, address conflict, and improve team interaction.

.7 Work Performance Information

As part of the Direct and Manage Project Execution process (Section 4.4), the project management team directly observes team member performance as it occurs. Observations related to areas such as a team member's meeting participation, follow-up on action items, and communication clarity are considered when managing the project team.

.8 Performance Reports

Performance reports (Section 10.3.3.1) provide documentation about performance against the project management plan. Examples of performance areas that can help with project team management include results from schedule control, cost control, quality control, scope verification, and procurement audits. The information from performance reports and related forecasts assists in determining future human resource requirements, recognition and rewards, and updates to the staffing management plan.

9.4.2 Manage Project Team: Tools and Techniques

.1 Observation and Conversation

Observation and conversation are used to stay in touch with the work and attitudes of project team members. The project management team monitors indicators such as progress toward project deliverables, accomplishments that are a source of pride for team members, and interpersonal issues.

.2 Project Performance Appraisals

The need for formal or informal project performance appraisals depends on the length of the project, complexity of the project, organizational policy, labor contract requirements, and the amount and quality of regular communication. Project team members receive feedback from the people who supervise their project work. Evaluation information also can be gathered from people who interact with project team members by using 360-degree feedback principles. The term "360-degree" means that feedback regarding performance is provided to the person being evaluated from many sources, including superiors, peers, and subordinates.

Objectives for conducting performance appraisals during the course of a project can include reclarification of roles and responsibilities, structured time to ensure team members receive positive feedback in what might otherwise be a hectic environment, discovery of unknown or unresolved issues, development of individual training plans, and the establishment of specific goals for future time periods.

.3 Conflict Management

Successful conflict management results in greater productivity and positive working relationships. Sources of conflict include scarce resources, scheduling priorities, and personal work styles. Team ground rules, group norms, and solid project management practices, like communication planning and role definition, reduce the amount of conflict. When managed properly, differences of opinion are healthy, and can lead to increased creativity and better decision-making. When the differences become a negative factor, project team members are initially responsible for resolving their own conflicts. If conflict escalates, the project manager should help facilitate a satisfactory resolution. Conflict should be addressed early and usually in private, using a direct, collaborative approach. If disruptive conflict continues, increasingly formal procedures will need to be used, including the possible use of disciplinary actions.

.4 Issue Log

As issues arise in the course of managing the project team, a written log can document persons responsible for resolving specific issues by a target date. The log helps the project team monitor issues until closure. Issue resolution addresses obstacles that can block the team from achieving its goals. These obstacles can include factors such as differences of opinion, situations to be investigated, and emerging or unanticipated responsibilities that need to be assigned to someone on the project team.

9.4.3 Manage Project Team: Outputs

.1 Requested Changes

Staffing changes, whether by choice or by uncontrollable events, can affect the rest of the project plan. When staffing issues are going to disrupt the project plan, such as causing the schedule to be extended or the budget to be exceeded, a change request can be processed through the Integrated Change Control process (Section 4.6).

.2 Recommended Corrective Actions

Corrective action for human resource management includes items such as staffing changes, additional training, and disciplinary actions. Staffing changes can include moving people to different assignments, outsourcing some work, and replacing team members who leave. The project management team also determines how and when to give out recognition and rewards based on the team's performance.

.3 Recommended Preventive Actions

When the project management team identifies potential or emerging human resource issues, preventive action can be developed to reduce the probability and/or impact of problems before they occur. Preventive actions can include cross-training in order to reduce problems during project team member absences, additional role clarification to ensure all responsibilities are fulfilled, and added personal time in anticipation of extra work that may be needed in the near future to meet project deadlines.

.4 Organizational Process Assets (Updates)

- **Input to organizational performance appraisals.** Project staff generally should be prepared to provide input for regular organizational performance appraisals of any project team member with whom they interact in a significant way.

A Guide to the Project Management Body of Knowledge (PMBOK® Guide) Third Edition
©2004 Project Management Institute, Four Campus Boulevard, Newtown Square, PA 19073-3299 USA

- **Lessons learned documentation.** All knowledge learned during the project should be documented so it becomes part of the historical database of the organization. Lessons learned in the area of human resources can include:
  - ◆ Project organization charts, position descriptions, and staffing management plans that can be saved as templates
  - ◆ Ground rules, conflict management techniques, and recognition events that were particularly useful
  - ◆ Procedures for virtual teams, co-location, negotiation, training, and team building that proved to be successful
  - ◆ Special skills or competencies by team members that were discovered during the project
  - ◆ Issues and solutions documented in the project issue log.

.5 Project Management Plan (Updates)

Approved change requests and corrective actions can result in updates to the staffing management plan, a part of the project management plan. Examples of plan update information include new project team member roles, additional training, and reward decisions.

9

CHAPTER 10

Project Communications Management

Project Communications Management is the Knowledge Area that employs the processes required to ensure timely and appropriate generation, collection, distribution, storage, retrieval, and ultimate disposition of project information. The Project Communications Management processes provide the critical links among people and information that are necessary for successful communications. Project managers can spend an inordinate amount of time communicating with the project team, stakeholders, customer, and sponsor. Everyone involved in the project should understand how communications affect the project as a whole. Figure 10-1 provides an overview of the Project Communications Management processes, and Figure 10-2 provides a process flow diagram of those processes and their inputs, outputs, and other related Knowledge Area processes. The Project Communications Management processes include the following:

10.1 Communications Planning – determining the information and communications needs of the project stakeholders.

10.2 Information Distribution – making needed information available to project stakeholders in a timely manner.

10.3 Performance Reporting – collecting and distributing performance information. This includes status reporting, progress measurement, and forecasting.

10.4 Manage Stakeholders – managing communications to satisfy the requirements of and resolve issues with project stakeholders.

These processes interact with each other and with the processes in the other Knowledge Areas as well. Each process can involve effort from one or more persons or groups of persons based on the needs of the project. Each process occurs at least once in every project and occurs in one or more project phases, if the project is divided into phases. Although the processes are presented here as discrete elements with well-defined interfaces, in practice they may overlap and interact in ways not detailed here. Process interactions are discussed in detail in Chapter 3.

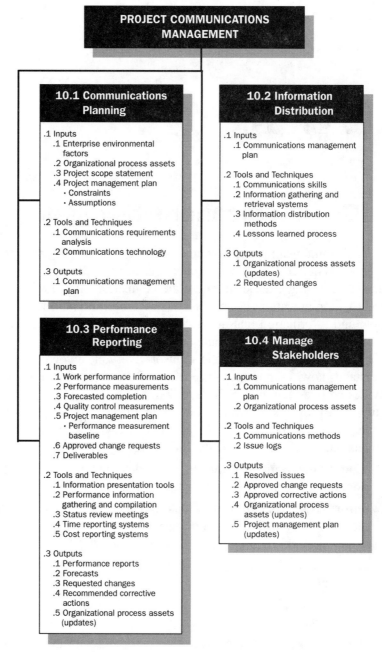

Figure 10-1. Project Communications Management Overview

A Guide to the Project Management Body of Knowledge (PMBOK® Guide) Third Edition
©2004 Project Management Institute, Four Campus Boulevard, Newtown Square, PA 19073-3299 USA

Note: Not all process interactions and data flow among the processes are shown.

Figure 10-2. Project Communications Management Process Flow Diagram

Communications skills are related to, but are not the same as, project management communications. The art of communications is a broad subject and involves a substantial body of knowledge including:

- **Sender-receiver models.** Feedback loops and barriers to communication.
- **Choice of media.** When to communicate in writing versus orally, when to write an informal memo versus a formal report, and when to communicate face-to-face versus by e-mail. The media chosen for communication activities will depend upon the situation.
- **Writing style.** Active versus passive voice, sentence structure, and word choice.

- **Presentation techniques.** Body language and design of visual aids.
- **Meeting management techniques.** Preparing an agenda and dealing with conflict.

A basic model of communication, shown in Figure 10-3, demonstrates how ideas or information is sent and received between two parties, defined as the sender and the receiver. The key components of the model include:

- **Encode.** To translate thoughts or ideas into a language that is understood by others.
- **Message.** The output of encoding.
- **Medium.** The method used to convey the message.
- **Noise.** Anything that interferes with the transmission and understanding of the message (e.g., distance).
- **Decode.** To translate the message back into meaningful thoughts or ideas.

Inherent in the model shown in Figure 10-3 is an action to acknowledge a message. Acknowledgement means that the receiver signals receipt of the message, but not necessarily agreement with the message. Another action is the response to a message, which means that the receiver has decoded, understands, and is replying to the message.

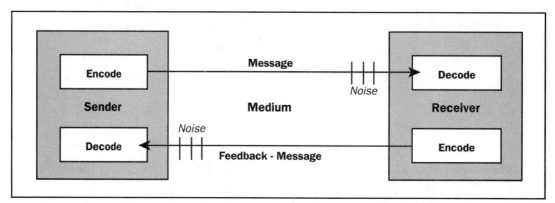

Figure 10-3. Communication – Basic Model

The components in the communications model need to be taken into account when discussing project communications. There are many challenges in using these components to effectively communicate with project stakeholders. Consider a highly technical, multi-national project team. For one team member to successfully communicate a technical concept to another team member in a different country can involve encoding the message in the appropriate language, sending the message using a variety of technologies, and having the receiver decode the message. Any noise introduced along the way compromises the original meaning of the message. A breakdown in communications can negatively impact the project.

10.1 Communications Planning

The Communications Planning process determines the information and communications needs of the stakeholders; for example, who needs what information, when they will need it, how it will be given to them, and by whom. While all projects share the need to communicate project information, the informational needs and methods of distribution vary widely. Identifying the informational needs of the stakeholders and determining a suitable means of meeting those needs is an important factor for project success.

On most projects, the majority of Communications Planning is done as part of the earliest project phases. However, the results of this planning process are reviewed regularly throughout the project and revised as needed to ensure continued applicability.

Communications Planning is often tightly linked with enterprise environmental factors (Section 4.1.1.3) and organizational influences (Section 2.3), since the project's organizational structure will have a major effect on the project's communications requirements.

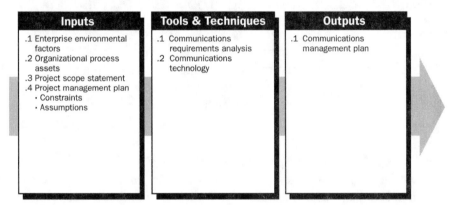

Figure 10-4. Communications Planning: Inputs, Tools & Techniques, and Outputs

10.1.1 Communications Planning: Inputs

.1 Enterprise Environmental Factors
All the factors described in Section 4.1.1.3 are used as inputs for this process.

.2 Organizational Process Assets
While all of the assets described in Section 4.1.1.4 are used as inputs for this process, lessons learned and historical information are of particular importance. Lessons learned and historical information can provide both decisions and results based on previous similar projects concerning communications issues.

.3 Project Scope Statement

The project scope statement (Section 5.2.3.1) provides a documented basis for future project decisions and for confirming a common knowledge of project scope among the stakeholders. Stakeholder analysis is completed as part of the Scope Definition process.

.4 Project Management Plan

The project management plan (Section 4.3) provides background information about the project, including dates and constraints that may be relevant to Communications Planning.

- **Constraints.** Constraints are factors that can limit the project management team's options. Examples of constraints include team members situated in different geographic locations, incompatible communication software versions, or limited communications technical capabilities.
- **Assumptions.** Specific assumptions that affect Communications Planning will depend upon the particular project.

10.1.2 Communications Planning: Tools and Techniques

.1 Communications Requirements Analysis

The analysis of the communications requirements results in the sum of the information needs of the project stakeholders. These requirements are defined by combining the type and format of information needed with an analysis of the value of that information. Project resources are expended only on communicating information that contributes to success, or where a lack of communication can lead to failure. This does not mean that "bad news" should not be shared; rather, the intent is to prevent overwhelming stakeholders with minutiae.

The project manager should consider the number of potential communication channels or paths as an indicator of the complexity of a project's communications.

The total number of communication channels is $n(n-1)/2$, where n = number of stakeholders. Thus, a project with 10 stakeholders has 45 potential communication channels. A key component of planning the project's communications, therefore, is to determine and limit who will communicate with whom and who will receive what information. Information typically required to determine project communications requirements includes:

- Organization charts
- Project organization and stakeholder responsibility relationships
- Disciplines, departments, and specialties involved in the project
- Logistics of how many persons will be involved with the project and at which locations
- Internal information needs (e.g., communicating across organizations)
- External information needs (e.g., communicating with the media or contractors)
- Stakeholder information.

A Guide to the Project Management Body of Knowledge (PMBOK® Guide) Third Edition
©2004 Project Management Institute, Four Campus Boulevard, Newtown Square, PA 19073-3299 USA

.2 Communications Technology

The methodologies used to transfer information among project stakeholders can vary significantly. For example, a project management team may include brief conversations all the way through to extended meetings, or simple written documents to material (e.g., schedules and databases) that is accessible online as methods of communication.

Communications technology factors that can affect the project include:

- **The urgency of the need for information.** Is project success dependent upon having frequently updated information available on a moment's notice, or would regularly issued written reports suffice?
- **The availability of technology.** Are the systems already in place appropriate, or do project needs warrant change?
- **The expected project staffing.** Are the proposed communications systems compatible with the experience and expertise of the project participants, or is extensive training and learning required?
- **The length of the project.** Is the available technology likely to change before the project is over?
- **The project environment.** Does the team meet and operate on a face-to-face basis or in a virtual environment?

10.1.3 Communications Planning: Outputs

.1 Communications Management Plan

The communications management plan is contained in, or is a subsidiary plan of, the project management plan (Section 4.3). The communications management plan provides:

- Stakeholder communication requirements
- Information to be communicated, including format, content, and level of detail
- Person responsible for communicating the information
- Person or groups who will receive the information
- Methods or technologies used to convey the information, such as memoranda, e-mail, and/or press releases
- Frequency of the communication, such as weekly
- Escalation process-identifying time frames and the management chain (names) for escalation of issues that cannot be resolved at a lower staff level
- Method for updating and refining the communications management plan as the project progresses and develops
- Glossary of common terminology.

The communications management plan can also include guidelines for project status meetings, project team meetings, e-meetings, and e-mail. The communications management plan can be formal or informal, highly detailed or broadly framed, and based on the needs of the project. The communications management plan is contained in, or is a subsidiary plan of, the overall project management plan (Section 4.3). Sample attributes of a communications management plan can include:

- **Communications item.** The information that will be distributed to stakeholders.
- **Purpose.** The reason for the distribution of that information.
- **Frequency.** How often that information will be distributed.
- **Start/end dates.** The time frame for the distribution of the information.
- **Format/medium.** The layout of the information and the method of transmission.
- **Responsibility.** The team member charged with the distribution of information.

Communication Planning often entails creation of additional deliverables that, in turn, require additional time and effort. Thus, the project's work breakdown structure, project schedule, and project budget are updated accordingly.

10.2 Information Distribution

Information Distribution involves making information available to project stakeholders in a timely manner. Information distribution includes implementing the communications management plan, as well as responding to unexpected requests for information.

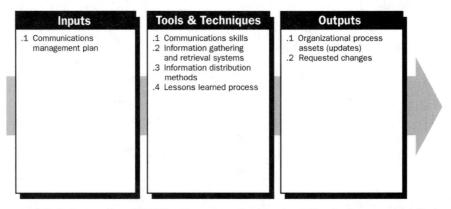

Inputs	Tools & Techniques	Outputs
.1 Communications management plan	.1 Communications skills .2 Information gathering and retrieval systems .3 Information distribution methods .4 Lessons learned process	.1 Organizational process assets (updates) .2 Requested changes

Figure 10-5. Information Distribution: Inputs, Tools & Techniques, and Outputs

A Guide to the Project Management Body of Knowledge (PMBOK® Guide) Third Edition
©2004 Project Management Institute, Four Campus Boulevard, Newtown Square, PA 19073-3299 USA

10.2.1 Information Distribution: Inputs

.1 Communications Management Plan
Described in Section 10.1.3.1.

10.2.2 Information Distribution: Tools and Techniques

.1 Communications Skills
Communications skills are part of general management skills and are used to exchange information. General management skills related to communications include ensuring that the right persons get the right information at the right time, as defined in the communications management plan. General management skills also include the art of managing stakeholder requirements.

As part of the communications process, the sender is responsible for making the information clear and complete so that the receiver can receive it correctly, and for confirming that it is properly understood. The receiver is responsible for making sure that the information is received in its entirety and understood correctly. Communicating has many dimensions:

- Written and oral, listening, and speaking
- Internal (within the project) and external (customer, the media, the public)
- Formal (reports, briefings) and informal (memos, ad hoc conversations)
- Vertical (up and down the organization) and horizontal (with peers).

.2 Information Gathering and Retrieval Systems
Information can be gathered and retrieved through a variety of media including manual filing systems, electronic databases, project management software, and systems that allow access to technical documentation, such as engineering drawings, design specifications, and test plans.

.3 Information Distribution Methods
Information Distribution is information collection, sharing, and distribution to project stakeholders in a timely manner across the project life cycle. Project information can be distributed using a variety of methods, including:

- Project meetings, hard-copy document distribution, manual filing systems, and shared-access electronic databases
- Electronic communication and conferencing tools, such as e-mail, fax, voice mail, telephone, video and Web conferencing, and Web publishing
- Electronic tools for project management, such as Web interfaces to scheduling and project management software, meeting and virtual office support software, portals, and collaborative work management tools.

10

.4 Lessons Learned Process

A lessons learned session focuses on identifying project successes and project failures, and includes recommendations to improve future performance on projects. During the project life cycle, the project team and key stakeholders identify lessons learned concerning the technical, managerial, and process aspects of the project. The lessons learned are compiled, formalized, and stored through the project's duration.

The focus of lessons learned meetings can vary. In some cases, the focus is on strong technical or product development processes, while in other cases, the focus is on the processes that aided or hindered performance of the work. Teams can gather information more frequently if they feel that the increased quantity of data merits the additional investment of time and money. Lessons learned provide future project teams with the information that can increase effectiveness and efficiency of project management. In addition, phase-end lessons learned sessions provide a good team-building exercise. Project managers have a professional obligation to conduct lessons learned sessions for all projects with key internal and external stakeholders, particularly if the project yielded less than desirable results. Some specific results from lessons learned include:

- Update of the lessons learned knowledge base
- Input to knowledge management system
- Updated corporate policies, procedures, and processes
- Improved business skills
- Overall product and service improvements
- Updates to the risk management plan.

10.2.3 Information Distribution: Outputs

.1 Organizational Process Assets (Updates)

- **Lessons learned documentation.** Documentation includes the causes of issues, reasoning behind the corrective action chosen, and other types of lessons learned about Information Distribution. Lessons learned are documented so that they become part of the historical database for both this project and the performing organization.
- **Project records.** Project records can include correspondence, memos, and documents describing the project. This information should, to the extent possible and appropriate, be maintained in an organized fashion. Project team members can also maintain records in a project notebook.
- **Project reports.** Formal and informal project reports detail project status, and include lessons learned, issues logs, project closure reports, and outputs from other Knowledge Areas (Chapters 4–12).

- **Project presentations.** The project team provides information formally or informally to any or all of the project stakeholders. The information is relevant to the needs of the audience, and the method of presentation is appropriate.
- **Feedback from stakeholders.** Information received from stakeholders concerning project operations can be distributed and used to modify or improve future performance of the project.
- **Stakeholder notifications.** Information may be provided to stakeholders about resolved issues, approved changes, and general project status.

.2 Requested Changes

Changes to the Information Distribution process should trigger changes to the project management plan and the communications management plan. Requested changes (additions, modifications, revisions) to the project management plan and its subsidiary plans are reviewed, and the disposition is managed through the Integrated Change Control process (Section 4.6).

10.3 Performance Reporting

The performance reporting process involves the collection of all baseline data, and distribution of performance information to stakeholders. Generally, this performance information includes how resources are being used to achieve project objectives. Performance reporting should generally provide information on scope, schedule, cost, and quality. Many projects also require information on risk and procurement. Reports may be prepared comprehensively or on an exception basis.

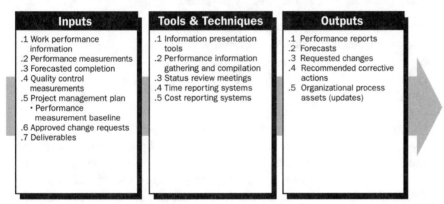

Inputs	Tools & Techniques	Outputs
.1 Work performance information .2 Performance measurements .3 Forecasted completion .4 Quality control measurements .5 Project management plan • Performance measurement baseline .6 Approved change requests .7 Deliverables	.1 Information presentation tools .2 Performance information gathering and compilation .3 Status review meetings .4 Time reporting systems .5 Cost reporting systems	.1 Performance reports .2 Forecasts .3 Requested changes .4 Recommended corrective actions .5 Organizational process assets (updates)

Figure 10-6. Performance Reporting: Inputs, Tools & Techniques, and Outputs

10.3.1 Performance Reporting: Inputs

.1 Work Performance Information

Work performance information on the completion status of the deliverables and what has been accomplished is collected as part of project execution, and is fed into the Performance Reporting process. Collecting the work performance information is discussed in further detail in the Direct and Manage Project Execution process (Section 4.4).

.2 Performance Measurements

Described in Section 6.6.3.3 and Section 7.3.3.3.

.3 Forecasted Completion

Described in Section 7.3.3.4.

.4 Quality Control Measurements

Described in Section 8.3.3.1.

.5 Project Management Plan

The project management plan provides baseline information (Section 4.3).

- **Performance measurement baseline.** An approved plan for the project work against which project execution is compared, and deviations are measured for management control. The performance measurement baseline typically integrates scope, schedule, and cost parameters of a project, but may also include technical and quality parameters.

.6 Approved Change Requests

Approved change requests (Section 4.6.3.1) are requested changes to expand or contract project scope, to modify the estimated cost, or to revise activity duration estimates that have been approved and are ready for implementation by the project team.

.7 Deliverables

Deliverables (Section 4.4.3.1) are any unique and verifiable product, result, or capability to perform a service that must be produced to complete a process, phase, or project. The term is often used more narrowly in reference to an external deliverable that is subject to approval by the project sponsor or customer.

10.3.2 Performance Reporting: Tools and Techniques

.1 Information Presentation Tools

Software packages that include table reporting, spreadsheet analysis, presentations, or graphic capabilities can be used to create presentation-quality images of project performance data.

A Guide to the Project Management Body of Knowledge (PMBOK® Guide) Third Edition
©2004 Project Management Institute, Four Campus Boulevard, Newtown Square, PA 19073-3299 USA

.2 Performance Information Gathering and Compilation

Information can be gathered and compiled from a variety of media including manual filing systems, electronic databases, project management software, and systems that allow access to technical documentation, such as engineering drawings, design specifications and test plans, to produce forecasts as well as performance, status and progress reports.

.3 Status Review Meetings

Status review meetings are regularly scheduled events to exchange information about the project. On most projects, status review meetings will be held at various frequencies and on different levels. For example, the project management team can meet weekly by itself and monthly with the customer.

.4 Time Reporting Systems

Time reporting systems record and provide time expended for the project.

.5 Cost Reporting Systems

Cost reporting systems record and provide the cost expended for the project.

10.3.3 Performance Reporting: Outputs

.1 Performance Reports

Performance reports organize and summarize the information gathered, and present the results of any analysis as compared to the performance measurement baseline. Reports should provide the status and progress information, and the level of detail required by various stakeholders, as documented in the communications management plan. Common formats for performance reports include bar charts, S-curves, histograms, and tables. Earned value analysis data is often included as part of performance reporting. While S-curves, such as those in Figure 7-7, can display one view of earned value analysis data, Figure 10-7 gives a tabular view of earned value data.

WBS Element	Planned	Earned	Cost	Cost Variance		Schedule Variance		Performance Index	
	Budget	Earned Value	Actual Cost					Cost	Schedule
	($) (PV)	($) (EV)	($) (AC)	($) (EV – AC)	(%) (CV ÷ EV)	($) (EV – PV)	(%) (SV ÷ PV)	CPI (EV ÷ AC)	SPI (EV ÷ PV)
1.0 Pre-Pilot Plan	63,000	58,000	62,500	-4,500	-7.8	-5,000	-7.9	0.93	0.92
2.0 Checklists	64,000	48,000	46,800	1,200	2.5	-16,000	-25.0	1.03	0.75
3.0 Curriculum	23,000	20,000	23,500	-3,500	-17.5	-3,000	-13.0	0.85	0.87
4.0 Mid-Term Evaluation	68,000	68,000	72,500	-4,500	-6.6	0	0.0	0.94	1.00
5.0 Implementation Support	12,000	10,000	10,000	0	0.0	-2,000	-16.7	1.00	0.83
6.0 Manual of Practice	7,000	6,200	6,000	200	3.2	-800	-11.4	1.03	0.89
7.0 Roll-Out Plan	20,000	13,500	18,100	-4,600	-34.1	-6,500	-32.5	.075	0.68
Totals	257,000	223,700	239,400	-15,700	-7.0	-33,300	-13.0	0.93	0.87

Note: All figures are project-to-date
*Other units of measure that may be used in these calculations may include: labor hours, cubic yards of concrete, etc.

Figure 10-7 Tabular Performance Report Sample

.2 Forecasts

Forecasts are updated and reissued based on work performance information provided as the project is executed. This information is about the project's past performance that could impact the project in the future, for example, estimate at completion and estimate to complete.

.3 Requested Changes

Analysis of project performance often generates requested changes (Section 4.4.3.2) to some aspect of the project. These requested changes are processed and dispositioned through the Integrated Change Control process (Section 4.6).

.4 Recommended Corrective Actions

Recommended corrective actions (Section 4.5.3.1) include changes that bring the expected future performance of the project in line with the project management plan.

.5 Organizational Process Assets (Updates)

Lessons learned documentation includes the causes of issues, reasoning behind the corrective action chosen, and other types of lessons learned about performance reporting. Lessons learned are documented so that they become part of the historical database for both this project and the performing organization.

A Guide to the Project Management Body of Knowledge (PMBOK® Guide) Third Edition
©2004 Project Management Institute, Four Campus Boulevard, Newtown Square, PA 19073-3299 USA

10.4 Manage Stakeholders

Stakeholder management refers to managing communications to satisfy the needs of, and resolve issues with, project stakeholders. Actively managing stakeholders increases the likelihood that the project will not veer off track due to unresolved stakeholder issues, enhances the ability of persons to operate synergistically, and limits disruptions during the project. The project manager is usually responsible for stakeholder management.

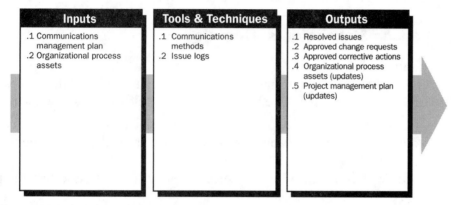

Figure 10-8. Manage Stakeholders: Inputs, Tools & Techniques, and Outputs

10.4.1 Manage Stakeholders: Inputs

.1 Communications Management Plan

Stakeholder requirements and expectations provide an understanding of stakeholder goals, objectives, and level of communication during the project. The needs and expectations are identified, analyzed, and documented in the communications management plan (Section 10.1.3.1), which is a subsidiary of the project management plan.

.2 Organizational Process Assets

As project issues arise, the project manager should address and resolve them with the appropriate project stakeholders.

10.4.2 Manage Stakeholders: Tools and Techniques

.1 Communications Methods

The methods of communications identified for each stakeholder in the communications management plan are utilized during stakeholder management.

Face-to-face meetings are the most effective means for communicating and resolving issues with stakeholders. When face-to-face meetings are not warranted or practical (such as on international projects), telephone calls, electronic mail, and other electronic tools are useful for exchanging information and dialoguing.

.2 Issue Logs

An issue log or action-item log is a tool that can be used to document and monitor the resolution of issues. Issues do not usually rise to the importance of becoming a project or activity, but are usually addressed in order to maintain good, constructive working relationships among various stakeholders, including team members.

An issue is clarified and stated in a way that it can be resolved. An owner is assigned and a target date is usually established for closure. Unresolved issues can be a major source of conflict and project delays.

10.4.3 Manage Stakeholders: Outputs

.1 Resolved Issues

As stakeholder requirements are identified and resolved, the issues log will document concerns that have been addressed and closed. Examples include:

- Customers agree to a follow-on contract, which ends protracted discussion of whether requested changes to project scope are within or outside the scope of the current project
- More staff is added to the project, thus closing the issue that the project is short on required skills
- Negotiations with functional managers in the organization competing for scarce human resources end in a mutually satisfactory solution before causing project delays
- Issues raised by board members about the financial viability of the project have been answered, allowing the project to move forward as planned.

.2 Approved Change Requests

Approved change requests (Section 4.6.3.1) include stakeholder issue status changes in the staffing management plan, which are necessary to reflect changes to how communications with stakeholders will occur.

.3 Approved Corrective Actions

Approved corrective actions (Section 4.6.3.5) include changes that bring the expected future performance of the project in line with the project management plan.

.4 Organizational Process Assets (Updates)

Lessons learned documentation includes the causes of issues, the reasoning behind the corrective action chosen, and other types of lessons learned about stakeholder management. Lessons learned are documented so that they become part of the historical database for both this project and the performing organization.

.5 Project Management Plan (Updates)

The project management plan is updated to reflect the changes made to the communications plan.

CHAPTER 11

Project Risk Management

Project Risk Management includes the processes concerned with conducting risk management planning, identification, analysis, responses, and monitoring and control on a project; most of these processes are updated throughout the project. The objectives of Project Risk Management are to increase the probability and impact of positive events, and decrease the probability and impact of events adverse to the project. Figure 11-1 provides an overview of the Project Risk Management processes, and Figure 11-2 provides a process flow diagram of those processes and their inputs, outputs, and other related Knowledge Area processes. The Project Risk Management processes include the following:

11.1 Risk Management Planning – deciding how to approach, plan, and execute the risk management activities for a project.

11.2 Risk Identification – determining which risks might affect the project and documenting their characteristics.

11.3 Qualitative Risk Analysis – prioritizing risks for subsequent further analysis or action by assessing and combining their probability of occurrence and impact.

11.4 Quantitative Risk Analysis – numerically analyzing the effect on overall project objectives of identified risks.

11.5 Risk Response Planning – developing options and actions to enhance opportunities, and to reduce threats to project objectives.

11.6 Risk Monitoring and Control – tracking identified risks, monitoring residual risks, identifying new risks, executing risk response plans, and evaluating their effectiveness throughout the project life cycle.

These processes interact with each other and with the processes in the other Knowledge Areas as well. Each process can involve effort from one or more persons or groups of persons based on the needs of the project. Each process occurs at least once in every project and occurs in one or more project phases, if the project is divided into phases. Although the processes are presented here as discrete elements with well-defined interfaces, in practice they may overlap and interact in ways not detailed here. Process interactions are discussed in detail in Chapter 3.

11

Project risk is an uncertain event or condition that, if it occurs, has a positive or a negative effect on at least one project objective, such as time, cost, scope, or quality (i.e., where the project time objective is to deliver in accordance with the agreed-upon schedule; where the project cost objective is to deliver within the agreed-upon cost; etc.). A risk may have one or more causes and, if it occurs, one or more impacts. For example, a cause may be requiring an environmental permit to do work, or having limited personnel assigned to design the project. The risk event is that the permitting agency may take longer than planned to issue a permit, or the design personnel available and assigned may not be adequate for the activity. If either of these uncertain events occurs, there may be an impact on the project cost, schedule, or performance. Risk conditions could include aspects of the project's or organization's environment that may contribute to project risk, such as poor project management practices, lack of integrated management systems, concurrent multiple projects, or dependency on external participants who cannot be controlled.

A Guide to the Project Management Body of Knowledge (PMBOK® Guide) Third Edition
©2004 Project Management Institute, Four Campus Boulevard, Newtown Square, PA 19073-3299 USA

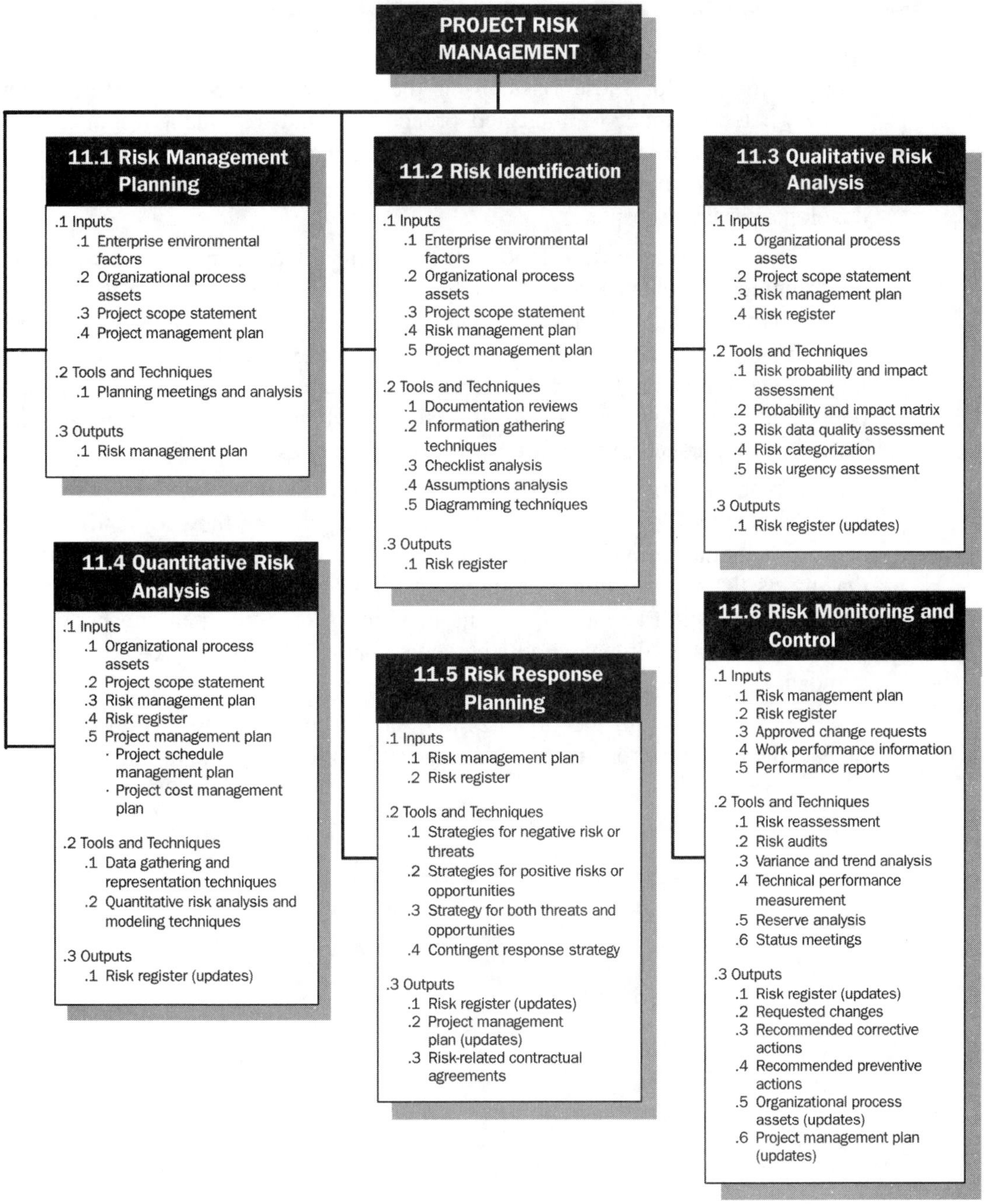

PROJECT RISK MANAGEMENT

11.1 Risk Management Planning

.1 Inputs
  .1 Enterprise environmental factors
  .2 Organizational process assets
  .3 Project scope statement
  .4 Project management plan

.2 Tools and Techniques
  .1 Planning meetings and analysis

.3 Outputs
  .1 Risk management plan

11.2 Risk Identification

.1 Inputs
  .1 Enterprise environmental factors
  .2 Organizational process assets
  .3 Project scope statement
  .4 Risk management plan
  .5 Project management plan

.2 Tools and Techniques
  .1 Documentation reviews
  .2 Information gathering techniques
  .3 Checklist analysis
  .4 Assumptions analysis
  .5 Diagramming techniques

.3 Outputs
  .1 Risk register

11.3 Qualitative Risk Analysis

.1 Inputs
  .1 Organizational process assets
  .2 Project scope statement
  .3 Risk management plan
  .4 Risk register

.2 Tools and Techniques
  .1 Risk probability and impact assessment
  .2 Probability and impact matrix
  .3 Risk data quality assessment
  .4 Risk categorization
  .5 Risk urgency assessment

.3 Outputs
  .1 Risk register (updates)

11.4 Quantitative Risk Analysis

.1 Inputs
  .1 Organizational process assets
  .2 Project scope statement
  .3 Risk management plan
  .4 Risk register
  .5 Project management plan
    · Project schedule management plan
    · Project cost management plan

.2 Tools and Techniques
  .1 Data gathering and representation techniques
  .2 Quantitative risk analysis and modeling techniques

.3 Outputs
  .1 Risk register (updates)

11.5 Risk Response Planning

.1 Inputs
  .1 Risk management plan
  .2 Risk register

.2 Tools and Techniques
  .1 Strategies for negative risk or threats
  .2 Strategies for positive risks or opportunities
  .3 Strategy for both threats and opportunities
  .4 Contingent response strategy

.3 Outputs
  .1 Risk register (updates)
  .2 Project management plan (updates)
  .3 Risk-related contractual agreements

11.6 Risk Monitoring and Control

.1 Inputs
  .1 Risk management plan
  .2 Risk register
  .3 Approved change requests
  .4 Work performance information
  .5 Performance reports

.2 Tools and Techniques
  .1 Risk reassessment
  .2 Risk audits
  .3 Variance and trend analysis
  .4 Technical performance measurement
  .5 Reserve analysis
  .6 Status meetings

.3 Outputs
  .1 Risk register (updates)
  .2 Requested changes
  .3 Recommended corrective actions
  .4 Recommended preventive actions
  .5 Organizational process assets (updates)
  .6 Project management plan (updates)

11

Figure 11-1. Project Risk Management Overview

Project risk has its origins in the uncertainty that is present in all projects. Known risks are those that have been identified and analyzed, and it may be possible to plan for those risks using the processes described in this chapter. Unknown risks cannot be managed proactively, and a prudent response by the project team can be to allocate general contingency against such risks, as well as against any known risks for which it may not be cost-effective or possible to develop a proactive response.

Organizations perceive risk as it relates to threats to project success, or to opportunities to enhance chances of project success. Risks that are threats to the project may be accepted if the risk is in balance with the reward that may be gained by taking the risk. For example, adopting a fast track schedule (Section 6.5.2.3) that may be overrun is a risk taken to achieve an earlier completion date. Risks that are opportunities, such as work acceleration that may be gained by assigning additional staff, may be pursued to benefit the project's objectives.

Persons and, by extension, organizations have attitudes toward risk that affect both the accuracy of the perception of risk and the way they respond. Attitudes about risk should be made explicit wherever possible. A consistent approach to risk that meets the organization's requirements should be developed for each project, and communication about risk and its handling should be open and honest. Risk responses reflect an organization's perceived balance between risk-taking and risk-avoidance.

To be successful, the organization should be committed to addressing the management of risk proactively and consistently throughout the project.

A Guide to the Project Management Body of Knowledge (PMBOK® Guide) Third Edition
©2004 Project Management Institute, Four Campus Boulevard, Newtown Square, PA 19073-3299 USA

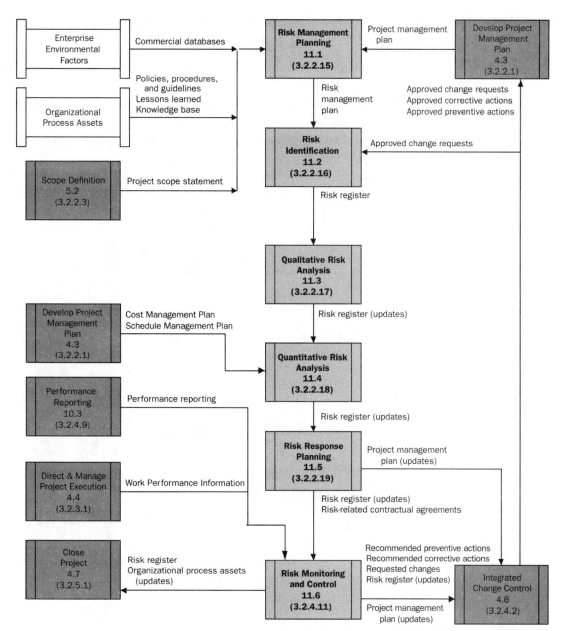

Note: Not all process interactions and data flow among the processes are shown.

Figure 11-2. Project Risk Management Process Flow Diagram

11.1　Risk Management Planning

Careful and explicit planning enhances the possibility of success of the five other risk management processes. Risk Management Planning is the process of deciding how to approach and conduct the risk management activities for a project. Planning of risk management processes is important to ensure that the level, type, and visibility of risk management are commensurate with both the risk and importance of the project to the organization, to provide sufficient resources and time for risk management activities, and to establish an agreed-upon basis for evaluating risks. The Risk Management Planning process should be completed early during project planning, since it is crucial to successfully performing the other processes described in this chapter.

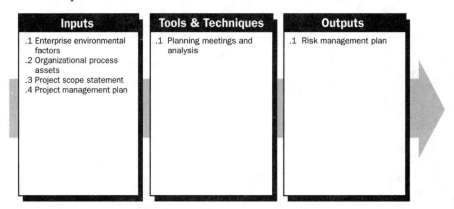

Figure 11-3. Risk Management Planning: Inputs, Tools & Techniques, and Outputs

11.1.1　Risk Management Planning: Inputs

.1　Enterprise Environmental Factors
The attitudes toward risk and the risk tolerance of organizations and people involved in the project will influence the project management plan (Section 4.3). Risk attitudes and tolerances may be expressed in policy statements or revealed in actions (Section 4.1.1.3).

.2　Organizational Process Assets
Organizations may have predefined approaches to risk management such as risk categories, common definition of concepts and terms, standard templates, roles and responsibilities, and authority levels for decision-making.

.3　Project Scope Statement
Described in Section 5.2.3.1.

.4　Project Management Plan
Described in Section 4.3.

11.1.2 Risk Management Planning: Tools and Techniques

.1 Planning Meetings and Analysis

Project teams hold planning meetings to develop the risk management plan. Attendees at these meetings may include the project manager, selected project team members and stakeholders, anyone in the organization with responsibility to manage the risk planning and execution activities, and others, as needed.

Basic plans for conducting the risk management activities are defined in these meetings. Risk cost elements and schedule activities will be developed for inclusion in the project budget and schedule, respectively. Risk responsibilities will be assigned. General organizational templates for risk categories and definitions of terms such as levels of risk, probability by type of risk, impact by type of objectives, and the probability and impact matrix will be tailored to the specific project. The outputs of these activities will be summarized in the risk management plan.

11.1.3 Risk Management Planning: Outputs

.1 Risk Management Plan

The risk management plan describes how risk management will be structured and performed on the project. It becomes a subset of the project management plan (Section 4.3). The risk management plan includes the following:

- **Methodology.** Defines the approaches, tools, and data sources that may be used to perform risk management on the project.
- **Roles and responsibilities.** Defines the lead, support, and risk management team membership for each type of activity in the risk management plan, assigns people to these roles, and clarifies their responsibilities.
- **Budgeting.** Assigns resources and estimates costs needed for risk management for inclusion in the project cost baseline (Section 7.2.3.1).
- **Timing.** Defines when and how often the risk management process will be performed throughout the project life cycle, and establishes risk management activities to be included in the project schedule (Section 6.5.3.1).
- **Risk categories.** Provides a structure that ensures a comprehensive process of systematically identifying risk to a consistent level of detail and contributes to the effectiveness and quality of Risk Identification. An organization can use a previously prepared categorization of typical risks. A risk breakdown structure (RBS) (Figure 11-4) is one approach to providing such a structure, but it can also be addressed by simply listing the various aspects of the project. The risk categories may be revisited during the Risk Identification process. A good practice is to review the risk categories during the Risk Management Planning process prior to their use in the Risk Identification process. Risk categories based on prior projects may need to be tailored, adjusted, or extended to new situations before those categories can be used on the current project.

11

- **Definitions of risk probability and impact.** The quality and credibility of the Qualitative Risk Analysis process requires that different levels of the risks' probabilities and impacts be defined. General definitions of probability levels and impact levels are tailored to the individual project during the Risk Management Planning process for use in the Qualitative Risk Analysis process (Section 11.3).

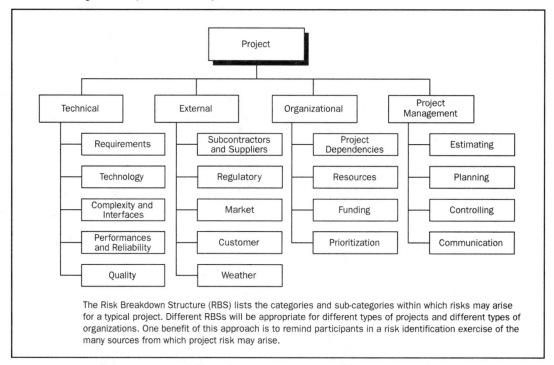

The Risk Breakdown Structure (RBS) lists the categories and sub-categories within which risks may arise for a typical project. Different RBSs will be appropriate for different types of projects and different types of organizations. One benefit of this approach is to remind participants in a risk identification exercise of the many sources from which project risk may arise.

Figure 11-4. Example of a Risk Breakdown Structure (RBS)

A relative scale representing probability values from "very unlikely" to "almost certainty" could be used. Alternatively, assigned numerical probabilities on a general scale (e.g., 0.1, 0.3, 0.5, 0.7, 0.9) can be used. Another approach to calibrating probability involves developing descriptions of the state of the project that relate to the risk under consideration (e.g., the degree of maturity of the project design).

A Guide to the Project Management Body of Knowledge (PMBOK® Guide) Third Edition
©2004 Project Management Institute, Four Campus Boulevard, Newtown Square, PA 19073-3299 USA

The impact scale reflects the significance of impact, either negative for threats or positive for opportunities, on each project objective if a risk occurs. Impact scales are specific to the objective potentially impacted, the type and size of the project, the organization's strategies and financial state, and the organization's sensitivity to particular impacts. Relative scales for impact are simply rank-ordered descriptors such as "very low," "low," "moderate," "high," and "very high," reflecting increasingly extreme impacts as defined by the organization. Alternatively, numeric scales assign values to these impacts. These values may be linear (e.g., 0.1, 0.3, 0.5, 0.7, 0.9) or nonlinear (e.g., 0.05, 0.1, 0.2, 0.4, 0.8). Nonlinear scales may represent the organization's desire to avoid high-impact threats or exploit high-impact opportunities, even if they have relatively low probability. In using nonlinear scales, it is important to understand what is meant by the numbers and their relationship to each other, how they were derived, and the effect they may have on the different objectives of the project.

Figure 11-5 is an example of negative impacts of definitions that might be used in evaluating risk impacts related to four project objectives. That figure illustrates both relative and numeric (in this case, nonlinear) approaches. The figure is not intended to imply that the relative and numeric terms are equivalent, but to show the two alternatives in one figure rather than two.

- **Probability and impact matrix.** Risks are prioritized according to their potential implications for meeting the project's objectives. The typical approach to prioritizing risks is to use a look-up table or a Probability and Impact Matrix (Figure 11-8 and Section 11.3.2.2). The specific combinations of probability and impact that lead to a risk being rated as "high," "moderate," or "low" importance—with the corresponding importance for planning responses to the risk (Section 11.5)—are usually set by the organization. They are reviewed and can be tailored to the specific project during the Risk Management Planning process.

11

Defined Conditions for Impact Scales of a Risk on Major Project Objectives (Examples are shown for negative impacts only)					
Project Objective	Relative or numerical scales are shown				
	Very low /.05	Low /.10	Moderate /.20	High /.40	Very high /.80
Cost	Insignificant cost increase	<10% cost increase	10-20% cost increase	20-40% cost increase	>40% cost lincrease
Time	Insignificant time increase	<5% time increase	5-10% time increase	10-20% time ilncrease	>20% time increase
Scope	Scope decrease barely noticeable	Minor areas of scope affected	Major areas of scope affected	Scope reduction unacceptable to sponsor	Project end item is effectively useless
Quality	Quality degradation barely noticeable	Only very demanding applications are affected	Quality reduction requires sponsor approval	Quality reduction unacceptable to sponsor	Project end item is effectively useless

This table presents examples of risk impact definitions for four different project objectives. They should be tailored in the Risk Management Planning process to the individual project and to the organization's risk thresholds. Impact definitions can be developed for opportunities in a similar way.

Figure 11-5. Definition of Impact Scales for Four Project Objectives

- **Revised stakeholders' tolerances.** Stakeholders' tolerances may be revised in the Risk Management Planning process, as they apply to the specific project.
- **Reporting formats.** Describes the content and format of the risk register (Sections 11.2, 11.3, 11.4, and 11.5) as well as any other risk reports required. Defines how the outcomes of the risk management processes will be documented, analyzed, and communicated.
- **Tracking.** Documents how all facets of risk activities will be recorded for the benefit of the current project, future needs, and lessons learned. Documents whether and how risk management processes will be audited.

11.2 Risk Identification

Risk Identification determines which risks might affect the project and documents their characteristics. Participants in risk identification activities can include the following, where appropriate: project manager, project team members, risk management team (if assigned), subject matter experts from outside the project team, customers, end users, other project managers, stakeholders, and risk management experts. While these personnel are often key participants for risk identification, all project personnel should be encouraged to identify risks.

Risk Identification is an iterative process because new risks may become known as the project progresses through its life cycle (Section 2.1). The frequency of iteration and who participates in each cycle will vary from case to case. The project team should be involved in the process so that they can develop and maintain a sense of ownership of, and responsibility for, the risks and associated risk response actions. Stakeholders outside the project team may provide additional objective information. The Risk Identification process usually leads to the Qualitative Risk Analysis process (Section 11.3). Alternatively, it can lead directly to the Quantitative Risk Analysis process (Section 11.4) when conducted by an experienced risk manager. On some occasions, simply the identification of a risk may suggest its response, and these should be recorded for further analysis and implementation in the Risk Response Planning process (Section 11.5).

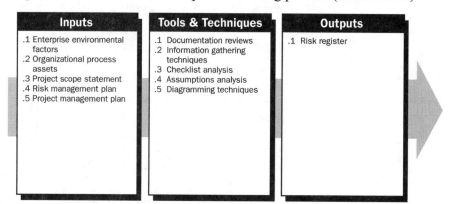

Figure 11-6. Risk Identification: Inputs, Tools & Techniques, and Outputs

A Guide to the Project Management Body of Knowledge (PMBOK® Guide) Third Edition
©2004 Project Management Institute, Four Campus Boulevard, Newtown Square, PA 19073-3299 USA

11.2.1 Risk Identification: Inputs

.1 Enterprise Environmental Factors
Published information, including commercial databases, academic studies, benchmarking, or other industry studies, may also be useful in identifying risks (Section 4.1.1.3).

.2 Organizational Process Assets
Information on prior projects may be available from previous project files, including actual data and lessons learned (Section 4.1.1.4).

.3 Project Scope Statement
Project assumptions are found in the project scope statement (Section 5.2.3.1). Uncertainty in project assumptions should be evaluated as potential causes of project risk.

.4 Risk Management Plan
Key inputs from the risk management plan to the Risk Identification process are the assignments of roles and responsibilities, provision for risk management activities in the budget and schedule, and categories of risk (Section 11.1.3.1), which are sometimes expressed in an RBS (Figure 11-4).

.5 Project Management Plan
The Risk Identification process also requires an understanding of the schedule, cost, and quality management plans found in the project management plan (Section 4.3). Outputs of other Knowledge Area processes should be reviewed to identify possible risks across the entire project.

11.2.2 Risk Identification: Tools and Techniques

.1 Documentation Reviews
A structured review may be performed of project documentation, including plans, assumptions, prior project files, and other information. The quality of the plans, as well as consistency between those plans and with the project requirements and assumptions, can be indicators of risk in the project.

.2 Information Gathering Techniques
Examples of information gathering techniques used in identifying risk can include:
- **Brainstorming.** The goal of brainstorming is to obtain a comprehensive list of project risks. The project team usually performs brainstorming, often with a multidisciplinary set of experts not on the team. Ideas about project risk are generated under the leadership of a facilitator. Categories of risk (Section 11.1), such as a risk breakdown structure, can be used as a framework. Risks are then identified and categorized by type of risk and their definitions are sharpened.

- **Delphi technique.** The Delphi technique is a way to reach a consensus of experts. Project risk experts participate in this technique anonymously. A facilitator uses a questionnaire to solicit ideas about the important project risks. The responses are summarized and are then recirculated to the experts for further comment. Consensus may be reached in a few rounds of this process. The Delphi technique helps reduce bias in the data and keeps any one person from having undue influence on the outcome.

- **Interviewing.** Interviewing experienced project participants, stakeholders, and subject matter experts can identify risks. Interviews are one of the main sources of risk identification data gathering.

- **Root cause identification.** This is an inquiry into the essential causes of a project's risks. It sharpens the definition of the risk and allows grouping risks by causes. Effective risk responses can be developed if the root cause of the risk is addressed.

- **Strengths, weaknesses, opportunities, and threats (SWOT) analysis.** This technique ensures examination of the project from each of the SWOT perspectives, to increase the breadth of considered risks.

.3 Checklist Analysis

Risk identification checklists can be developed based on historical information and knowledge that has been accumulated from previous similar projects and from other sources of information. The lowest level of the RBS can also be used as a risk checklist. While a checklist can be quick and simple, it is impossible to build an exhaustive one. Care should be taken to explore items that do not appear on the checklist. The checklist should be reviewed during project closure to improve it for use on future projects.

.4 Assumptions Analysis

Every project is conceived and developed based on a set of hypotheses, scenarios, or assumptions. Assumptions analysis is a tool that explores the validity of assumptions as they apply to the project. It identifies risks to the project from inaccuracy, inconsistency, or incompleteness of assumptions.

.5 Diagramming Techniques

Risk diagramming techniques may include:

- **Cause-and-effect diagrams** (Section 8.3.2.1). These are also known as Ishikawa or fishbone diagrams, and are useful for identifying causes of risks.

- **System or process flow charts.** These show how various elements of a system interrelate, and the mechanism of causation (Section 8.3.2.3).

- **Influence diagrams.** These are graphical representations of situations showing causal influences, time ordering of events, and other relationships among variables and outcomes.

A Guide to the Project Management Body of Knowledge (PMBOK® Guide) Third Edition
©2004 Project Management Institute, Four Campus Boulevard, Newtown Square, PA 19073-3299 USA

11.2.3 Risk Identification: Outputs

The outputs from Risk Identification are typically contained in a document that can be called a risk register.

.1 Risk Register

The primary outputs from Risk Identification are the initial entries into the risk register, which becomes a component of the project management plan (Section 4.3). The risk register ultimately contains the outcomes of the other risk management processes as they are conducted. The preparation of the risk register begins in the Risk Identification process with the following information, and then becomes available to other project management and Project Risk Management processes.

- **List of identified risks.** The identified risks, including their root causes and uncertain project assumptions, are described. Risks can cover nearly any topic, but a few examples include the following: A few large items with long lead times are on critical path. There could be a risk that industrial relations disputes at the ports will delay the delivery and, subsequently, delay completion of the construction phase. Another example is a project management plan that assumes a staff size of ten, but there are only six resources available. The lack of resources could impact the time required to complete the work and the activities would be late.
- **List of potential responses.** Potential responses to a risk may be identified during the Risk Identification process. These responses, if identified, may be useful as inputs to the Risk Response Planning process (Section 11.5).
- **Root causes of risk.** These are the fundamental conditions or events that may give rise to the identified risk.
- **Updated risk categories.** The process of identifying risks can lead to new risk categories being added to the list of risk categories. The RBS developed in the Risk Management Planning process may have to be enhanced or amended, based on the outcomes of the Risk Identification process.

11.3 Qualitative Risk Analysis

Qualitative Risk Analysis includes methods for prioritizing the identified risks for further action, such as Quantitative Risk Analysis (Section 11.4) or Risk Response Planning (Section 11.5). Organizations can improve the project's performance effectively by focusing on high-priority risks. Qualitative Risk Analysis assesses the priority of identified risks using their probability of occurring, the corresponding impact on project objectives if the risks do occur, as well as other factors such as the time frame and risk tolerance of the project constraints of cost, schedule, scope, and quality.

Definitions of the levels of probability and impact, and expert interviewing, can help to correct biases that are often present in the data used in this process. The time criticality of risk-related actions may magnify the importance of a risk. An evaluation of the quality of the available information on project risks also helps understand the assessment of the risk's importance to the project.

Qualitative Risk Analysis is usually a rapid and cost-effective means of establishing priorities for Risk Response Planning, and lays the foundation for Quantitative Risk Analysis, if this is required. Qualitative Risk Analysis should be revisited during the project's life cycle to stay current with changes in the project risks. Qualitative Risk Analysis requires outputs of the Risk Management Planning (Section 11.1) and Risk Identification (Section 11.2) processes. This process can lead into Quantitative Risk Analysis (Section 11.4) or directly into Risk Response Planning (Section 11.5).

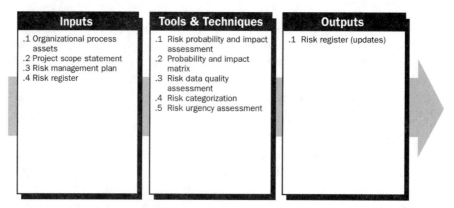

Figure 11-7. Qualitative Risk Analysis: Inputs, Tools & Techniques, and Outputs

11.3.1 Qualitative Risk Analysis: Inputs

.1 Organizational Process Assets
Data about risks on past projects and the lessons learned knowledge base can be used in the Qualitative Risk Analysis process.

.2 Project Scope Statement
Projects of a common or recurrent type tend to have more well-understood risks. Projects using state-of-the-art or first-of-its-kind technology, and highly complex projects, tend to have more uncertainty. This can be evaluated by examining the project scope statement (Section 5.2.3.1).

.3 Risk Management Plan
Key elements of the risk management plan for Qualitative Risk Analysis include roles and responsibilities for conducting risk management, budgets, and schedule activities for risk management, risk categories, definition of probability and impact, the probability and impact matrix, and revised stakeholders' risk tolerances (also enterprise environmental factors in Section 4.1.1.3). These inputs are usually tailored to the project during the Risk Management Planning process. If they are not available, they can be developed during the Qualitative Risk Analysis process.

.4 Risk Register
A key item from the risk register for Qualitative Risk Analysis is the list of identified risks (Section 11.2.3.1).

A Guide to the Project Management Body of Knowledge (PMBOK® Guide) Third Edition
©2004 Project Management Institute, Four Campus Boulevard, Newtown Square, PA 19073-3299 USA

11.3.2 Qualitative Risk Analysis: Tools and Techniques

.1 Risk Probability and Impact Assessment

Risk probability assessment investigates the likelihood that each specific risk will occur. Risk impact assessment investigates the potential effect on a project objective such as time, cost, scope, or quality, including both negative effects for threats and positive effects for opportunities.

Probability and impact are assessed for each identified risk. Risks can be assessed in interviews or meetings with participants selected for their familiarity with the risk categories on the agenda. Project team members and, perhaps, knowledgeable persons from outside the project, are included. Expert judgment is required, since there may be little information on risks from the organization's database of past projects. An experienced facilitator may lead the discussion, since the participants may have little experience with risk assessment.

The level of probability for each risk and its impact on each objective is evaluated during the interview or meeting. Explanatory detail, including assumptions justifying the levels assigned, is also recorded. Risk probabilities and impacts are rated according to the definitions given in the risk management plan (Section 11.1.3.1). Sometimes, risks with obviously low ratings of probability and impact will not be rated, but will be included on a watchlist for future monitoring.

.2 Probability and Impact Matrix

Risks can be prioritized for further quantitative analysis (Section 11.4) and response (Section 11.5), based on their risk rating. Ratings are assigned to risks based on their assessed probability and impact (Section 11.3.2.2). Evaluation of each risk's importance and, hence, priority for attention is typically conducted using a look-up table or a probability and impact matrix (Figure 11-8). Such a matrix specifies combinations of probability and impact that lead to rating the risks as low, moderate, or high priority. Descriptive terms or numeric values can be used, depending on organizational preference.

The organization should determine which combinations of probability and impact result in a classification of high risk ("red condition"), moderate risk ("yellow condition"), and low risk ("green condition"). In a black-and-white matrix, these conditions can be denoted by different shades of gray. Specifically, in Figure 11-8, the dark gray area (with the largest numbers) represents high risk; the medium gray area (with the smallest numbers) represents low risk; and the light gray area (with in-between numbers) represents moderate risk. Usually, these risk-rating rules are specified by the organization in advance of the project, and included in organizational process assets (Section 4.1.1.4). Risk rating rules can be tailored in the Risk Management Planning process (Section 11.1) to the specific project.

A probability and impact matrix, such as the one shown in Figure 11-8, is often used.

11

Probability and Impact Matrix

Probability	Threats					Opportunities				
0.90	0.05	0.09	0.18	0.36	0.72	0.72	0.36	0.18	0.09	0.05
0.70	0.04	0.07	0.14	0.28	0.56	0.56	0.28	0.14	0.07	0.04
0.50	0.03	0.05	0.10	0.20	0.40	0.40	0.20	0.10	0.05	0.03
0.30	0.02	0.03	0.06	0.12	0.24	0.24	0.12	0.06	0.03	0.02
0.10	0.01	0.01	0.02	0.04	0.08	0.08	0.04	0.02	0.01	0.01
	0.05	0.10	0.20	0.40	0.80	0.80	0.40	0.20	0.10	0.05

Impact (ratio scale) on an objective (e.g., cost, time, scope or quality)

Each risk is rated on its probability of occurring and impact on an objective if it does occur. The organization's thresholds for low, moderate or high risks are shown in the matrix and determine whether the risk is scored as high, moderate or low for that objective.

Figure 11-8. Probability and Impact Matrix

As illustrated in Figure 11-8, an organization can rate a risk separately for each objective (e.g., cost, time, and scope). In addition, it can develop ways to determine one overall rating for each risk. Finally, opportunities and threats can be handled in the same matrix using definitions of the different levels of impact that are appropriate for each.

The risk score helps guide risk responses. For example, risks that have a negative impact on objectives if they occur (threats), and that are in the high-risk (dark gray) zone of the matrix, may require priority action and aggressive response strategies. Threats in the low-risk (medium gray) zone may not require proactive management action beyond being placed on a watchlist or adding a contingency reserve.

Similarly for opportunities, those in the high-risk (dark gray) zone that can be obtained most easily and offer the greatest benefit should, therefore, be targeted first. Opportunities in the low-risk (medium gray) zone should be monitored.

.3 Risk Data Quality Assessment

A qualitative risk analysis requires accurate and unbiased data if it is to be credible. Analysis of the quality of risk data is a technique to evaluate the degree to which the data about risks is useful for risk management. It involves examining the degree to which the risk is understood and the accuracy, quality, reliability, and integrity of the data about the risk.

The use of low-quality risk data may lead to a qualitative risk analysis of little use to the project. If data quality is unacceptable, it may be necessary to gather better data. Often, collection of information about risks is difficult, and consumes time and resources beyond that originally planned.

.4 Risk Categorization

Risks to the project can be categorized by sources of risk (e.g., using the RBS), the area of the project affected (e.g., using the WBS), or other useful category (e.g., project phase) to determine areas of the project most exposed to the effects of uncertainty. Grouping risks by common root causes can lead to developing effective risk responses.

.5 Risk Urgency Assessment

Risks requiring near-term responses may be considered more urgent to address. Indicators of priority can include time to effect a risk response, symptoms and warning signs, and the risk rating.

11.3.3 Qualitative Risk Analysis: Outputs

.1 Risk Register (Updates)

The risk register is initiated during the Risk Identification process. The risk register is updated with information from Qualitative Risk Analysis and the updated risk register is included in the project management plan. The risk register updates from Qualitative Risk Analysis include:

- **Relative ranking or priority list of project risks.** The probability and impact matrix can be used to classify risks according to their individual significance. The project manager can then use the prioritized list to focus attention on those items of high significance to the project, where responses can lead to better project outcomes. Risks may be listed by priority separately for cost, time, scope, and quality, since organizations may value one objective over another. A description of the basis for the assessed probability and impact should be included for risks assessed as important to the project.

- **Risks grouped by categories.** Risk categorization can reveal common root causes of risk or project areas requiring particular attention. Discovering concentrations of risk may improve the effectiveness of risk responses.

- **List of risks requiring response in the near-term.** Those risks that require an urgent response and those that can be handled at a later date may be put into different groups.

- **List of risks for additional analysis and response.** Some risks might warrant more analysis, including Quantitative Risk Analysis, as well as response action.

- **Watchlists of low priority risks.** Risks that are not assessed as important in the Qualitative Risk Analysis process can be placed on a watchlist for continued monitoring.

- **Trends in qualitative risk analysis results.** As the analysis is repeated, a trend for particular risks may become apparent, and can make risk response or further analysis more or less urgent/important.

11.4 Quantitative Risk Analysis

Quantitative Risk Analysis is performed on risks that have been prioritized by the Qualitative Risk Analysis process as potentially and substantially impacting the project's competing demands. The Quantitative Risk Analysis process analyzes the effect of those risk events and assigns a numerical rating to those risks. It also presents a quantitative approach to making decisions in the presence of uncertainty. This process uses techniques such as Monte Carlo simulation and decision tree analysis to:

- Quantify the possible outcomes for the project and their probabilities
- Assess the probability of achieving specific project objectives
- Identify risks requiring the most attention by quantifying their relative contribution to overall project risk
- Identify realistic and achievable cost, schedule, or scope targets, given the project risks
- Determine the best project management decision when some conditions or outcomes are uncertain.

Quantitative Risk Analysis generally follows the Qualitative Risk Analysis process, although experienced risk managers sometimes perform it directly after Risk Identification. In some cases, Quantitative Risk Analysis may not be required to develop effective risk responses. Availability of time and budget, and the need for qualitative or quantitative statements about risk and impacts, will determine which method(s) to use on any particular project. Quantitative Risk Analysis should be repeated after Risk Response Planning, as well as part of Risk Monitoring and Control, to determine if the overall project risk has been satisfactorily decreased. Trends can indicate the need for more or less risk management action. It is an input to the Risk Response Planning process.

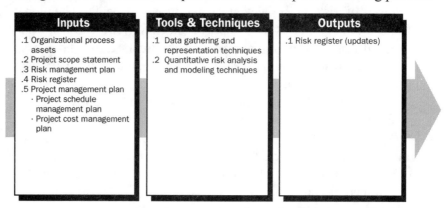

Inputs	Tools & Techniques	Outputs

.1 Organizational process assets
.2 Project scope statement
.3 Risk management plan
.4 Risk register
.5 Project management plan
  · Project schedule management plan
  · Project cost management plan
	.1 Data gathering and representation techniques
	.2 Quantitative risk analysis and modeling techniques
		.1 Risk register (updates)

Figure 11-9. Quantitative Risk Analysis: Inputs, Tools & Techniques, and Outputs

A Guide to the Project Management Body of Knowledge (PMBOK® Guide) Third Edition
©2004 Project Management Institute, Four Campus Boulevard, Newtown Square, PA 19073-3299 USA

11.4.1 Quantitative Risk Analysis: Inputs

.1 Organizational Process Assets
Information on prior, similar completed projects, studies of similar projects by risk specialists, and risk databases that may be available from industry or proprietary sources.

.2 Project Scope Statement
Described in Section 5.2.3.1.

.3 Risk Management Plan
Key elements of the risk management plan for Quantitative Risk Analysis include roles and responsibilities for conducting risk management, budgets, and schedule activities for risk management, risk categories, the RBS, and revised stakeholders' risk tolerances.

.4 Risk Register
Key items from the risk register for Quantitative Risk Analysis include the list of identified risks, the relative ranking or priority list of project risks, and the risks grouped by categories.

.5 Project Management Plan
The project management plan includes:

- **Project schedule management plan.** The project schedule management plan sets the format and establishes criteria for developing and controlling the project schedule (described in the Chapter 6 introductory material).
- **Project cost management plan.** The project cost management plan sets the format and establishes criteria for planning, structuring, estimating, budgeting, and controlling project costs (described in the Chapter 7 introductory material).

11.4.2 Quantitative Risk Analysis: Tools and Techniques

.1 Data Gathering and Representation Techniques

- **Interviewing.** Interviewing techniques are used to quantify the probability and impact of risks on project objectives. The information needed depends upon the type of probability distributions that will be used. For instance, information would be gathered on the optimistic (low), pessimistic (high), and most likely scenarios for some commonly used distributions, and the mean and standard deviation for others. Examples of three-point estimates for a cost estimate are shown in Figure 11-10. Documenting the rationale of the risk ranges is an important component of the risk interview, because it can provide information on reliability and credibility of the analysis.

Range of Project Cost Estimates

WBS Element	Low	Most Likely	High
Design	$4M	$6M	$10M
Build	$16M	$20M	$35M
Test	$11M	$15M	$23M
Total Project		$41M	

The risk interview determines the three-point estimates for each WBS element for triangular or other asymmetrical distributions. In this example, the likelihood of completing the project at or below the traditional estimate of $41 million is relatively small as shown in the simulation results (Figure 11-13).

Figure 11-10. Range of Project Cost Estimates Collected During the Risk Interview

- **Probability distributions.** Continuous probability distributions represent the uncertainty in values, such as durations of schedule activities and costs of project components. Discrete distributions can be used to represent uncertain events, such as the outcome of a test or a possible scenario in a decision tree. Two examples of widely used continuous distributions are shown in Figure 11-11. These asymmetrical distributions depict shapes that are compatible with the data typically developed during the project risk analysis. Uniform distributions can be used if there is no obvious value that is more likely than any other between specified high and low bounds, such as in the early concept stage of design.

Beta Distribution

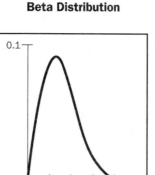

Triangular Distribution

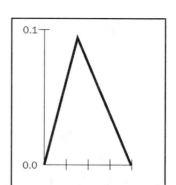

Beta and triangular distributions are frequently used in quantitative risk analysis. The data shown here is one example of a family of such distributions determined by two "shape parameters". Other commonly used distributions include the uniform, normal and lognormal. In these charts the horizontal (X) axes represent possible values of time or cost and the vertical (Y) axes represent relative likelihood.

Figure 11-11. Examples of Commonly Used Probability Distributions

- **Expert judgment.** Subject matter experts internal or external to the organization, such as engineering or statistical experts, validate data and techniques.

.2 Quantitative Risk Analysis and Modeling Techniques

Commonly used techniques in Quantitative Risk Analysis include:

- **Sensitivity analysis.** Sensitivity analysis helps to determine which risks have the most potential impact on the project. It examines the extent to which the uncertainty of each project element affects the objective being examined when all other uncertain elements are held at their baseline values. One typical display of sensitivity analysis is the tornado diagram, which is useful for comparing relative importance of variables that have a high degree of uncertainty to those that are more stable.

- **Expected monetary value analysis.** Expected monetary value (EMV) analysis is a statistical concept that calculates the average outcome when the future includes scenarios that may or may not happen (i.e., analysis under uncertainty). The EMV of opportunities will generally be expressed as positive values, while those of risks will be negative. EMV is calculated by multiplying the value of each possible outcome by its probability of occurrence, and adding them together. A common use of this type of analysis is in decision tree analysis (Figure 11-12). Modeling and simulation are recommended for use in cost and schedule risk analysis, because they are more powerful and less subject to misuse than EMV analysis.

- **Decision tree analysis.** Decision tree analysis is usually structured using a decision tree diagram (Figure 11-12) that describes a situation under consideration, and the implications of each of the available choices and possible scenarios. It incorporates the cost of each available choice, the probabilities of each possible scenario, and the rewards of each alternative logical path. Solving the decision tree provides the EMV (or other measure of interest to the organization) for each alternative, when all the rewards and subsequent decisions are quantified.

11

Decision Definition	Decision Node	Chance Node	Net Path Value
Decision to be Made	Input: Cost of Each Option Output: Decision Made (TRUE, FALSE)	Input: Scenario Probability, Reward if it Occurs Output: Expected Monetary Value (EMV)	Computed: (Payoffs minus Costs) along Path

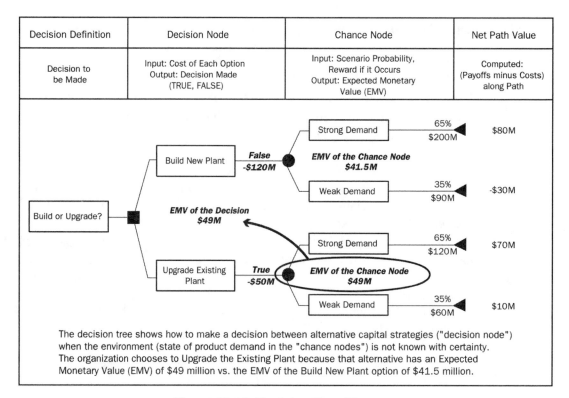

The decision tree shows how to make a decision between alternative capital strategies ("decision node") when the environment (state of product demand in the "chance nodes") is not known with certainty. The organization chooses to Upgrade the Existing Plant because that alternative has an Expected Monetary Value (EMV) of $49 million vs. the EMV of the Build New Plant option of $41.5 million.

Figure 11-12. Decision Tree Diagram

- **Modeling and simulation.** A project simulation uses a model that translates the uncertainties specified at a detailed level of the project into their potential impact on project objectives. Simulations are typically performed using the Monte Carlo technique. In a simulation, the project model is computed many times (iterated), with the input values randomized from a probability distribution function (e.g., cost of project elements or duration of schedule activities) chosen for each iteration from the probability distributions of each variable. A probability distribution (e.g., total cost or completion date) is calculated.

For a cost risk analysis, a simulation can use the traditional project WBS (Section 5.3.3.2) or a cost breakdown structure as its model. For a schedule risk analysis, the precedence diagramming method (PDM) schedule is used (Section 6.2.2.1). A cost risk simulation is shown in Figure 11-13.

A Guide to the Project Management Body of Knowledge (PMBOK® Guide) Third Edition
©2004 Project Management Institute, Four Campus Boulevard, Newtown Square, PA 19073-3299 USA

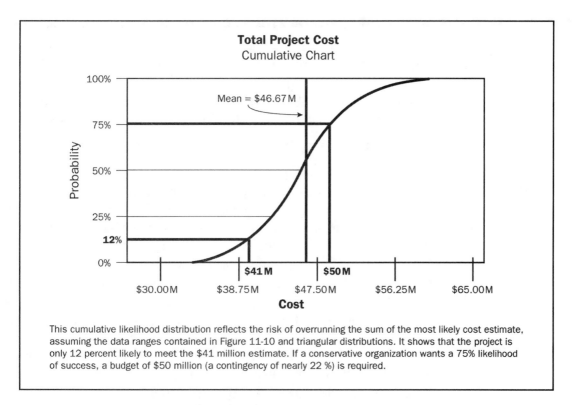

This cumulative likelihood distribution reflects the risk of overrunning the sum of the most likely cost estimate, assuming the data ranges contained in Figure 11-10 and triangular distributions. It shows that the project is only 12 percent likely to meet the $41 million estimate. If a conservative organization wants a 75% likelihood of success, a budget of $50 million (a contingency of nearly 22 %) is required.

Figure 11-13. Cost Risk Simulation Results

11.4.3 Quantitative Risk Analysis: Outputs

.1 Risk Register (Updates)

The risk register is initiated in the Risk Identification process (Section 11.2) and updated in Qualitative Risk Analysis (Section 11.3). It is further updated in Quantitative Risk Analysis. The risk register is a component of the project management plan. Updates include the following main components:

- **Probabilistic analysis of the project.** Estimates are made of potential project schedule and cost outcomes, listing the possible completion dates and costs with their associated confidence levels. This output, typically expressed as a cumulative distribution, is used with stakeholder risk tolerances to permit quantification of the cost and time contingency reserves. Such contingency reserves are needed to bring the risk of overrunning stated project objectives to a level acceptable to the organization. For instance, in Figure 11-13, the cost contingency to the 75th percentile is $9 million, or about 22% versus the $41 million sum of the most likely estimates.

- **Probability of achieving cost and time objectives.** With the risks facing the project, the probability of achieving project objectives under the current plan can be estimated using quantitative risk analysis results. For instance, in Figure 11-13, the likelihood of achieving the cost estimate of $41 million (from Figure 11-10) is about 12%.

- **Prioritized list of quantified risks.** This list of risks includes those that pose the greatest threat or present the greatest opportunity to the project. These include the risks that require the greatest cost contingency and those that are most likely to influence the critical path.
- **Trends in quantitative risk analysis results.** As the analysis is repeated, a trend may become apparent that leads to conclusions affecting risk responses.

11.5 Risk Response Planning

Risk Response Planning is the process of developing options, and determining actions to enhance opportunities and reduce threats to the project's objectives. It follows the Qualitative Risk Analysis and Quantitative Risk Analysis processes. It includes the identification and assignment of one or more persons (the "risk response owner") to take responsibility for each agreed-to and funded risk response. Risk Response Planning addresses the risks by their priority, inserting resources and activities into the budget, schedule, and project management plan, as needed.

Planned risk responses must be appropriate to the significance of the risk, cost effective in meeting the challenge, timely, realistic within the project context, agreed upon by all parties involved, and owned by a responsible person. Selecting the best risk response from several options is often required.

The Risk Response Planning section presents commonly used approaches to planning responses to the risks. Risks include threats and opportunities that can affect project success, and responses are discussed for each.

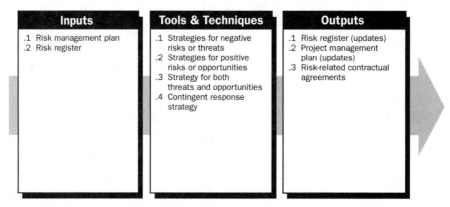

Figure 11-14. Risk Response Planning: Inputs, Tools & Techniques, and Outputs

11.5.1 Risk Response Planning: Inputs

.1 Risk Management Plan

Important components of the risk management plan include roles and responsibilities, risk analysis definitions, risk thresholds for low, moderate, and high risks, and the time and budget required to conduct Project Risk Management.

Some components of the Risk Management Plan that are important inputs to Risk Response Planning may include risk thresholds for low, moderate, and high risks to help understand those risks for which responses are needed, assignment of personnel and scheduling and budgeting for risk response planning.

.2 Risk Register

The risk register is first developed in the Risk Identification process, and is updated during the Qualitative and Quantitative Risk Analysis processes. The Risk Response Planning process may have to refer back to identified risks, root causes of risks, lists of potential responses, risk owners, symptoms, and warning signs in developing risk responses.

Important inputs to Risk Response Planning include the relative rating or priority list of project risks, a list of risks requiring response in the near term, a list of risks for additional analysis and response, trends in qualitative risk analysis results, root causes, risks grouped by categories, and a watchlist of low priority risks. The risk register is further updated during the Quantitative Risk Analysis process.

11.5.2 Risk Response Planning: Tools and Techniques

Several risk response strategies are available. The strategy or mix of strategies most likely to be effective should be selected for each risk. Risk analysis tools, such as decision tree analysis, can be used to choose the most appropriate responses. Then, specific actions are developed to implement that strategy. Primary and backup strategies may be selected. A fallback plan can be developed for implementation if the selected strategy turns out not to be fully effective, or if an accepted risk occurs. Often, a contingency reserve is allocated for time or cost. Finally, contingency plans can be developed, along with identification of the conditions that trigger their execution.

.1 Strategies for Negative Risks or Threats

Three strategies typically deal with threats or risks that may have negative impacts on project objectives if they occur. These strategies are to avoid, transfer, or mitigate:

- **Avoid.** Risk avoidance involves changing the project management plan to eliminate the threat posed by an adverse risk, to isolate the project objectives from the risk's impact, or to relax the objective that is in jeopardy, such as extending the schedule or reducing scope. Some risks that arise early in the project can be avoided by clarifying requirements, obtaining information, improving communication, or acquiring expertise.

- **Transfer.** Risk transference requires shifting the negative impact of a threat, along with ownership of the response, to a third party. Transferring the risk simply gives another party responsibility for its management; it does not eliminate it. Transferring liability for risk is most effective in dealing with financial risk exposure. Risk transference nearly always involves payment of a risk premium to the party taking on the risk. Transference tools can be quite diverse and include, but are not limited to, the use of insurance, performance bonds, warranties, guarantees, etc. Contracts may be used to transfer liability for specified risks to another party. In many cases, use of a cost-type contract may transfer the cost risk to the buyer, while a fixed-price contract may transfer risk to the seller, if the project's design is stable.

- **Mitigate.** Risk mitigation implies a reduction in the probability and/or impact of an adverse risk event to an acceptable threshold. Taking early action to reduce the probability and/or impact of a risk occurring on the project is often more effective than trying to repair the damage after the risk has occurred. Adopting less complex processes, conducting more tests, or choosing a more stable supplier are examples of mitigation actions. Mitigation may require prototype development to reduce the risk of scaling up from a bench-scale model of a process or product. Where it is not possible to reduce probability, a mitigation response might address the risk impact by targeting linkages that determine the severity. For example, designing redundancy into a subsystem may reduce the impact from a failure of the original component.

.2 Strategies for Positive Risks or Opportunities

Three responses are suggested to deal with risks with potentially positive impacts on project objectives. These strategies are to exploit, share, or enhance.

- **Exploit.** This strategy may be selected for risks with positive impacts where the organization wishes to ensure that the opportunity is realized. This strategy seeks to eliminate the uncertainty associated with a particular upside risk by making the opportunity definitely happen. Directly exploiting responses include assigning more talented resources to the project to reduce the time to completion, or to provide better quality than originally planned.

- **Share.** Sharing a positive risk involves allocating ownership to a third party who is best able to capture the opportunity for the benefit of the project. Examples of sharing actions include forming risk-sharing partnerships, teams, special-purpose companies, or joint ventures, which can be established with the express purpose of managing opportunities.

- **Enhance.** This strategy modifies the "size" of an opportunity by increasing probability and/or positive impacts, and by identifying and maximizing key drivers of these positive-impact risks. Seeking to facilitate or strengthen the cause of the opportunity, and proactively targeting and reinforcing its trigger conditions, might increase probability. Impact drivers can also be targeted, seeking to increase the project's susceptibility to the opportunity.

.3 Strategy for Both Threats and Opportunities

Acceptance: A strategy that is adopted because it is seldom possible to eliminate all risk from a project. This strategy indicates that the project team has decided not to change the project management plan to deal with a risk, or is unable to identify any other suitable response strategy. It may be adopted for either threats or opportunities. This strategy can be either passive or active. Passive acceptance requires no action, leaving the project team to deal with the threats or opportunities as they occur. The most common active acceptance strategy is to establish a contingency reserve, including amounts of time, money, or resources to handle known—or even sometimes potential, unknown—threats or opportunities.

.4 Contingent Response Strategy

Some responses are designed for use only if certain events occur. For some risks, it is appropriate for the project team to make a response plan that will only be executed under certain predefined conditions, if it is believed that there will be sufficient warning to implement the plan. Events that trigger the contingency response, such as missing intermediate milestones or gaining higher priority with a supplier, should be defined and tracked.

11.5.3 Risk Response Planning: Outputs

.1 Risk Register (Updates)

The risk register is developed in Risk Identification, and is updated during Qualitative Risk Analysis and Quantitative Risk Analysis. In the Risk Response Planning process, appropriate responses are chosen, agreed-upon, and included in the risk register. The risk register should be written to a level of detail that corresponds with the priority ranking and the planned response. Often, the high and moderate risks are addressed in detail. Risks judged to be of low priority are included in a "watchlist" for periodic monitoring. Components of the risk register at this point can include:

- Identified risks, their descriptions, area(s) of the project (e.g., WBS element) affected, their causes (e.g., RBS element), and how they may affect project objectives
- Risk owners and assigned responsibilities
- Outputs from the Qualitative and Quantitative Risk Analysis processes, including prioritized lists of project risks and probabilistic analysis of the project
- Agreed-upon response strategies
- Specific actions to implement the chosen response strategy
- Symptoms and warning signs of risks' occurrence
- Budget and schedule activities required to implement the chosen responses
- Contingency reserves of time and cost designed to provide for stakeholders' risk tolerances

- Contingency plans and triggers that call for their execution
- Fallback plans for use as a reaction to a risk that has occurred, and the primary response proves to be inadequate
- Residual risks that are expected to remain after planned responses have been taken, as well as those that have been deliberately accepted
- Secondary risks that arise as a direct outcome of implementing a risk response
- Contingency reserves that are calculated based on the quantitative analysis of the project and the organization's risk thresholds.

.2 Project Management Plan (Updates)

The project management plan is updated as response activities are added after review and disposition through the Integrated Change Control process (Section 4.6). Integrated change control is applied in the Direct and Manage Project Execution process (Section 4.4) to ensure that agreed-upon actions are implemented and monitored as part of the ongoing project. Risk response strategies, once agreed to, must be fed back into the appropriate processes in other Knowledge Areas, including the project's budget and schedule.

.3 Risk-Related Contractual Agreements

Contractual agreements, such as agreements for insurance, services, and other items as appropriate, can be prepared to specify each party's responsibility for specific risks, should they occur.

11.6 Risk Monitoring and Control

Planned risk responses (Section 11.5) that are included in the project management plan are executed during the life cycle of the project, but the project work should be continuously monitored for new and changing risks.

Risk Monitoring and Control (Section 4.4) is the process of identifying, analyzing, and planning for newly arising risks, keeping track of the identified risks and those on the watchlist, reanalyzing existing risks, monitoring trigger conditions for contingency plans, monitoring residual risks, and reviewing the execution of risk responses while evaluating their effectiveness. The Risk Monitoring and Control process applies techniques, such as variance and trend analysis, which require the use of performance data generated during project execution. Risk Monitoring and Control, as well as the other risk management processes, is an ongoing process for the life of the project. Other purposes of Risk Monitoring and Control are to determine if:

- Project assumptions are still valid
- Risk, as assessed, has changed from its prior state, with analysis of trends
- Proper risk management policies and procedures are being followed
- Contingency reserves of cost or schedule should be modified in line with the risks of the project.

Risk Monitoring and Control can involve choosing alternative strategies, executing a contingency or fallback plan, taking corrective action, and modifying the project management plan. The risk response owner reports periodically to the project manager on the effectiveness of the plan, any unanticipated effects, and any mid-course correction needed to handle the risk appropriately. Risk Monitoring and Control also includes updating the organizational process assets (Section 4.1.1.4), including project lessons-learned databases and risk management templates for the benefit of future projects.

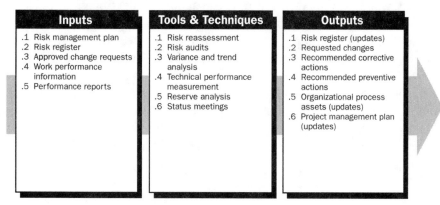

Inputs	Tools & Techniques	Outputs
.1 Risk management plan .2 Risk register .3 Approved change requests .4 Work performance information .5 Performance reports	.1 Risk reassessment .2 Risk audits .3 Variance and trend analysis .4 Technical performance measurement .5 Reserve analysis .6 Status meetings	.1 Risk register (updates) .2 Requested changes .3 Recommended corrective actions .4 Recommended preventive actions .5 Organizational process assets (updates) .6 Project management plan (updates)

Figure 11-15. Risk Monitoring and Control: Inputs, Tools & Techniques, and Outputs

11.6.1 Risk Monitoring and Control: Inputs

.1 Risk Management Plan

This plan has key inputs that include the assignment of people, including the risk owners, time, and other resources to project risk management.

.2 Risk Register

The risk register has key inputs that include identified risks and risk owners, agreed-upon risk responses, specific implementation actions, symptoms and warning signs of risk, residual and secondary risks, a watchlist of low priority risks, and the time and cost contingency reserves.

.3 Approved Change Requests

Approved change requests (Section 4.6.3.1) can include modifications such as work methods, contract terms, scope, and schedule. Approved changes can generate risks or changes in identified risks, and those changes need to be analyzed for any effects upon the risk register, risk response plan, or risk management plan. All changes should be formally documented. Any verbally discussed, but undocumented, changes should not be processed or implemented.

.4 Work Performance Information

Work performance information (Section 4.4.3.7), including project deliverables' status, corrective actions, and performance reports, are important inputs to Risk Monitoring and Control.

.5 Performance Reports

Performance reports (Section 10.3.3.1) provide information on project work performance, such as an analysis that may influence the risk management processes.

11.6.2 Risk Monitoring and Control: Tools and Techniques

.1 Risk Reassessment

Risk Monitoring and Control often requires identification of new risks and reassessment of risks, using the processes of this chapter as appropriate. Project risk reassessments should be regularly scheduled. Project Risk Management should be an agenda item at project team status meetings. The amount and detail of repetition that is appropriate depends on how the project progresses relative to its objectives. For instance, if a risk emerges that was not anticipated in the risk register or included on the watchlist, or if its impact on objectives is different from what was expected, the planned response may not be adequate. It will then be necessary to perform additional response planning to control the risk.

.2 Risk Audits

Risk audits examine and document the effectiveness of risk responses in dealing with identified risks and their root causes, as well as the effectiveness of the risk management process.

.3 Variance and Trend Analysis

Trends in the project's execution should be reviewed using performance data. Earned value analysis (Section 7.3.2.4) and other methods of project variance and trend analysis may be used for monitoring overall project performance. Outcomes from these analyses may forecast potential deviation of the project at completion from cost and schedule targets. Deviation from the baseline plan may indicate the potential impact of threats or opportunities.

.4 Technical Performance Measurement

Technical performance measurement compares technical accomplishments during project execution to the project management plan's schedule of technical achievement. Deviation, such as demonstrating more or less functionality than planned at a milestone, can help to forecast the degree of success in achieving the project's scope.

.5 Reserve Analysis

Throughout execution of the project, some risks may occur, with positive or negative impacts on budget or schedule contingency reserves (Section 11.5.2.4). Reserve analysis compares the amount of the contingency reserves remaining to the amount of risk remaining at any time in the project, in order to determine if the remaining reserve is adequate.

A Guide to the Project Management Body of Knowledge (PMBOK® Guide) Third Edition
©2004 Project Management Institute, Four Campus Boulevard, Newtown Square, PA 19073-3299 USA

.6 Status Meetings

Project risk management can be an agenda item at periodic status meetings. That item may take no time or a long time, depending on the risks that have been identified, their priority, and difficulty of response. Risk management becomes easier the more often it is practiced, and frequent discussions about risk make talking about risks, particularly threats, easier and more accurate.

11.6.3 Risk Monitoring and Control: Outputs

.1 Risk Register (Updates)

An updated risk register contains:

- Outcomes of risk reassessments, risk audits, and periodic risk reviews. These outcomes may include updates to probability, impact, priority, response plans, ownership, and other elements of the risk register. Outcomes can also include closing risks that are no longer applicable.

- The actual outcomes of the project's risks, and of risk responses that can help project managers plan for risk throughout the organization, as well as on future projects. This completes the record of risk management on the project, is an input to the Close Project process (Section 4.7), and becomes part of the project closure documents.

.2 Requested Changes

Implementing contingency plans or workarounds frequently results in a requirement to change the project management plan to respond to risks. Requested changes are prepared and submitted to the Integrated Change Control process (Section 4.6) as an output of the Risk Monitoring and Control process. Approved change requests are issued and become inputs to the Direct and Manage Project Execution process (Section 4.4) and to the Risk Monitoring and Control process.

.3 Recommended Corrective Actions

Recommended corrective actions include contingency plans and workaround plans. The latter are responses that were not initially planned, but are required to deal with emerging risks that were previously unidentified or accepted passively. Workarounds should be properly documented and included in both the Direct and Manage Project Execution (Section 4.4) and Monitor and Control Project Work (Section 4.5) processes. Recommended corrective actions are inputs to the Integrated Change Control process (Section 4.6).

.4 Recommended Preventive Actions

Recommended preventive actions are used to bring the project into compliance with the project management plan.

11

.5 Organizational Process Assets (Updates)

The six Project Risk Management processes produce information that can be used for future projects, and should be captured in the organizational process assets (Section 4.1.1.4). The templates for the risk management plan, including the probability and impact matrix, and risk register, can be updated at project closure. Risks can be documented and the RBS updated. Lessons learned from the project risk management activities can contribute to the lessons learned knowledge database of the organization. Data on the actual costs and durations of project activities can be added to the organization's databases. The final versions of the risk register and the risk management plan templates, checklists, and RBSs are included.

.6 Project Management Plan (Updates)

If the approved change requests have an effect on the risk management processes, then the corresponding component documents of the project management plan are revised and reissued to reflect the approved changes.

CHAPTER 12

Project Procurement Management

Project Procurement Management includes the processes to purchase or acquire the products, services, or results needed from outside the project team to perform the work. This chapter presents two perspectives of procurement. The organization can be either the buyer or seller of the product, service, or results under a contract.

Project Procurement Management includes the contract management and change control processes required to administer contracts or purchase orders issued by authorized project team members.

Project Procurement Management also includes administering any contract issued by an outside organization (the buyer) that is acquiring the project from the performing organization (the seller), and administering contractual obligations placed on the project team by the contract.

Figure 12-1 provides an overview of the Project Procurement Management processes, and Figure 12-2 provides a process flow view of the processes and their inputs, outputs, and related processes from other Knowledge Areas.

The Project Procurement Management processes include the following:

12.1 Plan Purchases and Acquisitions – determining what to purchase or acquire and determining when and how.

12.2 Plan Contracting – documenting products, services, and results requirements and identifying potential sellers.

12.3 Request Seller Responses – obtaining information, quotations, bids, offers, or proposals, as appropriate.

12.4 Select Sellers – reviewing offers, choosing among potential sellers, and negotiating a written contract with each seller.

12.5 Contract Administration – managing the contract and relationship between the buyer and seller, reviewing and documenting how a seller is performing or has performed to establish required corrective actions and provide a basis for future relationships with the seller, managing contract-related changes and, when appropriate, managing the contractual relationship with the outside buyer of the project.

12.6 Contract Closure – completing and settling each contract, including the resolution of any open items, and closing each contract applicable to the project or a project phase.

These processes interact with each other and with the processes in the other Knowledge Areas as well. Each process can involve effort from one or more persons or groups of persons, based on the requirements of the project. Each process occurs at least once in every project and occurs in one or more project phases, if the project is divided into phases. Although the processes are presented here as discrete components with well-defined interfaces, in practice they overlap and interact in ways not detailed here. Process interactions are discussed in detail in Chapter 3.

The Project Procurement Management processes involve contracts that are legal documents between a buyer and a seller. A contract is a mutually binding agreement that obligates the seller to provide the specified products, services, or results, and obligates the buyer to provide monetary or other valuable consideration. A contract is a legal relationship subject to remedy in the courts. The agreement can be simple or complex, and can reflect the simplicity or complexity of the deliverables. A contract includes terms and conditions, and can include other items such as the seller's proposal or marketing literature, and any other documentation that the buyer is relying upon to establish what the seller is to perform or provide. It is the project management team's responsibility to help tailor the contract to the specific needs of the project. Depending upon the application area, contracts can also be called an agreement, subcontract, or purchase order. Most organizations have documented policies and procedures specifically defining who can sign and administer such agreements on behalf of the organization.

Although all project documents are subject to some form of review and approval, the legally binding nature of a contract usually means that it will be subjected to a more extensive approval process. In all cases, the primary focus of the review and approval process ensures that the contract language describes products, services, or results that will satisfy the identified project need. In the case of major projects undertaken by public agencies, the review process can include public review of the agreement.

The project management team may seek support early from specialists in the disciplines of contracting, purchasing, and law. Such involvement can be mandated by an organization's policy.

The various activities involved in the Project Procurement Management processes form the life cycle of a contract. By actively managing the contract life cycle and carefully wording the terms and conditions of the contract, some identifiable project risks can be avoided or mitigated. Entering into a contract for products or services is one method of allocating the responsibility for managing or assuming potential risks.

A Guide to the Project Management Body of Knowledge (PMBOK® Guide) **Third Edition**
©2004 Project Management Institute, Four Campus Boulevard, Newtown Square, PA 19073-3299 USA

A complex project can involve managing multiple contracts or subcontracts simultaneously or in sequence. In such cases, each contract life cycle can end during any phase of the project life cycle (see Chapter 2). Project Procurement Management is discussed within the perspective of the buyer-seller relationship. The buyer-seller relationship can exist at many levels on any one project, and between organizations internal to and external to the acquiring organization. Depending on the application area, the seller can be called a contractor, subcontractor, vendor, service provider, or supplier. Depending on the buyer's position in the project acquisition cycle, the buyer can be called a client, customer, prime contractor, contractor, acquiring organization, governmental agency, service requestor, or purchaser. The seller can be viewed during the contract life cycle first as a bidder, then as the selected source, and then as the contracted supplier or vendor.

The seller will typically manage the work as a project if the acquisition is not just for materiel, goods, or common products. In such cases:

- Buyer becomes the customer, and is thus a key project stakeholder for the seller
- Seller's project management team is concerned with all the processes of project management, not just with those of this Knowledge Area
- Terms and conditions of the contract become key inputs to many of the seller's management processes. The contract can actually contain the inputs (e.g., major deliverables, key milestones, cost objectives), or it can limit the project team's options (e.g., buyer approval of staffing decisions is often required on design projects).

This chapter assumes that the buyer of items for the project is within the project team and that the seller is external to the project team. This relationship is true if the performing organization is the seller of a project to a customer. This relationship is also true if the performing organization is the buyer from other vendors or suppliers of products, services, results, or subproject components used on a project.

This chapter assumes that a formal contractual relationship is developed and exists between the buyer and the seller. However, most of the discussion in this chapter is equally applicable to non-contractual formal agreements entered into with other units of the project team's organizations.

12

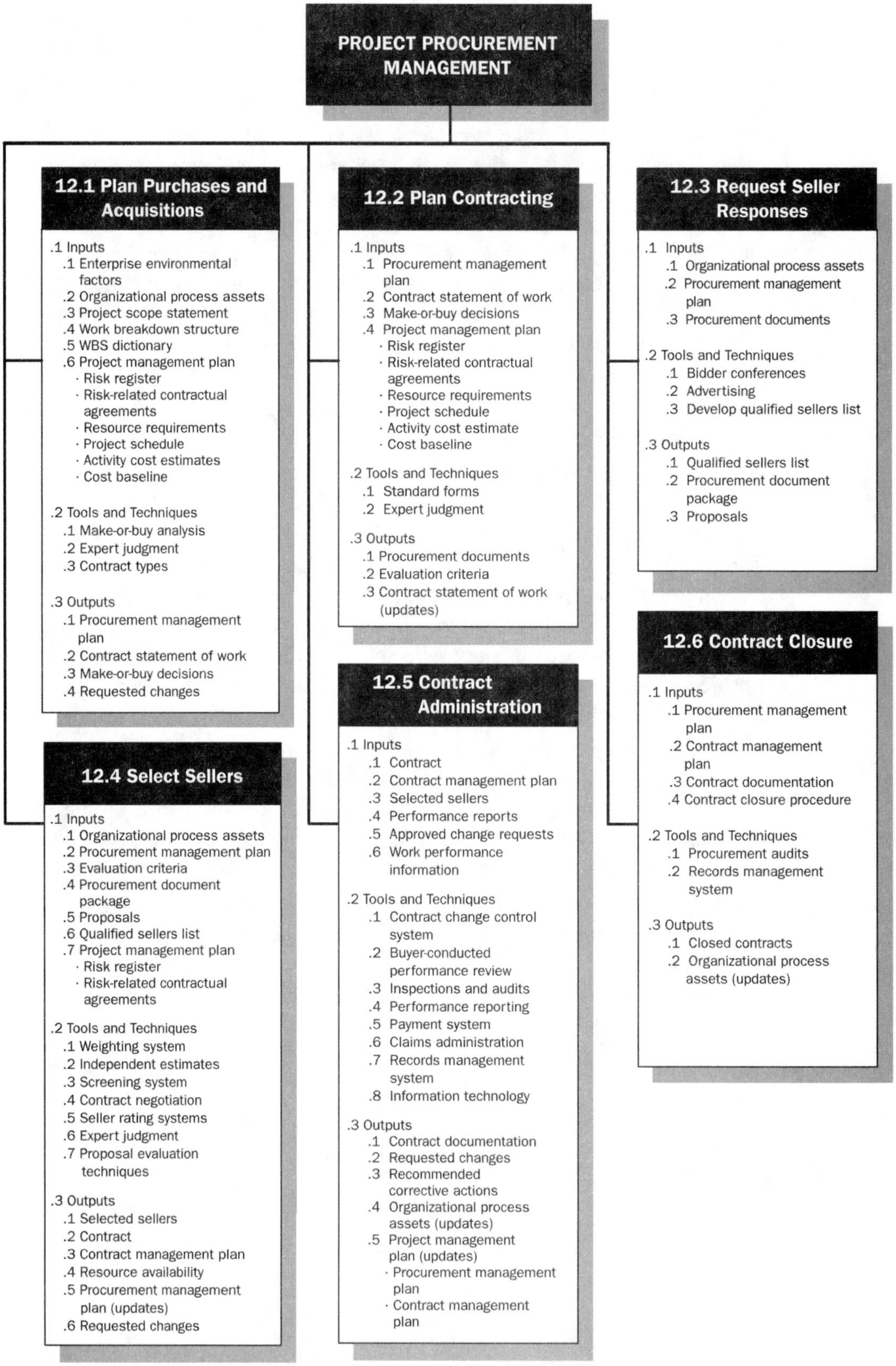

PROJECT PROCUREMENT MANAGEMENT

12.1 Plan Purchases and Acquisitions

.1 Inputs
  .1 Enterprise environmental factors
  .2 Organizational process assets
  .3 Project scope statement
  .4 Work breakdown structure
  .5 WBS dictionary
  .6 Project management plan
    · Risk register
    · Risk-related contractual agreements
    · Resource requirements
    · Project schedule
    · Activity cost estimates
    · Cost baseline

.2 Tools and Techniques
  .1 Make-or-buy analysis
  .2 Expert judgment
  .3 Contract types

.3 Outputs
  .1 Procurement management plan
  .2 Contract statement of work
  .3 Make-or-buy decisions
  .4 Requested changes

12.2 Plan Contracting

.1 Inputs
  .1 Procurement management plan
  .2 Contract statement of work
  .3 Make-or-buy decisions
  .4 Project management plan
    · Risk register
    · Risk-related contractual agreements
    · Resource requirements
    · Project schedule
    · Activity cost estimate
    · Cost baseline

.2 Tools and Techniques
  .1 Standard forms
  .2 Expert judgment

.3 Outputs
  .1 Procurement documents
  .2 Evaluation criteria
  .3 Contract statement of work (updates)

12.3 Request Seller Responses

.1 Inputs
  .1 Organizational process assets
  .2 Procurement management plan
  .3 Procurement documents

.2 Tools and Techniques
  .1 Bidder conferences
  .2 Advertising
  .3 Develop qualified sellers list

.3 Outputs
  .1 Qualified sellers list
  .2 Procurement document package
  .3 Proposals

12.6 Contract Closure

.1 Inputs
  .1 Procurement management plan
  .2 Contract management plan
  .3 Contract documentation
  .4 Contract closure procedure

.2 Tools and Techniques
  .1 Procurement audits
  .2 Records management system

.3 Outputs
  .1 Closed contracts
  .2 Organizational process assets (updates)

12.4 Select Sellers

.1 Inputs
  .1 Organizational process assets
  .2 Procurement management plan
  .3 Evaluation criteria
  .4 Procurement document package
  .5 Proposals
  .6 Qualified sellers list
  .7 Project management plan
    · Risk register
    · Risk-related contractual agreements

.2 Tools and Techniques
  .1 Weighting system
  .2 Independent estimates
  .3 Screening system
  .4 Contract negotiation
  .5 Seller rating systems
  .6 Expert judgment
  .7 Proposal evaluation techniques

.3 Outputs
  .1 Selected sellers
  .2 Contract
  .3 Contract management plan
  .4 Resource availability
  .5 Procurement management plan (updates)
  .6 Requested changes

12.5 Contract Administration

.1 Inputs
  .1 Contract
  .2 Contract management plan
  .3 Selected sellers
  .4 Performance reports
  .5 Approved change requests
  .6 Work performance information

.2 Tools and Techniques
  .1 Contract change control system
  .2 Buyer-conducted performance review
  .3 Inspections and audits
  .4 Performance reporting
  .5 Payment system
  .6 Claims administration
  .7 Records management system
  .8 Information technology

.3 Outputs
  .1 Contract documentation
  .2 Requested changes
  .3 Recommended corrective actions
  .4 Organizational process assets (updates)
  .5 Project management plan (updates)
    · Procurement management plan
    · Contract management plan

Figure 12-1. Project Procurement Management Overview

A Guide to the Project Management Body of Knowledge (PMBOK® Guide) Third Edition
©2004 Project Management Institute, Four Campus Boulevard, Newtown Square, PA 19073-3299 USA

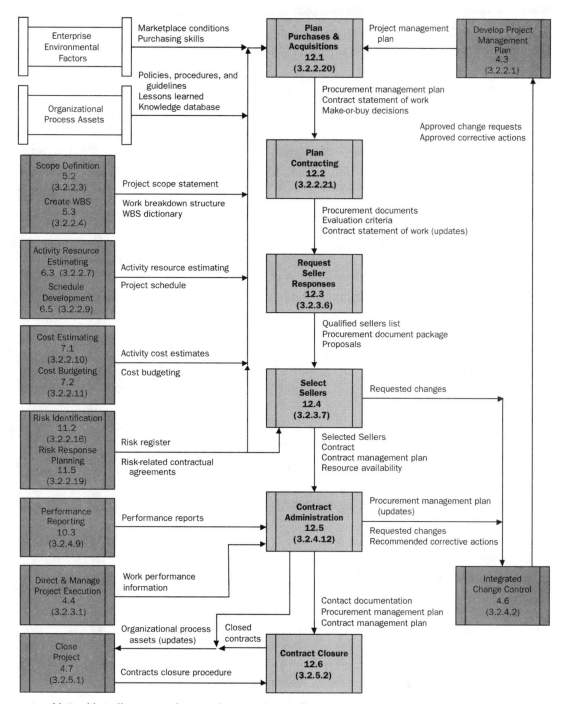

Note: Not all process interactions and data flow among the processes are shown.

Figure 12-2. Project Procurement Management Process Flow Diagram

12.1   Plan Purchases and Acquisitions

The Plan Purchases and Acquisitions process identifies which project needs can best be met by purchasing or acquiring products, services, or results outside the project organization, and which project needs can be accomplished by the project team during project execution. This process involves consideration of whether, how, what, how much, and when to acquire.

When the project obtains products, services, and results required for project performance from outside the performing organization, the processes from Plan Purchases and Acquisitions through Contract Closure are performed for each item to be purchased or acquired.

The Plan Purchases and Acquisitions process also includes consideration of potential sellers, particularly if the buyer wishes to exercise some degree of influence or control over contracting decisions. Consideration should also be given to who is responsible for obtaining or holding any relevant permits and professional licenses that may be required by legislation, regulation, or organizational policy in executing the project.

The project schedule can significantly influence the Plan Purchases and Acquisitions process. Decisions made in developing the procurement management plan can also influence the project schedule and are integrated with Schedule Development (Section 6.5), Activity Resource Estimating (Section 6.3), and make-or-buy decisions.

The Plan Purchases and Acquisitions process includes reviewing the risks involved in each make-or-buy decision; it also includes reviewing the type of contract planned to be used with respect to mitigating risks and transferring risks to the seller.

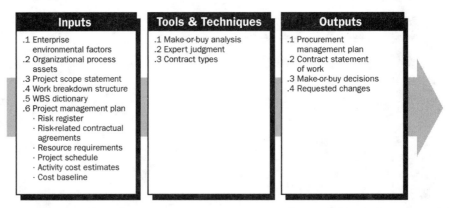

Inputs	Tools & Techniques	Outputs
.1 Enterprise environmental factors .2 Organizational process assets .3 Project scope statement .4 Work breakdown structure .5 WBS dictionary .6 Project management plan · Risk register · Risk-related contractual agreements · Resource requirements · Project schedule · Activity cost estimates · Cost baseline	.1 Make-or-buy analysis .2 Expert judgment .3 Contract types	.1 Procurement management plan .2 Contract statement of work .3 Make-or-buy decisions .4 Requested changes

Figure 12-3. Plan Purchases and Acquisitions: Inputs, Tools & Techniques, and Outputs

A Guide to the Project Management Body of Knowledge (PMBOK® Guide) Third Edition
©2004 Project Management Institute, Four Campus Boulevard, Newtown Square, PA 19073-3299 USA

12.1.1 Plan Purchases and Acquisitions: Inputs

.1 Enterprise Environmental Factors

Enterprise environmental factors (Section 4.1.1.3) that are considered include the conditions of the marketplace and what products, services, and results are available in the marketplace, from whom and under what terms and conditions. If the performing organization does not have formal purchasing or contracting groups, then the project team will have to supply both the resources and the expertise to perform project procurement activities.

.2 Organizational Process Assets

Organizational process assets (Section 4.1.1.4) provide the existing formal and informal procurement-related policies, procedures, guidelines, and management systems that are considered in developing the procurement management plan and selecting the contract types to be used. Organizational policies frequently constrain procurement decisions. These policy constraints can include limiting the use of simple purchase orders and requiring all purchases above a certain value to use a longer form of contract, requiring specific forms of contracts, limiting the ability to make specific make-or-buy decisions, and limiting, or requiring, specific types or sizes of sellers.

Organizations in some application areas also have an established multi-tier supplier system of selected and pre-qualified sellers to reduce the number of direct sellers to the organization and establish an extended supply chain.

.3 Project Scope Statement

The project scope statement (Section 5.2.3.1) describes the project boundaries, requirements, constraints, and assumptions related to the project scope. Constraints are specific factors that can limit both the buyer's and seller's options. One of the most common constraints for many projects is availability of funds. Other constraints can involve required delivery dates, available skilled resources, and organizational policies. Assumptions are factors that will be considered to be true, and which can include items such as the assumed availability of multiple sellers or a sole-source seller. Requirements with contractual and legal implications can include health, safety, security, performance, environmental, insurance, intellectual property rights, equal employment opportunity, licenses, and permits.

The project scope statement provides important information about project needs and strategies that are considered during the Plan Purchases and Acquisitions process. The project scope statement also provides the list of deliverables and acceptance criteria for the project and its products, services, and results. Consideration is given to all such factors that may need to be included in the procurement documentation and flowed down within a contract to sellers.

The product scope description component of the project scope statement provides important information about any technical issues or concerns related to the products, services, and results of the project that are considered during the Plan Purchases and Acquisitions process.

The work breakdown structure (WBS) and WBS dictionary components of the project scope statement provide the structured and detailed plan for the project scope:

.4 Work Breakdown Structure

The Work Breakdown Structure (Section 5.3.3.2) provides the relationship among all the components of the project and the project deliverables (Section 4.4).

.5 WBS Dictionary

The WBS dictionary (Section 5.3.3.3) provides detailed statements of work that provide an identification of the deliverables and a description of the work within each WBS component required to produce each deliverable.

.6 Project Management Plan

The project management plan (Section 4.3) provides the overall plan for managing the project and includes subsidiary plans such as a scope management plan, procurement management plan, quality management plan, and contract management plans, which provide guidance and direction for procurement management planning. To the extent that other planning outputs are available, those other planning outputs are considered during the Plan Purchases and Acquisitions process. Other planning outputs that are often considered include:

- **Risk register** (Section 11.2.3.1). Contains risk-related information such as the identified risks, risk owners, and risk responses.
- **Risk-related contractual agreements** (Section 11.5.3.3). Includes agreements for insurance, services, and other items as appropriate, that are prepared to specify each party's responsibility for specific risks, should they occur.
- **Activity resource requirements** (Section 6.3.3.1).
- **Project schedule** (Section 6.5.3.1).
- **Activity cost estimates** (Section 7.1.3.1).
- **Cost baseline** (Section 7.2.3.1).

12.1.2 Plan Purchases and Acquisitions: Tools and Techniques

.1 Make-or-Buy Analysis

The make-or-buy analysis is a general management technique and a part of the project Plan Purchases and Acquisition process that can be used to determine whether a particular product or service can be produced by the project team or can be purchased. Any project budget constraints are factored in the make-or-buy decisions. If a buy decision is to be made, then a further decision of whether to purchase or rent is also made. The analysis includes both indirect as well as direct costs. For example, the buy-side of the analysis includes both the actual out-of-pocket costs to purchase the product as well as the indirect costs of managing the purchasing process.

A Guide to the Project Management Body of Knowledge (PMBOK® Guide) Third Edition
©2004 Project Management Institute, Four Campus Boulevard, Newtown Square, PA 19073-3299 USA

In a make-or-buy analysis, if a buy decision is to be made, it also reflects the perspective of the project team's organization as well as the immediate needs of the project. For example, purchasing an item (anything from a construction crane to a personal computer) rather than renting or leasing it may or may not be cost effective from the perspective of the project. However, if the project team's organization has an ongoing need for the item, the portion of the purchase cost allocated to the project could be less than the cost of the rental. The cost allocation could be based upon a margin analysis.

The long-range strategy of the project team's organization is also a component in the make-or-buy analysis. Items needed for the performance of the project may not be available within the organization. However, the organization may anticipate future requirements for those items and the organization's plans may also be based on making the items in the future. Such considerations can lead to a make decision in spite of the current project constraints and requirements. When this occurs, the costs charged to the project can be less than the actual costs, with the difference representing the organization's investment for the future.

.2 Expert Judgment

Expert technical judgment will often be required to assess the inputs to and outputs from this process. Expert purchasing judgment can also be used to develop or modify the criteria that will be used to evaluate offers or proposals made by sellers. Expert legal judgment may involve the services of a lawyer to assist with non-standard procurement terms and conditions. Such judgment and expertise, including business expertise and technical expertise, can be applied to both the technical details of the procured products, services, or results and to various aspects of the procurement management processes.

.3 Contract Types

Different types of contracts are more or less appropriate for different types of purchases. The type of contract used and the specific contract terms and conditions set the degree of risk being assumed by both the buyer and seller. Contracts generally fall into one of three broad categories:

- **Fixed-price or lump-sum contracts.** This category of contract involves a fixed total price for a well-defined product. Fixed-price contracts can also include incentives for meeting or exceeding selected project objectives, such as schedule targets. The simplest form of a fixed-price contract is a purchase order for a specified item to be delivered by a specified date for a specified price.

12

- **Cost-reimbursable contracts.** This category of contract involves payment (reimbursement) to the seller for seller's actual costs, plus a fee typically representing seller profit. Costs are usually classified as direct costs or indirect costs. Direct costs are costs incurred for the exclusive benefit of the project (e.g., salaries of full-time project staff). Indirect costs, also called overhead and general and administrative costs, are costs allocated to the project by the project team as a cost of doing business (e.g., salaries of management indirectly involved in the project, cost of electric utilities for the office). Indirect costs are usually calculated as a percentage of direct costs. Cost-reimbursable contracts often include incentive clauses where if the seller meets or exceeds selected project objectives, such as schedule targets or total cost, then the seller receives an incentive or bonus payment. Three common types of cost-reimbursable contracts are CPF, CPFF, and CPIF.

  a. **Cost-Plus-Fee (CPF) or Cost-Plus-Percentage of Cost (CPPC).** Seller is reimbursed for allowable costs for performing the contract work and receives a fee calculated as an agreed-upon percentage of the costs. The fee varies with the actual cost.

  b. **Cost-Plus-Fixed-Fee (CPFF).** Seller is reimbursed for allowable costs for performing the contract work and receives a fixed fee payment calculated as a percentage of the estimated project costs. The fixed fee does not vary with actual costs unless the project scope changes.

  c. **Cost-Plus-Incentive-Fee (CPIF).** Seller is reimbursed for allowable costs for performing the contract work and receives a predetermined fee, an incentive bonus, based upon achieving certain performance objective levels set in the contract. In some CPIF contracts, if the final costs are less than the expected costs, then both the buyer and seller benefit from the cost savings based upon a pre-negotiated sharing formula.

- **Time and Material (T&M) contracts.** T&M contracts are a hybrid type of contractual arrangement that contains aspects of both cost-reimbursable and fixed-price type arrangements. These types of contracts resemble cost-reimbursable type arrangements in that they are open ended. The full value of the agreement and the exact quantity of items to be delivered are not defined by the buyer at the time of the contract award. Thus, T&M contracts can grow in contract value as if they were cost-reimbursable type arrangements. Conversely, T&M arrangements can also resemble fixed-price arrangements. For example, unit rates can be preset by the buyer and seller when both parties agree on the rates for a specific resource category.

A Guide to the Project Management Body of Knowledge (PMBOK® Guide) Third Edition
©2004 Project Management Institute, Four Campus Boulevard, Newtown Square, PA 19073-3299 USA

The requirements (e.g., standard or custom product version, performance reporting, cost data submittals) that a buyer imposes on a seller, along with other planning considerations such as the degree of market competition and degree of risk, will also determine which type of contract will be used. In addition, the seller can consider some of those specific requirements as items that have additional costs. Another consideration relates to the future potential purchase of the product or service being acquired by the project team. Where such potential can be significant, sellers may be inclined or induced to charge prices that are less than would be the case without such future sale potential. While this can reduce the costs to the project, there are legal ramifications if the buyer promises such potential and it is not, in fact, realized.

12.1.3 Plan Purchases and Acquisitions: Outputs

.1 Procurement Management Plan

The procurement management plan describes how the procurement processes will be managed from developing procurement documentation through contract closure. The procurement management plan can include:

- Types of contracts to be used
- Who will prepare independent estimates and if they are needed as evaluation criteria
- Those actions the project management team can take on its own, if the performing organization has a procurement, contracting, or purchasing department
- Standardized procurement documents, if they are needed
- Managing multiple providers
- Coordinating procurement with other project aspects, such as scheduling and performance reporting
- Constraints and assumptions that could affect planned purchases and acquisitions
- Handling the lead times required to purchase or acquire items from sellers and coordinating them with the project schedule development
- Handling the make-or-buy decisions and linking them into the Activity Resource Estimating and Schedule Development processes
- Setting the scheduled dates in each contract for the contract deliverables and coordinating with the schedule development and control processes
- Identifying performance bonds or insurance contracts to mitigate some forms of project risk
- Establishing the direction to be provided to the sellers on developing and maintaining a contract work breakdown structure
- Establishing the form and format to be used for the contract statement of work
- Identifying pre-qualified selected sellers, if any, to be used
- Procurement metrics to be used to manage contracts and evaluate sellers.

12

A procurement management plan can be formal or informal, can be highly detailed or broadly framed, and is based upon the needs of the project. The procurement management plan is a subsidiary component of the project management plan (Section 4.3).

.2 Contract Statement of Work

Each contract statement of work defines, for those items being purchased or acquired, just the portion of the project scope that is included within the related contract. The statement of work (SOW) for each contract is developed from the project scope statement, the project work breakdown structure (WBS), and WBS dictionary. The contract SOW describes the procurement item in sufficient detail to allow prospective sellers to determine if they are capable of providing the item. Sufficient detail can vary, based on the nature of the item, the needs of the buyer, or the expected contract form. A contract SOW describes the products, services, or results to be supplied by the seller. Information included in a contract SOW can include specifications, quantity desired, quality levels, performance data, period of performance, work location, and other requirements.

The contract SOW is written to be clear, complete, and concise. It includes a description of any collateral services required, such as performance reporting or post-project operational support for the procured item. In some application areas, there are specific content and format requirements for a contract SOW. Each individual procurement item requires a contract SOW. However, multiple products or services can be grouped as one procurement item within a single contract SOW.

The contract SOW can be revised and refined as required as it moves through the procurement process until incorporated into a signed contract. For example, a prospective seller can suggest a more efficient approach or a less costly product than that originally specified.

.3 Make-or-Buy Decisions

The documented decisions of what project products, services, or results will be either be acquired or will be developed by the project team. This may include decisions to buy insurance policies or performance bonds contracts to address some of the identified risks. The make-or-buy decisions document can be as simple as a listing that includes a short justification for the decision. These decisions can be iterative as subsequent procurement activities indicate a need for a different approach.

.4 Requested Changes

Requested changes (Section 4.4) to the project management plan and its subsidiary plans and other components may result from the Plan Purchases and Acquisition process. Requested changes are processed for review and disposition through the Integrated Change Control process (Section 4.6).

A Guide to the Project Management Body of Knowledge (PMBOK® Guide) Third Edition
©2004 Project Management Institute, Four Campus Boulevard, Newtown Square, PA 19073-3299 USA

12.2 Plan Contracting

The Plan Contracting process prepares the documents needed to support the Request Seller Responses process and Select Sellers process.

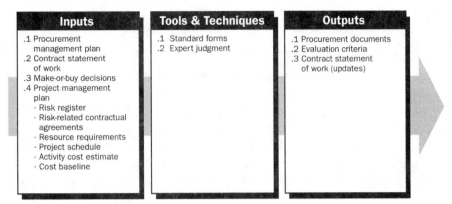

Inputs	Tools & Techniques	Outputs

.1 Procurement management plan
.2 Contract statement of work
.3 Make-or-buy decisions
.4 Project management plan
  · Risk register
  · Risk-related contractual agreements
  · Resource requirements
  · Project schedule
  · Activity cost estimate
  · Cost baseline
	.1 Standard forms
	.2 Expert judgment
		.1 Procurement documents
		.2 Evaluation criteria
		.3 Contract statement of work (updates)

Figure 12-4. Plan Contracting: Inputs, Tools & Techniques, and Outputs

12.2.1 Plan Contracting: Inputs

.1 Procurement Management Plan
Described in Section 12.1.3.1.

.2 Contract Statement of Work
Described in Section 12.1.

.3 Make-or-Buy Decisions
The make-or-buy decisions (Section 12.1) are documented in the issued list of items to be purchased or acquired and those items to be produced by the project team.

.4 Project Management Plan
The project management plan (Section 4.3) provides other planning output documents, which may have been modified and may need to be reviewed again as part of the procurement documentation development. In particular, development of procurement documentation is closely aligned with scheduled delivery dates in the project schedule (Section 6.5).

- **Risk register.** Contains risk-related information such as the identified risks, root causes of risks, risk owners, risk analyses results, risk prioritization, risk categorization, and risk responses generated by the risk management processes.

- **Risk-related contractual agreements** (Section 11.5.3.3). Includes agreements for insurance, services, and other items as appropriate that are prepared to specify each party's responsibility for specific risks, should they occur.

- **Activity resource requirements** (Section 6.3.3.1).
- **Project schedule** (Section 6.5.3.1).
- **Activity cost estimates** (Section 7.1.3.1).
- **Cost baseline** (Section 7.2.3.1).

12.2.2 Plan Contracting: Tools and Techniques

.1 Standard Forms

Standard forms include standard contracts, standard descriptions of procurement items, non-disclosure agreements, proposal evaluation criteria checklists, or standardized versions of all parts of the needed bid documents. Organizations that perform substantial amounts of procurement can have many of these documents standardized. Buyer and seller organizations performing intellectual property transactions ensure that non-disclosure agreements are approved and accepted before disclosing any project specific intellectual property information to the other party.

.2 Expert Judgment

Described in Section 12.1.2.2.

12.2.3 Plan Contracting: Outputs

.1 Procurement Documents

Procurement documents are used to seek proposals from prospective sellers. A term such as bid, tender, or quotation is generally used when the seller selection decision will be based on price (as when buying commercial or standard items), while a term such as proposal is generally used when other considerations, such as technical skills or technical approach, are paramount. However, the terms are often used interchangeably and care is taken not to make unwarranted assumptions about the implications of the term used. Common names for different types of procurement documents include invitation for bid, request for proposal, request for quotation, tender notice, invitation for negotiation, and contractor initial response.

The buyer structures procurement documents to facilitate an accurate and complete response from each prospective seller and to facilitate easy evaluation of the bids. These documents include a description of the desired form of the response, the relevant contract statement of work and any required contractual provisions (e.g., a copy of a model contract, non-disclosure provisions). With government contracting, some or all of the content and structure of procurement documents can be defined by regulation.

The complexity and level of detail of the procurement documents should be consistent with the value of, and risk associated with, the planned purchase or acquisition. Procurement documents are rigorous enough to ensure consistent, comparable responses, but flexible enough to allow consideration of seller suggestions for better ways to satisfy the requirements. Inviting the sellers to submit a proposal that is wholly responsive to the request for bid and to provide a proposed alternative solution in a separate proposal can do this.

A Guide to the Project Management Body of Knowledge (PMBOK® Guide) Third Edition
©2004 Project Management Institute, Four Campus Boulevard, Newtown Square, PA 19073-3299 USA

Issuing a request to potential sellers to submit a proposal or bid is done formally in accordance with the policies of the buyer's organization, which can include publication of the request in public newspapers, in magazines, in public registries, or on the Internet.

.2 Evaluation Criteria

Evaluation criteria are developed and used to rate or score proposals. They can be objective (e.g., "The proposed project manager needs to be a certified Project Management Professional, PMP®") or subjective (e.g., "The proposed project manager needs to have documented previous experience with similar projects"). Evaluation criteria are often included as part of the procurement documents.

Evaluation criteria can be limited to purchase price if the procurement item is readily available from a number of acceptable sellers. Purchase price in this context includes both the cost of the item and ancillary expenses such as delivery.

Other selection criteria can be identified and documented to support an assessment for a more complex product or service. For example:

- **Understanding of need.** How well does the seller's proposal address the contract statement of work?
- **Overall or life-cycle cost.** Will the selected seller produce the lowest total cost (purchase cost plus operating cost)?
- **Technical capability.** Does the seller have, or can the seller be reasonably expected to acquire, the technical skills and knowledge needed?
- **Management approach.** Does the seller have, or can the seller be reasonably expected to develop, management processes and procedures to ensure a successful project?
- **Technical approach.** Do the seller's proposed technical methodologies, techniques, solutions, and services meet the procurement documentation requirements or are they likely to provide more than the expected results?
- **Financial capacity.** Does the seller have, or can the seller reasonably be expected to obtain, the necessary financial resources?
- **Production capacity and interest.** Does the seller have the capacity and interest to meet potential future requirements?
- **Business size and type.** Does the seller's enterprise meet a specific type or size of business, such as small business, women-owned, or disadvantaged small business, as defined by the buyer or established by governmental agency and set as a condition of being award a contract?
- **References.** Can the seller provide references from prior customers verifying the seller's work experience and compliance with contractual requirements?
- **Intellectual property rights.** Does the seller assert intellectual property rights in the work processes or services they will use or in the products they will produce for the project?
- **Proprietary rights.** Does the seller assert proprietary rights in the work processes or services they will use or in the products they will produce for the project?

12

.3 Contract Statement of Work (Updates)
Modifications to one or more contract statements of work (Section 12.1.3.2) can be identified during procurement documentation development.

12.3 Request Seller Responses

The Request Seller Responses process obtains responses, such as bids and proposals, from prospective sellers on how project requirements can be met. The prospective sellers, normally at no direct cost to the project or buyer, expend most of the actual effort in this process.

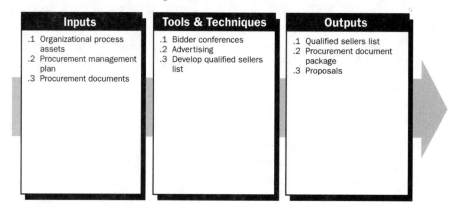

Figure 12-5. Request Seller Responses: Inputs, Tools & Techniques, and Outputs

12.3.1 Request Seller Responses: Inputs

.1 Organizational Process Assets
Some organizations, as part of their organizational process assets, maintain lists or files with information on prospective and previously qualified sellers, sometimes called bidders, who can be asked to bid, propose, or quote on work. These lists will generally have information on relevant past experience and other characteristics of the prospective sellers. Some organizations maintain preferred sellers lists that include only sellers already selected through some qualification methodology.

.2 Procurement Management Plan
Described in Section 12.1.3.1.

.3 Procurement Documents
Described in Section 12.2.3.1.

A Guide to the Project Management Body of Knowledge (PMBOK® Guide) Third Edition
©2004 Project Management Institute, Four Campus Boulevard, Newtown Square, PA 19073-3299 USA

12.3.2 Request Seller Responses: Tools and Techniques

.1 Bidder Conferences

Bidder conferences (also called contractor conferences, vendor conferences, and pre-bid conferences) are meetings with prospective sellers prior to preparation of a bid or proposal. They are used to ensure that all prospective sellers have a clear, common understanding of the procurement (e.g., technical requirements and contract requirements). Responses to questions can be incorporated into the procurement documents as amendments. All potential sellers are given equal standing during this initial buyer and seller interaction to produce the best bid.

.2 Advertising

Existing lists of potential sellers can often be expanded by placing advertisements in general circulation publications such as newspapers or in specialty publications such as professional journals. Some government jurisdictions require public advertising of certain types of procurement items; most government jurisdictions require public advertising of pending government contracts.

.3 Develop Qualified Sellers List

Qualified sellers lists can be developed from the organizational assets if such lists or information are readily available. Whether or not that data is available, the project team can also develop its own sources. General information is widely available through the Internet, library directories, relevant local associations, trade catalogs, and similar sources. Detailed information on specific sources can require more extensive effort, such as site visits or contact with previous customers. Procurement documents (Section 12.2.3.1) can also be sent to determine if some or all of the prospective sellers have an interest in becoming a qualified potential seller.

12

12.3.3 Request Seller Responses: Outputs

.1 Qualified Sellers List

The qualified sellers list are those sellers who are asked to submit a proposal or quotation.

.2 Procurement Document Package

The procurement document package is a buyer-prepared formal request sent to each seller and is the basis upon which a seller prepares a bid for the requested products, services, or results that are defined and described in the procurement documentation.

.3 Proposals

Proposals are seller-prepared documents that describe the seller's ability and willingness to provide the requested products, services, or results described in the procurement documentation. Proposals are prepared in accordance with the requirements of the relevant procurement documents and reflect the application of applicable contract principles. The seller's proposal constitutes a formal and legal offer in response to a buyer's request. After a proposal is formally submitted, the buyer sometimes requests the seller to supplement its proposals with an oral presentation. The oral presentation is meant to provide additional information with respect to the seller's proposed staff, management proposal, and technical proposal, which can be used by the buyer in evaluating the seller's proposal.

12.4 Select Sellers

The Select Sellers process receives bids or proposals and applies evaluation criteria, as applicable, to select one or more sellers who are both qualified and acceptable as a seller. Many factors such as the following can be evaluated in the seller selection decision process:

- Price or cost can be the primary determinant for an off-the-shelf item, but the lowest proposed price may not be the lowest cost if the seller proves unable to deliver the products, services, or results in a timely manner.
- Proposals are often separated into technical (approach) and commercial (price) sections, with each evaluated separately. Sometimes, management sections are required as part of the proposal and also have to be evaluated.
- Multiple sources could be required for critical products, services, and results to mitigate risks that can be associated with issues such as delivery schedules and quality requirements. The potentially higher cost associated with such multiple sellers, including any loss of possible quantity discounts, and replacement and maintenance issues, are considered.

The tools and techniques described here can be used alone or in combination to select sellers. For example, a weighting system can be used to:

- Select a single seller that will be asked to sign a standard contract.
- Establish a negotiating sequence by ranking all proposals by the weighed evaluation scores assigned to each proposal.

On major procurement items, the overall process of requesting responses from sellers and evaluating sellers' responses can be repeated. A short list of qualified sellers can be established based on a preliminary proposal. A more detailed evaluation can then be conducted based on a more detailed and comprehensive proposal that is requested from the sellers on the short list.

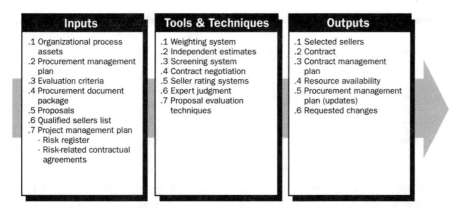

Inputs	Tools & Techniques	Outputs
.1 Organizational process assets .2 Procurement management plan .3 Evaluation criteria .4 Procurement document package .5 Proposals .6 Qualified sellers list .7 Project management plan · Risk register · Risk-related contractual agreements	.1 Weighting system .2 Independent estimates .3 Screening system .4 Contract negotiation .5 Seller rating systems .6 Expert judgment .7 Proposal evaluation techniques	.1 Selected sellers .2 Contract .3 Contract management plan .4 Resource availability .5 Procurement management plan (updates) .6 Requested changes

Figure 12-6. Select Sellers: Inputs, Tools & Techniques, and Outputs

12.4.1 Select Sellers: Inputs

.1 Organizational Process Assets

The organizational process assets of the organizations involved in project procurement typically have formal policies that affect the evaluation of proposals.

.2 Procurement Management Plan

Described in Section 12.1.3.1.

.3 Evaluation Criteria

Evaluation criteria (Section 12.2.3.2) can include samples of the supplier's previously produced products, services, or results for the purpose of providing a way to evaluate the supplier's capabilities and quality of products. Evaluation criteria also can include a review of the supplier's history with the contracting organization and others.

.4 Procurement Document Package

Described in Section 12.3.3.2.

.5 Proposals

Seller proposals prepared in response to a procurement document package (Section 12.3.3.3) form the basic set of information that will be used by an evaluation body to select one or more successful bidders (sellers).

.6 Qualified Sellers List

Described in Section 12.3.3.1.

.7 Project Management Plan

The project management plan provides the overall plan for managing the project and includes subsidiary plans and other components. To the extent that other component documents are available, they are considered during the Select Sellers process. Other documents that are often considered include:

- **Risk register** (Section 11.5.1.2).
- **Risk-related contractual agreements** (Section 11.5.3.3).

12.4.2 Select Sellers: Tools and Techniques

.1 Weighting System

A weighting system is a method for quantifying qualitative data to minimize the effect of personal prejudice on seller selection. Most such systems involve assigning a numerical weight to each of the evaluation criteria, rating the prospective sellers on each criterion, multiplying the weight by the rating, and totaling the resultant products to compute an overall score.

.2 Independent Estimates

For many procurement items, the procuring organization can either prepare its own independent estimates or have prepared an independent estimate of the costs as a check on proposed pricing. This independent estimate is sometimes referred to as a "should-cost" estimate. Significant differences from these cost estimates can be an indication that the contract statement of work was not adequate, that the prospective seller either misunderstood or failed to respond fully to the contract statement of work, or that the marketplace changed.

.3 Screening System

A screening system involves establishing minimum requirements of performance for one or more of the evaluation criteria, and can employ a weighting system and independent estimates. For example, a prospective seller might be required to propose a project manager who has specific qualifications before the remainder of the proposal would be considered. These screening systems are used to provide a weighted ranking from best to worst for all sellers who submitted a proposal.

.4 Contract Negotiation

Contract negotiation clarifies the structure and requirements of the contract so that mutual agreement can be reached prior to signing the contract. Final contract language reflects all agreements reached. Subjects covered include responsibilities and authorities, applicable terms and law, technical and business management approaches, proprietary rights, contract financing, technical solution, overall schedule, payments, and price. Contract negotiations conclude with a document that can be signed by both buyer and seller, that is, the contract. The final contract can be a revised offer by the seller or a counter offer by the buyer.

For complex procurement items, contract negotiation can be an independent process with inputs (e.g., an issues or open items list) and outputs (e.g., documented decisions) of its own. For simple procurement items, the terms and conditions of the contract can be fixed and non-negotiable, and only need to be accepted by the seller.

The project manager may not be the lead negotiator on the contract. The project manager and other members of the project management team may be present during negotiations to provide, if needed, any clarification of the project's technical, quality, and management requirements.

A Guide to the Project Management Body of Knowledge (PMBOK® Guide) Third Edition
©2004 Project Management Institute, Four Campus Boulevard, Newtown Square, PA 19073-3299 USA

.5 Seller Rating Systems

Seller rating systems are developed by many organizations and use information such as the seller's past performance, quality ratings, delivery performance, and contractual compliance. The seller performance evaluation documentation generated during the Contract Administration process for previous sellers is one source of relevant information. These rating systems are used in addition to the proposal evaluations screening system to select sellers.

.6 Expert Judgment

Expert judgment is used in evaluating seller proposals. The evaluation of proposals is accomplished by a multi-discipline review team with expertise in each of the areas covered by the procurement documents and proposed contract. This can include expertise from functional disciplines, such as contracts, legal, finance, accounting, engineering, design, research, development, sales, and manufacturing.

.7 Proposal Evaluation Techniques

Many different techniques can be used to rate and score proposals, but all will use some expert judgment and some form of evaluation criteria (Section 12.2.3.2). The evaluation criteria can involve both objective and subjective components. Evaluation criteria, when used for a formalized proposal evaluation, are usually assigned predefined weightings with respect to each other. The proposal evaluation then uses inputs from multiple reviewers that are obtained during the Select Sellers process, and any significant differences in scoring are resolved. An overall assessment and comparison of all proposals can then be developed using a weighting system that determines the total weighted score for each proposal. These proposal evaluation techniques also can employ a screening system and use data from a seller rating system.

12.4.3 Select Sellers: Outputs

.1 Selected Sellers

The sellers selected are those sellers who have been judged to be in a competitive range based upon the outcome of the proposal or bid evaluation, and who have negotiated a draft contract, which will be the actual contract when an award is made.

.2 Contract

A contract is awarded to each selected seller. The contract can be in the form of a complex document or a simple purchase order. Regardless of the document's complexity, a contract is a mutually binding legal agreement that obligates the seller to provide the specified products, services, or results, and obligates the buyer to pay the seller. A contract is a legal relationship subject to remedy in the courts. The major components in a contract document generally include, but are not limited to, section headings, statement of work, schedule, period of performance, roles and responsibilities, pricing and payment, inflation adjustments, acceptance criteria, warranty, product support, limitation of liability, fees, retainage, penalties, incentives, insurance, performance bonds, subcontractor approval, change request handling, and a termination and disputes resolution mechanism.

.3 Contract Management Plan

For significant purchases or acquisitions, a plan to administer the contract is prepared based upon the specific buyer-specified items within the contract such as documentation, and delivery and performance requirements that the buyer and seller must meet. The plan covers the contract administration activities throughout the life of the contract. Each contract management plan is a subset of the project management plan.

.4 Resource Availability

The quantity and availability of resources and those dates on which each specific resource can be active or idle are documented.

.5 Procurement Management Plan (Updates)

The procurement management plan (Section 12.1.3.1) is updated to reflect any approved change requests (Section 4.4.1.4) that affect procurement management.

.6 Requested Changes

Requested changes to the project management plan and its subsidiary plans and other components, such as the project schedule (Section 6.5.3.1) and procurement management plan, may result from the Select Sellers process. Requested changes are processed for review and disposition through the Integrated Change Control process (Section 4.6).

12.5 Contract Administration

Both the buyer and the seller administer the contract for similar purposes. Each party ensures that both it and the other party meet their contractual obligations and that their own legal rights are protected. The Contract Administration process ensures that the seller's performance meets contractual requirements and that the buyer performs according to the terms of the contract. On larger projects with multiple products, services, and results providers, a key aspect of contract administration is managing interfaces among the various providers.

The legal nature of the contractual relationship makes it imperative that the project management team is acutely aware of the legal implications of actions taken when administering any contract. Because of the legal considerations, many organizations treat contract administration as an administrative function separate from the project organization. While a contract administrator may be on the project team, this individual typically reports to a supervisor from a different department. This is usually true if the performing organization is also the seller of the project to an external customer.

Contract Administration includes application of the appropriate project management processes to the contractual relationship(s), and integration of the outputs from these processes into overall management of the project. This integration will often occur at multiple levels when there are multiple sellers and multiple products, services, or results involved. The project management processes that are applied include, but are not limited to:

A Guide to the Project Management Body of Knowledge (PMBOK® Guide) Third Edition
©2004 Project Management Institute, Four Campus Boulevard, Newtown Square, PA 19073-3299 USA

- Direct and Manage Project Execution (Section 4.4) to authorize the contractor's work at the appropriate time
- Performance Reporting (Section 10.3) to monitor contractor cost, schedule, and technical performance
- Perform Quality Control (Section 8.3) to inspect and verify the adequacy of the contractor's product
- Integrated Change Control (Section 4.6) to assure that changes are properly approved, and that all those with a need to know are aware of such changes
- Risk Monitoring and Control (Section 11.6) to ensure that risks are mitigated.

Contract administration also has a financial management component that involves monitoring of payments to the seller. This ensures that payment terms defined within the contract are met and that seller compensation is linked to seller progress, as defined in the contract.

The Contract Administration process reviews and documents how well a seller is performing or has performed based on the contract and established corrective actions. Also, the performance is documented as a basis for future relationships with the seller. Seller performance evaluation by the buyer is primarily carried out to confirm the competency or lack of competency of the seller, relative to performing similar work on the project or other projects. Similar evaluations are also carried out when it is necessary to confirm that a seller is not meeting the seller's contractual obligations, and when the buyer contemplates corrective actions. Contract administration includes managing any early termination (Section 12.6) of the contracted work (for cause, convenience, or default) in accordance with the termination clause of the contract.

Contracts can be amended any time prior to contract closure by mutual consent, in accordance with the change control terms of the contract. Such amendments may not always be equally beneficial to both the seller and the buyer.

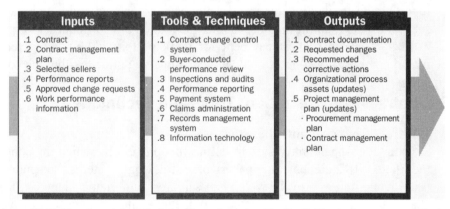

Figure 12-7. Contract Administration: Inputs, Tools & Techniques, and Outputs

12.5.1 Contract Administration: Inputs

.1 Contract
Described in Section 12.4.3.2.

.2 Contract Management Plan
Described in Section 12.4.3.3.

.3 Selected Sellers
Described in Section 12.4.3.1.

.4 Performance Reports
Seller performance-related documentation includes:

- Seller-developed technical documentation and other deliverables information provided in accordance with the terms of the contract
- Seller performance reports (Section 10.3.3.1).

.5 Approved Change Requests
Approved changes requests can include modifications to the terms and conditions of the contract, including the contract statement of work, pricing, and description of the products, services, or results to be provided. All changes are formally documented in writing and approved before being implemented. Any verbally discussed, but undocumented, changes do not need to be processed or implemented.

.6 Work Performance Information
Work performance information (Section 4.4.3.7), including the extent to which quality standards are being met, what costs have been incurred or committed, seller invoices, etc., is collected as part of project execution. The seller's performance reports indicate which deliverables have been completed and which have not. The seller must also submit invoices (sometimes called bills or requests for payment) on a timely basis to request payment for work performed. Invoicing requirements, including necessary supporting documentation, are defined within the contract.

12.5.2 Contract Administration: Tools and Techniques

.1 Contract Change Control System
A contract change control system defines the process by which the contract can be modified. It includes the paperwork, tracking systems, dispute resolution procedures, and approval levels necessary for authorizing changes. The contract change control system is integrated with the integrated change control system.

.2 Buyer-Conducted Performance Review

A procurement performance review is a structured review of the seller's progress to deliver project scope and quality, within cost and on schedule, as compared to the contract. It can include a review of seller-prepared documentation and buyer inspections, as well as quality audits conducted during seller's execution of the work. The objective of a performance review is to identify performance successes or failures, progress with respect to the contract statement of work, and contract non-compliance that allows the buyer to quantify the seller's demonstrated ability or inability to perform work.

.3 Inspections and Audits

Inspections and audits (Section 8.2.2.2), required by the buyer and supported by the seller as specified in the contract documentation, can be conducted during execution of the project to identify any weaknesses in the seller's work processes or deliverables. If authorized by contract, some inspection and audit teams can include buyer procurement personnel.

.4 Performance Reporting

Performance reporting provides management with information about how effectively the seller is achieving the contractual objectives. Contract performance reporting is integrated into performance reporting (Section 10.3.3.1).

.5 Payment System

Payments to the seller are usually handled by the accounts payable system of the buyer. On larger projects with many or complex procurement requirements, the project can develop its own payment system. In either case, the payment system includes appropriate reviews and approvals by the project management team, and payments are made in accordance with the terms of the contract (Section 12.4.3.2).

12

.6 Claims Administration

Contested changes and constructive changes are those requested changes (Section 4.4.3.2) where the buyer and seller cannot agree on compensation for the change, or cannot agree that a change has even occurred. These contested changes are variously called claims, disputes, or appeals. Claims are documented, processed, monitored, and managed throughout the contract life cycle, usually in accordance with the terms of the contract. If the parties themselves do not resolve a claim, it may have to be handled in accordance with the dispute resolution procedures established in the contract. These contract clauses can involve arbitration or litigation, and can be invoked prior to or after contract closure.

.7 Records Management System

A records management system is a specific set of processes, related control functions, and automation tools that are consolidated and combined into a whole, as part of the project management information system (Section 4.2.2.2). A records management system is used by the project manager to manage contract documentation and records. The system is used to maintain an index of contract documents and correspondence, and assist with retrieving and archiving that documentation.

.8 Information Technology

The use of information and communication technologies can enhance the efficiency and effectiveness of contract administration by automating portions of the records management system, payment system, claims administration, or performance reporting and providing electronic data interchange between the buyer and seller.

12.5.3 Contract Administration: Outputs

.1 Contract Documentation

Contract documentation includes, but is not limited to, the contract (Section 12.4.3.2), along with all supporting schedules, requested unapproved contract changes, and approved change requests. Contract documentation also includes any seller-developed technical documentation and other work performance information, such as deliverables, seller performance reports, warranties, financial documents including invoices and payment records, and the results of contract-related inspections.

.2 Requested Changes

Requested changes to the project management plan and its subsidiary plans and other components, such as the project schedule (Section 6.5.3.1) and procurement management plan (Section 12.1.3.1), may result from the Contract Administration process. Requested changes are processed for review and approval through the Integrated Change Control process (Section 4.6).

Requested changes can include direction provided by the buyer, or actions taken by the seller, that the other party considers a constructive change to the contract. Since any of these constructive changes may be disputed by one party and can lead to a claim against the other party, such changes are uniquely identified and documented by project correspondence.

.3 Recommended Corrective Actions

A recommended corrective action is anything that needs to be done to bring the seller in compliance with the terms of the contract.

.4 Organizational Process Assets (Updates)

- **Correspondence.** Contract terms and conditions often require written documentation of certain aspects of buyer/seller communications, such as warnings of unsatisfactory performance and requests for contract changes or clarifications. This can include the reported results of buyer audits and inspections that indicate weaknesses the seller needs to correct. In addition to specific contract requirements for documentation, a complete and accurate written record of all written and oral contract communications, as well as actions taken and decisions made, are maintained by both parties.
- **Payment schedules and requests.** This assumes that the project is using an external payment system. If the project has its own internal system, the output here would simply be payments.

- **Seller performance evaluation documentation.** Seller performance evaluation documentation is prepared by the buyer. Such performance evaluations document the seller's ability to continue to perform work on the current contract, indicate if the seller can be allowed to perform work on future projects, or rate how well the seller is performing the project work. These documents can form the basis for early termination of the seller's contract, or determining how contract penalties, fees, or incentives are administered. The results of these performance evaluations can also be included in the appropriate qualified seller lists (Section 12.3.3.1).

.5 Project Management Plan (Updates)

- **Procurement management plan.** The procurement management plan (Section 12.1.3.1) is updated to reflect any approved change requests that affect procurement management.
- **Contract management plan.** Each contract management plan (Section 12.4.3.3) is updated to reflect any approved change requests that affect contract administration.

12.6 Contract Closure

The Contract Closure process supports the Close Project process (Section 4.7), since it involves verification that all work and deliverables were acceptable. The Contract Closure process also involves administrative activities, such as updating records to reflect final results and archiving such information for future use. Contract closure addresses each contract applicable to the project or a project phase. In multi-phase projects, the term of a contract may only be applicable to a given phase of the project. In these cases, the Contract Closure process closes the contract(s) applicable to that phase of the project. Unresolved claims may be subject to litigation after contract closure. The contract terms and conditions can prescribe specific procedures for contract closure.

Early termination of a contract is a special case of contract closure, and can result from a mutual agreement of the parties or from the default of one of the parties. The rights and responsibilities of the parties in the event of an early termination are contained in a terminations clause of the contract. Based upon those contract terms and conditions, the buyer may have the right to terminate the whole contract or a portion of the project, for cause or convenience, at any time. However, based upon those contract terms and conditions, the buyer may have to compensate the seller for seller's preparations and for any completed and accepted work related to the terminated part of the contract.

12

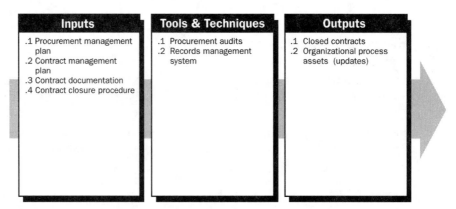

Figure 12-8. Contract Closure: Inputs, Tools & Techniques, and Outputs

12.6.1 Contract Closure: Inputs

.1 Procurement Management Plan
Described in Section 12.1.3.1

.2 Contract Management Plan
Described in Section 12.4.3.3.

.3 Contract Documentation
Described in Section 12.5.3.1.

.4 Contract Closure Procedure
Described in Section 4.7.3.2.

12.6.2 Contract Closure: Tools and Techniques

.1 Procurement Audits
A procurement audit is a structured review of the procurement process from the Plan Purchases and Acquisitions process (Section 12.1) through Contract Administration (Section 12.5). The objective of a procurement audit is to identify successes and failures that warrant recognition in the preparation or administration of other procurement contracts on the project, or on other projects within the performing organization.

.2 Records Management System
Described in Section 12.5.

12.6.3 Contract Closure: Outputs

.1 Closed Contracts

The buyer, usually through its authorized contract administrator, provides the seller with formal written notice that the contract has been completed. Requirements for formal contract closure are usually defined in the terms of the contract, and would be included in the contract management plan, if one was prepared.

.2 Organizational Process Assets (Updates)

- **Contract file.** A complete set of indexed contract documentation, including the closed contract, is prepared for inclusion with the final project files (Section 4.7.3.4).
- **Deliverable acceptance.** The buyer, usually through its authorized contract administrator, provides the seller with formal written notice that the deliverables have been accepted or rejected. Requirements for formal deliverable acceptance, and how to address non-conforming deliverables, are usually defined in the contract.
- **Lessons learned documentation.** Lessons learned analysis and process improvement recommendations are developed for future purchasing and acquisition planning and implementation.

12

Section IV

Appendices

Appendix A   Third Edition Changes

Appendix B   Evolution of PMI's A Guide to the Project
Management Body of Knowledge

Appendix C   Contributors and Reviewers of
PMBOK® Guide – Third Edition

Appendix D   Application Area Extensions

Appendix E   Additional Sources of Information on
Project Management

Appendix F   Summary of Project Management Knowledge Areas

APPENDIX A – THIRD EDITION CHANGES

The purpose of this appendix is to give a detailed explanation of the detailed changes made to *A Guide to the Project Management Body of Knowledge (PMBOK® Guide)* – 2000 Edition to create the *PMBOK® Guide* – Third Edition.

Structural Changes

One of the most pronounced changes to the Third Edition of the *PMBOK® Guide* is the structure. The Third Edition is structured to emphasize the importance of the Process Groups as described in Table 1, which displays a side-by-side comparison of the changes. Chapter 3 is renamed "Project Management Processes for a Project" and has been moved from Section I to a new Section II, which is now called "The Standard for Project Management of a Project." As part of this change, Chapter 3 has been extensively revised to clearly indicate that the processes, inputs, and outputs called out in the chapter are the basis of the standard for project management of a single project.

2000 Edition Sections	Third Edition Sections
Section I - The Project Management Framework Chapters 1, 2, and 3	Section I - The Project Management Framework Chapters 1 and 2
	Section II - The Standard for Project Management of a Project Chapter 3 - Project Management Processes for a Project
Section II - The Project Management Knowledge Areas Chapters 4 through 12	Section III - The Project Management Knowledge Areas Chapters 4 through 12
Section III - Appendices Appendix D - Notes Appendix E - Application Area Extensions	Section IV - Appendices Appendix D - Application Area Extensions
Section IV - Glossary and Index	Section V – References, Glossary, and Index

Table 1 – Structural Changes

Process Name Changes

In the Third Edition, seven processes have been added, thirteen renamed, and two deleted for a net gain of five processes.

The names of processes in the various chapters of the *PMBOK® Guide* – 2000 Edition are in different formats and styles. Inconsistent naming styles can cause confusion for project management students and experienced individuals as well. As an example, the processes in the Scope Knowledge Area are Initiation, Scope Planning, Scope Definition, Scope Verification, and Scope Change Control. Some of these are active voice; some are present participles. The effect of these different styles is that readers are unable, at a glance, to determine whether a term is an activity (a process) or a deliverable (a work-product or artifact). The project team proposed a wholesale change of all process names to the verb-object format in the *PMBOK® Guide* – Third Edition. However, PMI was concerned that changing all of the names would be too large a change; therefore, PMI authorized only an incremental change in the *PMBOK® Guide* – Third Edition to include only those approved new processes and a small number of other processes for specific reasons explained later in this appendix.

Elimination of Facilitating and Core Process Designations

The terms "Facilitating Processes" and "Core Processes" are no longer used. These terms have been eliminated to ensure that all project management processes in the Project Management Process Groups have the same level of importance. The project management processes are still grouped within the Project Management Process Groups, as indicated in Figure 3-5 Initiating Process Group; Figure 3-6 Planning Process Group; Figure 3-7 Executing Process Group; Figure 3-8 Monitoring and Controlling Process Group; and Figure 3-9 Closing Process Group. The 44 project management processes are mapped into both the Project Management Process Groups and the Knowledge Areas, as shown in Table 3-45.

Writing Styles

A Style Guide was developed and used by the project team to create and finalize the input. Attention was focused on using active voice language and content consistency throughout the document to prevent an occurrence of different writing styles.

Chapter 1 - Introduction Changes

Chapter 1 changes clarify and improve organization within the chapter. Chapter 1 clarifies the differences between a project and operations. The changes provide standard definitions for program and program management, portfolio and portfolio management, and include a more detailed discussion of project management office (PMO) variations. Additional revisions include the following:

- General management skills have been moved to Chapter 1
- A section identifying the many areas of expertise needed by the project team has been added.

Chapter 2 - Project Life Cycle and Organization Changes

Chapter 2 changes clarify the distinctions between project life cycles and product life cycles, and explain project phases. Stakeholders are defined in relation to the project team. A PMO's role and responsibility in the organization are defined, and the concept of a project management system is introduced.

Chapter 3 - Project Management Processes for a Project Changes

Chapter 3 has been completely rewritten and expanded to focus on the Project Management Process Groups and processes within the Knowledge Areas. For emphasis, Chapter 3 has been renamed "Project Management Processes for a Project" and moved into a new Section II, "The Standard for Project Management of a Project." Chapter 3 has been extensively revised to serve as a standard for managing a single project and clearly indicates the five required Project Management Process Groups and their constituent processes. The Initiating Process Group and the Closing Process Group are given more emphasis than in previous editions. The Controlling Process Group has been expanded to include Monitoring and is retitled the "Monitoring and Controlling Process Group." Material has been added to clarify the distinction between the Project Management Process Groups and project phases, which have sometimes mistakenly been viewed as one and the same.

Chapter 4 - Project Integration Management Changes

Chapter 4 has been completely rewritten and enhances the discussion of integrating project management processes and activities. The chapter describes integration from the aspect of the Project Management Process Groups, and provides a clear description of integration across all Project Management Process Groups and among all project management processes. Four new processes are included in the chapter and two processes have been renamed:

- Develop Project Charter process formally authorizes a project.
- Develop Preliminary Project Scope Statement process provides a high-level scope narrative.
- Develop Project Management Plan process documents the actions necessary to define, prepare, integrate, and coordinate all subsidiary plans into the project management plan.
- Direct and Manage Project Execution process executes the work defined in the project management plan to achieve the project's objectives.
- Monitor and Control Project Work process defines the processes to monitor and control the project activities needed to initiate, plan, execute, and close a project.
- Close Project process finalizes all activities across all of the Process Groups to formally close the project.

The following table summarizes the Chapter 4 changes:

2000 Edition Sections	Third Edition Sections
	4.1 Develop Project Charter
	4.2 Develop Preliminary Project Scope Statement
4.1 Project Plan Development	4.3 Develop Project Management Plan
4.2 Project Plan Execution	4.4 Direct and Manage Project Execution
	4.5 Monitor and Control Project Work
4.3 Integrated Change Control	4.6 Integrated Change Control
	4.7 Close Project

Table 2 – Chapter 4 Changes

Chapter 5 - Project Scope Management Changes

Chapter 5 has been modified to clarify the role of the project scope management plan in developing the project scope statement. The chapter expands the discussion and clarifies the importance of a work breakdown structure (WBS), with the addition of a new section on creating the WBS. The Initiation section has been rewritten and moved to Chapter 4. The following table summarizes the Chapter 5 changes:

2000 Edition Sections	Third Edition Sections
5.1 Initiation	Rewritten and moved to Chapter 4
5.2 Scope Planning	5.1 Scope Planning
5.3 Scope Definition	5.2 Scope Definition
	5.3 Create WBS
5.4 Scope Verification	5.4 Scope Verification
5.5 Scope Change Control	5.5 Scope Control

Table 3 – Chapter 5 Changes

A Guide to the Project Management Body of Knowledge (PMBOK® Guide) Third Edition
©2004 Project Management Institute, Four Campus Boulevard, Newtown Square, PA 19073-3299 USA

Chapter 6 - Project Time Management Changes

Chapter 6 changes include moving the Resource Planning section into the chapter and renaming it Activity Resource Estimating. Several figures have been deleted (e.g., PERT) and other figures reworked to clarify the use and meaning (e.g., bar or Gantt chart, milestone chart). Another figure has been added to show the difference between a milestone schedule, summary schedule, and detailed schedule. The chapter introduction describes the need for a schedule management plan, a subsidiary component of the project management plan. Subsections have also been added to provide information on project cost estimates, resource leveling, and progress reporting to reflect how these processes influence the project's schedule. The following table summarizes the Chapter 6 changes:

2000 Edition Sections	Third Edition Sections
6.1 Activity Definition	6.1 Activity Definition
6.2 Activity Sequencing	6.2 Activity Sequencing
	6.3 Activity Resource Estimating
6.3 Activity Duration Estimating	6.4 Activity Duration Estimating
6.4 Schedule Development	6.5 Schedule Development
6.5 Schedule Control	6.6 Schedule Control

Table 4 – Chapter 6 Changes

Chapter 7 - Project Cost Management Changes

Chapter 7 processes have been expanded to integrate project budget directly with the WBS and to cover controlling costs. There are significant structural changes to the inputs, tools and techniques, as well. The chapter introduction describes the need for a cost management plan, a subsidiary component of the project management plan. The Resource Planning process has been moved to Chapter 6 and renamed Activity Resource Estimating. This chapter contains the majority of the information on Earned Value Management. The following table summarizes the Chapter 7 changes:

2000 Edition Sections	Third Edition Sections
7.1 Resource Planning	Moved to Project Time Management (Chapter 6)
7.2 Cost Estimating	7.1 Cost Estimating
7.3 Cost Budgeting	7.2 Cost Budgeting
7.4 Cost Control	7.3 Cost Control

Table 5 – Chapter 7 Changes

A

Chapter 8 - Project Quality Management Changes

Chapter 8 includes two revised project management process names to better reflect the activities of those processes. An emphasis has been made to integrate quality activities with the overall Monitoring and Controlling process, as defined in Chapter 4. The following table summarizes the Chapter 8 changes:

2000 Edition Sections	Third Edition Sections
8.1 Quality Planning	8.1 Quality Planning
8.2 Quality Assurance	8.2 Perform Quality Assurance
8.3 Quality Control	8.3 Perform Quality Control

Table 6 – Chapter 8 Changes

Chapter 9 - Project Human Resource Management Changes

Chapter 9 identifies several aspects of human resource planning, as well as the staffing management plan. Manage Project Team has been added as a Monitoring and Controlling process. Several key explanations have also been added, including organizational charts and position descriptions. The figures in this chapter now reflect current project management techniques, such as virtual teams, ground rules, and issues log. The following table summarizes the Chapter 9 changes:

2000 Edition Sections	Third Edition Sections
9.1 Organizational Planning	9.1 Human Resource Planning
9.2 Staff Acquisition	9.2 Acquire Project Team
9.3 Team Development	9.3 Develop Project Team
	9.4 Manage Project Team

Table 7 – Chapter 9 Changes

Chapter 10 - Project Communications Management Changes

Chapter 10 has been updated with the addition of a Manage Stakeholders process. The Manage Stakeholders process manages communications to satisfy the needs of, and resolve issues with, project stakeholders. The following table summarizes the Chapter 10 changes:

2000 Edition Sections	Third Edition Sections
10.1 Communications Planning	10.1 Communications Planning
10.2 Information Distribution	10.2 Information Distribution
10.3 Performance Reporting	10.3 Performance Reporting
10.4 Administrative Closure	10.4 Manage Stakeholders

Table 8 – Chapter 10 Changes

A Guide to the Project Management Body of Knowledge (PMBOK® Guide) Third Edition
©2004 Project Management Institute, Four Campus Boulevard, Newtown Square, PA 19073-3299 USA

Chapter 11 - Project Risk Management Changes

Chapter 11 has been updated to increase focus on opportunities (versus threats). It includes options based on project complexity, enhances Risk Management Planning activities, adds the risk register, and provides closer integration with other processes. The following table summarizes the Chapter 11 changes:

2000 Edition Sections	Third Edition Sections
11.1 Risk Management Planning	11.1 Risk Management Planning
11.2 Risk Identification	11.2 Risk Identification
11.3 Qualitative Risk Analysis	11.3 Qualitative Risk Analysis
11.4 Quantitative Risk Analysis	11.4 Quantitative Risk Analysis
11.5 Risk Response Planning	11.5 Risk Response Planning
11.6 Risk Monitoring and Control	11.6 Risk Monitoring and Control

Table 9 – Chapter 11 Changes (no name changes were made)

Chapter 12 - Project Procurement Management Changes

Chapter 12 has been updated to include a consistent use of the terms "buyer" and "seller." The chapter now clarifies the difference between the project team as a buyer of products and services, and as the seller of products and services. The chapter now includes a process on seller performance evaluation to contract administration, and has removed the words "procure," "solicit," and "solicitation" to recognize the negative connotation of these words in various areas around the world. The following table summarizes the Chapter 12 changes:

2000 Edition Sections	Third Edition Sections
12.1 Procurement Planning	12.1 Plan Purchases and Acquisitions
12.2 Solicitation Planning	12.2 Plan Contracting
12.3 Solicitation	12.3 Request Seller Responses
12.4 Source Selection	12.4 Select Sellers
12.5 Contract Administration	12.5 Contract Administration
12.6 Contract Closeout	12.6 Contract Closure

Table 10 – Chapter 12 Changes

Glossary

The glossary has been expanded and updated to:

- Include those terms within the *PMBOK® Guide* that need to be defined to support an understanding of the document's contents
- Clarify meaning and improve the quality and accuracy of any translations
- Eliminate terms not used within the *PMBOK® Guide* – Third Edition.

A

APPENDIX B

Evolution of PMI's *A Guide to the Project Management Body of Knowledge*

B.1 Initial Development

The Project Management Institute (PMI) was founded in 1969 on the premise that there were many management practices that were common to projects in application areas as diverse as construction and pharmaceuticals. By the time of the PMI Montreal Seminars/Symposium in 1976, the idea that such common practices might be documented as standards began to be widely discussed. This led, in turn, to consideration of project management as a distinct profession.

It was not until 1981, however, that the PMI Board of Directors approved a project to develop the procedures and concepts necessary to support the profession of project management. The project proposal suggested three areas of focus:

- The distinguishing characteristics of a practicing professional (ethics)
- The content and structure of the profession's body of knowledge (standards)
- Recognition of professional attainment (accreditation).

The project team thus came to be known as the Ethics, Standards, and Accreditation (ESA) Management Group. The ESA Management Group consisted of the following individuals:

Matthew H. Parry, Chair	David C. Aird	Frederick R. Fisher
David Haeney	Harvey Kolodney	Charles E. Oliver
William H. Robinson	Douglas J. Ronson	Paul Sims
Eric W. Smythe		

More than twenty-five volunteers in several local chapters assisted this group. The Ethics statement was developed and submitted by a committee in Washington, DC, chaired by Lew Ireland. The Time Management statement was developed through extensive meetings of a group in Southern Ontario, including Dave MacDonald, Dave Norman, Bob Spence, Bob Hall, and Matt Parry. The Cost Management statement was developed through extensive meetings within the cost department of Stelco, under the direction of Dave Haeney and Larry Harrison. Other statements were developed by the ESA Management Group. Accreditation was taken up by John Adams and his group at Western Carolina University, which resulted in the development of accreditation guidelines. It also resulted in a program of Project Management Professional (PMP®) certification, under the guidance of Dean Martin.

The results of the ESA Project were published in a Special Report in the Project Management Journal in August 1983. The report included:

- A Code of Ethics, plus a procedure for code enforcement
- A standards baseline consisting of six major Knowledge Areas: Scope Management, Cost Management, Time Management, Quality Management, Human Resources Management, and Communications Management
- Guidelines for both accreditation (recognition of the quality of programs provided by educational institutions) and certification (recognition of the professional qualifications of individuals).

This report subsequently served as the basis for PMI's initial Accreditation and Certification programs. Western Carolina University's Master's Degree in Project Management was accredited in 1983, and the first PMP certifications were awarded in 1984.

B.2   1986–87 Update

Publication of the ESA Baseline Report gave rise to much discussion within PMI about the adequacy of the standards. In 1984, the PMI Board of Directors approved a second standards-related project "to capture the knowledge applied to project management … within the existing ESA framework." Six committees were then recruited to address each of the six identified Knowledge Areas. In addition, a workshop was scheduled as part of the PMI 1985 Annual Seminars/Symposium.

As a result of these efforts, a revised document was approved in principle by the PMI Board of Directors and published for comment in the Project Management Journal in August 1986. The primary contributors to this version of the document were:

R. Max Wideman, Chair *(during development)*	John R. Adams, Chair *(when issued)*	
Joseph R. Beck	Peter Bibbes	Jim Blethen
Richard Cockfield	Peggy Day	William Dixon
Peter C. Georgas	Shirl Holingsworth	William Kane
Colin Morris	Joe Muhlberger	Philip Nunn
Pat Patrick	David Pym	Linn C. Stuckenbruck
George Vallance	Larry C. Woolslager	Shakir Zuberi

In addition to expanding and restructuring the original material, the revised document included three new sections:

- Project Management Framework was added to cover the relationships between the project and its external environment, and between project management and general management
- Risk Management was added as a separate Knowledge Area in order to provide better coverage of this subject
- Contract/Procurement Management was added as a separate Knowledge Area in order to provide better coverage of this subject.

Subsequently, a variety of editorial changes and corrections were incorporated into the material, and the PMI Board of Directors approved it in March 1987. The final manuscript was published in August 1987 as a stand-alone document titled "The Project Management Body of Knowledge."

B.3 1996 Update

Discussion about the proper form, content, and structure of PMI's key standards document continued after publication of the 1987 version. In August 1991, PMI's Director of Standards Alan Stretton initiated a project to update the document based on comments received from the membership. The revised document was developed over several years through a series of widely circulated working drafts and through workshops at the PMI Seminars/Symposia in Dallas, Pittsburgh, and San Diego.

In August 1994, the PMI Standards Committee issued an exposure draft of the document that was distributed for comment to all 10,000 PMI members and to more than twenty other professional and technical associations.

The publication of A Guide to the Project Management Body of Knowledge (PMBOK® Guide) in 1996 represented the completion of the project initiated in 1991. Contributors and reviewers are listed later in this section. A summary of the differences between the 1987 document and the 1996 document, which was included in the Preface of the 1996 edition, also is listed later in this section.

The document superseded PMI's "The Project Management Body of Knowledge (PMBOK®)" document that was published in 1987. To assist users of the 1996 document, who may have been familiar with its predecessor, we have summarized the major differences here:

1. We changed the title to emphasize that this document is not the project management body of knowledge. The 1987 document defined the project management body of knowledge as "all those topics, subject areas and intellectual processes which are involved in the application of sound management principles to … projects." Clearly, one document will never contain the entire project management body of knowledge.

B

2.   We completely rewrote the Framework section. The new section consists of three chapters:
   - Introduction, which sets out the purpose of the document and defines at length the terms project and project management
   - The Project Management Context, which covers the context in which projects operate—the project life cycle, stakeholder perspectives, external influences, and key general management skills
   - Project Management Processes, which describes how the various elements of project management interrelate.

3.   We developed a revised definition of project. We wanted a definition that was both inclusive ("It should not be possible to identify any undertaking generally thought of as a project that does not fit the definition.") and exclusive ("It should not be possible to describe any undertaking that satisfies the definition and is not generally thought of as a project."). We reviewed many of the definitions of project in the existing literature and found all of them unsatisfactory in some way. The new definition is driven by the unique characteristics of a project: a project is a temporary endeavor undertaken to create a unique product or service.

4.   We developed a revised view of the project life cycle. The 1987 document defined project phases as subdivisions of the project life cycle. We have reordered this relationship and defined project life cycle as a collection of phases whose number and names are determined by the control needs of the performing organization.

5.   We changed the name of the major sections from Function to Knowledge Area. The term Function had been frequently misunderstood to mean an element of a functional organization. The name change should eliminate this misunderstanding.

6.   We formally recognized the existence of a ninth Knowledge Area. There has been widespread consensus for some time that project management is an integrative process. Chapter 4, Project Integration Management, recognizes the importance of this subject.

7.   We added the word Project to the title of each Knowledge Area. Although this may seem redundant, it helps to clarify the scope of the document. For example, Project Human Resource Management covers only those aspects of managing human resources that are unique or nearly unique to the project context.

8.   We chose to describe the Knowledge Areas in terms of their component processes. The search for a consistent method of presentation led us to completely restructure the 1987 document into thirty-seven project management processes. Each process is described in terms of its inputs, outputs, and tools and techniques. Inputs and outputs are documents (e.g., a scope statement) or documentable items (e.g., activity dependencies). Tools and techniques are the mechanisms applied to the inputs to create the outputs. In addition to its fundamental simplicity, this approach offers several other benefits:

- It emphasizes the interactions among the Knowledge Areas. Outputs from one process become inputs to another.

- The structure is flexible and robust. Changes in knowledge and practice can be accommodated by adding a new process, by resequencing processes, by subdividing processes, or by adding descriptive material within a process.

- Processes are at the core of other standards. For example, the International Organization for Standardization's quality standards (the ISO 9000 series) are based on identification of business processes.

9. We added some illustrations. When it comes to work breakdown structures, network diagrams, and S-curves, a picture is worth a thousand words.

10. We significantly reorganized the document. The following table provides a comparison of the major headings of the 1987 document and the corresponding headings and/or content sources of the 1996 version:

1987 Number and Name	1996 Number and Name
0. PMBOK® Standards	B. Evolution of PMI's *A Guide to the Project Management Body of Knowledge*
1. Framework: The Rationale	1. Introduction (basic definitions)
	2. The Project Context (life cycles)
2. Framework: An Overview	1. Various portions
	2. Various portions
	3. Various portions
3. Framework: An Integrative Model	3. Project Management Processes
	4. Project Integration Management
4. Glossary of General Terms	IV. Glossary
A. Scope Management	5. Project Scope Management
B. Quality Management	8. Project Quality Management
C. Time Management	6. Project Time Management
D. Cost Management	7. Project Cost Management
E. Risk Management	11. Project Risk Management
F. Human Resource Management	9. Project Human Resource Management
G. Contract/Procurement Management	12. Project Procurement Management
H. Communications Management	10. Project Communications Management

11. We removed "to classify" from the list of purposes. Both the 1996 document and the 1987 version provide a structure for organizing project management knowledge, but neither is particularly effective as a classification tool. First, the topics included are not comprehensive—they do not include innovative or unusual practices. Second, many elements have relevance in more than one Knowledge Area or process, such that the categories are not unique.

The following individuals, as listed in Appendix C of the 1996 document, contributed in many different ways to various drafts of the 1996 document. PMI is indebted to them for their support.

Standards Committee

The following individuals served as members of the PMI Standards Committee during development of the 1996 update of the PMBOK® document:

William R. Duncan	Frederick Ayer	Cynthia Berg
Mark Burgess	Helen Cooke	Judy Doll
Drew Fetters	Brian Fletcher	Earl Glenwright
Eric Jenett	Deborah O'Bray	Diane Quinn
Anthony Rizzotto	Alan Stretton	Douglas E. Tryloff

Contributors

In addition to the members of the Standards Committee, the following individuals provided original text or key concepts for one or more sections in the chapters indicated:

John Adams (Chapter 3)	Keely Brunner (Chapter 7)
Louis J. Cabano (Chapter 5)	David Curling (Chapter 12)
Douglas Gordon (Chapter 7)	David T. Hulett (Chapter 11)
Edward Ionata (Chapter 10)	John M. Nevison (Chapter 9)
Hadley Reynolds (Chapter 2)	Agnes Salvo (Chapter 11)
W. Stephen Sawle (Chapter 5)	Leonard Stolba (Chapter 8)
Ahmet Taspinar (Chapter 6)	Francis M. Webster Jr. (Chapter 1)

Reviewers

In addition to the Standards Committee and the contributors, the following individuals and organizations provided comments on various drafts of the 1996 document:

Edward L. Averill	C. "Fred" Baker	F. J. "Bud" Baker
Tom Belanger	John A. Bing	Brian Bock
Paul Bosakowski	Dorothy J. Burton	Kim Colenso
Samuel K. Collier	Karen Condos-Alfonsi	E. J. Coyle
Darlene Crane	Russ Darnall	Maureen Dougherty
John J. Downing	Daniel D. Dudek	Lawrence East
Quentin W. Fleming	Rick Fletcher	Greg Githens
Leo Giulianeti	Martha D. Hammonds	Abdulrazak Hajibrahim
G. Alan Hellawell	Paul Hinkley	Wayne L. Hinthorn
Mark E. Hodson	Lew Ireland	Elvin Isgrig
Murray Janzen	Frank Jenes	Walter Karpowski
William F. Kerrigan	Harold Kerzner	Robert L. Kimmons
Richard King	J. D. "Kaay" Koch	Lauri Koskela
Richard E. Little	Lyle W. Lockwood	Lawrence Mack
Christopher Madigan	Michael L. McCauley	Hugh McLaughlin

Frank McNeely
Raymond Miller
R. Bruce Morris
John P. Nolan
JoAnn C. Osmer
John G. Phippen
PMI Houston Chapter
Charles J. Pospisil
Christopher Quaife
William S. Ruggles
Darryl M. Selleck
Craig T. Stone
Dick Thiel
Janet Toepfer
Jack Way
Hugh M. Woodward
Dirk Zwart

Pierre Menard
Alan Minson
David J. Mueller
Louise C. Novakowski
Jon V. Palmquist
Hans E. Picard
PMI Manitoba Chapter
Janice Y. Preston
Peter E. Quinn
Ralph B. Sackman
Melvin Silverman
Hiroshi Tanaka
Saul Thomashow
Vijay K. Verma
R. Max Wideman
Robert Youker

Rick Michaels
Colin Morris
Gary Nelson
James O'Brien
Matthew Parry
Serge Y. Piotte
PMI New Zealand Chapter
Mark T. Price
Steven F. Ritter
Alice Sapienza
Roy Smith
Robert Templeton
J. Tidhar
Alex Walton
Rebecca Winston
Shakir H. Zuberi

Production Staff

Special mention is due to the following employees of PMI Communications:

Jeannette M. Cabanis, Editor, Book Division

Linda V. Gillman, Office Administrator

Jonathan Hicks, Systems Administrator

Dewey L. Messer, Managing Editor

Mark S. Parker, Production Coordinator

Melissa Pendergast, Information Services Coordinator

Michelle Triggs, Graphic Designer

Misty N. Dillard, Administrative Assistant

Bobby R. Hensley, Publications Coordinator

Sandy Jenkins, Associate Editor

Danell Moses, Marketing Promotion Coordinator

Shirley B. Parker, Business/Marketing Manager

James S. Pennypacker, Publisher/Editor-In-Chief

Lisa Woodring, Administrative Assistant

B

B.4   2000 Update

This document superseded the Project Management Institute's (PMI®) A Guide to the Project Management Body of Knowledge (PMBOK® Guide), published in 1996.

The scope of the project using the 1996 publication as its starting point, was to:

- Add new material, reflecting the growth of the knowledge and practices in the field of project management by capturing those practices, tools, techniques, and other relevant items that have become generally accepted. (Generally accepted means being applicable to most projects most of the time, and having widespread consensus about their value and usefulness.)
- Add clarification to text and figures to make this document more beneficial to users.
- Correct existing errors in the predecessor document.

Major Changes to the document are as follows:

1.   Throughout the document, we clarified that projects manage to requirements, which emerge from needs, wants, and expectations.
2.   We strengthened linkages to organizational strategy throughout the document.
3.   We provided more emphasis on progressive elaboration in Section 1.2.3.
4.   We acknowledged the role of the Project Office in Section 2.3.4.
5.   We added references to project management involving developing economies, as well as social, economic, and environmental impacts, in Section 2.5.4.
6.   We added expanded treatment of Earned Value Management in Chapter 4 (Project Integration Management), Chapter 7 (Project Cost Management), and Chapter 10 (Project Communications Management).
7.   We rewrote Chapter 11 (Project Risk Management). The chapter now contains six processes instead of the previous four processes. The six processes are Risk Management Planning, Risk Identification, Qualitative Risk Analysis, Quantitative Risk Analysis, Risk Response Planning, and Risk Monitoring and Control.
8.   We moved scope verification from an Executing process to a Controlling process.
9.   We changed the name of Process 4.3 from Overall Change Control to Integrated Change Control to emphasize the importance of change control throughout the entirety of the project.
10.   We added a chart that maps the thirty-nine Project Management processes against the five Project Management Process Groups and the nine Project Management Knowledge Areas in Figure 3-9.
11.   We standardized terminology throughout the document from "supplier" to "seller."

12.   We added several Tools and Techniques:

Chapter 4 - Project Integration Management	*Earned Value Management (EVM)* *Preventive Action*
Chapter 5 - Project Scope Management	*Scope Statement Updates* *Project Plan* *Adjusted Baseline*
Chapter 6 - Project Time Management	*Quantitatively Based Durations* *Reserve Time (Contingency)* *Coding Structure* *Variance Analysis* *Milestones* *Activity Attributes* *Computerized Tools*
Chapter 7 - Project Cost Management	*Estimating Publications* *Earned Value Measurement*
Chapter 8 - Project Quality Management	*Cost of Quality*
Chapter 10 - Project Communications Management	*Project Reports* *Project Presentations* *Project Closure*

PMI Project Management Standards Program Member Advisory Group

The following individuals served as members of the PMI Standards Program Member Advisory Group during development of this edition of A Guide to the Project Management Body of Knowledge (PMBOK® Guide) document:

George Belev	Cynthia A. Berg, PMP	Sergio Coronado Arrechedera
Judith A. Doll, PMP	J. Brian Hobbs, PMP	David Hotchkiss, PMP

PMBOK® Guide Update Project Team

The following individuals served as members of the project team for this 2000 Edition of the PMBOK® Guide, under the leadership of Cynthia A. Berg, PMP, as Project Manager:

Cynthia A. Berg, PMP	Judith A. Doll, PMP	Daniel Dudek, PMP
Quentin Fleming	Greg Githens, PMP	Earl Glenwright
David T. Hulett, PhD	Gregory J. Skulmoski	

B

Contributors

In addition to the members of the PMI Standards Program Member Advisory Group and the PMBOK® Guide Project Team, the following individuals provided original text or key concepts for one or more sections in the chapters indicated. Also, the PMI Risk Management Specific Interest Group provided leadership for the rewrite of Chapter 11, Project Risk Management.

Alfredo del Caño (Chapter 11)
Roger Graves (Chapter 11)
David Hulett (Chapter 11)
Janice Preston (Chapter 11)
David Shuster (Chapter 8)
Mike Wakshull (Chapter 11)

Quentin Fleming (Chapters 4 and 12)
David Hillson (Chapter 11)
Sam Lane (Chapter 11)
Stephen Reed (Chapter 11)
Ed Smith (Chapter 11)
Robert Youker (several chapters)

Reviewers

In addition to the PMI Standards Program Member Advisory Group, the PMBOK® Guide Project Team, and the Contributors, the following individuals provided comments on the Exposure Draft of this document:

Muhamed Abdomerovic, PMP, D. Eng.
Frank Allen, PMP
MaryGrace Allenchey, PMP
Ichizo Aoki
Ronald Auffrédou, PMP
Frederick L. Ayer, PMP
A. C. "Fred" Baker, PMP
Berndt Bellman
Nigel Blampied, PE, PMP
Patrick Brown, PMP
Bruce C. Chadbourne, PMP
Raymond C. Clark, PE
David Coates, PMP
Edmund H. Conrow, PMP
John Cornman, PMP
Kevin Daly, PMP
Thomas Diethelm, PMP
Frank D. Einhorn, PMP
Christian Frankenberg, PMP
Jean-Luc Frere, PMP
Chikako Futamura, PMP
Brian L. Garrison, PMP
Peter Bryan Goldsbury

Yassir Afaneh
Jon D. Allen, PMP
Robert A. Andrejko, PMP
Paul C. Aspinwall
Edward Averill, PMP
William W. Bahnmaier, PMP
Carole J. Bass, PMP
Sally Bernstein, PMP
John Blatta
Chris Cartwright, PMP
Michael T. Clark, PMP
Elizabeth Clarke
Kim Colenso, PMP
Kenneth G. Cooper
Richard F. Cowan, PMP
Mario Damiani, PMP
David M. Drevinsky, PMP
Edward Fern, PMP
Scott D. Freauf, PMP
Ichiro Fujita, PMP
Serge Garon, PEng, PMP
Eric Glover
Michael Goodman, PMP

A Guide to the Project Management Body of Knowledge (PMBOK® Guide) Third Edition
©2004 Project Management Institute, Four Campus Boulevard, Newtown Square, PA 19073-3299 USA

Jean Gouix, PMP
Franz X. Hake
Chris Herbert, PMP
J. Brian Hobbs, PMP
Robin Hornby
Charles L. Hunt
George Jackelen
Elden F. Jones II, PMP, CMII
Lewis Kana, PMP
Ronald L. Kempf, PMP
Kurt V. Kloecker
Blase Kwok, PMP
Philip A. Lindeman
Lyle W. Lockwood, PMP
Arif Mahmood, PMP
Stephen S. Mattingly
Peter McCarthy
Krik D. McManus
Mary F. Miekoski, PMP
Gordon R. Miller, PMP
Jim Morris, PMP
William A. Moylan, PMP
Wolfgang Obermeier
Masato Ohori, PMP
Edward Oliver
Francisco Perez-Polo, PMP
Crispin (Kik) Piney, PMP
David L. Prater, PMP
Samuel L. Raisch, PMP
G. Ramachandran, PMP
Bernice L. Rocque, PMP
Fernando Romero Peñailillo
Linda Rust, PMP
James N. Salapatas, PMP
Bradford N. Scales
John R. Schuyler, PMP
Shoukat Sheikh, MBA, PMP
Larry Sieck
Melvin Silverman, PhD, PE
Keith Skilling, PE, PMP
Kenneth F. Smith, PMP
Paul J. Solomon
Christopher Wessley Sours, PMP
Joyce Statz, PMP
Thangavel Subbu
Ahmet N. Taspinar, PMP
Alan D. Uren, PMP
S. Rao Vallabhaneni
Ana Isabel Vazquez Urbina
Stephen E. Wall, PMP
Tammo T. Wilkens, PE, PMP

Alexander Grassi Sr., PMP
Peter Heffron
Dr. David Hillson, PMP, FAPM
Marion Diane Holbrook
Bill Hubbard
Thomas P. Hurley, PMP
Angyan P. Jagathnarayanan
Sada Joshi, PMP
Subramaniam Kandaswamy, PhD, PMP
Robert Dohn Kissinger, PhD, PMP
Jan Kristrom
Lawrence P. Leach
Gábor Lipi
J. W. Lowthian, PMP
James Martin (on behalf of INCOSE)
Glen Maxfield
Rob McCormack, PMP
David Michaud
Oscar A. Mignone
Roy E. Morgan, PMP
Bert Mosterd, PMP
John D. Nelson, PMP
Cathy Oest, PMP
Kazuhiko Okubo, PE, PMP
Jerry Partridge, PMP
James M. Phillips, PMP
George Pitagorsky, PMP
Bradford S. Price, PMP
Naga Rajan
Bill Righter, PMP
Wolfgang Theodore Roesch
Jon Rude
Fabian Sagristani, PMP
Seymour Samuels
H. Peter Schiller
Maria Scott, PMP
Kazuo Shimizu, PMP
  (on behalf of the PMI Tokyo, Japan Chapter)
Loren J. Simer Jr.
Greg Skulmoski
Barry Smythe, PMP
Joe Soto Sr., PMP
Charlene Spoede, PMP
Emmett Stine, PMP
Jim Szpakowski
John A. Thoren Jr., PMP
Juan Luis Valero, PMP
William Simon Vaughan Robinson
Ricardo Viana Vargas, PMP
William W. Wassel, PMP
Robert Williford, PMP

B

Contributions to Predecessor Documents

Portions of the 1996 edition and other predecessor documents are included in the 2000 edition. PMI wishes to acknowledge the following volunteers as substantial contributors to the 2000 Edition:

John R. Adams	William R. Duncan	Matthew H. Parry
Alan Stretton	R. Max Wideman	

Production Staff

Special mention is due to the following employees of PMI:

Steven L. Fahrenkrog, Standards Manager

Lisa Fisher, Assistant Editor

Lewis M. Gedansky, Research Manager

Linda V. Gillman, Advertising Coordinator/*PMBOK*® *Guide* Copyright Permissions Coordinator

Eva T. Goldman, Technical Research & Standards Associate

Paul Grace, Certification Manager

Sandy Jenkins, Managing Editor

Toni D. Knott, Book Editor

John McHugh, Interim Publisher

Dewey L. Messer, Design and Production Manager

Mark S. Parker, Production Coordinator

Shirley B. Parker, Business/Book Publishing Manager

Michelle Triggs Owen, Graphic Designer

Iesha D. Turner-Brown, Standards Administrator

APPENDIX C

Contributors and Reviewers of *PMBOK®Guide* – Third Edition

PMI volunteers first attempted to codify the Project Management Body of Knowledge in the *Special Report on Ethics, Standards, and Accreditation*, published in 1983. Since that time, other volunteers have come forward to update and improve that original document and contribute the now de facto standard for project management, PMI's *A Guide to the Project Management Body of Knowledge* (*PMBOK® Guide*). This appendix lists, alphabetically within groupings, those individuals who have contributed to the development and production of the *PMBOK® Guide* – Third Edition. No simple list or even multiple lists can adequately portray all the contributions of those who have volunteered to develop the *PMBOK® Guide* – Third Edition. Appendix B describes specific contributions of many of the individuals listed below and should be consulted for further information about individual contributions to the project.

The Project Management Institute is grateful to all of these individuals for their support and acknowledges their contributions to the project management profession.

C.1 *PMBOK® Guide* 2004 Update Project Leadership Team

The following individuals served as members were contributors of text or concepts and served as leaders within the Project Leadership Team (PLT):

Dennis Bolles, PMP, Project Manager
Darrel G. Hubbard, PE, Deputy Project Manager
J. David Blaine, PMP (Quality Control Coordinator)
Theodore R. Boccuzzi, PMP (Document Research Team Leader)
Elden Jones, PMP (Configuration Management Coordinator)
Dorothy Kangas, PMP (Product Overview Team Leader)
Carol Steuer, PMP (Framework Team Leader)
Geree Streun, PMP (Process Groups Team Leader)
Lee Towe, PMP (Special Appointment)

C

C.2 *PMBOK® Guide* 2004 Update Project Core Team

In addition to the Project Leadership Team, the following individuals served as contributors of text or concepts and as Co-Leaders within the Project Core Team (PCT):

Nigel Blampied, PE, PMP (Framework Team Co-Leader)
J. David Blaine, PMP (Product Overview Team Co-Leader)
Andrea Giulio Demaria, PMP (Document Research Team Co-Leader)
Greg Githens, PMP (Framework Team Co-Leader)
Dana J. Goulston, PMP (Framework Team Co-Leader)
David T. Hulett, PhD (Knowledge Areas Team Co-Leader)
Elden Jones, MSPM, PMP (Process Groups Team Co-Leader)
Carol Rauh, PhD, PMP (Knowledge Areas Team Co-Leader)
Michael J. Schollmeyer, PMP (Product Overview Team Co-Leader)

C.3 *PMBOK® Guide* 2004 Update Project Sub-Teams

The following individuals served as contributors of text or concepts and as leaders of the Project Sub-Teams (PST):

W. Clifton Baldwin, PMP (Index and Input Guidance Leader)
Barbara Borgmann, PMP (Knowledge Areas Chapter 8 Leader)
Kim D. Colenso, PMP, CSQE (Glossary Leader)
Earl Glenwright, PE, VEA (Knowledge Areas Chapter 7 Leader)
Darrel G. Hubbard, PE (Knowledge Areas Chapter 12 Leader)
David T. Hulett, PhD, (Knowledge Areas Chapter 11 Leader)
Jim O'Brien, PMP (Knowledge Areas Chapter 6 Leader)
Brian Salk, M.A. Ed., PMP (Knowledge Areas Chapter 5 Leader)
Geree Streun, PMP (Knowledge Areas Chapters 3 and 4 Leader)
John A. Thoren, Jr., PMP, PhD (Knowledge Areas Chapter 10 Leader)
Lee Towe, PMP, MBA (Knowledge Areas Chapter 9 Leader)

C.4 Significant Contributors

In addition to the members of the Project Leadership Team, the Project Core Team, and the Sub-Team Leaders, the following individuals provided significant input or concepts:

Sumner Alpert, PMP, CMC
Cynthia A. Berg, PMP
Edmund H. Conrow, PhD, PMP
Bradford Eichhorn, PMP
Steve Grey, PhD, PMP
David Hillson, PhD, PMP
Yan Bello Mendez, PMP
Crispin "Kik" Piney, BSc, PMP
Massimo Torre, PhD, PMP
Cornelis (Kees) Vonk, PMP
Linda Westfall, PE, CSQE

A Guide to the Project Management Body of Knowledge (PMBOK® Guide) Third Edition
©2004 Project Management Institute, Four Campus Boulevard, Newtown Square, PA 19073-3299 USA

C.5 *PMBOK® Guide* 2004 Update Project Team Members

In addition to those listed above, the following PMBOK® Guide 2004 Update Project Team Members provided input to and recommendations on drafts of the PMBOK® Guide – Third Edition, or submitted Enterprise Change Requests (ECRs):

Abdallah Abi-Aad, PMP, P.Eng.	Muhamed Abdomerovic, PMP
Adrian Abramovici, PMP	Jamie K. Allen, PMP
Mark Allyn, PMP	Scott C. Anderson, PMP
Lionel Andrew, MBA, ISP	Russell Archibald, PMP
Prabu V. Ayyagari, PhD, PMP	Ernest Baker, PMP
Pamela M. Baker, PMP	Kevin E. Bast, PMP
James S. Bennett, PMP	Ionut C. Bibac
Howland Blackiston	Ray Blake, PMP
Charles W. Bosler, Jr.	Rollin O. Bowen, Jr.
Carolyn Boyles, MBA, PMP	Wayne R. Brantley, PMP, MS Ed
Alex S. Brown, PMP	Timothy S. Brown
Stephen C. Burgan, PMP	Anne Cagle, PMP
Dean J. Calabrese, PMP	Neil R. Caldwell
Giuseppe A. Caruso, PMP	Bill Chadick, PMP
Clare Chan	Porfirio Chen Chang, MBA, PMP
Gene Chiappetta, PMP	Tomio Chiba, PMP
Mark T. Chism, PMP	Andy Crowe, PMP
Robert L. Cutler, PMP	Darren Dalcher, PhD, MAPM
Mario Damiani, PMP	Pranab Das, PMP
Robert de Jong, PMP	Connie Delisle
John M. Dery, PMP	Barbara De Vries, PMP
Jerry Dimos, PMP	James A. Doanes
Capt. Nick Doralp, PMP	Magnus Karl Drengwitz, PMP
Peter Duignan, PMP	Lloyd R. Duke, Jr., PMP
Suhas Dutta, PMP	Bradford R. Eichhorn, PMP
Gary S. Elliott, M.S., M.D.	Gregory William Fabian, PMP
Morten Fangel, PhD	Martin Christopher Fears, PMP
Eve Featherman	AnnaMaria Felici
Flynn M. Fernandes, PMP, MSPM	John C. "Buck" Field, MBA, PMP
David Foley, MBA	Kirby Fortenberry, PMP
Gary W. Fortune, PMP	John M. Foster, PMP, MBA
Scott D. Freauf, PMP	Denis Freeland
Ichiro Fujita, PMP	John S. Galliano
Donald G. Gardner, PMP	Stainslaw Gasik
Jose A. George, Btech, PGDM	Dan Georgopulos
Leo A.Giulianetti, PMP	Christopher A. Goetz, PMP
Donna Golden	Neil P. Goldman, PMP
Dr. Margarida Goncalves	John C. Goodpasture, PMP
Neal S. Gray, PMP	Robert J. Gries, PE, PMP
Patrick D. Guest, PMP	Jinendra Gunathilaka, PE
Navneet Gupta, PMP	Aaron S. Hall, PMP
J. Ray Harwood, PMP	Ali Hassan, PMP
Ralph Hernandez	Pat Hillcoat, PMP
Bobby Tsan Fai Ho, PMP, CISM	Gopi V. Hombal
Keith D. Hornbacher, MBA	Kenneth Alan Hudacsko, PMP
Clinton in't Veld	Adesh Jain, PMP, MPD
Don R. James, PMP	Noel C. Jensen, PMP
Wei Jing	Bruce Johnson, PMP

C

Granville H. Jones, Sr., MBA, PMP

Tom Kerr, PMP

Asadullah Khan, PMP

Mihail Kitanovski

Takahiko Kuki, PMP, PE

Avis Kunz

John S. Layman, PMP

Elizabeth Ann Long, PMP

Pier Paolo Lo Valvo, PMP

Sajith K. Madapatu, PMP

Enrique Martinez

David L. McPeters, PMP

Godfrey I. Meertens, PMP

Gordon R. Miller, PMP, CCP

Andrew H. Moore, MBA, PMP

Mhlabaniseni Moses Mitmunye

K.S. Keshava Murthy

AnathaKrishnan S. Nallepally, PMP

Vijayalakshimi Neela, MCA, PMP

Brian D. Nelson, PMP

Kazuhiko Okubo, PE, PMP

Rodger Oren, MBA, PMP

Michael T. Ozeranic

Glen R. Palmer

George Pasieka, PMP

Sreenivasa Rao Potti, MCA, PMP

Patrick J. Quairoli

Vara Prasad Raju Kunada

Raju Rao, PMP

Tony Raymond

J. Logan C. Rice

Thad B. Ring, PMP

Susan Rizzi

Alexandre G. Rodrigues, PhD

Scott A. Rose, PMP

Samuel S. Roth, PMP

Gurdev Roy, PMP

James J. Rutushni, PMP

Anjali Sabharwal, PMP

Nashaat A. Salman, PMP

John Schmitt, PMP

Randa Schollmeyer, PMP

Benjamin R. Sellers, PMP, CPCM

Sanjay Shah, PMP

Kazuo Shimizu, PMP

Ganga Siebertz

Melvin Silverman, PhD, PE

Raghavendra Singh

Patricia Smith

Allison St. Jean

Sambasivam S., PMP, CSQA

Karen Tate, PMP, MBA

James E. Teer, Jr

Surendra Tipparaju, ME

Rogerio Carlos Traballi

Kevin B. Jones, BMath, PMP

Ajmal Afzal Khan

Lucy Kim, PMP, PE

Jennifer Eileen Kraft

Polisetty V.S. Kumar, Mtech, PMP

Antonio Carlos Laranjo da Silva

Erik D. Lindquist, PMP, PE

Raul S. Lopez, PE, PMP

Karen Griffin MacNeil, PMP

Vijaya Kumar Mani, PMP

Victor J. Matheron, PMP

Ed Mechler, PMP

Richard Meertens, MBA, PMP

Liu Min

Colin Morris, PE, PMP

Charles L. Munch, PMP

Jo Musto, PMP

NB Narayanan

Beatrice Nelson, PMP

Isabella Nizza, PMP

David M. Olson, MBA (ITM)

Jeffery L. Ottesen, PE

Laura Dorival Paglione

Jerry L. Partridge, PMP

Eric Patel

Manohar Powar, PMP

Ge Qun

Prem Ranganath, PMP

Ulka Rathi

Vijay Sai Reddy, PMP, CSQA

Steven Ricks, PMP

Dee Rizor

Michael C. Roach

Cheryl N. Rogers, PMP

Ed Rosenstein, PMP

Joseph A. Roushdi

Paul S. Royer, PMP

Frank Ryle, PMP

Srinivasa R. Sajja, PMP

Markus Scheibel, PMP, Dipl.-Ing.

Amy Schneider, PMP

Andrea R. Scott

Tufan Sevim, PMP

Mundaje S. Shetty, PMP

Rali Shital

Larry Sieck

Richard L. Sinatra, PMP, PhD

Edward Smith

Richard Spector, PMP

Donglin Su

Karen Z. Sullivan, PMP

David E. Taylor, PMP

Sai K. Thallam, MBA, PMP

Massimo Torre, PhD, PMP

Rufis A. Turpin, CQA, CSQE

Marion J. Tyler, PMP
Eric Uyttewaal, PMP
Gerrit van Otterdijk, BSc. Mgt Science
Paula X. Varas, PMP
Mark M. Vertin, PE, PMP
Roberto Viale, PMP
Desmond Joseph Vize, PMP
J. Wendell Wagner, PMP
Patrick Weaver, PMP, FAICD
Timothy E. Welker, PMP
Tammo T. Wilkens, PE, PMP
Charles M. Williamson, MBA, PMP
Robert Wood
Uma S. Yalamanchili, PMP
Kathy Zandbergen

M. Raj Ullagaraj, PhD
JR Vanden Eynde, PMP
Thomas G. Van Scoyoc, PMP
Ricardo Viana Vargas, MSc, PMP
Craig Veteto, PMP, CPIM
Eduardo Newton Vieira, PMP
Cornelius (Kees) Vonk, PMP
Thomas M. Walsh, PMP
Kevin R. Wegryn, PMP, CPM
Gwen Whitman, PMP
Alan K. Williams, Sr., PMP
Stephen D. Wise
Thomas Wuttke, PMP, CPM
Angela F. Young, PMP
Eire E. Zimmermann, PMP

C.6   Final Exposure Draft reviewers and contributors

In addition to team members, the following individuals provided recommendations for improving the Exposure Draft of the PMBOK® Guide – Third Edition:

Fred Abrams, PMP, CPL
Mohammed Abdulla Al-Kuwari, Eur Ing, CEng
Frank Anbari
Alfred Baker
Jefferson Bastreghi
Cynthia A. Berg, PMP
Mamoun A. Besaiso, CE
Nigel Blampied, PE, PMP
Stephen Bonk
David Bradford, PMP
Gary D. Brawley, P.Eng., PMP
Bruce Chadbourne
Aaron Coffman, PMP, CQM
Edmund H. Conrow, PhD, PMP
Michael Corish
John Cornman, PMP, MBA
Mario Damiani
Allan E. Dean
Juan De La Cruz
Ravi Kumar Dikshit, PMP
Daniel Dudek
Robert L. Emerson, PMP
Keith Farndale, PEng, PMP
Quentin W. Fleming
Ichiro Fujita, PMP
Jackelen George
David R. Haas, PMP, FLMI
Delbert K. Hardy, PMP
Bob Hillier, PMP
Danny N. Hinton, PMP
J. Brian Hobbs, PhD, PMP
Martin Hopkinson, BSc, APMP
Grant Jefferson

Yassir Afaneh
Hussain Ali Al-Ansari, Eur Ing, CEng
William W. Bahnmaier, PMP
B. D. Barnes
Mohammed Safi Batley, MIM
Sally Bernstein, PMP
J. David Blaine, PMP, CSQE
Dennis Bolles, PMP
Gregory M. Bowen, CSDP
James (Jim) P. Branden, MBA, PMP
Edgard P. Cerqueira Neto, PhD, PMP
Tomio Chiba, PMP
Kim D. Colenso, PMP, CSQE
Helen S. Cooke, PMP
John E. Cormier, PMP
Aloysio da Silva
Arindam Das
Alfredo del Cano, PE, PhD
M. Pilar De La Cruz
John Downing
Judith Edwards, PhD, PMP
Alison Evanish
Linda Fitzgerald
Scott D. Freauf, PMP
Paul H. Gil, MCP, PMP
Mike Griffiths, PMP
Robert W. Harding, RA
Rick Hiett
Guy N. Hindley, MAPM, MILT
Ho Lee Cheong, PhD, MIMech E
Piet Holbrouck, MSc
Darrel G. Hubbard, PE
Howard J. Kalinsky, PMP, MPM

C

Constance Katsanis
Takahiko Kuki, PMP, PE
Craig Letavec
Pier Paolo Lo Valvo, PMP
Enrique Lopez-Mingueza, PMP
Stephen S. Mattingly
Giuseppe Mauri
Santosh Kumar Mishra, PMP, CSQA
Saradhi Motamarri, MTech, PMP
Jeffrey S. Nielsen, PMP
Peter Ostrom, PhD, PMP
Ravindranath Palahalli
Nick Palumbo, PMP
Francisco Perez-Polo
Crispin (Kik) Piney, BSc, PMP
Gurdev Randhawa, PMP
Steven F. Ritter, PMP
David W. Ross, PMP
Kyoichi Sato
Benjamin R. Sellers, PMP, CPCM
Kazuo Shimizu, PMP
Fernando Demattio de O. Simoes, PMP
Cynthia Snyder, PMP, MBA
Paul Solomon, PMP
Juergen Sturany
Luis Eduardo Torres Calzada, PMP, MBA
Gary Van Eck
J.R. Vanden Eynde, PMP
Aloysio Vianna, Jr.
Thomas M. Walsh, PMP
Patrick Weaver, PMP, FAICD
Linda Westfall, PE, CSQE
Clement C.L. Yeung, PMP
Cristine Zerpa

Roger Kent
Lawrence (Larry) P. Leach, PMP
Ben Linders
Mary K. Lofsness
Mark Marlin, PMP
Christopher J. Maughan, CEng, PMP
Yves Mboda, PMP
Colin Morris, P.Eng., PMP
Rita Mulcahy, PMP
Kazuhiko Okubo, PE, PMP
Ravindranath P S
Jon Palmquist
Anil Peer, P.Eng., PMP
Paul W. Phister, Jr., PhD, PE
Polisetty V.S. Kumar, MTech, PMP
Raju Rao, PMP
Hans (Ron) Ronhovde, PMP
Robbi Ryan
Suzanne Lee Schmidt, PMP
Tufan Sevim, PMP
Melvin Silverman
John E. Singley, PhD, PMP
Antonio Soares
Michael Stefanovic, P.Eng., PMP
George Sukumar, MSChe, OE
Dalton L. Valeriano-Alves, M.E.
Judy Van Meter
Ricardo Vargas
Dave Violette, MPM, PMP
William W. Wassel, PE, PMP
Kevin R. Wegryn, PMP, CPM
Allan Wong
John Zachar, BSc, APMP
Paul Zilmer

C.7 PMI Project Management Standards Program Member Advisory Group

The following individuals served as members of the PMI Standards Program Member Advisory Group during development of A Guide to the Project Management Body of Knowledge (PMBOK® Guide) – Third Edition:

Julia M. Bednar, PMP
J. Brian Hobbs, PMP
Thomas Kurihara
Bobbye Underwood, PMP

Sergio R. Coronado
Carol Holliday, PMP
Asbjorn Rolstadas, PhD
Dave Violette, MPM, PMP

C.8   Production Staff

Special mention is due to the following employees of PMI:

Steven L. Fahrenkrog, PMP, Manager, Standards
Kristin L. Wright, Standards Program Administrator
Shari M. Daniel, PMP, Project Manager—Translations
Dan Goldfischer, Editor-in-Chief
Patti Harter, Project Manager
David Parker, Manager, Publications
Natasha Pollard, Translation Verification Committee Coordinator
Richard E. Schwartz, Product Editor
Barbara Walsh, Publications Planner

C

APPENDIX D

Application Area Extensions

D.1 Need for Application Area Extensions

Application area extensions are necessary when there are generally accepted knowledge and practices for a category of projects in one application area that are not generally accepted across the full range of project types in most application areas. Application area extensions reflect:

- Unique or unusual aspects of the project environment of which the project management team must be aware, in order to manage the project efficiently and effectively
- Common knowledge and practices that, if followed, will improve the efficiency and effectiveness of the project (e.g., standard work breakdown structures).

Application area-specific knowledge and practices can arise as a result of many factors, including, but not limited to, differences in cultural norms, technical terminology, societal impact, or project life cycles. For example:

- In construction, where virtually all work is accomplished under contract, there are common knowledge and practices related to procurement that do not apply to all categories of projects
- In bioscience, there are common knowledge and practices driven by the regulatory environment that do not apply to all categories of projects
- In government contracting, there are common knowledge and practices driven by government acquisition regulations that do not apply to all categories of projects
- In consulting, there are common knowledge and practices created by the project manager's sales and marketing responsibilities that do not apply to all categories of projects.

D

Application area extensions are:

- Additions to the core material of *PMBOK® Guide* Chapters 1 through 12, not substitutes for it
- Organized in a fashion similar to the *PMBOK® Guide*—that is, by identifying and describing the project management processes unique to that application area
- Unique additions to the core material. Such content may:
  - ◆ Identify new or modified processes
  - ◆ Subdivide existing processes
  - ◆ Describe different sequences or interactions of processes
  - ◆ Increase elements or modifying the common process definitions
  - ◆ Define special inputs, tools and techniques, and/or outputs for the existing processes.

Application area extensions are not:

- "How-to" documents or "practice guidelines"—such documents may be issued as PMI Standards, but they are not what are intended as extensions
- A lower level of detail than is addressed in the *PMBOK® Guide*—such details may be addressed in handbooks or guidebooks that may be issued as PMI Standards, but they are not what is intended as extensions.

D.2 Criteria for Development of Application Area Extensions

Extensions will be developed under the following criteria:

- There is a substantial body of knowledge that is both project-oriented and unique or nearly unique to that application area.
- There is an identifiable PMI component (e.g., a PMI Specific Interest Group, College, or Chapter) or an identifiable external organization willing and able to commit the necessary resources to subscribe to and support the PMI Standards Program with the development and maintenance of a specific PMI Standard. Or, the extension may be developed by PMI itself.
- The proposed extension is able to pass the same level of rigorous PMI Project Management Standard-Setting Process as any other PMI Standard.

A Guide to the Project Management Body of Knowledge (PMBOK® Guide) Third Edition
©2004 Project Management Institute, Four Campus Boulevard, Newtown Square, PA 19073-3299 USA

D.3 Publishing and Format of Application Area Extensions

Application area extensions are developed and/or published by PMI, or they are developed and/or published by either a PMI component or an external organization under a formal agreement with PMI.

- Extensions match the *PMBOK® Guide* in style and content. They use the same paragraph and subparagraph numbers for the material that has been extended.
- Sections and paragraphs of the *PMBOK® Guide* that are not extended are not repeated in extensions.
- Extensions contain a rationale/justification about the need for an extension and its material.
- Extensions are delimited in terms of what they are not intended to do.

D.4 Process for Development and Maintenance of Application Area Extensions

When approved in accordance with the PMI Standards-Setting Process, application area extensions become PMI Standards. They will be developed and maintained in accordance with the process described below.

- An extension must be sponsored by PMI, a formally chartered PMI component (e.g., a Specific Interest Group, College, or Chapter), or another organization external to PMI, which has been approved by the PMI Standards Program Member Advisory Group and the PMI Standards Manager. Co-sponsorship with PMI is the preferred arrangement. All approvals will be by formal written agreement between PMI and the sponsoring entity; such agreement will include, among other things, the parties' agreement as to intellectual property ownership rights and publications rights to the extension.
- A project to develop, publish, and/or maintain an extension must be approved by the PMI Standards Program. Permission to initiate, develop, and maintain an extension must be received from PMI and will be the subject of an agreement between or among the organizations. If there is no other sponsoring organization, the PMI Standards Program may elect to proceed alone.
- The sponsoring group will notify and solicit advice and support from the PMI Standards Program Member Advisory Group and PMI Standards Manager throughout the development and maintenance process. They will concur with the appropriateness of the sponsoring organization for the proposed extension and will review the extension during its development to identify any conflicts or overlaps with other similar projects that may be under way.

D

- The sponsoring group will prepare a proposal to develop the extension. The proposal will include a justification for the project with a matrix of application-area-specific processes and the affected sections of this document (i.e., the *PMBOK® Guide*). It will also contain the commitment of sufficient qualified drafters and reviewers; identification of funding requirements, including reproduction, postage, telephone costs, desktop publishing, etc.; commitment to the PMI procedures for PMI Standards extension development and maintenance; and a plan and schedule for extension development and maintenance.

- Following acceptance of the proposal, the project team will prepare a project charter for approval by the sponsoring group and the PMI Standards Program Team. The charter will include sources of funding and any funding proposed to be provided by PMI. It will include a requirement for periodic review of the extension with reports to the PMI Standards Program Team and a "Sunset Clause" that specifies when, and under what conditions, the extension will be removed from active status as a PMI Standard.

- The proposal will be submitted to the PMI Standards Manager in accordance with the PMI Standards-Setting Process. The PMI Standards Manager will determine if the proposal can be expected to result in a document that will meet the requirements for a PMI Standard and if adequate resources and sources of support have been identified. To help with this determination, the PMI Standards Manager will seek review and comment by the PMI Standards Program Member Advisory Group and, if appropriate, a panel of knowledgeable persons not involved with the extension.

- The PMI Standards Manager, with the support of the PMI Standards Program Member Advisory Group, will monitor and support the development of the approved project.

- The sponsoring organization will develop the extension according to the approved project charter, including coordinating with the PMI Standards Program Team for support, review, and comment.

- When the extension has been completed to the satisfaction of the sponsoring organization, it will be submitted to the PMI Standards Manager, who will manage the final approval and publication processes in accordance with the PMI Standards-Setting Process. This final submittal will include listing of, and commitment by, the sponsoring organization to the PMI extension maintenance processes and efforts.

- Following approval of the extension as a PMI Standard, the sponsoring organization will implement the extension maintenance process in accordance with the approved plan.

APPENDIX E

Additional Sources of Information on Project Management

Project management is a growing, dynamic field; books and articles on the subject are published regularly. The entities listed below provide a variety of products and services that may be of use to those interested in project management.

E.1 Professional and Technical Organizations

This document was developed and published by the Project Management Institute (PMI). PMI can be contacted at:

Project Management Institute
Four Campus Boulevard
Newtown Square, PA 19073-3299 USA
Phone: +1-610-356-4600
Fax: +1-610-356-4647
E-mail: pmihq@pmi.org
Internet: http://www.pmi.org

PMI currently has cooperative agreements with the following organizations:

Association for the Advancement of Cost Engineering (AACE International)
        Phone: +1-304-296-8444   Fax: +1-304-291-5728
        http://www.aacei.org/
Asociacion Espanola de Ingenieria de Proyectos (AEIPRO)
        Phone: +3476-976-761-910   Fax: +347-6976-761861
        www.aeipro.org
Australian Institute of Project Management (AIPM)
        Phone: +61-2-9252-7277   Fax: +61-2-9252-7077
        www.aipm.com.au
Construction & Economy Research Institute of Korea (CERIK)
        Phone: +822-3441-0801   Fax: +822-544-6234
        www.cerik.re.kr
Defense Systems Management College Alumni Association (DSMCAA)
        Phone: +1-703-960-6802   Fax: +1-703-960-6807
Engineering Advancement Association of Japan (ENAA)
        Phone: +81-4-5682-8071   Fax: +81-4-5682-8710
        www.enaa.or.jp

E

Institute of Project Management (IPM-Ireland)
    Phone: +353-1-661-4677   Fax: +353-1-661-3588
International Project Management Association (IPMA)
    Phone: +44-1594-531-007   Fax: +44-1594-531-008
Korean Institute of Project Management & Technology (PROMAT)
    Phone: +822-523-16446   Fax: +822-523-1680
    www.promat.or.kr
National Contract Management Association (NCMA)
    Phone: +703-448-9231   Fax: +703-448-0939
The NORDNET National Associations
(Denmark, Finland, Iceland, Norway, and Sweden)
    Fax: +468-719-9316
Project Management Associates (PMA-India)
    Phone: +91-11-852-6673   Fax: +91-11-646-4481
    www.pma-india.org
Project Management Association of Slovakia (SPPR)
    Phone: +421-805-599-1806   Fax: +421-805-599-1-818
Project Management South Africa
    Phone:+2711-706-6813   Fax: +2711-706-6813
    www.pmisa.co.za
Projekt Management Austria
    Phone: +43-1-319-29-210   Fax: +43-1-319-29-21-29
    www.p-m-a.at
Russian Project Management Association (SOVNET)
    Phone: +7-095-215-37-18   Fax: +7-095-215-37-18
    www.sovnet.ru
Slovenian Project Management Association (ZPM)
    Phone: +61-1767-134   Fax: +61-217-341
    www.ipma.ch
Ukrainian Project Management Association (UPMA)
    Phone: +38-044-459-3464 or +38-044-241-5400
    www.upma.kiev.ua

In addition, there are numerous other organizations in related fields, which may be able to provide additional information about project management. For example:

    Academy of Management

    American Management Association International

    American Society for Quality Control

    Construction Industry Institute

    Construction Management Association of America (CMAA)

    Institute of Electrical and Electronics Engineers (IEEE)

    Institute of Industrial Engineers (IIE)

    International Council on Systems Engineering (INCOSE)

    National Association for Purchasing Management

    National Contract Management Association

A Guide to the Project Management Body of Knowledge (PMBOK® Guide) Third Edition
©2004 Project Management Institute, Four Campus Boulevard, Newtown Square, PA 19073-3299 USA

Society for Human Resource Management

American Society of Civil Engineers

Current contact information for these and other professional and technical organizations worldwide can generally be found on the Internet.

E.2 Commercial Publishers

PMI is the premier publisher of books on project management. Many commercial publishers produce books on project management and related fields. Commercial publishers that regularly produce such materials include:

Addison-Wesley

AMACOM

Gower Press

John Wiley & Sons

Marcel Dekker

McGraw-Hill

Prentice-Hall

Probus

Van Nostrand Reinhold

Most project management books from these publishers are available from PMI. Many of the books available from these sources include extensive bibliographies or lists of suggested readings.

E.3 Product and Service Vendors

Companies that provide software, training, consulting, and other products and services to the project management profession often provide monographs or reprints.

The PMI Registered Education Provider (R.E.P.) program facilitates the ongoing professional development of PMI members, Project Management Professional (PMP®) certificants, and other project management stakeholders by linking stakeholders and training coordinators with qualified educational providers and products. A listing of R.E.P.s and their associated educational offerings is found at http://www.pmi.org/education/rep.

E.4 Educational Institutions

Many universities, colleges, and junior colleges offer continuing education programs in project management and related disciplines. Many of these institutions also offer graduate or undergraduate degree programs.

E

APPENDIX F

Summary of Project Management Knowledge Areas

Project Integration Management

Project Integration Management includes the processes and activities needed to identify, define, combine, unify and coordinate the various processes and project management activities within the Project Management Process Groups. In the project management context, integration includes characteristics of unification, consolidation, articulation and integrative actions that are crucial to project completion, successfully meeting customer and stakeholder requirements and managing expectations. The Project Integration Management processes include:

- Develop Project Charter – developing the project charter that formally authorizes a project
- Develop Preliminary Project Scope Statement – developing the preliminary project scope statement that provides a high-level scope narrative
- Develop Project Management Plan – documenting the actions necessary to define, prepare, integrate, and coordinate all subsidiary plans into a project management plan
- Direct and Manage Project Execution – executing the work defined in the project management plan to achieve the project's requirements defined in the project scope statement
- Monitor and Control Project Work – monitoring and controlling the processes required to initiate, plan, execute, and close a project to meet the performance objectives defined in the project management plan
- Integrated Change Control – reviewing all change requests, approving changes, and controlling changes to the deliverables and organizational process assets
- Close Project – finalizing all activities across all of the Project Process Groups to formally close the project.

F

Project Scope Management

Project Scope Management includes the processes required to ensure that the project includes all the work required, and only the work required, to complete the project successfully. Project Scope Management is primarily concerned with defining and controlling what is and is not included in the project. The Project Scope Management processes include:

- Scope Planning - creating a project scope management plan that documents how the project scope will be defined, verified, and controlled, and how the work breakdown structure (WBS) will be created and defined
- Scope Definition - developing a detailed project scope statement as the basis for future project decisions
- Create WBS - subdividing the major project deliverables and project work into smaller, more manageable components
- Scope Verification - formalizing acceptance of the completed project deliverables
- Scope Control - controlling changes to the project scope.

Project Time Management

Project Time Management includes the processes required to accomplish timely completion of the project. The Project Time Management processes include:

- Activity Definition - identifying the specific schedule activities that need to be performed to produce the various project deliverables
- Activity Sequencing - identifying and documenting dependencies among schedule activities
- Activity Resource Estimating - estimating the type and quantities of resources required to perform each schedule activity
- Activity Duration Estimating - estimating the number of work periods that will be needed to complete individual schedule activities
- Schedule Development - analyzing activity sequences, durations, resource requirements, and schedule constraints to create the project schedule
- Schedule Control - controlling changes to the project schedule.

Project Cost Management

Project Cost Management includes the processes involved in planning, estimating, budgeting, and controlling costs so that the project can be completed within the approved budget. The Project Cost Management processes include:

- Cost Estimating - developing an approximation of the costs of the resources needed to complete project activities
- Cost Budgeting - aggregating the estimated costs of individual activities or work packages to establish a cost baseline
- Cost Control - influencing the factors that create cost variances and controlling changes to the project budget.

Project Quality Management

Project Quality Management includes the processes and activities of the performing organization that determine quality policies, objectives, and responsibilities so that the project will satisfy the needs for which it was undertaken. It implements the quality management system through policy and procedures, with continuous process improvement activities conducted throughout, as appropriate. The Project Quality Management processes include:

- Quality Planning - identifying which quality standards are relevant to the project and determining how to satisfy them
- Perform Quality Assurance - applying the planned, systematic quality activities to ensure that the project employs all processes needed to meet requirements
- Perform Quality Control - monitoring specific project results to determine whether they comply with relevant quality standards and identifying ways to eliminate causes of unsatisfactory performance.

Project Human Resource Management

Project Human Resource Management includes the processes that organize and manage the project team. The project team is comprised of the people who have assigned roles and responsibilities for completing the project. While it is common to speak of roles and responsibilities being assigned, team members should be involved in much of the project's planning and decision-making. Early involvement of team members adds expertise during the planning process and strengthens commitment to the project. The type and number of project team members can often change as the project progresses. Project team members can be referred to as the project's staff. Project Human Resource Management processes include:

- Human Resource Planning - Identifying and documenting project roles, responsibilities, and reporting relationships, as well as creating the staffing management plan
- Acquire Project Team - Obtaining the human resources needed to complete the project
- Develop Project Team - Improving the competencies and interaction of team members to enhance project performance
- Manage Project Team - Tracking team member performance, providing feedback, resolving issues, and coordinating changes to enhance project performance.

F

Project Communications Management

Project Communications Management includes the processes required to ensure timely and appropriate generation, collection, distribution, storage, retrieval, and ultimate disposition of project information. The Project Communications Management processes provide the critical links among people and information that are necessary for successful communications. Project managers can spend an inordinate amount of time communicating with the project team, stakeholders, customer, and sponsor. Everyone involved in the project should understand how communications affect the project as a whole. Project Communications Management processes include:

- Communications Planning - determining the information and communications needs of the project stakeholders
- Information Distribution - making needed information available to project stakeholders in a timely manner
- Performance Reporting - collecting and distributing performance information, including status reporting, progress measurement, and forecasting
- Manage Stakeholders - managing communications to satisfy the requirements of, and resolve issues with, project stakeholders.

Project Risk Management

Project Risk Management includes the processes concerned with conducting risk management planning, identification, analysis, responses, and monitoring and control on a project. The objectives of Project Risk Management are to increase the probability and impact of positive events and decrease the probability and impact of events adverse to project objectives. Project Risk Management processes include:

- Risk Management Planning - deciding how to approach, plan, and execute the risk management activities for a project
- Risk Identification - determining which risks might affect the project and documenting their characteristics
- Qualitative Risk Analysis - prioritizing risks for subsequent further analysis or action by assessing and combining their probability of occurrence and impact
- Quantitative Risk Analysis - numerically analyzing the effect on overall project objectives of identified risks
- Risk Response Planning - developing options and actions to enhance opportunities and to reduce threats to project objectives
- Risk Monitoring and Control - tracking identified risks, monitoring residual risks, identifying new risks, executing risk response plans, and evaluating their effectiveness throughout the project life cycle.

Project Procurement Management

Project Procurement Management includes the processes to purchase or acquire the products, services, or results needed from outside the project team to perform the work. This chapter presents two perspectives of procurement. The organization can be either the buyer or seller of the product, service, or results under a contract.

Project Procurement Management includes the contract management and change control processes required to administer contracts or purchase orders issued by authorized project team members. Project Procurement Management also includes administering any contract issued by an outside organization (the buyer) that is acquiring the project from the performing organization (the seller) and administering contractual obligations placed on the project team by the contract. Project Procurement Management processes include:

- Plan Purchases and Acquisitions - determining what to purchase or acquire, and determining when and how
- Plan Contracting - documenting products, services, and results requirements and identifying potential sellers
- Request Seller Responses - obtaining information, quotations, bids, offers, or proposals, as appropriate
- Select Sellers - reviewing offers, choosing from among potential sellers, and negotiating a written contract with a seller
- Contract Administration - managing the contract and the relationship between the buyer and the seller, reviewing and documenting how a seller is performing or has performed to establish required corrective actions and provide a basis for future relationships with the seller, managing contract related changes and, when appropriate, managing the contractual relationship with the outside buyer of the project
- Contract Closure - completing and settling each contract, including the resolution of any open items, and closing each contract.

F

Section V

Glossary and Index

References

Glossary

Index

REFERENCES

Chapter 1. Introduction

[1] The American Heritage Dictionary of the English Language, 3rd ed. Boston: Houghton Mifflin Company, 1992.

[2] International Organization for Standardization/International Electrotechnical Commission (ISO/IEC) Guide 2. Geneva: ISO Press, 1996.

[3] Turner, J. Rodney. The Handbook of Project-Based Management. New York: McGraw-Hill, 1992.

Chapter 2. Project Life Cycle and Organization

No references for this chapter.

Chapter 3. Project Management Processes for a Project

No references for this chapter.

Chapter 4. Project Integration Management

[4] İyigün, M. Güven. A Decision Support System for R&D Project Selection and Resource Allocation Under Uncertainty. *Project Management Journal* 24, no. 4 (1993).

Chapter 5. Project Scope Management

[5] Turner, J. Rodney. *The Handbook of Project-Based Management.* New York: McGraw-Hill, 1992.

Chapter 6. Project Time Management

No references for this chapter.

Chapter 7. Project Cost Management

No references for this chapter.

Chapter 8. Project Quality Management

[6] American Society for Quality, 2000.

[7] International Organization for Standardization. ISO 8402. *Quality Management and Quality Assurance.* Geneva: ISO Press, 1994.

Chapter 9. Project Human Resource Management

No references for this chapter.

Chapter 10. Project Communications Management

No references for this chapter.

Chapter 11. Project Risk Management

No references for this chapter.

Chapter 12. Project Procurement Management

No references for this chapter.

A Guide to the Project Management Body of Knowledge (PMBOK® Guide) Third Edition
©2004 Project Management Institute, Four Campus Boulevard, Newtown Square, PA 19073-3299 USA

346

GLOSSARY

1. Inclusions and Exclusions

This glossary includes terms that are:

- Unique or nearly unique to project management (e.g., project scope statement, work package, work breakdown structure, critical path method)
- Not unique to project management, but used differently or with a narrower meaning in project management than in general everyday usage (e.g., early start date, schedule activity).

This glossary generally does not include:

- Application area-specific terms (e.g., project prospectus as a legal document—unique to real estate development)
- Terms whose uses in project management do not differ in any material way from everyday use (e.g., calendar day, delay)
- Compound terms whose meaning is clear from the combined meanings of the component parts
- Variants when the meaning of the variant is clear from the base term (e.g., exception report is included, exception reporting is not).

As a result of the above inclusions and exclusions, this glossary includes:

- A preponderance of terms related to Project Scope Management, Project Time Management, and Project Risk Management, since many of the terms used in these knowledge areas are unique or nearly unique to project management
- Many terms from Project Quality Management, since these terms are used more narrowly than in their everyday usage
- Relatively few terms related to Project Human Resource Management and Project Communications Management, since most of the terms used in these knowledge areas do not differ significantly from everyday usage
- Relatively few terms related to Project Cost Management, Project Integration Management, and Project Procurement Management, since many of the terms used in these knowledge areas have narrow meanings that are unique to a particular application area.

Glossary

2. Common Acronyms

AC	Actual Cost
ACWP	Actual Cost of Work Performed
AD	Activity Description
ADM	Arrow Diagramming Method
AE	Apportioned Effort
AF	Actual Finish date
AOA	Activity-on-Arrow
AON	Activity-on-Node
AS	Actual Start date
BAC	Budget at Completion
BCWP	Budgeted Cost of Work Performed
BCWS	Budgeted Cost of Work Scheduled
BOM	Bill Of Materials
CA	Control Account
CAP	Control Account Plan
CCB	Change Control Board
COQ	Cost of Quality
CPF	Cost-Plus-Fee
CPFF	Cost-Plus-Fixed-Fee
CPI	Cost Performance Index
CPIF	Cost-Plus-Incentive-Fee
CPM	Critical Path Method
CPPC	Cost-Plus-Percentage of Cost
CV	Cost Variance
CWBS	Contract Work Breakdown Structure
DD	Data Date
DU	Duration
DUR	Duration
EAC	Estimate at Completion
EF	Early Finish date
EMV	Expected Monetary Value
ES	Early Start date
ETC	Estimate to Complete
EV	Earned Value
EVM	Earned Value Management
EVT	Earned Value Technique
FF	Finish-to-Finish
FF	Free Float
FFP	Firm-Fixed-Price
FMEA	Failure Mode and Effect Analysis
FPIF	Fixed-Price-Incentive-Fee
FS	Finish-to-Start

A Guide to the Project Management Body of Knowledge (PMBOK® Guide) Third Edition
©2004 Project Management Institute, Four Campus Boulevard, Newtown Square, PA 19073-3299 USA

IFB	Invitation for Bid
LF	Late Finish date
LOE	Level of Effort
LS	Late Start date
OBS	Organizational Breakdown Structure
OD	Original Duration
PC	Percent Complete
PCT	Percent Complete
PDM	Precedence Diagramming Method
PF	Planned Finish date
PM	Project Management
PM	Project Manager
PMBOK®	Project Management Body of Knowledge
PMIS	Project Management Information System
PMO	Program Management Office
PMO	Project Management Office
PMP®	Project Management Professional
PS	Planned Start date
PSWBS	Project Summary Work Breakdown Structure
PV	Planned Value
QA	Quality Assurance
QC	Quality Control
RAM	Responsibility Assignment Matrix
RBS	Resource Breakdown Structure
RBS	Risk Breakdown Structure
RD	Remaining Duration
RFP	Request for Proposal
RFQ	Request for Quotation
SF	Scheduled Finish date
SF	Start-to-Finish
SOW	Statement of Work
SPI	Schedule Performance Index
SS	Scheduled Start date
SS	Start-to-Start
SV	Schedule Variance
SWOT	Strengths, Weaknesses, Opportunities, and Threats
TC	Target Completion date
TF	Target Finish date
TF	Total Float
T&M	Time and Material
TQM	Total Quality Management
TS	Target Start date
VE	Value Engineering
WBS	Work Breakdown Structure

Glossary

3. Definitions

Many of the words defined here have broader, and in some cases different, dictionary definitions.

The definitions use the following conventions:

- Terms used as part of the definitions and that are defined in the glossary are shown in *italics*.
  - ◆ When the same glossary term appears more than once in a given definition, only the first occurrence is italicized.
  - ◆ In some cases, a single glossary term consists of multiple words (e.g., risk response planning).
  - ◆ In many cases, there are multiple, consecutive glossary terms within a given definition. For example, *duration estimate* denotes two separate glossary entries, one for "duration" and another for "estimate." (There are even some definitions with a string of consecutive italicized words, not separated by commas, that represent multiple, consecutive glossary terms, at least one of which consists of multiple words. For example, *critical path method late finish date* denotes two separate glossary entries, one for "critical path method" and another for "late finish date.")

    In situations with multiple, consecutive glossary terms, an asterisk (*) will follow the last italicized word in the string to denote that multiple glossary terms are referenced.

- When synonyms are included, no definition is given and the reader is directed to the preferred term (i.e., see preferred term).

- Related terms that are not synonyms are cross-referenced at the end of the definition (i.e., see also related term).

Accept. The act of formally receiving or acknowledging something and regarding it as being true, sound, suitable, or complete.

Acceptance. See *accept*.

Acceptance Criteria. Those *criteria*, including performance *requirements* and essential conditions, which must be met before project *deliverables* are accepted.

Acquire Project Team [Process]. The process of obtaining the human resources needed to complete the *project*.

Activity. A *component* of *work* performed during the course of a *project*. See also *schedule activity*.

Activity Attributes [Output/Input]. Multiple attributes associated with each *schedule activity* that can be included within the *activity list*. Activity attributes include *activity codes*, *predecessor activities*, *successor activities*, *logical relationships*, *leads* and *lags*, *resource requirements, imposed dates, constraints,* and *assumptions*.

Activity Code. One or more numerical or text values that identify characteristics of the *work* or in some way categorize the *schedule activity* that allows filtering and ordering of activities within reports.

Activity Definition [Process]. The *process* of identifying the specific *schedule activities* that need to be performed to produce the various project *deliverables*.

Activity Description (AD). A short phrase or label for each *schedule activity* used in conjunction with an *activity identifier* to differentiate that project schedule activity from

A Guide to the Project Management Body of Knowledge (PMBOK® Guide) Third Edition
©2004 Project Management Institute, Four Campus Boulevard, Newtown Square, PA 19073-3299 USA

other schedule activities. The activity description normally describes the *scope* of work of the schedule activity.

Activity Duration. The time in *calendar* units between the start and finish of a *schedule activity*. See also *actual duration*, *original duration*, and *remaining duration*.

Activity Duration Estimating [Process]. The *process* of estimating the number of work periods that will be needed to complete individual *schedule activities*.

Activity Identifier. A short unique numeric or text identification assigned to each *schedule activity* to differentiate that *project activity** from other activities. Typically unique within any one *project schedule network diagram*.

Activity List [Output/Input]. A documented tabulation of *schedule activities* that shows the *activity description*, *activity identifier*, and a sufficiently detailed scope of work description so *project team members* understand what *work* is to be performed.

Activity-on-Arrow (AOA). See *arrow diagramming method*.

Activity-on-Node (AON). See *precedence diagramming method*.

Activity Resource Estimating [Process]. The *process* of estimating the types and quantities of *resources* required to perform each *schedule activity*.

Activity Sequencing [Process]. The *process* of identifying and documenting *dependencies* among *schedule activities*.

Actual Cost (AC). Total costs actually incurred and recorded in accomplishing work performed for a *schedule activity* or *work breakdown structure component*. Actual cost can sometimes be direct labor hours alone, direct costs alone, or all costs including indirect costs. Also referred to as the actual cost of work performed (ACWP). See also *earned value management* and *earned value technique*.

Actual Cost of Work Performed (ACWP). See *actual cost (AC)*.

Actual Duration. The time in *calendar units* between the *actual start date* of the *schedule activity* and either the *data date* of the *project schedule* if the schedule activity is in progress or the *actual finish date* if the schedule activity is complete.

Actual Finish Date (AF). The point in time that *work* actually ended on a *schedule activity*. (Note: In some application areas, the schedule activity is considered "finished" when work is "substantially complete.")

Actual Start Date (AS). The point in time that *work* actually started on a *schedule activity*.

Analogous Estimating [Technique]. An estimating *technique* that uses the values of parameters, such as *scope*, *cost*, *budget*, and *duration* or measures of scale such as size, weight, and complexity from a previous, similar *activity* as the basis for estimating the same parameter or measure for a future activity. It is frequently used to estimate a parameter when there is a limited amount of detailed information about the project (e.g., in the early *phases*). Analogous estimating is a form of *expert judgment*. Analogous estimating is most reliable when the previous activities are similar in fact and not just in appearance, and the *project team* members preparing the *estimates* have the needed expertise.

Application Area. A category of *projects* that have common *components* significant in such projects, but are not needed or present in all projects. Application areas are usually defined in terms of either the *product* (i.e., by similar technologies or production methods) or the type of *customer* (i.e., internal versus external, government versus commercial) or industry sector (i.e., utilities, automotive, aerospace, information technologies). Application areas can overlap.

Glossary

Apportioned Effort (AE). *Effort* applied to project *work* that is not readily divisible into discrete efforts for that work, but which is related in direct proportion to measurable discrete work efforts. Contrast with *discrete effort*.

Approval. See *approve*.

Approve. The act of formally confirming, sanctioning, ratifying, or agreeing to something.

Approved Change Request [Output/Input]. A *change request* that has been processed through the *integrated change control* process and *approved*. Contrast with *requested change*.

Arrow. The graphic presentation of a *schedule activity* in the *arrow diagramming method* or a *logical relationship* between schedule activities in the *precedence diagramming method*.

Arrow Diagramming Method (ADM) [Technique]. A schedule network diagramming *technique* in which *schedule activities* are represented by *arrows*. The tail of the arrow represents the start, and the head represents the finish of the schedule activity. (The length of the arrow does **not** represent the expected duration of the schedule activity.) Schedule activities are connected at points called nodes (usually drawn as small circles) to illustrate the sequence in which the schedule activities are expected to be performed. See also *precedence diagramming method*.

As-of Date. See *data date*.

Assumptions [Output/Input]. Assumptions are factors that, for planning purposes, are considered to be true, real, or certain without proof or demonstration. Assumptions affect all aspects of *project* planning, and are part of the *progressive elaboration* of the project. *Project teams* frequently identify, document, and validate assumptions as part of their planning *process*. Assumptions generally involve a degree of *risk*.

Assumptions Analysis [Technique]. A *technique* that explores the accuracy of *assumptions* and identifies *risks* to the project from inaccuracy, inconsistency, or incompleteness of assumptions.

Authority. The right to apply *project resources**, expend *funds*, make decisions, or give *approvals*.

Backward Pass. The calculation of *late finish dates* and *late start dates* for the uncompleted portions of all *schedule activities*. Determined by working backwards through the schedule *network logic* from the project's end date. The end date may be calculated in a *forward pass* or set by the *customer* or *sponsor*. See also *schedule network analysis*.

Bar Chart [Tool]. A graphic display of schedule-related information. In the typical bar chart, *schedule activities* or *work breakdown structure components* are listed down the left side of the chart, *dates* are shown across the top, and *activity durations* are shown as date-placed horizontal bars. Also called a Gantt chart.

Baseline. The approved time phased plan (for a *project*, a *work breakdown structure component*, a *work package*, or a *schedule activity*), plus or minus approved *project scope*, *cost*, schedule, and technical changes. Generally refers to the current baseline, but may refer to the original or some other baseline. Usually used with a modifier (e.g., cost baseline, schedule baseline, performance measurement baseline, technical baseline). See also *performance measurement baseline*.

Baseline Finish Date. The finish date of a *schedule activity* in the approved *schedule baseline*. See also *scheduled finish date*.

Baseline Start Date. The start date of a *schedule activity* in the approved *schedule baseline*. See also *scheduled start date*.

A Guide to the Project Management Body of Knowledge (PMBOK® Guide) Third Edition
©2004 Project Management Institute, Four Campus Boulevard, Newtown Square, PA 19073-3299 USA

Bill of Materials (BOM). A documented formal hierarchical tabulation of the physical assemblies, subassemblies, and *components* needed to fabricate a *product*.

Bottom-up Estimating [Technique]. A method of estimating a *component* of *work*. The work is *decomposed* into more detail. An *estimate* is prepared of what is needed to meet the *requirements* of each of the lower, more detailed pieces of work, and these estimates are then aggregated into a total quantity for the component of work. The accuracy of bottom-up estimating is driven by the size and complexity of the work identified at the lower levels. Generally smaller work scopes increase the accuracy of the estimates.

Brainstorming [Technique]. A general data gathering and creativity *technique* that can be used to identify *risks*, ideas, or solutions to *issues* by using a group of *team members* or subject-matter experts. Typically, a brainstorming session is structured so that each participant's ideas are recorded for later analysis.

Budget. The approved *estimate* for the *project* or any *work breakdown structure* component or any *schedule activity*. See also *estimate*.

Budget at Completion (BAC). The sum of all the *budgets* established for the *work* to be performed on a *project* or a *work breakdown structure component* or a *schedule activity*. The total *planned value* for the project.

Budgeted Cost of Work Performed (BCWP). See *earned value (EV)*.

Budgeted Cost of Work Scheduled (BCWS). See *planned value (PV)*.

Buffer. See *reserve*.

Buyer. The acquirer of *products*, *services*, or *results* for an organization.

Calendar Unit. The smallest unit of time used in scheduling the *project*. Calendar units are generally in hours, days, or weeks, but can also be in quarter years, months, shifts, or even in minutes.

Change Control. Identifying, documenting, approving or rejecting, and controlling changes to the *project baselines**.

Change Control Board (CCB). A formally constituted group of *stakeholders* responsible for reviewing, evaluating, approving, delaying, or rejecting changes to the *project*, with all decisions and recommendations being recorded.

Change Control System [Tool]. A collection of formal documented *procedures* that define how project *deliverables* and documentation will be controlled, changed, and approved. In most *application areas* the change control system is a subset of the *configuration management system*.

Change Request. Requests to expand or reduce the *project scope*, modify policies, *processes*, plans, or *procedures*, modify *costs* or *budgets*, or revise *schedules*. Requests for a change can be direct or indirect, externally or internally initiated, and legally or contractually mandated or optional. Only formally documented requested changes are processed and only approved change requests are implemented.

Chart of Accounts [Tool]. Any numbering *system* used to monitor *project costs** by category (e.g., labor, supplies, materials, and equipment). The project chart of accounts is usually based upon the corporate chart of accounts of the primary *performing organization*. Contrast with *code of accounts*.

Charter. See *project charter*.

Checklist [Output/Input]. Items listed together for convenience of comparison, or to ensure the actions associated with them are managed appropriately and not forgotten.

Glossary

An example is a list of items to be inspected that is created during *quality* planning and applied during quality *control.*

Claim. A request, demand, or assertion of rights by a *seller* against a *buyer*, or vice versa, for consideration, compensation, or payment under the terms of a legally binding *contract,* such as for a disputed change.

Close Project [Process]. The *process* of finalizing all *activities* across all of the project *process groups* to formally close the *project* or *phase.*

Closing Processes [Process Group]. Those *processes* performed to formally terminate all *activities* of a *project* or *phase*, and transfer the completed *product* to others or close a cancelled *project.*

Code of Accounts [Tool]. Any numbering *system* used to uniquely identify each *component* of the *work breakdown structure.* Contrast with *chart of accounts.*

Co-location [Technique]. An organizational placement strategy where the *project team members* are physically located close to one another in order to improve *communication*, working relationships, and productivity.

Common Cause. A source of variation that is inherent in the *system* and predictable. On a *control chart*, it appears as part of the random process variation (i.e., variation from a *process* that would be considered normal or not unusual), and is indicated by a random pattern of points within the *control limits.* Also referred to as random cause. Contrast with *special cause.*

Communication. A *process* through which information is exchanged among persons using a common system of symbols, signs, or behaviors.

Communication Management Plan [Output/Input]. The *document* that describes: the *communications* needs and expectations for the *project*; how and in what format information will be communicated; when and where each communication will be made; and who is responsible for providing each type of communication. A communication management plan can be formal or informal, highly detailed or broadly framed, based on the requirements of the project *stakeholders.* The communication management plan is contained in, or is a subsidiary plan of, the *project management plan.*

Communications Planning [Process]. The *process* of determining the information and *communications* needs of the project *stakeholders*: who they are, what is their level of interest and influence on the *project*, who needs what information, when will they need it, and how it will be given to them.

Compensation. Something given or received, a payment or recompense, usually something monetary or in kind for *products*, *services*, or *results* provided or received.

Component. A constituent part, element, or piece of a complex whole.

Configuration Management System [Tool]. A subsystem of the overall *project management system.* It is a collection of formal documented *procedures* used to apply technical and administrative direction and surveillance to: identify and document the functional and physical characteristics of a *product, result, service,* or *component*; control any changes to such characteristics; record and report each change and its implementation status; and support the audit of the products, results, or components to verify conformance to *requirements.* It includes the documentation, tracking *systems*, and defined approval levels necessary for authorizing and controlling changes. In most *application areas*, the configuration management system includes the *change control system.*

A Guide to the Project Management Body of Knowledge (PMBOK® Guide) Third Edition
©2004 Project Management Institute, Four Campus Boulevard, Newtown Square, PA 19073-3299 USA

Constraint [Input]. The state, quality, or sense of being restricted to a given course of action or inaction. An applicable restriction or limitation, either internal or external to the project, that will affect the performance of the *project* or a *process*. For example, a schedule constraint is any limitation or restraint placed on the *project schedule* that affects when a s*chedule activity* can be scheduled and is usually in the form of fixed *imposed dates*. A cost constraint is any limitation or restraint placed on the *project budget* such as *funds* available over time. A project *resource* constraint is any limitation or restraint placed on resource usage, such as what resource *skills* or *disciplines* are available and the amount of a given resource available during a specified time frame.

Contingency. See *reserve*.

Contingency Allowance. See *reserve*.

Contingency Reserve [Output/Input]. The amount of *funds*, *budget*, or time needed above the *estimate* to reduce the *risk* of overruns of project *objectives* to a level acceptable to the *organization*.

Contract [Output/Input]. A contract is a mutually binding agreement that obligates the *seller* to provide the specified *product* or *service* or *result* and obligates the *buyer* to pay for it.

Contract Administration [Process]. The process of managing the *contract* and the relationship between the *buyer* and *seller*, reviewing and documenting how a seller is performing or has performed to establish required *corrective actions* and provide a basis for future relationships with the seller, managing contract related changes and, when appropriate, managing the contractual relationship with the outside buyer of the *project*.

Contract Closure [Process]. The process of completing and settling the *contract*, including resolution of any open items and closing each contract.

Contract Management Plan [Output/Input]. The *document* that describes how a specific *contract* will be administered and can include items such as required documentation delivery and performance requirements. A contract management plan can be formal or informal, highly detailed or broadly framed, based on the requirements in the contract. Each contract management plan is a subsidiary plan of the *project management plan*.

Contract Statement of Work (SOW) [Output/Input]. A narrative description of *products, services, or results* to be supplied under contract.

Contract Work Breakdown Structure (CWBS) [Output/Input]. A portion of the *work breakdown structure* for the *project* developed and maintained by a *seller* contracting to provide a *subproject* or project *component*.

Control [Technique]. Comparing actual performance with planned performance, analyzing *variances*, assessing trends to effect *process* improvements, evaluating possible alternatives, and recommending appropriate *corrective action* as needed.

Control Account (CA) [Tool]. A management control point where *scope*, *budget* (resource plans), *actual cost*, and *schedule* are integrated and compared to *earned value* for performance measurement. Control accounts are placed at selected management points (specific *components* at selected levels) of the *work breakdown structure*. Each control account may include one or more *work packages*, but each work package may be associated with only one control account. Each control account is associated with a specific single organizational *component* in the *organizational breakdown structure* (OBS). Previously called a cost account. See also *work package*.

Control Account Plan (CAP) [Tool]. A plan for all the *work* and *effort* to be performed in a control account. Each CAP has a definitive *statement of work*, *schedule*, and time-phased *budget*. Previously called a Cost Account Plan.

Control Chart [Tool]. A graphic display of process data over time and against established *control limits*, and that has a centerline that assists in detecting a trend of plotted values toward either *control limit*.

Control Limits. The area composed of three standard deviations on either side of the centerline, or mean, of a normal distribution of data plotted on a *control chart* that reflects the expected variation in the data. See also *specification limits*.

Controlling. See *control*.

Corrective Action. Documented direction for *executing* the *project work* to bring expected future performance of the project *work* in line with the *project management plan*.

Cost. The monetary value or price of a *project activity** or *component* that includes the monetary worth of the *resources* required to perform and complete the activity or component, or to produce the component. A specific cost can be composed of a combination of cost components including direct labor hours, other direct costs, indirect labor hours, other indirect costs, and purchased price. (However, in the *earned value management* methodology, in some instances, the term cost can represent only labor hours without conversion to monetary worth.) See also *actual cost* and *estimate*.

Cost Baseline. See *baseline*.

Cost Budgeting [Process]. The *process* of aggregating the estimated costs of individual activities or *work packages* to establish a cost *baseline*.

Cost Control [Process]. The *process* of influencing the factors that create variances, and controlling changes to the project budget.

Cost Estimating [Process]. The *process* of developing an approximation of the cost of the *resources* needed to complete *project activities**.

Cost Management Plan [Output/Input]. The document that sets out the format and establishes the *activities* and *criteria* for planning, structuring, and controlling the *project costs*. A cost management plan can be formal or informal, highly detailed or broadly framed, based on the requirements of the project stakeholders. The cost management plan is contained in, or is a subsidiary plan, of the *project management plan*.

Cost of Quality (COQ) [Technique]. Determining the costs incurred to ensure *quality*. Prevention and appraisal costs (cost of conformance) include costs for quality planning, quality control (QC), and quality assurance to ensure compliance to requirements (i.e., training, QC *systems*, etc.). Failure costs (cost of non-conformance) include costs to rework *products*, *components*, or *processes* that are non-compliant, costs of warranty work and waste, and loss of reputation.

Cost Performance Index (CPI). A measure of cost efficiency on a *project*. It is the ratio of *earned value* (EV) to *actual costs* (AC). CPI = EV divided by AC. A value equal to or greater than one indicates a favorable condition and a value less than one indicates an unfavorable condition.

Cost-Plus-Fee (CPF). A type of *cost reimbursable contract* where the *buyer* reimburses the *seller* for seller's allowable costs for performing the contract work and seller also receives a fee calculated as an agreed upon percentage of the costs. The fee varies with the actual cost.

Cost-Plus-Fixed-Fee (CPFF) Contract. A type of *cost-reimbursable contract* where the *buyer* reimburses the *seller* for the seller's allowable costs (allowable costs are defined by the contract) plus a fixed amount of profit (fee).

Cost-Plus-Incentive-Fee (CPIF) Contract. A type of *cost-reimbursable contract* where the *buyer* reimburses the *seller* for the seller's allowable costs (allowable costs are defined by the contract), and the seller earns its profit if it meets defined performance criteria.

Cost-Plus-Percentage of Cost (CPPC). See *cost-plus-fee*.

Cost-Reimbursable Contract. A type of *contract* involving payment (reimbursement) by the *buyer* to the *seller* for the seller's actual costs, plus a fee typically representing seller's profit. Costs are usually classified as direct costs or indirect costs. Direct costs are costs incurred for the exclusive benefit of the project, such as salaries of full-time project staff. Indirect costs, also called overhead and general and administrative cost, are costs allocated to the project by the performing organization as a cost of doing business, such as salaries of management indirectly involved in the project, and cost of electric utilities for the office. Indirect costs are usually calculated as a percentage of direct costs. Cost-reimbursable contracts often include incentive clauses where, if the seller meets or exceeds selected project objectives, such as schedule targets or total cost, then the seller receives from the buyer an incentive or bonus payment.

Cost Variance (CV). A measure of cost performance on a *project*. It is the algebraic difference between *earned value* (EV) and *actual cost* (AC). CV = EV minus AC. A positive value indicates a favorable condition and a negative value indicates an unfavorable condition.

Crashing [Technique]. A specific type of project *schedule compression technique* performed by taking action to decrease the total *project schedule duration** after analyzing a number of alternatives to determine how to get the maximum schedule duration compression for the least additional cost. Typical approaches for crashing a schedule include reducing *schedule activity durations* and increasing the assignment of *resources* on schedule activities. See *schedule compression* and see also *fast tracking*.

Create WBS (Work Breakdown Structure) [Process]. The *process* of subdividing the major project *deliverables* and project *work* into smaller, more manageable *components*.

Criteria. *Standards*, rules, or tests on which a judgment or decision can be based, or by which a *product*, *service*, *result*, or *process* can be evaluated.

Critical Activity. Any *schedule activity* on a *critical path* in a *project schedule*. Most commonly determined by using the *critical path method*. Although some activities are "critical," in the dictionary sense, without being on the critical path, this meaning is seldom used in the project context.

Critical Chain Method [Technique]. A *schedule network analysis technique** that modifies the project schedule to account for limited resources. The critical chain method mixes deterministic and probabilistic approaches to *schedule network analysis*.

Critical Path [Output/Input]. Generally, but not always, the sequence of *schedule activities* that determines the duration of the *project*. Generally, it is the longest path through the project. However, a critical path can end, as an example, on a *schedule milestone* that is in the middle of the project schedule and that has a finish-no-later-than *imposed date* schedule *constraint*. See also *critical path method*.

Critical Path Method (CPM) [Technique]. A *schedule network analysis technique** used to determine the amount of scheduling flexibility (the amount of *float*) on various logical *network paths* in the *project schedule* network, and to determine the minimum total project *duration. Early start and finish dates** are calculated by means of a *forward pass*, using a specified *start date. Late start and finish dates** are calculated by means of a *backward pass*, starting from a specified completion date, which sometimes is the project *early finish date* determined during the forward pass calculation.

Current Finish Date. The current *estimate* of the point in time when a *schedule activity* will be completed, where the estimate reflects any reported work progress. See also *scheduled finish date* and *baseline finish date*.

Current Start Date. The current *estimate* of the point in time when a *schedule activity* will begin, where the estimate reflects any reported work progress. See also *scheduled start date* and *baseline start date*.

Customer. The person or *organization* that will use the project's *product* or *service* or *result*. (See also *user*).

Data Date (DD). The *date* up to or through which the project's reporting *system* has provided actual status and accomplishments. In some reporting *systems*, the status information for the data date is included in the past and in some systems the status information is in the future. Also called *as-of date* and *time-now date*.

Date. A term representing the day, month, and year of a calendar, and, in some instances, the time of day.

Decision Tree Analysis [Technique]. The decision tree is a diagram that describes a decision under consideration and the implications of choosing one or another of the available alternatives. It is used when some future scenarios or outcomes of actions are uncertain. It incorporates probabilities and the costs or rewards of each logical path of *events* and future decisions, and uses *expected monetary value analysis* to help the *organization* identify the relative values of alternate actions. See also *expected monetary value analysis*.

Decompose. See *decomposition*.

Decomposition [Technique]. A planning technique that subdivides the *project scope* and project *deliverables* into smaller, more manageable *components*, until the project *work* associated with accomplishing the project scope and providing the deliverables is defined in sufficient detail to support *executing*, *monitoring*, and *controlling* the *work*.

Defect. An imperfection or deficiency in a project *component* where that component does not meet its *requirements* or *specifications* and needs to be either repaired or replaced.

Defect Repair. Formally documented identification of a *defect* in a project *component* with a recommendation to either repair the defect or completely replace the component.

Deliverable [Output/Input]. Any unique and verifiable *product, result*, or capability to perform a *service* that must be produced to complete a process, phase, or project. Often used more narrowly in reference to an external *deliverable*, which is a deliverable that is subject to approval by the project sponsor or customer. See also product, service, and result.

Delphi Technique [Technique]. An information gathering technique used as a way to reach a consensus of experts on a subject. Experts on the subject participate in this technique anonymously. A facilitator uses a questionnaire to solicit ideas about the important project points related to the subject. The responses are summarized and are then re-circulated to the experts for further comment. Consensus may be reached in a few rounds of this *process*. The Delphi technique helps reduce bias in the data and keeps any one person from having undue influence on the outcome.

Dependency. See *logical relationship*.

Design Review [Technique]. A management *technique* used for evaluating a proposed design to ensure that the design of the *system* or *product* meets the *customer requirements*, or to assure that the design will perform successfully, can be produced, and can be maintained.

A Guide to the Project Management Body of Knowledge (PMBOK® Guide) Third Edition
©2004 Project Management Institute, Four Campus Boulevard, Newtown Square, PA 19073-3299 USA

Develop Project Charter [Process]. The *process* of developing the *project charter* that formally authorizes a *project*.

Develop Project Management Plan [Process]. The *process* of documenting the actions necessary to define, prepare, integrate, and coordinate all subsidiary plans into a *project management plan*.

Develop Preliminary Project Scope Statement [Process]. The *process* of developing the preliminary *project scope statement* that provides a high level *scope* narrative.

Develop Project Team [Process]. The *process* of improving the competencies and interaction of team members to enhance *project* performance.

Direct and Manage Project Execution [Process]. The *process* of executing the *work* defined in the *project management plan* to achieve the project's *requirements* defined in the *project scope statement*.

Discipline. A field of work requiring specific knowledge and that has a set of rules governing work conduct (e.g., mechanical engineering, computer programming, cost estimating, etc.).

Discrete Effort. *Work effort* that is separate, distinct, and related to the completion of specific *work breakdown structure* components and *deliverables*, and that can be directly planned and measured. Contrast with *apportioned effort*.

Document. A medium and the information recorded thereon, that generally has permanence and can be read by a person or a machine. Examples include *project management plans*, *specifications*, *procedures*, studies, and manuals.

Documented Procedure. A formalized written description of how to carry out an *activity*, *process*, *technique*, or *methodology*.

Dummy Activity. A *schedule activity* of zero *duration* used to show a *logical relationship* in the *arrow diagramming method*. Dummy activities are used when logical relationships cannot be completely or correctly described with schedule activity *arrows*. Dummy activities are generally shown graphically as a dashed line headed by an arrow.

Duration (DU or DUR). The total number of *work* periods (not including holidays or other nonworking periods) required to complete a *schedule activity* or *work breakdown structure component*. Usually expressed as workdays or workweeks. Sometimes incorrectly equated with elapsed time. Contrast with *effort*. See also *original duration*, *remaining duration*, and *actual duration*.

Early Finish Date (EF). In the *critical path method*, the earliest possible point in time on which the uncompleted portions of a *schedule activity* (or the *project*) can finish, based on the schedule *network logic*, the *data date*, and any schedule *constraints*. Early finish dates can change as the project progresses and as changes are made to the *project management plan*.

Early Start Date (ES). In the *critical path method*, the earliest possible point in time on which the uncompleted portions of a *schedule activity* (or the *project*) can start, based on the schedule *network logic*, the *data date*, and any schedule *constraints*. Early start dates can change as the project progresses and as changes are made to the *project management plan*.

Earned Value (EV). The value of *work* performed expressed in terms of the approved *budget* assigned to that work for a *schedule activity* or *work breakdown structure component*. Also referred to as the *budgeted cost of work performed* (BCWP).

Earned Value Management (EVM). A management methodology for integrating *scope, schedule*, and *resources*, and for objectively measuring project performance and progress. Performance is measured by determining the budgeted cost of work performed (i.e., *earned value*) and comparing it to the actual cost of work performed (i.e., *actual cost*). Progress is measured by comparing the *earned value* to the *planned value*.

Earned Value Technique (EVT) [Technique]. A specific technique for measuring the performance of work and used to establish the *performance measurement baseline* (PMB). Also referred to as the earning rules and crediting method.

Effort. The number of labor units required to complete a *schedule activity* or *work breakdown structure component*. Usually expressed as staff hours, staff days, or staff weeks. Contrast with *duration*.

Enterprise. A company, business, firm, partnership, corporation, or governmental agency.

Enterprise Environmental Factors [Output/Input]. Any or all external environmental factors and internal organizational environmental factors that surround or influence the project's success. These factors are from any or all of the enterprises involved in the project, and include organizational culture and structure, infrastructure, existing resources, commercial databases, market conditions, and *project management software*.

Estimate [Output/Input]. A quantitative assessment of the likely amount or outcome. Usually applied to project *costs, resources, effort*, and *durations* and is usually preceded by a modifier (i.e., preliminary, conceptual, feasibility, order-of-magnitude, definitive). It should always include some indication of accuracy (e.g., ±x percent).

Estimate at Completion (EAC) [Output/Input]. The expected total cost of a *schedule activity*, a *work breakdown structure component*, or the *project* when the defined *scope* of *work* will be completed. EAC is equal to the *actual cost* (AC) plus the *estimate to complete* (ETC) for all of the remaining work. EAC = AC plus ETC. The EAC may be calculated based on performance to date or estimated by the *project team* based on other factors, in which case it is often referred to as the latest revised estimate. See also *earned value technique* and *estimate to complete*.

Estimate to Complete (ETC) [Output/Input]. The expected cost needed to complete all the remaining work for a schedule *activity*, *work breakdown structure* component, or the *project*. See also *earned value technique* and *estimate at completion*.

Event. Something that happens, an occurrence, an outcome.

Exception Report. *Document* that includes only major variations from the plan (rather than all variations).

Execute. Directing, managing, performing, and accomplishing the *project work,* providing the *deliverables,* and providing *work performance information*.

Executing. See *execute*.

Executing Processes [Process Group]. Those *processes* performed to complete the *work* defined in the *project management plan* to accomplish the project's *objectives* defined in the *project scope statement*.

Execution. See *execute*.

Expected Monetary Value (EMV) Analysis. A statistical *technique* that calculates the average outcome when the future includes scenarios that may or may not happen. A common use of this technique is within *decision tree analysis*. Modeling and simulation are recommended for *cost* and schedule *risk* analysis because it is more powerful and less subject to misapplication than expected monetary value analysis.

Expert Judgment [Technique]. Judgment provided based upon expertise in an *application area, knowledge area, discipline*, industry, etc. as appropriate for the activity being performed. Such expertise may be provided by any group or person with specialized

A Guide to the Project Management Body of Knowledge (PMBOK® Guide) Third Edition
©2004 Project Management Institute, Four Campus Boulevard, Newtown Square, PA 19073-3299 USA

education, *knowledge*, *skill*, experience, or training, and is available from many sources, including: other units within the performing organization; consultants; *stakeholder*s, including *customers*; professional and technical associations; and industry groups.

Failure Mode and Effect Analysis (FMEA) [Technique]. An analytical *procedure* in which each potential failure mode in every *component* of a *product* is analyzed to determine its effect on the reliability of that component and, by itself or in combination with other possible failure modes, on the reliability of the product or system and on the required function of the component; or the examination of a *product* (at the *system* and/or lower levels) for all ways that a failure may occur. For each potential failure, an estimate is made of its effect on the total *system* and of its impact. In addition, a review is undertaken of the action planned to minimize the probability of failure and to minimize its effects.

Fast Tracking [Technique]. A specific project *schedule compression technique* that changes *network logic* to overlap *phases* that would normally be done in sequence, such as the design phase and construction phase, or to perform *schedule activities* in parallel. See *schedule compression* and see also *crashing*.

Finish Date. A point in time associated with a *schedule activity's* completion. Usually qualified by one of the following: actual, planned, estimated, scheduled, early, late, baseline, target, or current.

Finish-to-Finish (FF). The *logical relationship* where completion of *work* of the *successor activity* cannot finish until the completion of work of the *predecessor* activity. See also *logical relationship*.

Finish-to-Start (FS). The *logical relationship* where initiation of *work* of the *successor activity* depends upon the completion of work of the *predecessor activity*. See also *logical relationship*.

Firm-Fixed-Price (FFP) Contract. A type of *fixed price contract* where the *buyer* pays the *seller* a set amount (as defined by the *contract*), regardless of the seller's costs.

Fixed-Price-Incentive-Fee (FPIF) Contract. A type of *contract* where the *buyer* pays the *seller* a set amount (as defined by the contract), and the seller can earn an additional amount if the seller meets defined performance *criteria*.

Fixed-Price or Lump-Sum Contract. A type of *contract* involving a fixed total price for a well-defined *product*. Fixed-price contracts may also include incentives for meeting or exceeding selected *project objectives*, such as schedule targets. The simplest form of a fixed price contract is a purchase order.

Float. Also called slack. See *total float* and see also *free float*.

Flowcharting [Technique]. The depiction in a diagram format of the *inputs*, *process* actions, and *outputs* of one or more processes within a *system*.

Forecasts. *Estimates* or predictions of conditions and *events* in the *project's* future based on information and knowledge available at the time of the forecast. Forecasts are updated and reissued based on *work performance information* provided as the project is *executed*. The information is based on the project's past performance and expected future performance, and includes information that could impact the project in the future, such as *estimate at completion* and *estimate to complete*.

Forward Pass. The calculation of the *early start* and *early finish dates* for the uncompleted portions of all network activities. See also *schedule network analysis* and *backward pass*.

Free Float (FF). The amount of time that a *schedule activity* can be delayed without delaying the early start of any immediately following schedule activities. See also *total float*.

Functional Manager. Someone with management *authority* over an organizational unit within a *functional organization*. The manager of any group that actually makes a *product* or performs a *service*. Sometimes called a line manager.

Functional Organization. A hierarchical *organization* where each employee has one clear superior, staff are grouped by areas of specialization, and managed by a person with expertise in that area.

Funds. A supply of money or pecuniary resources immediately available.

Gantt Chart. See *bar chart*.

Goods. Commodities, wares, merchandise.

Grade. A category or rank used to distinguish items that have the same functional use (e.g., "hammer"), but do not share the same requirements for quality (e.g., different hammers may need to withstand different amounts of force).

Ground Rules [Tool]. A list of acceptable and unacceptable behaviors adopted by a *project team* to improve working relationships, effectiveness, and *communication*.

Hammock Activity. See *summary activity*.

Historical Information. Documents and data on prior projects including project files, records, correspondence, closed contracts, and closed projects.

Human Resource Planning [Process]. The *process* of identifying and documenting *project roles*, responsibilities and reporting relationships, as well as creating the *staffing management plan*.

Imposed Date. A fixed date imposed on a *schedule activity* or *schedule milestone*, usually in the form of a "start no earlier than" and "finish no later than" date.

Influence Diagram [Tool]. Graphical representation of situations showing causal influences, time ordering of *events*, and other relationships among variables and outcomes.

Influencer. Persons or groups that are not directly related to the acquisition or use of the project's *product*, but, due to their position in the *customer organization**, can influence, positively or negatively, the course of the *project*.

Information Distribution [Process]. The *process* of making needed information available to *project stakeholders* in a timely manner.

Initiating Processes [Process Group]. Those *processes* performed to authorize and define the *scope* of a new *phase* or *project* or that can result in the continuation of halted project *work*. A large number of the initiating processes are typically done outside the project's scope of control by the *organization*, *program*, or *portfolio* processes and those processes provide input to the project's initiating processes group.

Initiator. A person or *organization* that has both the ability and *authority* to start a *project*.

Input [Process Input]. Any item, whether internal or external to the project that is required by a *process* before that process proceeds. May be an *output* from a predecessor process.

Inspection [Technique]. Examining or measuring to verify whether an *activity*, *component*, *product*, *result* or *service* conforms to specified *requirements*.

Integral. Essential to completeness; requisite; constituent with; formed as a unit with another component.

A Guide to the Project Management Body of Knowledge (PMBOK® Guide) Third Edition
©2004 Project Management Institute, Four Campus Boulevard, Newtown Square, PA 19073-3299 USA

Integrated. Interrelated, interconnected, interlocked, or meshed components blended and unified into a functioning or unified whole.

Integrated Change Control [Process]. The *process* of reviewing all *change requests*, approving changes and controlling changes to *deliverables* and *organizational process assets*.

Invitation for Bid (IFB). Generally, this term is equivalent to *request for proposal*. However, in some *application areas*, it may have a narrower or more specific meaning.

Issue. A point or matter in question or in dispute, or a point or matter that is not settled and is under discussion or over which there are opposing views or disagreements.

Knowledge. Knowing something with the familiarity gained through experience, education, observation, or investigation, it is understanding a *process*, *practice*, or *technique*, or how to use a *tool*.

Knowledge Area Process. An identifiable project management *process* within a *knowledge area*.

Knowledge Area, Project Management. See *Project Management Knowledge Area*.

Lag [Technique]. A modification of a *logical relationship* that directs a delay in the *successor activity*. For example, in a *finish-to-start* dependency with a ten-day lag, the successor activity cannot start until ten days after the *predecessor* activity has finished. See also *lead*.

Late Finish Date (LF). In the *critical path method*, the latest possible point in time that a *schedule activity* may be completed based upon the schedule *network logic*, the project completion date, and any *constraints* assigned to the schedule activities without violating a schedule constraint or delaying the project completion date. The late finish dates are determined during the *backward pass* calculation of the project schedule network.

Late Start Date (LS). In the critical path method, the latest possible point in time that a *schedule activity* may begin based upon the schedule *network logic*, the project completion date, and any *constraints* assigned to the schedule activities without violating a schedule constraint or delaying the project completion date. The late start dates are determined during the *backward pass* calculation of the project schedule network.

Latest Revised Estimate. See *estimate at completion*.

Lead [Technique]. A modification of a *logical relationship* that allows an acceleration of the *successor activity*. For example, in a *finish-to-start* dependency with a ten-day lead, the *successor activity* can start ten days before the *predecessor activity* has finished. See also *lag*. A negative lead is equivalent to a positive lag.

Lessons Learned [Output/Input]. The learning gained from the process of performing the project. Lessons learned may be identified at any point. Also considered a project record, to be included in the *lessons learned knowledge base*.

Lessons Learned Knowledge Base. A store of historical information and *lessons learned* about both the outcomes of previous *project* selection decisions and previous project performance.

Level of Effort (LOE). Support-type *activity* (e.g., *seller* or *customer* liaison, project cost accounting, project management, etc.), which does not produce definitive end *products*. It is generally characterized by a uniform rate of *work* performance over a period of time determined by the activities supported.

Leveling. See *resource leveling*.

Life Cycle. See *project life cycle*.

Log. A document used to record and describe or denote selected items identified during execution of a process or activity. Usually used with a modifier, such as issue, quality control, action, or defect.

Logic. See *network logic*.

Logic Diagram. See *project schedule network diagram*.

Logical Relationship. A *dependency* between two *project schedule activities*, or between a project schedule activity and a *schedule milestone*. See also *precedence relationship*. The four possible types of logical relationships are: *Finish-to-Start*; *Finish-to-Finish*; *Start-to-Start*; and *Start-to-Finish*.

Manage Project Team [Process]. The *process* of tracking team member performance, providing feedback, resolving issues, and coordinating changes to enhance project performance.

Manage Stakeholders [Process]. The *process* of managing *communications* to satisfy the *requirements* of, and resolve *issues* with, project *stakeholders*.

Master Schedule [Tool]. A summary-level *project schedule* that identifies the major *deliverables* and *work breakdown structure components* and key *schedule milestones*. See also *milestone schedule*.

Materiel. The aggregate of things used by an *organization* in any undertaking, such as equipment, apparatus, tools, machinery, gear, material, and supplies.

Matrix Organization. Any organizational structure in which the *project manager* shares responsibility with the *functional managers* for assigning priorities and for directing the *work* of persons assigned to the *project*.

Methodology. A *system* of *practices*, *techniques*, *procedures*, and rules used by those who work in a *discipline*.

Milestone. A significant point or *event* in the *project*. See also *schedule milestone*.

Milestone Schedule [Tool]. A summary-level *schedule* that identifies the major *schedule milestones*. See also *master schedule*.

Monitor. Collect *project* performance data with respect to a plan, produce performance measures, and report and disseminate performance information.

Monitor and Control Project Work [Process]. The process of *monitoring* and *controlling* the processes required to initiate, plan, execute, and close a *project* to meet the performance *objectives* defined in the *project management plan* and *project scope statement*.

Monitoring. See *monitor*.

Monitoring and Controlling Processes [Process Group]. Those *processes* performed to measure and *monitor project execution** so that corrective action can be taken when necessary to *control* the execution of the *phase* or project.

Monte Carlo Analysis. A *technique* that computes, or iterates, the *project* cost or *project schedule* many times using input values selected at random from probability distributions of possible *costs* or *durations*, to calculate a distribution of possible total project cost or completion dates.

Near-Critical Activity. A *schedule activity* that has low *total float*. The concept of near-critical is equally applicable to a *schedule activity* or schedule *network path*. The limit below which *total float* is considered near critical is subject to *expert judgment* and varies from *project* to project.

Network. See *project schedule network diagram*.

Network Analysis. See *schedule network analysis*.

Network Logic. The collection of *schedule activity* dependencies that makes up a *project schedule network diagram*.

Network Loop. A schedule *network path* that passes the same *node* twice. Network loops cannot be analyzed using traditional *schedule network analysis* techniques such as *critical path method*.

Network Open End. A *schedule activity* without any *predecessor activities* or *successor activities* creating an unintended break in a schedule *network path*. Network open ends are usually caused by missing *logical relationships*.

Network Path. Any continuous series of *schedule activities* connected with *logical relationships* in a *project schedule network diagram*.

Networking [Technique]. Developing relationships with persons who may be able to assist in the achievement of *objectives* and responsibilities.

Node. One of the defining points of a schedule network; a junction point joined to some or all of the other *dependency* lines. See also *arrow diagramming method* and *precedence diagramming method*.

Objective. Something toward which *work* is to be directed, a strategic position to be attained, or a purpose to be achieved, a *result* to be obtained, a *product* to be produced, or a *service* to be performed.

Operations. An organizational function performing the ongoing execution of *activities* that produce the same *product* or provide a repetitive *service*. Examples are: production operations, manufacturing operations, and accounting operations.

Opportunity. A condition or situation favorable to the *project*, a positive set of circumstances, a positive set of *events*, a *risk* that will have a positive impact on project *objectives*, or a possibility for positive changes. Contrast with *threat*.

Organization. A group of persons organized for some purpose or to perform some type of *work* within an *enterprise*.

Organization Chart [Tool]. A method for depicting interrelationships among a group of persons working together toward a common *objective*.

Organizational Breakdown Structure (OBS) [Tool]. A hierarchically organized depiction of the *project organization* arranged so as to relate the *work packages* to the *performing organizational* units. (Sometimes OBS is written as Organization Breakdown Structure with the same definition.)

Organizational Process Assets [Output/Input]. Any or all *process* related assets, from any or all of the organizations involved in the *project* that are or can be used to influence the project's success. These process assets include formal and informal plans, policies, *procedures*, and guidelines. The process assets also include the organizations' knowledge bases such as *lessons learned* and *historical information*.

Original Duration (OD). The *activity duration* originally assigned to a schedule activity and not updated as progress is reported on the activity. Typically used for comparison with *actual duration* and *remaining duration* when reporting schedule progress.

Output [Process Output]. A *product*, *result*, or *service* generated by a *process*. May be an input to a successor process.

Parametric Estimating [Technique]. An estimating *technique* that uses a statistical relationship between historical data and other variables (e.g., square footage in construction, lines of code in software development) to calculate an *estimate* for activity parameters, such as *scope, cost, budget*, and *duration*. This technique can produce higher levels of accuracy depending upon the sophistication and the underlying data built into the model. An example for the cost parameter is multiplying the planned quantity of work to be performed by the historical cost per unit to obtain the estimated cost.

Pareto Chart [Tool]. A histogram, ordered by frequency of occurrence, that shows how many *results* were generated by each identified cause.

Path Convergence. The merging or joining of parallel schedule *network paths* into the same *node* in a *project schedule network diagram*. Path convergence is characterized by a *schedule activity* with more than one *predecessor activity*.

Path Divergence. Extending or generating parallel schedule *network paths* from the same *node* in a *project schedule network diagram*. Path divergence is characterized by a *schedule activity* with more than one *successor activity*.

Percent Complete (PC or PCT). An *estimate*, expressed as a percent, of the amount of *work* that has been completed on an *activity* or a *work breakdown structure component*.

Perform Quality Assurance (QA) [Process]. The *process* of applying the planned, systematic quality *activities* (such as audits or peer reviews) to ensure that the *project* employs all processes needed to meet requirements.

Perform Quality Control (QC) [Process]. The *process* of *monitoring* specific *project results** to determine whether they comply with relevant quality standards and identifying ways to eliminate causes of unsatisfactory performance.

Performance Measurement Baseline. An approved integrated *scope-schedule-cost** plan for the *project work* against which project execution is compared to measure and manage performance. Technical and *quality* parameters may also be included.

Performance Reporting [Process]. The *process* of collecting and distributing performance information. This includes status reporting, progress measurement, and *forecasting*.

Performance Reports [Output/Input]. *Documents* and presentations that provide organized and summarized *work performance information, earned value management* parameters and calculations, and analyses of *project work* progress and status. Common formats for performance reports include *bar charts, S-curves, histograms*, tables, and *project schedule network diagram* showing current schedule status.

Performing Organization. The *enterprise* whose personnel are most directly involved in doing the *work* of the *project*.

Phase. See *project phase*.

Plan Contracting [Process]. The *process* of documenting the *products, services,* and *results* requirements and identifying potential *sellers*.

Plan Purchases and Acquisitions [Process]. The *process* of determining what to purchase or acquire, and determining when and how to do so.

Planned Finish Date (PF). See *scheduled finish date*.

Planned Start Date (PS). See *scheduled start date*.

Planned Value (PV). The authorized *budget* assigned to the scheduled work to be accomplished for a *schedule activity* or *work breakdown structure component*. Also referred to as the budgeted cost of work scheduled (BCWS).

Planning Package. A WBS *component* below the *control account* with known *work* content but without detailed *schedule activities*. See also *control account*.

A Guide to the Project Management Body of Knowledge (PMBOK® Guide) Third Edition
©2004 Project Management Institute, Four Campus Boulevard, Newtown Square, PA 19073-3299 USA

Planning Processes [Process Group]. Those *processes* performed to define and mature the *project scope*, develop the *project management plan*, and identify and schedule the *project activities** that occur within the *project*.

Portfolio. A collection of *projects* or *programs* and other work that are grouped together to facilitate effective management of that *work* to meet strategic business *objectives*. The projects or programs of the portfolio may not necessarily be interdependent or directly related.

Portfolio Management [Technique]. The centralized management of one or more *portfolios*, which includes identifying, prioritizing, authorizing, managing, and controlling *projects*, *programs*, and other related work, to achieve specific strategic business *objectives*.

Position Description [Tool]. An explanation of a *project team* member's *roles* and responsibilities.

Practice. A specific type of professional or management *activity* that contributes to the execution of a *process* and that may employ one or more *techniques* and *tools*.

Precedence Diagramming Method (PDM) [Technique]. A schedule network diagramming *technique* in which *schedule activities* are represented by boxes (or *nodes*). Schedule activities are graphically linked by one or more *logical relationships* to show the sequence in which the activities are to be performed.

Precedence Relationship. The term used in the *precedence diagramming method* for a *logical relationship*. In current usage, however, precedence relationship, *logical relationship*, and *dependency* are widely used interchangeably, regardless of the diagramming method used.

Predecessor Activity. The *schedule activity* that determines when the logical *successor activity* can begin or end.

Preventive Action. Documented direction to perform an *activity* that can reduce the probability of negative consequences associated with *project risks**.

Probability and Impact Matrix [Tool]. A common way to determine whether a *risk* is considered low, moderate, or high by combining the two dimensions of a risk: its probability of occurrence, and its impact on objectives if it occurs.

Procedure. A series of steps followed in a regular definitive order to accomplish something.

Process. A set of interrelated actions and *activities* performed to achieve a specified set of *products, results, or services*.

Process Group. See *Project Management Process Groups*.

Procurement Documents [Output/Input]. Those *documents* utilized in bid and proposal activities, which include *buyer's* Invitation for Bid, Invitation for Negotiations, Request for Information, Request for Quotation, Request for Proposal and *seller's* responses.

Procurement Management Plan [Output/Input]. The *document* that describes how procurement *processes* from developing procurement documentation through *contract closure* will be managed.

Product. An artifact that is produced, is quantifiable, and can be either an end item in itself or a component item. Additional words for products are *materiel* and *goods*. Contrast with *result* and *service*. See also *deliverable*.

Product Life Cycle. A collection of generally sequential, non-overlapping *product phases** whose name and number are determined by the manufacturing and control needs of the *organization*. The last product life cycle phase for a product is generally the product's

Glossary

deterioration and death. Generally, a *project life cycle* is contained within one or more product life cycles.

Product Scope. The features and functions that characterize a *product*, *service* or *result*.

Product Scope Description. The documented narrative description of the *product scope*.

Program. A group of related *projects* managed in a coordinated way to obtain benefits and control not available from managing them individually. Programs may include elements of related *work* outside of the *scope* of the discrete projects in the program.

Program Management. The centralized coordinated management of a *program* to achieve the program's strategic *objectives* and benefits.

Program Management Office (PMO). The centralized management of a particular *program* or programs such that corporate benefit is realized by the sharing of *resources, methodologies, tools, and techniques*, and related high-level project management focus. See also *project management office*.

Progressive Elaboration [Technique]. Continuously improving and detailing a plan as more detailed and specific information and more accurate estimates become available as the project progresses, and thereby producing more accurate and complete plans that result from the successive iterations of the planning *process*.

Project. A temporary endeavor undertaken to create a unique *product*, *service*, or *result*.

Project Calendar. A calendar of working days or shifts that establishes those *dates* on which *schedule activities* are worked and nonworking days that determine those dates on which schedule activities are idle. Typically defines holidays, weekends and shift hours. See also *resource calendar*.

Project Charter [Output/Input]. A *document* issued by the project *initiator* or *sponsor* that formally authorizes the existence of a *project*, and provides the *project manager* with the authority to apply organizational *resources* to project *activities*.

Project Communications Management [Knowledge Area].

Project Cost Management [Knowledge Area].

Project Human Resource Management [Knowledge Area].

Project Initiation. Launching a *process* that can result in the authorization and *scope* definition of a new *project*.

Project Integration Management [Knowledge Area].

Project Life Cycle. A collection of generally sequential *project phases* whose name and number are determined by the *control* needs of the *organization* or organizations involved in the *project*. A life cycle can be documented with a *methodology*.

Project Management (PM). The application of *knowledge, skills, tools*, and *techniques* to *project activities** to meet the project *requirements*.

Project Management Body of Knowledge . An inclusive term that describes the sum of *knowledge* within the profession of *project management*. As with other professions, such as law, medicine, and accounting, the body of knowledge rests with the practitioners and academics that apply and advance it. The complete project management body of knowledge includes proven traditional *practices* that are widely applied and innovative practices that are emerging in the profession. The body of knowledge includes both published and unpublished materials. This body of knowledge is constantly evolving. PMI's *PMBOK® Guide* identifies that subset of the *project management body of knowledge* that is generally recognized as "good practice," as noted in Section 1.1.

Project Management Information System (PMIS) [Tool]. An information *system* consisting of the *tools* and *techniques* used to gather, integrate, and disseminate the

A Guide to the Project Management Body of Knowledge (PMBOK® Guide) Third Edition
©2004 Project Management Institute, Four Campus Boulevard, Newtown Square, PA 19073-3299 USA

outputs of project management *processes*. It is used to support all aspects of the project from initiating through closing, and can include both manual and automated *systems*.

Project Management Knowledge Area. An identified area of *project management* defined by its *knowledge requirements* and described in terms of its *component processes*, *practices*, *inputs*, *outputs*, *tools*, and *techniques*.

Project Management Office (PMO). An organizational body or entity assigned various responsibilities related to the centralized and coordinated management of those *projects* under its domain. The responsibilities of a PMO can range from providing project management support functions to actually being responsible for the direct management of a project. See also *program management office*.

Project Management Plan [Output/Input]. A formal, approved *document* that defines how the projected is executed, monitored and controlled. It may be summary or detailed and may be composed of one or more subsidiary management plans and other planning documents.

Project Management Process. One of the 44 *processes*, unique to *project management* and described in the *PMBOK® Guide*.

Project Management Process Group. A logical grouping of the *project management processes* described in the *PMBOK® Guide*. The project management process groups include *initiating processes*, *planning processes*, *executing processes*, *monitoring and controlling processes*, and *closing processes*. Collectively, these five groups are required for any *project*, have clear internal *dependencies*, and must be performed in the same sequence on each project, independent of the *application area* or the specifics of the applied *project life cycle*. Project management process groups are not *project phases*.

Project Management Professional (PMP®). A person certified as a PMP® by the Project Management Institute (PMI®).

Project Management Software [Tool]. A class of computer software applications specifically designed to aid the *project management team* with planning, monitoring, and controlling the project, including: *cost estimating*, scheduling, *communications*, collaboration, configuration management, document control, records management, and *risk* analysis.

Project Management System [Tool]. The aggregation of the *processes*, *tools*, *techniques*, *methodologies*, *resources*, and *procedures* to manage a project. The *system* is documented in the *project management plan* and its content will vary depending upon the *application area*, organizational influence, complexity of the project, and the availability of existing *systems*. A project management system, which can be formal or informal, aids a *project manager* in effectively guiding a *project* to completion. A project management system is a set of *processes* and the related monitoring and control functions that are consolidated and combined into a functioning, unified whole.

Project Management Team. The members of the *project team* who are directly involved in *project management activities*. On some smaller *projects*, the project management team may include virtually all of the *project team members*.

Project Manager (PM). The person assigned by the *performing organization* to achieve the *project objectives**.

Project Organization Chart [Output/Input]. A *document* that graphically depicts the *project team* members and their interrelationships for a specific *project*.

Project Phase. A collection of logically related *project activities**, usually culminating in the completion of a major *deliverable*. Project phases (also called phases) are mainly completed sequentially, but can overlap in some project situations. Phases can be subdivided into *subphases* and then *components*; this hierarchy, if the project or portions of the project are divided into phases, is contained in the *work breakdown structure*. A project phase is a component of a *project life cycle*. A project phase is not a *project management process group**.

Project Process Groups. The five *process groups* required for any project that have clear dependencies and that are required to be performed in the same sequence on each project, independent of the *application area* or the specifics of the applied *project life cycle*. The process groups are initiating, planning, executing, monitoring and controlling, and closing.

Project Procurement Management [Knowledge Area]. See Appendix F.

Project Quality Management [Knowledge Area]. See Appendix F.

Project Risk Management [Knowledge Area]. See Appendix F.

Project Schedule [Output/Input]. The planned *dates* for performing *schedule activities* and the planned dates for meeting *schedule milestones*.

Project Schedule Network Diagram [Output/Input]. Any schematic display of the *logical relationships* among the project *schedule activities*. Always drawn from left to right to reflect project *work* chronology.

Project Scope. The *work* that must be performed to deliver a *product, service, or result* with the specified features and functions.

Project Scope Management [Knowledge Area]. See Appendix F.

Project Scope Management Plan [Output/Input]. The *document* that describes how the *project scope* will be defined, developed, and verified and how the *work breakdown structure* will be created and defined, and that provides guidance on how the *project scope* will be managed and controlled by the *project management team*. It is contained in or is a subsidiary plan of the *project management plan*. The project scope management plan can be informal and broadly framed, or formal and highly detailed, based on the needs of the *project*.

Project Scope Statement [Output/Input]. The narrative description of the *project scope*, including major *deliverables*, project *objectives*, project *assumptions*, project *constraints*, and a *statement of work*, that provides a documented basis for making future project decisions and for confirming or developing a common understanding of *project scope* among the *stakeholders*. The definition of the *project scope* – what needs to be accomplished.

Project Sponsor. See *sponsor*.

Project Stakeholder. See *stakeholder*.

Project Summary Work Breakdown Structure (PSWBS) [Tool]. A *work breakdown structure* for the project that is only developed down to the *subproject* level of detail within some legs of the WBS, and where the detail of those subprojects are provided by use of *contract work breakdown structures*.

Project Team. All the *project team members*, including the *project management team*, the *project manager* and, for some projects, the *project sponsor*.

Project Team Directory. A documented list of *project team* members, their project *roles* and *communication* information.

A Guide to the Project Management Body of Knowledge (PMBOK® Guide) Third Edition
©2004 Project Management Institute, Four Campus Boulevard, Newtown Square, PA 19073-3299 USA

Project Team Members. The persons who report either directly or indirectly to the *project manager*, and who are responsible for performing *project work* as a regular part of their assigned duties.

Project Time Management [Knowledge Area]. See Appendix F.

Project Work. See *work*.

Projectized Organization. Any organizational structure in which the *project manager* has full authority to assign priorities, apply *resources*, and direct the *work* of persons assigned to the *project*.

Qualitative Risk Analysis [Process]. The *process* of prioritizing *risks* for subsequent further analysis or action by assessing and combining their probability of occurrence and impact.

Quality. The degree to which a set of inherent characteristics fulfills *requirements*.

Quality Management Plan [Output/Input]. The quality management plan describes how the *project management team* will implement the *performing organization's* quality policy. The quality management plan is a component or a subsidiary plan of the *project management plan*. The quality management plan may be formal or informal, highly detailed, or broadly framed, based on the *requirements* of the *project*.

Quality Planning [Process]. The *process* of identifying which quality standards are relevant to the *project* and determining how to satisfy them.

Quantitative Risk Analysis [Process]. The *process* of numerically analyzing the effect on overall project *objectives* of identified *risks*.

Regulation. Requirements imposed by a governmental body. These *requirements* can establish *product*, *process* or *service* characteristics—including applicable administrative provisions—that have government-mandated compliance.

Reliability. The probability of a *product* performing its intended function under specific conditions for a given period of time.

Remaining Duration (RD). The time in *calendar units*, between the *data date* of the *project schedule* and the *finish date* of a *schedule activity* that has an *actual start date*. This represents the time needed to complete a *schedule activity* where the *work* is in progress.

Request for Information. A type of *procurement document* whereby the *buyer* requests a potential *seller* to provide various pieces of information related to a *product* or *service* or *seller* capability.

Request for Proposal (RFP). A type of *procurement document* used to request proposals from prospective *sellers* of *products* or *services*. In some *application areas*, it may have a narrower or more specific meaning.

Request for Quotation (RFQ). A type of *procurement document* used to request price quotations from prospective *sellers* of common or standard *products* or *services*. Sometimes used in place of *request for proposal* and in some *application areas*, it may have a narrower or more specific meaning.

Request Seller Responses [Process]. The *process* of obtaining information, quotations, bids, offers, or proposals, as appropriate.

Requested Change [Output/Input]. A formally documented *change request* that is submitted for *approval* to the *integrated change control* process. Contrast with *approved change request*.

Requirement. A condition or capability that must be met or possessed by a *system, product, service, result,* or *component* to satisfy a *contract, standard, specification,* or other formally imposed *documents*. Requirements include the quantified and documented needs, wants, and expectations of the *sponsor*, *customer*, and other *stakeholders*.

Reserve. A provision in the *project management plan* to mitigate *cost* and/or schedule *risk*. Often used with a modifier (e.g., management reserve, contingency reserve) to provide further detail on what types of risk are meant to be mitigated. The specific meaning of the modified term varies by *application area*.

Reserve Analysis [Technique]. An analytical *technique* to determine the essential features and relationships of components in the *project management plan* to establish a *reserve* for the *schedule duration*, *budget*, estimated *cost*, or *funds* for a *project*.

Residual Risk. A *risk* that remains after risk responses have been implemented.

Resource. Skilled human resources (specific disciplines either individually or in crews or teams), equipment, *services*, supplies, *commodities*, *materiel*, *budgets*, or funds.

Resource Breakdown Structure (RBS). A hierarchical structure of *resources* by resource category and resource type used in *resource leveling* schedules and to develop resource-limited schedules, and which may be used to identify and analyze project human resource assignments.

Resource Calendar. A calendar of working days and nonworking days that determines those *dates* on which each specific *resource* is idle or can be active. Typically defines resource specific holidays and resource availability periods. See also *project calendar*.

Resource-Constrained Schedule. See *resource-limited schedule*.

Resource Histogram. A *bar chart* showing the amount of time that a *resource* is scheduled to work over a series of time periods. Resource availability may be depicted as a line for comparison purposes. Contrasting bars may show actual amounts of resource used as the project progresses.

Resource Leveling [Technique]. Any form of *schedule network analysis* in which scheduling decisions (start and finish dates) are driven by resource constraints (e.g., limited resource availability or difficult-to-manage changes in resource availability levels).

Resource-Limited Schedule. A *project schedule* whose *schedule activity*, *scheduled start dates* and *scheduled finish dates* reflect expected resource availability. A resource-limited schedule does not have any early or late start or finish dates. The resource-limited schedule *total float* is determined by calculating the difference between the *critical path method late finish date**** and the resource-limited scheduled finish date. Sometimes called resource-constrained schedule. See also *resource leveling*.

Resource Planning. See *activity resource estimating*.

Responsibility Assignment Matrix (RAM) [Tool]. A structure that relates the project *organizational breakdown structure* to the *work breakdown structure* to help ensure that each component of the project's *scope of work* is assigned to a responsible person/team.

Result. An output from performing project management *processes* and *activities*. Results include outcomes (e.g., integrated *systems*, revised *process*, restructured *organization*, tests, trained personnel, etc.) and *documents* (e.g., policies, plans, studies, *procedures*, *specifications*, reports, etc.). Contrast with *product* and *service*. See also *deliverable*.

Retainage. A portion of a *contract* payment that is withheld until contract completion to ensure full performance of the contract terms.

Rework. Action taken to bring a defective or nonconforming *component* into compliance with *requirements* or *specifications*.

A Guide to the Project Management Body of Knowledge (PMBOK® Guide) Third Edition
©2004 Project Management Institute, Four Campus Boulevard, Newtown Square, PA 19073-3299 USA

Risk. An uncertain *event* or condition that, if it occurs, has a positive or negative effect on a *project's objectives*. See also *risk category* and *risk breakdown structure*.

Risk Acceptance [Technique]. A *risk response planning technique** that indicates that the *project team* has decided not to change the *project management plan* to deal with a *risk*, or is unable to identify any other suitable response strategy.

Risk Avoidance [Technique]. A *risk response planning technique** for a *threat* that creates changes to the *project management plan* that are meant to either eliminate the *risk* or to protect the *project objectives* from its impact. Generally, risk avoidance involves relaxing the time, cost, scope, or quality *objectives*.

Risk Breakdown Structure (RBS) [Tool]. A hierarchically organized depiction of the identified *project risks** arranged by *risk category* and subcategory that identifies the various areas and causes of potential risks. The risk breakdown structure is often tailored to specific project types.

Risk Category. A group of potential causes of *risk*. Risk causes may be grouped into categories such as technical, external, organizational, environmental, or *project management*. A category may include subcategories such as technical maturity, weather, or aggressive estimating. See also *risk breakdown structure*.

Risk Database. A repository that provides for collection, maintenance, and analysis of data gathered and used in the risk management *processes*.

Risk Identification [Process]. The *process* of determining which *risks* might affect the *project* and documenting their characteristics.

Risk Management Plan [Output/Input]. The *document* describing how *project risk management* will be structured and performed on the *project*. It is contained in or is a subsidiary plan of the *project management plan*. The risk management plan can be informal and broadly framed, or formal and highly detailed, based on the needs of the project. Information in the risk management plan varies by *application area* and project size. The risk management plan is different from the *risk register* that contains the list of project *risks*, the *results* of risk analysis, and the risk responses.

Risk Management Planning [Process]. The *process* of deciding how to approach, plan, and execute *risk* management *activities* for a *project*.

Risk Mitigation [Technique]. A *risk response planning technique** associated with *threats* that seeks to reduce the probability of occurrence or impact of a *risk* to below an acceptable threshold.

Risk Monitoring and Control [Process]. The *process* of tracking identified *risks*, monitoring *residual risks*, identifying new risks, executing risk response plans, and evaluating their effectiveness throughout the *project life cycle*.

Risk Register [Output/Input]. The *document* containing the *results* of the *qualitative risk analysis*, *quantitative risk analysis*, and *risk response planning*. The risk register details all identified *risks*, including description, category, cause, probability of occurring, impact(s) on objectives, proposed responses, owners, and current status. The risk register is a component of the *project management plan*.

Risk Response Planning [Process]. The *process* of developing options and actions to enhance opportunities and to reduce threats to *project objectives*.

Risk Transference [Technique]. A *risk response planning technique** that shifts the impact of a *threat* to a third party, together with ownership of the response.

Role. A defined function to be performed by a *project team member*, such as testing, filing, inspecting, coding.

Rolling Wave Planning [Technique]. A form of *progressive elaboration* planning where the *work* to be accomplished in the near term is planned in detail at a low level of the *work breakdown structure,* while the work far in the future is planned at a relatively high level of the work breakdown structure, but the detailed planning of the work to be performed within another one or two periods in the near future is done as work is being completed during the current period.

Root Cause Analysis [Technique]. An analytical technique used to determine the basic underlying reason that causes a *variance* or a *defect* or a *risk.* A root cause may underlie more than one variance or defect or risk.

Schedule. See *project schedule* and see also *schedule model.*

Schedule Activity. A discrete scheduled *component* of *work* performed during the course of a *project.* A schedule activity normally has an estimated *duration,* an estimated *cost,* and estimated resource requirements. Schedule activities are connected to other schedule activities or schedule milestones with *logical relationships,* and are decomposed from *work packages.*

Schedule Analysis. See *schedule network analysis.*

Schedule Compression [Technique]. Shortening the *project schedule duration* without reducing the *project scope.* See also *crashing* and *fast tracking.*

Schedule Control [Process]. The *process* of controlling changes to the *project schedule.*

Schedule Development [Process]. The *process* of analyzing *schedule activity* sequences, schedule activity *durations, resource requirements,* and schedule *constraints* to create the *project schedule.*

Schedule Management Plan [Output/Input]. The *document* that establishes *criteria* and the *activities* for developing and controlling the *project schedule.* It is contained in, or is a subsidiary plan of, the *project management plan.* The schedule management plan may be formal or informal, highly detailed or broadly framed, based on the needs of the *project.*

Schedule Milestone. A significant *event* in the *project schedule,* such as an event restraining future work or marking the completion of a major *deliverable.* A schedule milestone has zero *duration.* Sometimes called a milestone *activity.* See also *milestone.*

Schedule Model [Tool]. A model used in conjunction with manual methods or *project management software* to perform *schedule network analysis* to generate the *project schedule* for use in managing the execution of a *project.* See also *project schedule.*

Schedule Network Analysis [Technique]. The *technique* of identifying *early and late start dates*,* as well as *early and late finish dates*,* for the uncompleted portions of project *schedule activities.* See also *critical path method, critical chain method, what-if analysis, and resource leveling.*

Schedule Performance Index (SPI). A measure of schedule efficiency on a project. It is the ratio of *earned value* (EV) to *planned value* (PV). The SPI = EV divided by PV. An SPI equal to or greater than one indicates a favorable condition and a value of less than one indicates an unfavorable condition. See also *earned value management.*

Schedule Variance (SV). A measure of schedule performance on a project. It is the algebraic difference between the *earned value* (EV) and the *planned value* (PV). SV = EV minus PV. See also *earned value management.*

Scheduled Finish Date (SF). The point in time that *work* was scheduled to finish on a *schedule activity.* The scheduled finish date is normally within the range of *dates* delimited by the *early finish date* and the *late finish date.* It may reflect *resource leveling* of scarce *resources.* Sometimes called planned finish date.

A Guide to the Project Management Body of Knowledge (PMBOK® Guide) Third Edition
©2004 Project Management Institute, Four Campus Boulevard, Newtown Square, PA 19073-3299 USA

Scheduled Start Date (SS). The point in time that *work* was scheduled to start on a *schedule activity*. The scheduled start date is normally within the range of *dates* delimited by the *early start date* and the *late start date*. It may reflect *resource leveling* of scarce *resources*. Sometimes called planned start date.

Scope. The sum of the *products*, *services*, and *results* to be provided as a *project*. See also *project scope* and *product scope*.

Scope Baseline. See *baseline.*

Scope Change. Any change to the *project scope*. A *scope* change almost always requires an adjustment to the project *cost* or *schedule*.

Scope Control [Process]. The *process* of *controlling* changes to the *project scope*.

Scope Creep. Adding features and functionality (*project scope*) without addressing the effects on time, *costs*, and *resources,* or without *customer* approval.

Scope Definition [Process]. The *process* of developing a detailed *project scope statement* as the basis for future project decisions.

Scope Planning [Process]. The *process* of creating a *project scope management plan*.

Scope Verification [Process]. The *process* of formalizing *acceptance* of the completed *project deliverables*.

S-Curve. Graphic display of cumulative *costs*, labor hours, percentage of *work*, or other quantities, plotted against time. Used to depict *planned value*, *earned value*, and *actual cost* of project work. The name derives from the S-like shape of the curve (flatter at the beginning and end, steeper in the middle) produced on a *project* that starts slowly, accelerates, and then tails off. Also a term for the cumulative likelihood distribution that is a *result* of a *simulation*, a *tool* of *quantitative risk analysis*.

Secondary Risk. A *risk* that arises as a direct *result* of implementing a risk response.

Select Sellers [Process]. The *process* of reviewing offers, choosing from among potential sellers, and negotiating a written *contract* with a *seller*.

Seller. A provider or supplier of *products*, *services*, or *results* to an organization.

Sensitivity Analysis. A *quantitative risk analysis* and modeling *technique* used to help determine which *risks* have the most potential impact on the *project*. It examines the extent to which the uncertainty of each project element affects the *objective* being examined when all other uncertain elements are held at their *baseline* values. The typical display of *results* is in the form of a tornado diagram.

Service. Useful *work* performed that does not produce a tangible *product* or *result,* such as performing any of the business functions supporting production or distribution. Contrast with product and result. See also *deliverable*.

Should-Cost Estimate. An *estimate* of the *cost* of a *product* or *service* used to provide an assessment of the reasonableness of a prospective *seller's* proposed cost.

Simulation. A simulation uses a *project* model that translates the uncertainties specified at a detailed level into their potential impact on *objectives* that are expressed at the level of the total *project*. Project simulations use computer models and *estimates* of *risk*, usually expressed as a probability distribution of possible *costs* or *durations* at a detailed work level, and are typically performed using *Monte Carlo analysis*.

Skill. Ability to use *knowledge*, a developed aptitude, and/or a capability to effectively and readily execute or perform an *activity*.

Slack. See *total float* and *free float*.

Special Cause. A source of variation that is not inherent in the *system*, is not predictable, and is intermittent. It can be assigned to a defect in the *system*. On a *control chart*, points

Glossary

beyond the *control limits*, or non-random patterns within the control limits, indicate it. Also referred to as assignable cause. Contrast with *common cause*.

Specification. A *document* that specifies, in a complete, precise, verifiable manner, the *requirements*, design, behavior, or other characteristics of a *system, component, product, result*, or *service* and, often, the *procedures* for determining whether these provisions have been satisfied. Examples are: requirement *specification*, design specification, product specification, and test specification.

Specification Limits. The area, on either side of the centerline, or mean, of data plotted on a *control chart* that meets the *customer's* requirements for a *product* or *service*. This area may be greater than or less than the area defined by the control limits. See also *control limits*.

Sponsor. The person or group that provides the financial resources, in cash or in kind, for the *project*.

Staffing Management Plan [Output/Input]. The *document* that describes when and how human *resource requirements* will be met. It is contained in, or is a subsidiary plan of, the *project management plan*. The staffing management plan can be informal and broadly framed, or formal and highly detailed, based on the needs of the *project*. Information in the staffing management plan varies by *application area* and project size.

Stakeholder. Person or *organization* (e.g., *customer, sponsor, performing organization*, or the public) that is actively involved in the *project*, or whose interests may be positively or negatively affected by execution or completion of the project. A stakeholder may also exert influence over the project and its *deliverables*.

Standard. A *document* established by consensus and approved by a recognized body that provides, for common and repeated use, rules, guidelines or characteristics for *activities* or their *results*, aimed at the achievement of the optimum degree of order in a given context.

Start Date. A point in time associated with a *schedule activity's* start, usually qualified by one of the following: actual, planned, estimated, scheduled, early, late, target, *baseline*, or current.

Start-to-Finish (SF). The *logical relationship* where completion of the *successor schedule activity* is dependent upon the initiation of the *predecessor schedule activity*. See also *logical relationship*.

Start-to-Start (SS). The *logical relationship* where initiation of the work of the *successor schedule activity* depends upon the initiation of the work of the *predecessor schedule activity*. See also *logical relationship*.

Statement of Work (SOW). A narrative description of *products, services, or results* to be supplied.

Strengths, Weaknesses, Opportunities, and Threats (SWOT) Analysis. This information gathering technique examines the project from the perspective of each project's strengths, weaknesses, *opportunities*, and *threats* to increase the breadth of the *risks* considered by risk management.

Subnetwork. A subdivision (fragment) of a *project schedule network diagram*, usually representing a *subproject* or a *work package*. Often used to illustrate or study some potential or proposed schedule condition, such as changes in preferential schedule *logic* or *project scope*.

Subphase. A subdivision of a *phase*.

Subproject. A smaller portion of the overall *project* created when a project is subdivided into more manageable *components* or pieces. Subprojects are usually represented in the *work breakdown structure*. A subproject can be referred to as a project, managed as a project, and acquired from a seller. May be referred to as a *subnetwork* in a *project schedule network diagram*.

Successor. See *successor activity*.

Successor Activity. The schedule activity that follows a *predecessor activity*, as determined by their *logical relationship*.

Summary Activity. A group of related *schedule activities* aggregated at some summary level, and displayed/reported as a single activity at that summary level. See also *subproject* and *subnetwork*.

System. An *integrated* set of regularly interacting or interdependent *components* created to accomplish a defined *objective*, with defined and maintained relationships among its components, and the whole producing or operating better than the simple sum of its components. Systems may be either physically *process* based or management process based, or more commonly a combination of both. Systems for *project management* are composed of *project management processes*, *techniques*, *methodologies*, and *tools* operated by the *project management team*.

Target Completion Date (TC). An *imposed date* that constrains or otherwise modifies the *schedule network analysis*.

Target Finish Date (TF). The *date* that *work* is planned (targeted) to finish on a *schedule activity*.

Target Schedule. A *schedule* adopted for comparison purposes during *schedule network analysis*, which can be different from the baseline schedule. See also *baseline*.

Target Start Date (TS). The *date* that *work* is planned (targeted) to start on a *schedule activity*.

Task. A term for *work* whose meaning and placement within a structured plan for project work varies by the *application area*, industry, and brand of *project management software*.

Team Members. See *project team members*.

Technical Performance Measurement [Technique]. A performance measurement *technique* that compares technical accomplishments during *project* execution to the *project management plan's schedule* of planned technical achievements. It may use key technical parameters of the *product* produced by the project as a *quality* metric. The achieved metric values are part of the *work performance information*.

Technique. A defined systematic *procedure* employed by a human *resource* to perform an *activity* to produce a *product* or *result* or deliver a *service*, and that may employ one or more *tools*.

Template. A partially complete *document* in a predefined format that provides a defined structure for collecting, organizing and presenting information and data. Templates are often based upon documents created during prior *projects*. Templates can reduce the *effort* needed to perform *work* and increase the consistency of *results*.

Threat. A condition or situation unfavorable to the *project*, a negative set of circumstances, a negative set of events, a *risk* that will have a negative impact on a project objective if it occurs, or a possibility for negative changes. Contrast with *opportunity*.

Three-Point Estimate [Technique]. An analytical *technique* that uses three *cost* or *duration estimates* to represent the optimistic, most likely, and pessimistic scenarios. This technique is applied to improve the accuracy of the *estimates* of cost or duration when the underlying *activity* or cost *component* is uncertain.

Threshold. A *cost*, time, *quality*, technical, or *resource* value used as a parameter, and which may be included in *product specifications*. Crossing the threshold should trigger some action, such as generating an exception report.

Time and Material (T&M) Contract. A type of *contract* that is a hybrid contractual arrangement containing aspects of both *cost-reimbursable* and *fixed-price contracts*. Time and material contracts resemble cost-reimbursable type arrangements in that they have no definitive end, because the full value of the arrangement is not defined at the time of the award. Thus, time and material contracts can grow in contract value as if they were cost-reimbursable-type arrangements. Conversely, time and material arrangements can also resemble fixed-price arrangements. For example, the unit rates are preset by the *buyer* and *seller*, when both parties agree on the rates for the category of senior engineers.

Time-Now Date. See *data date*.

Time-Scaled Schedule Network Diagram [Tool]. Any *project schedule network diagram* drawn in such a way that the positioning and length of the *schedule activity* represents its duration. Essentially, it is a *bar chart* that includes schedule *network logic*.

Tool. Something tangible, such as a template or software program, used in performing an *activity* to produce a *product* or *result*.

Total Float (TF). The total amount of time that a *schedule activity* may be delayed from its *early start date* without delaying the project *finish date*, or violating a schedule *constraint*. Calculated using the *critical path method* technique and determining the difference between the *early finish dates* and *late finish dates*. See also *free float*.

Total Quality Management (TQM) [Technique]. A common approach to implementing a *quality* improvement program within an *organization*.

Trend Analysis [Technique]. An analytical technique that uses mathematical models to forecast future outcomes based on historical *results*. It is a method of determining the *variance* from a *baseline* of a *budget*, *cost*, *schedule*, or *scope* parameter by using prior progress reporting periods' data and projecting how much that parameter's variance from baseline might be at some future point in the project if no changes are made in *executing* the *project*.

Triggers. Indications that a risk has occurred or is about to occur. Triggers may be discovered in the *risk identification* process and watched in the *risk monitoring and control* process. Triggers are sometimes called *risk* symptoms or warning signs.

Triple Constraint. A framework for evaluating competing demands. The triple constraint is often depicted as a triangle where one of the sides or one of the corners represent one of the parameters being managed by the project team.

User. The person or *organization* that will use the project's *product* or *service*. See also *customer*.

Validation [Technique]. The *technique* of evaluating a *component* or *product* during or at the end of a *phase* or *project* to ensure it complies with the specified *requirements*. Contrast with *verification*.

A Guide to the Project Management Body of Knowledge (PMBOK® Guide) Third Edition
©2004 Project Management Institute, Four Campus Boulevard, Newtown Square, PA 19073-3299 USA

Value Engineering (VE). A creative approach used to optimize *project life cycle* costs, save time, increase profits, improve *quality*, expand market share, solve problems, and/or use *resources* more effectively.

Variance. A quantifiable deviation, departure, or divergence away from a known *baseline* or expected value.

Variance Analysis [Technique]. A method for resolving the total *variance* in the set of *scope*, *cost*, and *schedule* variables into specific component variances that are associated with defined factors affecting the scope, cost, and schedule variables.

Verification [Technique]. The technique of evaluating a *component* or *product* at the end of a *phase* or *project* to assure or confirm it satisfies the conditions imposed. Contrast with *validation*.

Virtual Team. A group of persons with a shared *objective* who fulfill their *roles* with little or no time spent meeting face to face. Various forms of technology are often used to facilitate *communication* among team members. Virtual teams can be comprised of persons separated by great distances.

Voice of the Customer. A planning *technique* used to provide *products*, *services*, and *results* that truly reflect *customer requirements* by translating those customer requirements into the appropriate technical requirements for each *phase* of project product development.

War Room. A room used for *project* conferences and planning, often displaying charts of *cost*, *schedule* status, and other key project data.

Work. Sustained physical or mental effort, exertion, or exercise of *skill* to overcome obstacles and achieve an *objective*.

Work Authorization [Technique]. A permission and direction, typically written, to begin work on a specific *schedule activity* or *work package* or *control account*. It is a method for sanctioning *project work* to ensure that the work is done by the identified *organization*, at the right time, and in the proper sequence.

Work Authorization System [Tool]. A subsystem of the overall *project management system*. It is a collection of formal documented *procedures* that defines how *project work* will be authorized (committed) to ensure that the work is done by the identified *organization*, at the right time, and in the proper sequence. It includes the steps, *documents*, tracking *system*, and defined approval levels needed to issue work authorizations.

Work Breakdown Structure (WBS) [Output/Input]. A *deliverable*-oriented hierarchical *decomposition* of the *work* to be *executed* by the *project team* to accomplish the project *objectives* and create the required deliverables. It organizes and defines the total *scope* of the *project*. Each descending level represents an increasingly detailed definition of the *project work*. The WBS is decomposed into *work packages*. The deliverable orientation of the hierarchy includes both internal and external deliverables. See also *work package, control account, contract work breakdown structure, and project summary work breakdown structure.*

Work Breakdown Structure Component. An entry in the *work breakdown structure* that can be at any level.

Work Breakdown Structure Dictionary [Output/Input]. A *document* that describes each *component* in the *work breakdown structure* (WBS). For each WBS component, the WBS dictionary includes a brief definition of the *scope* or *statement of work*, defined *deliverable(s)*, a list of associated *activities*, and a list of *milestones*. Other information may include: responsible *organization*, start and end dates, *resources* required, an *estimate* of *cost*, charge number, *contract* information, *quality requirements*, and technical references to facilitate performance of the *work*.

Work Item. Term no longer in common usage. See *activity* and *schedule activity*.

Work Package. A *deliverable* or *project work component* at the lowest level of each branch of the *work breakdown structure*. The work package includes the *schedule activities* and *schedule milestones* required to complete the work package deliverable or project work component. See also *control account*.

Work Performance Information [Output/Input]. Information and data, on the status of the *project schedule activities* being performed to accomplish the *project work*, collected as part of the *direct and manage project execution processes**. Information includes: status of *deliverables*; implementation status for *change requests, corrective actions, preventive actions*, and *defect repairs*; forecasted *estimates to complete*; reported percent of *work* physically completed; achieved value of *technical performance measures*; start and finish dates of *schedule activities*.

Workaround [Technique]. A response to a negative *risk* that has occurred. Distinguished from *contingency* plan in that a workaround is not planned in advance of the occurrence of the risk event.

A Guide to the Project Management Body of Knowledge (PMBOK® Guide) Third Edition
©2004 Project Management Institute, Four Campus Boulevard, Newtown Square, PA 19073-3299 USA

INDEX

A

AC *See* actual cost (AC)

accept, 350

acceptance, 22, 41, 44-45, 62, 68, 86, 100-103, 108, 118-119, 185, 189, 207, 263, 297, 332, 338, 350

acceptance criteria, 84, 101-111, 118, 163, 184-185, 275, 289, 350

acquire project team, 10, 57, 199, 209-210, 212, 306, 339, 350

activity, 4, 10, 49-50, 58, 69, 123, 127-132, 135-144, 149, 151, 156, 164, 166-169, 186-187, 196, 204, 206-207, 214, 236, 238, 243, 274, 276, 279, 282, 348, 302, 312, 348, 350, 356

activity attributes, 130-131, 135-136, 138, 140, 143-144, 151, 156, 317, 350

activity code, 350

activity definition, 10, 49, 123, 127-130, 136, 305, 338, 351

activity description (AD), 130, 348, 350-351

activity duration, 10, 51, 58, 123-124, 139-147, 164, 200, 232, 351-352

activity duration estimating, 10, 50, 123-124, 139-142, 164, 305, 338, 351

activity identifier, 129-130, 350-351

activity list, 129, 131, 135-136, 140-141, 144, 156, 351

activity resource estimating, 10, 50, 123-124, 135-138, 141, 164, 274, 279, 305, 338, 351

activity sequencing, 10, 50-51, 123-124, 130-132, 135, 305, 338, 351

activity-on-arrow (AOA), 133, 348, 351

activity-on-node (AON), 132, 149, 348, 351

actual cost (AC), 158, 164, 172-173, 175-176, 234, 278, 348, 351, 355-357, 360

actual cost of work performed (ACWP), 172, 348, 351, 360

actual duration, 141, 151, 351, 359, 365

actual finish date (AF), 151, 348, 351

actual start date (AS), 151, 348, 351, 371

ACWP *See* actual cost of work performed (ACWP)

AD *See* activity description (AD)

ADM *See* arrow diagramming method (ADM),

AE *See* apportioned effort(AE)

AF *See* actual finish date (AF)

analogous estimating, 141, 164, 351

AOA *See* activity-on-arrow (AOA)

AON *See* activity-on-node (AON)

application area, 4, 12-13, 33, 38, 39, 84, 87-88, 91, 97, 104, 110, 113, 124, 130, 134, 138, 151, 158, 167, 184-185, 208, 270-271, 301, 329-332, 347, 351, 360, 369-370, 372-373, 376-377

apportioned effort (AE), 130, 348, 352, 359

approval *See* approve

approve, 20, 23, 86, 99, 112, 352

approved change request, 92-93, 99, 109, 112-113, 117-118, 120-122, 131, 135, 138, 152-153, 155, 167, 171-172, 178, 188-189, 192, 219, 232, 236, 265, 267-268, 290, 292, 294-295, 352, 353

arrow diagramming method (ADM), 133, 348, 351-352, 359, 365

AS *See* actual start date (AS)

as-of date *See* data date

assumptions, 43, 46, 78, 82, 86, 109, 111, 127, 130, 134, 138-140, 142-143, 146, 151, 163, 167, 175, 226, 247-249, 251, 264, 275, 279, 282, 350, 352, 370

assumptions analysis, 248, 352

authority, 14, 17, 25, 27, 29-30, 32, 81-82, 98, 206-207, 242, 352, 362, 368, 371

B

BAC *See* budget at completion (BAC)

backward pass, 145, 148, 352, 357, 361, 363

bar chart, 149, 154, 194, 208, 233, 352, 366, 372, 378

baseline, 51, 56, 59, 89, 96-97, 104, 110, 117, 120-122, 141, 143, 151, 153-155, 157, 167, 169-170-173, 177-178, 187, 197, 231-233, 243, 257, 266, 276, 282, 310, 317, 338, 352, 356, 358, 361, 366, 375-379
baseline finish date, 352, 358
baseline start date, 352, 358
BCWP *See* budgeted cost of work performed (BCWP)
BCWS *See* budgeted cost of work scheduled (BCWS)
bill of materials (BOM), 117, 348, 353
BOM *See* bill of materials (BOM)
bottom-up estimating, 137, 165, 353
brainstorming, 110, 186, 247, 353
budget, 8, 10, 56, 59, 63, 82, 93, 97, 100, 111, 157, 163-164, 167-170, 172-174, 176-178, 204, 218, 228, 234, 243, 247, 254, 260, 263-264, 266, 276, 305, 338, 348, 351, 353, 355-356, 359, 366, 372, 378
budget at completion (BAC), 173, 176, 348, 353
budgeted cost of work performed (BCWP), 172, 348, 353, 359, 360
budgeted cost of work scheduled (BCWS), 172, 348, 353, 366
buffer, 147, 166, 353
buyer, 65, 168, 262, 269-271, 274-275, 277-280, 282-286, 288-291, 293-295, 297, 307, 341, 353-357, 361, 367, 371, 378

C

CA *See* control account (CA)
calendar unit, 152, 351, 353, 371
CAP *See* control account plan (CAP)
CCB *See* change control board (CCB)
change control, 9, 59, 84, 88, 96-99, 101, 108, 112, 118-119, 121-122, 130, 135, 138, 153, 155, 167, 171-172, 177, 187, 190, 197-198, 218, 231, 234, 264, 267, 269, 280, 290-292, 294, 302, 304, 316, 337, 341, 352-354, 371
change control board (CCB), 98-99, 348, 353
change control system, 90, 121, 153, 172, 292, 353-354
change request, 56, 79, 92-93, 95, 99, 109, 189, 197, 218, 289, 352-353, 371
chart of accounts, 353
Charter *See* project charter
checklist, 187, 248, 353
claim, 293-294, 354
close project, 9, 67, 79, 100-101, 267, 295, 304, 337, 354
closing processes, 354, 369
code of accounts, 117, 353-354
co-location, 214-215, 219, 354
common cause, 191, 354, 376

communication, 15, 18, 52, 84, 88-89, 91, 149, 205-206, 211, 214, 216-217, 223-224, 226-229, 235, 240, 261, 294, 354, 362, 370, 379
communication management plan, 89, 354
communications planning, 10, 52, 211, 221, 225-227, 306, 340, 354
compensation, 15, 291, 293, 354
component, 5-6, 16, 20, 40, 90, 111-112, 115, 117-118, 122, 129, 130, 137, 144, 146, 152-154, 156, 158, 163, 167-173, 175, 186-187, 197, 206, 226, 249, 255, 259, 262, 268, 275-277, 280, 287, 291, 305, 312, 330-331, 347, 350-356, 358-362, 366-367, 369-373, 376, 378-380
configuration management system, 83, 90, 97, 102, 121, 353-354
constraint, 8, 18, 22, 43, 48, 51, 69, 78, 82, 86, 109, 111-112, 123, 127, 130, 140, 143-144, 147, 151, 163, 167-169, 189, 204, 226, 249, 275-277, 279, 338, 350, 355, 357, 359, 363, 370, 372, 374, 378
contingency allowance *See* reserve
contingency reserve, 142, 166, 169-170, 252, 261, 263, 355, 372
contingency *See* reserve
contract, 6-7, 10, 27, 58, 65, 67, 82, 84, 97-98, 100-102, 111, 115, 117, 121, 127, 130, 140, 144, 148, 165, 168, 172, 217, 232, 262, 265, 269, 270-271, 274-275, 277-280, 282-283, 285-286, 288-297, 311, 313, 329, 341, 354-357, 361, 367, 370-372, 375, 378-380
contract administration, 10, 65, 269, 289-292, 294-296, 307, 341, 355
contract closure, 10, 67, 100-102, 269, 274, 279, 291, 293, 295-297, 307, 341, 355, 367
contract management plan, 276, 290, 292, 295-297, 355
contract statement of work (SOW), 279-284, 288, 292-293, 355
contract work breakdown structure (CWBS), 115, 279, 348, 355, 379
control, 9-10, 16, 19-20, 22-23, 33, 37-38, 43, 59, 61, 63, 65, 78, 95, 88, 90-91, 94-96, 98-99, 107-108, 110, 114-115, 117-119, 121, 129, 149, 153, 155, 158, 161, 163, 170, 177, 179, 186-193, 196-198, 206, 209, 216, 232, 237, 254, 264-269, 274, 279, 291, 293, 304, 307, 316, 337, 340, 354-356, 362, 364, 366-369, 371
control account (CA), 117, 129, 155, 158, 168-169, 173, 175, 177, 348, 355-356, 360, 366, 379-380
control account plan (CAP), 129, 348, 356
control chart, 192-193, 354, 356, 375-376

control limits, 191, 354, 356, 376

controlling *See* control

COQ *See* cost of quality (COQ)

corrective action, 41, 59, 92-93, 96, 99, 119, 121-122, 154-155, 173, 177, 188-191, 195, 197, 218-219, 230, 234, 236, 265, 267, 269, 291, 294, 341, 355-356, 364, 380

cost, 8, 18, 20-21, 26, 37-38, 46, 51, 61, 63, 69, 85-86, 89, 91, 93-94, 97, 102, 111-112, 114, 117, 122, 135, 141, 145-146, 157-159, 161-178, 180, 183, 185-186, 189, 190, 193, 196, 209-210, 216, 231-234, 238, 243, 247, 249, 251-254, 256-257, 258-266, 271, 276-278, 282, 348, 355-357

cost baseline *See* baseline

cost budgeting, 10, 51, 157-158, 167-171, 305, 338, 356

cost control, 10, 63, 157, 171-173, 177, 216, 305, 338, 356

cost estimating, 10, 51, 83, 135, 148, 157-158, 161-167, 305, 338, 356, 359, 369

cost management plan, 89, 144, 158-159, 162, 167-168, 171-173, 176, 178, 255, 305, 356

cost of quality (COQ), 166, 180-181, 186, 189, 196, 317, 348, 356

cost performance index (CPI), 173, 175, 177, 234, 348, 356

cost-plus-fee (CPF), 278, 348, 356

cost variance (CV), 157, 166, 171, 173, 176-177, 193, 234, 338, 348, 357

cost-plus-fixed-fee (CPFF) contract, 278, 348, 356

cost-plus-incentive-fee (CPIF) contract, 278, 348, 357

cost-plus-percentage of cost (CPPC). *See* cost-plus-fee

cost-reimbursable contract, 278, 356-357

CPF *See* cost-plus-fee (CPF)

CPFF *See* cost-plus-fixed-fee (CPFF)

CPI *See* cost performance index (CPI)

CPIF *See* cost-plus-incentive-fee (CPIF)

CPM *See* critical path method (CPM)

CPPC *See* cost-plus-percentage of cost (CPPC)

crashing, 145, 357, 361, 374

create WBS (Work Breakdown Structure), 9, 49, 103, 112-113, 117-118, 128, 304, 338, 357

criteria, 44, 78, 81, 84, 86, 101-102, 111, 118-119, 124, 158-159, 163, 184-185, 202, 209, 255, 275, 277, 279, 282-283, 286-289, 330, 350, 356-357, 361, 374

critical activity, 154, 357

critical chain method, 145, 147, 166, 357, 374

critical path, 12, 145-149, 154, 249, 260, 350, 357

critical path method (CPM), 145-147, 347-348, 350, 357, 359, 363, 365, 372, 374, 378

current finish date, 151, 358

current start date, 151, 358

customer, 7, 26, 38, 44, 68, 77, 81-82, 86, 96, 100, 102, 110-112, 119, 144, 157, 169, 180-181, 185, 187, 189, 191, 203, 221, 229, 232-233, 236, 246, 271, 283, 285, 290, 337, 340, 351, 352, 358, 361-363, 372, 375-376, 378-379

CV *See* cost variance (CV)

CWBS *See* contract work breakdown structure (CWBS)

D

data date (DD), 151, 351-352, 358-359, 371

date, 89, 144, 147, 149, 151, 169, 174-176, 240, 253, 258, 277, 352, 357-358, 360

DD *See* data date (DD)

decision tree analysis, 254, 257, 261, 358, 360

decompose *See* decomposition

decomposition, 112, 114-116, 128, 358, 379

defect, 84-85, 92, 94, 181, 186, 197, 358, 364, 374-375

defect repair, 92-94, 96, 98-99, 189, 196-197, 358

deliverable, 5-6, 20, 22, 43-45, 49, 56, 62, 67, 76-77, 79, 86, 90-91, 93-94, 96-103, 108-116, 118-121, 123, 127-128, 133, 140, 144, 149, 157, 163, 165, 168, 172, 184-186, 188, 190-192, 198, 205, 217, 228, 232, 265, 270-271, 275-276, 279, 292-295, 297, 302, 337-338, 350, 353, 357-360, 363-364, 369, 370, 374-376, 379-380

delphi technique, 248, 358

dependency *See* logical relationship

design review, 157, 180, 193, 358

develop project charter, 9, 43, 45, 78, 81-82, 85-86, 304, 337, 359

develop project management plan, 9, 48, 78, 88-91, 124, 158, 304, 337, 359

develop preliminary project scope statement, 9, 43, 45, 78, 86-88, 304, 337, 358

develop project team, 10, 57, 199, 209, 212-213, 215, 306, 339, 359

direct and manage project execution, 9, 56, 78, 91-93, 119, 216, 232, 264, 267, 291, 304, 337, 359, 380

discipline, 12-13, 15, 83, 181, 203, 226, 270, 289, 335, 359-360, 364, 372

discrete effort, 130, 352, 359

document, 78, 285, 287, 359, 360

documented procedure, 90, 353-354, 359, 379

DU *See* duration (DU)

dummy activity, 133, 359

DUR *See* duration (DUR)

Index

duration (DU or DUR), 5, 7, 43, 133, 139-140, 141, 142-143, 147, 151, 158, 164, 166, 230, 258, 348, 351-352, 357, 359-360, 366, 374, 378

E

EAC *See* estimate at completion (EAC)
early finish date (EF), 348, 357, 359, 374
early start date (ES), 145, 347-348, 359, 375, 378
earned value (EV), 84, 153, 159, 169, 174-176, 233-234, 266, 317, 348, 353, 356-357, 359-360, 374
earned value management (EVM), 12, 95, 159, 305, 316-317, 348, 351, 356, 359, 366, 374
earned value technique (EVT), 95, 159, 172-176, 348, 351, 360
EF *See* early finish date (EF)
effort, 5, 16, 18-19, 22, 38, 40-41, 46, 59, 77, 85, 91, 103, 107, 114, 123-124, 128-130, 139, 157-159, 165, 179, 181, 186, 189, 197, 200, 212, 215, 221, 228, 237, 270, 284-285, 310, 332, 352, 356, 359-360, 377, 379
EMV *See* expected monetary value (EMV)
enterprise, 15, 17-18, 26, 81, 283, 323, 360, 365-366
enterprise environmental factors, 40, 74, 83, 87, 90, 101, 107, 127, 136, 140, 162, 184, 203, 210, 225, 242, 247, 250, 275, 360
ES *See* early start date (ES)
estimate, 77, 86, 112, 117, 138-142, 159, 161, 163-168, 175, 255, 259, 288, 350-351, 353, 355-356, 358, 360-361, 365-366, 375, 380
estimate at completion (EAC), 96, 173-175, 234, 348, 360-361, 363
estimate to complete (ETC), 96, 159, 173-175, 234, 348, 360-361
ETC *See* estimate to complete (ETC)
EV *See* earned value (EV)
event, 8, 164, 238, 262, 295, 360, 364, 373-374, 380
EVM *See* earned value management (EVM)
EVT *See* earned value technique (EVT)
exception report, 347, 360, 378
execute, 8, 9, 15, 17, 24, 33, 37-39, 46, 53, 56, 59, 65, 69, 74, 78, 81, 93-96, 100-101, 110, 127, 129-130, 163, 237, 265, 274, 304, 337, 340, 356, 358-360, 364, 370, 373, 375, 378
executing processes, 38, 40-41, 55-56, 67-68, 78, 302, 316, 360, 369
executing *See* execute
execution, *See* execute
expected monetary value (EMV) analysis, 257, 348, 358, 360

F

failure mode and effect analysis (FMEA), 180, 348, 361
fast tracking, 20, 22, 146, 357, 361, 374
FF *See* finish-to-finish (FF)
FF *See* free float (FF)
FFP *See* firm-fixed-price (FFP)
finish date, 59, 149, 151, 348-352, 359, 361, 363, 366, 371-372, 374, 377-378
finish-to-finish (FF), 132, 348, 361, 364
finish-to-start (FS), 132-134, 348, 361, 363-364
firm-fixed-price (FFP) contract, 348, 361
fixed-price or lump-sum contract, 361
fixed-price-incentive-fee (FPIF) contract, 348, 361
float *See* total float and *See also* free float
flowcharting, 193, 361
FMEA *See* failure mode and effect analysis (FMEA)
forecasts, 94-96, 174, 176, 216, 233-234, 361
forward pass, 145, 148, 352, 357, 361
FPIF *See* fixed-price-incentive-fee (FPIF)
free float (FF), 145, 348, 361-362, 375
FS *See* finish-to-start (FS)
functional manager, 28, 211, 215, 362
functional organization, 28-32, 312, 362
funds, 91, 168-170, 204, 275, 352, 355, 362, 372

G

gantt chart *See* bar chart
goods, 271, 362, 367
grade, 180, 362
ground rules, 204, 214, 217, 219, 306, 362

H

hammock activity, 149, 362
historical information, 39, 85, 102, 107-108, 127, 130, 134, 136, 140-141, 162, 169, 225, 248, 362, 363, 365
human resource planning, 10, 52, 199, 202-205, 207, 214, 306, 339, 362

I

IFB *See* invitation for bid (IFB)
imposed date, 169, 357, 362, 377
influence diagram, 248, 362
influencer, 362
information distribution, 10, 57, 221, 228-231, 306, 340, 362
initiating processes, 23, 38, 40-41, 43-46, 302-303, 362, 369
initiator, 81-82, 87, 98, 362, 368

A Guide to the Project Management Body of Knowledge (PMBOK® Guide) Third Edition
©2004 Project Management Institute, Four Campus Boulevard, Newtown Square, PA 19073-3299 USA

input, 37-39, 40-41, 43, 45, 48-58, 61-65, 67,
    69, 73-74, 78, 82, 86-89, 92, 95, 98, 100-101,
    103, 107, 109, 113, 118, 120, 123, 127-128,
    130-131, 134, 136-137, 139-140, 143, 147,
    152-153, 157, 161-162, 164, 167-168,
    171-172, 179-180, 184, 186-188, 191, 199,
    203, 209-210, 212-213, 215-216, 218, 221,
    225, 228-229, 230-232, 235, 237, 242,
    246-247, 249-250, 254-255, 258, 260-261,
    265, 267, 269, 271, 274-275, 277, 281, 284,
    287-289, 291-292, 296, 301-302, 305,
    312-313, 322, 330, 350-358, 360, 361-371,
    373-374, 379-380
inspection, 92, 96, 119, 181, 191, 196, 293, 362
integral, 17, 362
integrated, 38, 77-78, 86, 100, 104, 119, 121,
    172, 238, 274, 292-293, 363, 372, 377
integrated change control, 9, 59, 61, 79, 88,
    96-99, 101, 108, 112, 118-119, 121-122, 130,
    135, 138, 152-153, 155, 167, 171-172, 177,
    187, 190, 197-198, 218, 231, 234, 264, 267,
    280, 290-292, 294, 304, 316, 337, 352, 363,
    371
invitation for bid (IFB), 282, 349, 363, 367
issue, 16, 46, 63-64, 77, 81, 84-85, 88, 153, 163,
    185, 199, 202, 204, 212-213, 215-219, 221,
    225, 227, 230, 231, 234-236, 238, 275, 286,
    288, 306, 339-340, 353, 363-364, 379

K

knowledge, 3, 5, 8-9, 12, 15, 37, 39, 46, 70, 73,
    77, 83-86, 94, 96, 102, 108, 127, 134-137,
    163, 174, 190, 196, 219, 223, 226, 230, 248,
    250, 268, 283, 309-310, 313, 316, 329-330,
    347, 359, 361, 363, 365, 368-369, 375
knowledge area process, 74, 77-78, 103-104,
    123, 157, 179, 199, 221, 237, 247, 271, 302,
    311-313, 360, 363
knowledge area, project management See
    Project Management Knowledge Area

L

Lag, 134-135, 363
late finish date (LF), 349-350, 352, 363, 372,
    374, 378
late start date (LS), 349, 363, 375
latest revised estimate See estimate at
    completion
lead, 134-135, 249, 279, 363
lessons learned, 91, 94, 100, 102, 122, 155, 163,
    177, 184, 197, 204, 206, 215, 219, 225, 230,
    234, 236, 246-247, 265, 268, 297, 363, 365
lessons learned knowledge base, 85, 94, 102,
    108, 127, 230, 250, 268, 363
level of effort (LOE), 130, 349, 363

leveling See resource leveling
LF See late finish date (LF)
life cycle See project life cycle
LOE See level of effort (LOE)
log, 197, 218-219, 230, 236, 306, 364
logic diagram See project schedule network
    diagram
logic See network logic
logical relationship, 130, 133-135, 145, 350,
    352, 358-359, 361, 363, 364-365, 367, 370,
    374, 376-377
LS See late start date (LS)

M

manage project team, 10, 63, 199, 215-218, 306,
    339, 364
manage stakeholders, 10, 64, 221, 235-236, 306,
    340, 364
master schedule, 149, 364
materiel, 116, 135, 137-138, 141, 144, 164, 271,
    364, 367, 372
matrix organization, 30-31, 215, 364
methodology, 18, 85, 87, 90, 93, 95, 99, 101-
    102, 204, 243, 284, 356, 359, 364, 368
milestone, 89, 128, 130-131, 149, 151, 266, 305,
    364, 374
milestone schedule, 82, 149, 151, 305, 364
monitor, 8-10, 18, 22, 37-38, 40-41, 46, 59-61,
    63, 65, 78, 94-96, 127, 129, 154, 162-163
    170-171, 176, 179, 190, 192-193, 196,
    216-218, 236-237, 251, 253-254, 263-267,
    267, 291, 302-304, 306-307, 316, 332, 337,
    339-340, 353, 358, 364, 366, 369-370, 373,
    378
monitor and control project work, 9, 61, 78,
    94-96, 267, 304, 337, 364
monitoring and controlling processes, 59, 364,
    369
monitoring See monitor
monte carlo analysis, 146, 364, 375

N

near-critical activity, 154, 364
network, 84-85, 132-133, 135, 144-145, 147,
    149, 154, 166, 313, 351-352, 357, 359, 361,
    363-367, 370, 374, 376-378
network analysis, 143, 145-148, 151, 357, 361,
    365, 372, 374, 377
network logic, 133, 149, 352, 359, 361, 363-365,
    378
network loop, 145, 365
network open end, 145, 365
network path, 145, 147, 166, 357, 364-366
networking, 207, 365
node, 365-366

Index

O

objective, 7-8, 22, 39, 111, 189, 205, 214, 238, 245-246, 251-253, 257, 261, 278, 293, 296, 365, 375, 377, 379

OBS *See* organizational breakdown structure (OBS)

OD *See* original duration

operations, 6-8, 15-16, 19, 24, 27, 77, 101-102, 161, 169, 231, 303, 365

opportunity, 5, 18-19, 32, 163, 260, 262, 275, 365, 377

organization, 4, 7-8, 9, 14-15, 17-19, 22-24, 26-33, 38-39, 43, 45-46, 77-78, 81-86, 96, 100, 107, 109, 111-113, 117, 136, 140, 143, 155, 158, 161-162, 168-169, 175, 177, 179, 181, 184-190, 193, 196-197, 202, 204-205, 207-208, 210-212, 215-216, 219, 226, 229-230, 234, 236, 238, 240, 242-234, 245, 251-252, 257, 259, 262, 264, 267-271, 274-277, 279, 283, 287-288, 290, 296, 303, 312, 330-331-332, 339, 341, 353, 355, 357-358, 361-362, 364-365, 367-369, 371-372, 375-376, 378-379

Organization Chart, 205, 365

organizational breakdown structure (OBS), 117, 205, 349, 355, 365

organizational process assets, 40, 74, 79, 84, 87, 90, 101-102, 107, 109, 113, 122, 127, 136, 140, 143, 155, 162, 177, 184, 190-191, 204, 210, 216, 218, 225, 230, 234-236, 242, 247, 250, 255, 268, 275, 284, 287, 294, 297, 365

original duration (OD), 151, 349, 351, 359, 365

output, 23, 37-38, 40-41, 44-46, 48-58, 61-65, 67-68, 73-74, 78, 82, 86-89, 91-93, 95-96, 98-101, 103, 107-111, 113, 117-121, 123, 127-130, 135-136, 138-139, 192-193, 224, 259, 267, 281, 294, 350-360, 362-363, 365-373, 378-379

P

parametric estimating, 142, 165, 169, 365

pareto chart, 195, 366

path convergence, 145, 366

path divergence, 145, 366

PC *See* percent complete

PCT *See* percent complete

PDM *See* precedence diagramming method

percent complete (PC or PCT), 153, 349, 366

perform quality assurance (QA), 10, 56, 179, 187-190, 306, 339, 366

perform quality control (QC), 10, 63, 179, 190-192, 197, 291, 306, 339, 366

performance measurement baseline, 153, 187, 232-233, 352, 366

performance reporting, 10, 56, 64, 91, 176, 221, 231-234, 279, 280, 291, 293-294, 306, 340, 366

performance reports, 61, 120, 153, 172, 188, 216, 233, 265-266, 292, 294, 366

performing organization, 8, 14, 17, 19, 23-24, 26, 28, 33, 77, 83, 109, 111, 112, 136, 140, 143, 155, 158, 161, 169, 175, 177, 179, 181, 184-187, 189, 190, 197, 211, 230, 234, 236, 269, 271, 274-275, 279, 290, 296, 312, 339, 341, 353, 357, 361, 366, 369, 371, 376

PF *See* planned finish date (PF)

phase *See* project phase

plan contracting, 10, 55, 269, 281-282, 307, 341, 366

plan purchases and acquisitions, 10, 54, 269, 274-276, 279, 296, 307, 341, 366

planned finish date (PF) *See* scheduled finish date

planned start date (PS) *See* scheduled start date

planned value (PV), 173-176, 234, 349, 353, 366, 373-374

planning package, 129, 178, 366

planning processes, 46, 77, 88, 183, 367, 369

PM *See* project management (PM)

PM *See* project manager (PM)

PMBOK® *See* project management body of knowledge (PMBOK®)

PMIS *See* project management information system (PMIS)

PMO *See* program management office (PMO)

PMO *See* project management office (PMO)

PMP® *See* project management professional (PMP)

portfolio, 16-17, 43, 81, 362, 367

portfolio management, 16-17, 45, 303, 367

position description, 204-206, 219, 306, 367

practice, 3-4, 12, 20, 37, 39, 73, 77, 103, 113, 123, 157, 179, 200, 221, 234, 237, 243, 270, 313, 330, 363, 367

precedence diagramming method (PDM), 132, 258, 349 351-352, 365, 367

precedence relationship, 132, 364, 367

predecessor activity, 132, 134, 361, 363, 366-367, 377

preventive action, 41, 59, 92-93, 96, 98-99, 189, 197, 218, 267, 367

probability and impact matrix, 84, 243, 245, 250-253, 268, 367

procedure, 7, 14, 17-18, 27, 32-33, 46, 74, 78, 84-85, 90, 92-93, 96, 100-102, 107-108, 121, 127, 153, 158, 162, 172, 179, 184, 189-190, 209-210, 216-217, 219, 230, 264, 270, 275, 283, 292-293, 295-296, 309-310, 332, 339, 353-354, 359, 361, 364-365, 367, 369, 372, 376-377, 379

A Guide to the Project Management Body of Knowledge (PMBOK® Guide) Third Edition
©2004 Project Management Institute, Four Campus Boulevard, Newtown Square, PA 19073-3299 USA

process, 4-12, 14, 16-17, 19, 22-23, 33, 37-70, 73-74, 76-80, 82-104, 106-109, 111-113, 117-119, 121-124, 126-128, 130, 133-141, 143-144, 146-147, 149, 151-162, 164-165, 167, 169, 171-172, 177, 179, 181, 183-194, 196-200, 202, 204, 209-210, 213-214, 216, 218, 221, 223, 225-227, 229-237, 240-251, 253-255, 259-271, 273-277, 279-281, 283-284, 286-297, 301-307, 311-313, 316, 330-332, 337-341, 350-378, 380

process group *See* Project Management Process Groups

procurement documents, 279, 282-286, 289, 367

procurement management plan, 89, 274-276, 279-281, 284, 287, 290, 294-296, 367

product, 5-8, 10, 13-14, 16, 18, 21-26, 28, 37-38, 41, 45, 55, 66, 68, 78, 81-86, 90-94, 96-97, 100-102, 104, 110-111, 115, 117-119, 131, 148, 157-158, 161-163, 165, 168-169, 180-181, 183-186, 188-190, 193, 196, 230, 232, 262, 269-271, 274-277, 279-280, 283, 286-287, 289-292, 302, 307, 312, 333, 341, 351, 353-358, 361-362, 365-368, 370-372, 375-379

product life cycle, 23-24, 193, 303, 368

product scope, 6, 104, 120-121, 368, 375

product scope description, 83, 109, 111, 118, 131, 168, 185, 275, 368

program, 4, 16, 18, 24, 43, 45, 81, 129, 133, 148, 188, 303, 310, 362, 368, 378

program management, 16-17, 303, 349, 368

program management office (PMO), 17, 349, 368-369

progressive elaboration, 6, 8, 128, 316, 352, 368, 374

project, 3-5, 8-14, 16-27, 32-33, 37-40, 43, 45-46, 67-70, 77-95, 97-106, 108-113, 117-129, 131, 135, 137, 140-144, 148-150, 152, 154-160, 162-165, 168, 170-172, 176, 178-185, 187, 190, 193, 198-202, 204, 207, 210, 212-213, 216-219, 221-223, 226, 229-232, 236-243, 245, 247-251, 255-256, 260, 264, 266-273, 275-276, 281-283, 287, 291, 295, 347, 349, 352, 362, 367, 368-370, 375

project calendar, 85, 102, 139-140, 143, 148, 152, 353, 368, 372

project charter, 43, 45, 76, 78, 81, 83-87, 107-109, 111, 168, 210, 332, 337, 353, 359, 368

project communications management, 10, 221-223, 306, 313, 316-317, 340, 347, 368

project cost management, 10, 77, 157-160, 255, 305, 313, 316-317, 338, 347, 368

project human resource management, 10, 199-202, 306, 312-313, 339, 347, 368

project initiation, 61, 95, 109, 368

project integration management, 9, 77, 79-80, 303, 312-313, 316-317, 337, 347, 368

project life cycle, 9, 12, 17, 19-24, 38, 46, 65, 84, 88, 104, 113, 115, 124, 153, 158, 161, 197, 212, 229-230, 237, 243, 271, 303, 312, 329, 340, 363, 368-370, 373, 379

project management (PM), 3-4, 8-10, 12, 14-15, 17-20, 22, 24, 26-27, 32-33, 37-41, 43, 45, 349, 368

project management body of knowledge (PMBOK®), 3-4, 9, 12, 77-78, 311, 349, 368

project management information system (PMIS), 83, 86, 88, 90, 93, 95, 99, 101, 121, 127, 293, 349, 368

project management knowledge area, 9, 11, 69, 301, 316, 337, 363, 369

project management office (PMO), 4, 16-17, 27, 303, 349, 368-369

project management plan, 9, 33, 41, 46, 48, 55-56, 59, 67, 74, 76, 78, 88-102, 104, 107-108, 112, 121-122, 124, 128-130, 137, 141, 143-144, 149, 152-153, 155-156, 158-159, 163, 167-168, 170-173, 177-178, 183, 185-187, 190-191, 198, 204, 206, 208, 212, 216, 219, 226-228, 231-232, 234-236, 242-243, 247, 249, 253, 255, 259-261, 263-268, 276, 280-281, 287, 290, 294-295, 304-305, 337, 354-356, 359-360, 364, 367, 369-374, 376, 379

project management process, 4, 8-12, 19, 22, 37-41, 45, 56, 59-60, 67, 69-70, 77-79, 85, 88-89, 100, 193, 216, 290, 301-303, 306, 312-313, 316, 330, 367, 369

project management process group, 9, 12, 19, 23, 37-47, 55-56, 59-60, 66-70, 77-78, 85, 88, 100, 183, 354, 360, 362, 364, 366-368

project management professional (PMP®), 4, 8, 283, 349, 368

project management software, 18, 130, 132, 135, 137, 139, 144, 147-148, 154, 165, 176, 229, 233, 360, 369

project management system, 27, 33, 303, 354, 369, 379

project management team, 3-4, 8-9, 12, 14, 19-20, 24, 26-27, 43, 46, 78, 85-88, 90-91, 93-95, 97-99, 101, 107-108, 110, 114-115, 124, 127, 133-134, 143, 151, 158, 174-176, 180, 184-186, 190, 196, 199, 204, 208-211, 213, 215-218, 226-227, 233, 270-271, 279, 288, 290, 293, 329, 369-371, 377

project manager (PM), 4, 8, 14-15, 18-19, 22, 25-26, 28-30, 32-33, 37-39, 43-44, 77, 81-82, 91, 166, 169-170, 180, 199, 204, 215, 217, 221, 226, 230, 235, 243, 246, 253, 265, 267, 283, 288, 293, 329, 340, 349, 364, 368-371 project organization chart, 204, 207, 210, 212, 216, 219, 369

project phase, 19, 22, 41, 43-45, 59, 66-67, 69, 78-79, 82, 88, 100, 103, 123, 157, 179, 200, 221, 225, 237, 253, 269-270, 295, 303, 312, 366, 368-370

project process groups, 337, 354, 370

project procurement management, 10, 269-273, 307, 313, 341, 347, 370

project quality management, 10, 179-180, 182-183, 185, 306, 313, 317, 339, 347, 370

project risk management, 10, 77, 237, 239, 241, 249, 260, 265-268, 307, 313, 316, 318, 340, 347, 370

project schedule, 10, 51, 62, 84, 86, 89, 93-94, 112, 123, 130, 133, 135, 137-139, 143-145, 148-156, 158, 164, 168-169, 173-174, 178, 193, 234, 274, 279, 349, 352, 366, 369, 373-374

project schedule network diagram, 84-85, 132-133, 135, 144, 147, 149, 154, 351, 364-366, 370

project scope, 9, 43, 45, 78, 86-89, 99, 103, 105-106, 108-110, 112-113, 117-121, 127, 131, 140, 143, 163, 168, 180, 184, 226, 242, 247, 250, 255, 275, 347, 369

project scope management, 9, 103, 105-106, 108-109, 112-113, 118-119, 120, 180, 347, 369

project scope management plan, 108-109, 112-113, 118-120, 369

project scope statement, 9, 43, 45, 78, 86-89, 99, 108-110, 113, 117-118, 120-121, 127, 131, 140, 143, 163, 168, 184, 226, 242, 247, 250, 255, 275, 369

project sponsor. *See* sponsor

project stakeholder. *See* stakeholder

project summary work breakdown structure (PSWBS), 370

project team, 370

project team directory, 212, 370

project team members, 4, 8, 26, 32, 91, 100-102, 128-129, 141, 199-200, 202, 204, 206-208, 210-211, 213-214, 216-217, 230, 243, 246, 251, 269, 339, 341, 351, 354, 369-371, 377

project time management, 10, 77, 123-126, 152, 347, 370

project work *See* work

projectized organization, 29, 370

PS *See* planned start date (PS), 349

PSWBS *See* project summary work breakdown structure (PSWBS)

PV *See* planned value (PV)

Q

QA *See* quality assurance (QA)

QC *See* quality control (QC)

qualitative risk analysis, 10, 53, 237, 244, 246, 249-251, 253, 254, 259-260, 263, 370

quality, 10, 39, 52, 56, 63, 89, 118, 166, 179-181, 183-192, 197, 232, 252, 291, 348-350, 370

quality assurance (QA), 186-189, 197, 349

quality control (QC), 186, 190-191, 197-198, 349, 356

quality management plan, 186, 188, 191, 370

quality planning, 10, 52, 179, 183-186, 189, 370

quantitative risk analysis, 10, 54, 237, 246, 249-250, 253-255, 257, 259-261, 263, 370

R

RAM *See* responsibility assignment matrix (RAM)

RBS *See* resource breakdown structure (RBS)

RBS *See* risk breakdown structure (RBS)

RD *See* remaining duration (RD)

regulation, 12-15, 83, 184, 209, 274, 282, 329, 371

reliability, 186, 252, 255, 361, 371

remaining duration (RD), 151, 153-154, 349 351, 359, 365, 371

request for information, 82, 367, 371

request for proposal (RFP), 82, 282, 349, 363, 367, 371

request for quotation (RFQ), 282, 349, 367, 371

request seller responses, 10, 58, 269, 281, 284-285, 371

requested change, 93, 96, 98, 112, 118-119, 122, 130, 135, 138, 152, 155, 167, 171, 177, 190, 197, 218, 231, 234, 267, 280, 290, 294, 371

requirement, 7-8, 14, 17-18, 20, 22-25, 37-38, 43, 45-46, 51, 55-56, 64, 77-78, 81-84, 86-87, 90, 97, 102, 104, 109-112, 115, 117-119, 123, 130, 137-140, 144, 148, 151, 158, 163, 167, 170, 172, 179-181, 184-188, 190, 196-197, 204, 208, 212, 216-217, 221, 225-227, 229, 235-236, 240, 247, 261, 267, 269-270, 275-277, 279-280, 282-286, 288, 290, 292-294, 297, 316, 332, 337-341, 350, 353-356, 358-359, 362, 364, 366, 368-369, 371-372, 374, 376, 378-380

reserve, 142-143, 151, 166, 169, 263-264, 266, 355, 372

reserve analysis, 142, 166, 169, 266, 372

residual risk, 65, 237, 264, 340, 372

resource, 89, 94, 117, 137-138, 140-141, 144, 146-148, 151, 162, 165, 168, 199, 204, 208, 212-213, 290, 349, 372

A Guide to the Project Management Body of Knowledge (PMBOK® Guide) Third Edition
©2004 Project Management Institute, Four Campus Boulevard, Newtown Square, PA 19073-3299 USA

resource breakdown structure (RBS), 117, 138, 205, 243, 247-249, 253, 255, 263, 268, 349, 372

resource calendar, 138, 141, 144, 168, 372

resource constrained schedule *See* resource-limited schedule

resource histogram, 208, 372

resource leveling, 146, 372

resource planning. *See* activity resource estimating

resource-limited schedule, 147, 372

responsibility assignment matrix (RAM), 206, 349, 372

result, 102, 372

retainage, 289, 372

rework, 146, 180, 185-186, 305, 372

RFP *See* request for proposal (RFP)

RFQ *See* request for quotation (RFQ)

risk, 10, 53-54, 65, 84, 89, 117, 141, 144, 164, 237-238, 240, 242-256, 259-267, 276, 281, 287, 291, 349, 372-373

risk acceptance, 373

risk avoidance, 261, 373

risk breakdown structure (RBS), 117, 138, 205, 243-244, 247-249, 253, 255, 263, 268, 349, 372

risk category, 117, 373

risk database, 83, 255, 373

risk identification, 10, 53, 237, 243, 246-247, 249-250, 253-254, 259, 261, 263, 372

risk management plan, 10, 53, 237, 242-247, 249-251, 255, 260-261, 265, 372

risk management planning, 10, 53, 237, 242-246, 249-251, 261, 372

risk mitigation, 262, 373

risk monitoring and control, 10, 65, 237, 254, 264-267, 291, 372

risk register, 141, 144, 249-250, 253, 255, 259, 261, 263, 265, 267, 372

risk response planning, 10, 54, 237, 246, 249-250, 254, 260-261, 263, 373

risk transference, 262, 373

role, 32, 207, 373

rolling wave planning, 128, 373

root cause analysis, 155, 189, 374

S

schedule activity, 50, 133-134, 137-142, 145-146, 149, 151, 154-155, 158, 161, 164-169, 175-178, 338, 347, 352-353, 355, 373

schedule analysis *See* schedule network analysis

schedule compression, 145, 373

schedule control, 10, 62, 123, 152-154, 156, 373

schedule development, 10, 51, 123, 138-139, 143-145, 149, 151-152, 169, 274, 279, 373

schedule management plan, 152-153, 373

schedule milestone, 373

schedule model, 10, 51, 62, 86, 89, 94, 112, 123, 130, 133, 137-139, 143-145, 148-149, 151-156, 158, 164, 169, 173-174, 178, 234, 274, 279, 349, 352, 366, 373-374

schedule network analysis, 145, 373

schedule performance index (SPI), 154-155, 174, 177, 234, 349, 373,

schedule *See* project schedule and *See also* schedule model

schedule variance (SV), 154-155, 173,177, 234, 349, 374

scheduled finish date (SF), 349, 366, 374

scheduled start date (SS), 366, 374

scope, 9, 48-49, 62, 87, 103, 107-110, 112, 117-122, 226, 374

scope baseline *See* baseline

scope change, 18, 38, 108, 119, 121-122, 155, 193, 207, 278, 302, 304, 375

scope control, 9, 62, 103, 119-121, 374

scope creep, 6, 119, 375

scope definition, 9, 49, 87, 103, 109-110, 112, 226, 374

scope planning, 9, 48, 103, 107-108, 374

scope verification, 9, 62, 103, 118-119, 374

s-curve, 170, 174, 233, 313, 366, 375

secondary risk, 264-265, 375

select sellers, 10, 58, 269, 281, 286-290, 374

seller, 271, 278, 287, 289, 291-292, 295, 374

sensitivity analysis, 374

service, 102, 374

SF *See* scheduled finish date (SF)

SF *See* start-to-finish (SF)

should-cost estimate, 375

simulation, 146, 259, 375

skill, 375

slack *See* total float and free float

SOW *See* statement of work (SOW)

special cause, 191-192, 375

specification, 22, 111-112, 376

specification limits, 376

SPI *See* schedule performance index (SPI)

sponsor, 26, 375, 370, 376

SS *See* scheduled start date (SS)

SS *See* start-to-start (SS)

staffing management plan, 208, 210, 212, 213, 216, 376

stakeholder, 19, 24, 26, 82, 83, 109, 110, 111, 180, 226, 227, 231, 235, 370, 376

standard, 9, 113, 282, 376

start date, 145, 149, 151, 347, 376

start-to-finish (SF), 132, 349, 376

start-to-start (SS), 132, 349, 376

statement of work (SOW), 82, 280, 349, 376

strengths, weaknesses, opportunities, and threats (SWOT), 248-349, 376

subnetwork, 133, 376
subphase, 22, 376
subproject, 16, 41, 114, 271, 377
successor activity, 134, 145, 377
successor *See* successor activity
summary activity, 149, 362, 377
SV *See* schedule variance (SV)
SWOT *See* strengths, weaknesses, opportunities, and threats (SWOT)
system, 86, 88, 90, 93, 95, 99, 101, 248, 288, 293, 296, 349, 377

T

T&M *See* time and material (T&M)
target completion date (TC), 377
target finish date (TF), 377
target schedule, 149, 154, 377
target start date (TS), 377
TC *See* target completion date (TC)
team members *See* project team members
technical performance measurement, 266, 376
technique, 95, 348, 351-367, 371-373, 376-379
template, 113, 115, 128, 153, 162, 377
TF *See* target finish date (TF)
TF *See* total float (TF)
threat, 260-262, 377
three-point estimate, 142, 255, 378
threshold, 185, 262, 378
time and material (T&M) contract, 278, 349, 378
time-now date *See* data date
time-scaled schedule network diagram, 149, 378
tool, 3, 8, 12, 18-19, 33, 37, 82-83, 85-93, 95-96, 99-101, 104, 107-110, 113, 118-121, 124, 127-128, 130, 132, 136-137, 139, 141, 143, 145, 148, 152-154, 158, 162, 164-165, 167, 169, 171-172, 184-189, 191-192, 194, 196, 203, 205, 208-210, 212-213, 215, 217, 225-226, 228-229, 231-232, 235-236, 242-243, 246-248, 250-251, 254-255, 260-262, 265-266, 274, 276, 281-282, 288, 291-293, 296, 305, 312, 316-317, 330, 352-355, 361-373, 377-378
total float (TF), 134, 145, 147, 154, 349, 361-362, 364, 372, 375, 378

total quality management (TQM), 180-181, 350, 378
TQM *See* total quality management (TQM)
trend analysis, 266, 378
triggers, 264, 378
triple constraint, 8, 378
TS *See* target start date (TS)

U

user, 26, 180, 358, 378

V

validation, 44, 190, 378
value engineering (VE), 110, 157, 349, 379
variance, 121, 154, 158, 176, 234, 266, 348-349, 379
variance analysis, 121, 154, 379
VE *See* value engineering (VE)
verification, 97, 100, 108, 295, 378-379
virtual team, 211, 379
voice of the customer, 180, 379

W

war room, 214, 379
WBS *See* work breakdown structure (WBS)
work, 6, 27, 82, 87, 91, 94-95, 98, 101, 113-114, 116-117, 120-121, 128, 163, 168, 172, 188, 191, 205, 216, 232, 265, 276, 280-281, 284, 292, 348-350, 359, 370, 378-379
work authorization, 167, 379
work authorization system, 83, 379
work breakdown structure (WBS) , 9, 49, 86, 103-104, 108, 112-118, 120-121, 127-130, 149, 155, 158-159, 163, 168-169, 173, 175, 177, 205-206, 214, 234, 253, 258, 263, 276, 280, 350, 366, 370, 379
work breakdown structure component, 351-353, 359-360, 366, 379
work breakdown structure dictionary, 379
work item *See* activity and schedule activity
work package, 114, 175-176, 178, 380
work performance information, 94-95, 98, 101, 120, 172, 188, 191, 216, 232, 265, 292, 380
workaround, 267, 380

A Guide to the Project Management Body of Knowledge (PMBOK® Guide) Third Edition
©2004 Project Management Institute, Four Campus Boulevard, Newtown Square, PA 19073-3299 USA